CANADIAN CASES IN FINANCIAL MANAGEMENT

SECOND EDITION

CANADIAN CASES IN FINANCIAL MANAGEMENT

SECOND EDITION

David Shaw
James Hatch
John Humphrey
Larry Wynant
Paul Bishop

School of Business Administration
University of Western Ontario

Prentice-Hall Canada Inc.
Scarborough, Ontario

Canadian Cataloguing in Publication Data

Main entry under title:

Canadian cases in financial management

2nd ed.
ISBN 0-13-116534-8

1. Business enterprises — Canada — Finance —
Case studies. I. Shaw, David C., 1936—

HG4015.5.C3 1990   658.15'2'0971   C90-093903-6

"Bumpy ride for Air Canada issue" article reprinted with
permission The Financial Post, James Bagnall and Richard
Blackwell, August 5, 1988.

© 1991 Prentice-Hall Canada Inc., Scarborough, Ontario

Prentice Hall, Inc., Englewood Cliffs, New Jersey
Prentice-Hall International, Inc., London
Prentice-Hall of Australia, Pty., Ltd., Sydney
Prentice-Hall of India Pvt., Ltd., New Delhi
Prentice-Hall of Japan, Inc., Tokyo
Prentice-Hall of Southeast Asia (Pte.) Ltd., Singapore
Editora Prentice-Hall do Brasil Ltda., Rio de Janeiro
Prentice-Hall Hispanoamericana, S.A., Mexico

ISBN 0-13-116534-8

Production Coordinator: Kelly Dickson
Typesetting: Q Composition Inc.
Manufacturing Buyer: Florence Rousseau

1   2   3   AP   92   91   90

Printed and bound in Canada by Alger Press Limited

CONTENTS

PART 3 / Capital Structure Decisions

PART 4 / Cost of Capital

PART 5 / Capital Expenditures

PART 11 / Foreign Exchange Management

PREFACE

This book presents students with a variety of decisions typically faced by Canadian financial managers. The cases are drawn from a broad range of industries and reflect the various economic, market and behavioral factors which affect financial decision making. The decision maker in the case is sometimes a senior financial officer in the firm, or a potential investor in or lender to the company. In each case the student must adopt the role of the decision maker, define the problem and the options, consider the objectives for the company as they apply to the situation, analyze the relevant data for each option according to the objectives, and reach a decision.

The topics covered in this casebook are intended to complement an introductory course in corporate finance. We have taught these cases in our undergraduate and MBA degree programs, and in programs for managers. We have incorporated suggestions for changes and corrected errors in the original versions of these cases.

This second edition includes 30 cases. A new section includes three cases in foreign exchange management. In total the book includes 11 new cases and 11 significantly revised cases. Eight cases remain from the first edition in essentially the same form with only minor adjustments.

We are indebted to many persons for this book. First we wish to thank the many business executives who provided the material for the cases. Their generosity with time and data, some of which was confidential and controversial, was very much appreciated and critical to the success of each case.

Several colleagues have provided case materials and assistance in teaching and revising the cases in this book. Professor Robert White wrote Markborough Properties Limited. Professors Samuel Martin and James Taylor contributed in many ways to this book, but especially by writing original versions of cases we regard as "chestnuts." Professors Richard Bauer, John Graham, Terry Hildebrand, Gerald Higgins and Robert White have tested the cases in the classroom and suffered through the first-draft errors and misunderstandings which are inevitable. We appreciate all their efforts very much.

A number of case research assistants contributed to the development of this second edition. We are indebted to, and wish to thank, Charles Blair, Steven Cox, Laurie Dunk, Ann Groulx, John Harris, Roland Horst, Jay Katz, Vicki Mace, Richard Nason, Peter Nerby, David Porter, Margaret Sanderson, Derrick Strizic and William Volk.

We owe special thanks for the secretarial help we have received from Judy Ellis, Sue LeMoine, Sue O'Driscoll, Mary Jane Vonesh and Connie Zrini. Their assistance in typing the various drafts, setting the formats and making corrections, always offered in a cheerful and co-operative way, was invaluable.

We would especially like to thank C.B. (Bud) Johnston, the former Dean of the Western Business School, who was a great supporter of casewriting activities and encouraged us to publish this casebook. Funds and assistance provided by the School's Plan for Excellence, the Institute of Canadian Bankers, the Government of Canada's Secretary of State and the Royal Bank of Canada contributed greatly to the development of this casebook. The Plan for Excellence is supported by a large number of Canadian companies and individuals committed to excellence in management education.

An Assessment of the Firm and Its Cash Needs

CANFAB INC.

On November 20, 1987, Mr. Jim Kasmar, manager of the Confederation Bank in Edmonton, Alberta, was reviewing the credit file of Canfab Inc. The president of Canfab, Mr. Tom Kruger, had telephoned that morning with a request that the bank continue to extend a temporary line of credit of $1,000,000 for a further period of sixty days. "In two months' time, we should be pretty well out of the woods as far as our cash bind is concerned", said Mr. Kruger. "We've had some delays in collecting our holdbacks, but I'm expecting payment for sure about the middle of December. Then you can cut our line back to the normal $800,000 and we should be able to operate perfectly well within that limit from then on."

The regional credit office of the bank had extended Canfab a 30-day temporary line of $1,000,000 on October 20, 1987, when the company experienced difficulty in collecting $216,000 in holdbacks from a contract for two large school lockerroom installations in Calgary. Mr. Kasmar knew that the regional office of the bank had granted the 30-day extension reluctantly; in fact, the regional office made it crystal clear to Mr. Kasmar that it was relying entirely on the strong endorsement which he had given Canfab's new young president.

> On paper, nothing in the application warrants the extension of further credit; in fact, we are concerned about the safety of our existing line with the company. However, because of the confidence you have expressed in the new president of the company, your closeness to the situation, and the importance of Canfab to the community, we will authorize a 30-day credit line to a maximum of $1,000,000. . . . "

Mr. Kasmar knew that to convince the regional office to grant an extension of a further 60 days, it would be necessary to submit a comprehensive and compelling application to the senior credit officers in Calgary. In view of the responsibility he already carried for the first extension, he wanted to do so only if he himself was entirely convinced that Canfab, under Mr. Kruger's direction, was capable of overcoming the financial problems which had plagued it for almost ten years.

With these thoughts in mind, Mr. Kasmar proceeded to review all the information which he had accumulated in the file of the company.

2

Background

Canfab Inc. was reorganized under its present name after the bankruptcy of Canadian Metal Fabricators Limited in 1936. Canadian Metal Fabricators Limited had been the outgrowth of a blacksmith shop founded by the Blackwell family of Edmonton in 1868, and later incorporated as the Blackwell Wire and Iron Works Limited. By the late 1970's, control of Canfab Inc. had passed through five generations of the Blackwell family. At this time, none of the twenty-seven family shareholders expressed a keen desire to take an active role in the management of the company, and operating results deteriorated for a period of almost ten years.

In March, 1986, Mr. Tom Kruger convinced a group of influential Canfab shareholders to sell him their shares in Canfab Inc. For a cash payment of approximately $50,000 (and a complicated agreement for payment of the balance), Mr. Kruger acquired control of the company and assumed the position of president of the company on March 15, 1986.

Mr. Kruger, a native of Montreal, had earned the degrees of B. Com. (McGill, 1976) and M.B.A. (Harvard, 1978), and was a Certified Management Accountant. From 1979 to 1981, he worked for two management consulting firms in Montreal, where he gathered experience in organizational problems, production control, office and plant layout, and salary and wage incentives. In 1981, he joined the firm of Rodricks Associates, management consultants in Toronto; and from 1981 to 1985 he held the position of accountant, office manager, assistant to the secretary-treasurer, and general manager of that firm. Mr. Kruger had told Mr. Kasmar that his entire personal savings had been used up in acquiring control of Canfab.

Upon gaining control of Canfab in 1986, Mr. Kruger immediately applied himself to the problem of putting the company back on a profit-making basis. Although he was not completely satisfied with the performance of certain key employees, Mr. Kruger decided not to replace any of the senior management for the first year, in order to "preserve morale and build up good will". Mr. Charles Wilkes, a long time employee of the organization, continued as vice president and general manager in charge of production. The positions of secretary-treasurer and office manager were entrusted to Mrs. Ethyl Samson, another employee of long standing.

Production

Canfab manufactured lockers, school furniture, toilet partitions, and steel shelving. Cold rolled sheets were purchased from warehouses located in Edmonton and Calgary, in varying gauges and quality; current prices ranged from $122.57 per 100 kilograms for seconds to $145.00 per 100 kilograms for prime sheets. Mr. Kruger stated that delivery could be obtained on a day's notice from these sources, as opposed to three month's delivery by large steel producers. Also, warehouse credit terms were much more favourable –

60 to 90 days being common – whereas, the large producers demanded payment within 30 days. Prices from the warehouse averaged about 12 to 15% higher than purchase of similar quantities direct from steel producers. With both mills and warehouses, volume discounts reached their maximum at 40,000 pounds.

The manufacturing cycle, comprising seven operations in the case of a locker, required forty-four minutes to complete. First, the correct gauge of steel was selected, prime sheets being used for locker doors and seconds for locker backs. Shearing and cutting to size preceded the notching of the corners and the punching operations. Then the different pieces were bent for fitting so that they could be bolted or welded into place. At last, the lockers were ready for painting. Similar procedures were followed in manufacturing school furniture and toilet partitions.

The number of direct production workers varied at Canfab between twenty and twenty-five. Most of these employees were semi-skilled, but there were a few skilled mechanics who did the layout work. The production workers were organized by the Sheet Metal Workers' International Association. Mr. Kruger commented that "this union was no worse than any other union". In addition, there were eight to ten office workers and manufacturing supervisors employed by the firm.

According to Mr. Kruger, the steel fabricating industry was plagued with several problems. Scheduling was tied very closely to the construction industry which in turn was very dependent on the general economic climate. New institutional construction work in Alberta had been picking up since the recession of the early 1980's but there had been a 20% drop in such construction activity in 1987. It was thought that there could be a similar drop in 1988. Mr. Kruger was not certain how much impact the recent stock market crash would have on the Alberta economy. Paint touch-up presented another problem within the industry. It proved extremely difficult to match paint chipped off during transportation and erection. Because most products were shipped from the factory in knocked-down form, contractors had to be hired to erect them on the building sites, and thus the products were susceptible to chipping. Lags caused by numerous die changes presented the industry with a third headache. Because of the number of cuts to be made, the number and size of corners to be notched, and the varying shapes to be bent, the dies had to be altered fairly often, particularly when production runs were short. In addition, the industry was very competitive, with "anybody and their uncle" being able to manufacture lockers.

Rapid modernization had taken place in the industry as a result of mechanization and developments in the paint industry. In 1986, Canfab spent nearly $120,000 on a new oven for baking the enamel finishes. On the other hand, Canfab's punching and stamping equipment was rather old, but not obsolete by industry standards.

Production was divided equally among the three major items produced. Lockers, school furniture, and toilet partitions each accounted for about

30% of total production, while the specialty items such as steel shelving provided the remaining 10%.

Competition

Competition in the steel fabricating industry was very intense. Rising costs and severe price cutting minimized returns and demanded efficient operations for survival. The large conglomerates that were dominant players in the field were investing substantial amounts for new tooling and upgrading of facilities in an effort to become more efficient and to gain market share. However, the large players were not immune to the effects of the competitive industry. A recent Annual Report of GSW stated:

> "We have begun the difficult process of rationalizing our Building Products business, which continues to suffer from under-utilized facilities and some weak markets. This is our main area of concern for 1987."

(The Building Products division of GSW was an industry leader in products such as lockers, toilet partitions and other building products such as rain gutters.)

Marketing

Most companies distributed their products coast to coast because of the small Canadian market, but the majority of the business was carried out in Quebec, Ontario and the Western provinces, with large centres such as Calgary, Edmonton, Vancouver, Montreal and Toronto accounting for the bulk of sales.

As previously stated, Canfab's main product lines were lockers, school furnishings, and toilet partitions. Locker production was the most competitive, and Mr. Kruger commented that lockers were produced mainly as a contribution to overhead, with little realizable profit margin; they were a necessary product to carry in order to "round out the line".

Canfab's potential market was in schools, hospitals, motels, hotels, shopping centres, offices, and sports clubs. Normally, the architect for a particular building would determine the specifications, and the construction company would do the actual purchasing. However, in the school furnishings line, some school boards were doing the buying themselves, thus eliminating the commissions to the construction firms.

Service and delivery were very important factors for Canfab. When lockers were sold to a school, for example, Canfab was responsible for the erection and any re-touching of these lockers. Most of the erection jobs were subcontracted to local construction crews. In one case, Canfab had bid on an installation in Kitchener and lost it to a competitor. The competitor was unable to deliver in the allotted time, and the contract was therefore reassigned to Canfab (at Canfab's bid price) under the condition that delivery be made in one week. Canfab had been able to deliver the order and arrange for installation in six days.

Pricing for Canfab and its competitors was very crucial. When asked how some of the competitors bid, Mr. Kruger stated:

> "It depends on what kind of a crazy mood they are in. First a bid is sent in, but the first bid rarely brings any results. The purchaser, when he has received all the bids, usually plays one supplier against another, shaving the price down. In other words, you bid and then haggle."

Personal contact with the architect in some cases proved to be an influential factor, although price was the primary determinant.

Promotion and advertising were at a minimum. Catalogues were delivered personally by salesmen to architects, but little advertising was carried in trade magazines and commercial papers. Mr. Kruger referred to a recent advertisement by one of his competitors in *Construction Alberta News* as "a waste of money".

Selling was handled through fifteen manufacturers' agents across Canada. Mr. Kruger was not able to provide Mr. Kasmar with figures, although he indicated that sales per agent averaged $260,000. Recently, one of Canfab's leading agents had been made sales manager; and Mr. Kruger had released one, and intended to release another. One salesman was reassigned to cover the industrial aspect of the market. Mr. Kruger planned to visit his agents at least twice a year. Canfab's agents were paid on a straight commission basis.

Financial Position

Canfab was facing a tight working capital situation propagated by losses totaling $480,315 over the four-year period, 1984 to 1987. These losses had caused a heavy cash drain on the company with a resultant decrease in the current ratio from 2.33 to 1.12. Operations were being financed exclusively on bank credit with the company maintaining a cash fund of only $3,200. At the end of February 1987, outstanding bank loans of $784,000 exceeded the previous year's total by $248,000. Comparative balance sheets, income statements, and financial ratios are shown in Exhibits 1 to 3.

In 1987, a profit of $1,000 was earned. Mr. Kruger told Mr. Kasmar that he was expecting to break even or incur a small loss in fiscal 1988 because of the decline in new school, office and sport club construction, which he felt would be somewhat less than offset by an increase in new hospital construction. He anticipated sales of approximately $3.2 million to $3.4 million. Mr. Kruger attributed the improved operating picture of the company primarily to a new plant layout, which enabled production time and the number of production workers to be decreased. Three major contracts enabled Canfab to push sales above the break-even point in 1987.

Since taking over the company, Mr. Kruger had been working on a job cost system intended to give him the profit on each job and the contribution of each line. No standards had been developed within the plant; however, the president considered them no more useful than actual data, and proposed to use the latter in his cost control system. The company had been operating at between 50% and 70% of capacity over the last few years.

Canfab constantly operated under the threat of increasing steel prices and wage rates. Competition and contract bargaining forced sales prices down and depressed profit margins. In January 1987, Canfab employees received a five per cent increase in pay. This one-year contract was comparable to that negotiated by some of the larger competitors. In addition, sales fluctuated considerably following the cyclical trends in that sector of the construction industry which steel fabricators serviced. Since fixed costs constituted a large part of total costs, capacity operations were extremely important to the profitability of the company. Details of operations for the year ended February 28, 1987 are shown in Exhibit 4.

The age of receivables increased in February 1987 to 101 days over 77 days the previous year. Mr. Kruger attributed the increase to holdbacks on large accounts. The nature of the company's business was such that the supplying firm was not paid until the contractor had settled with the institution for which a building was erected. Government accounts were generally slow in payment and very little could be done to force settlement of an account. Mr. Kruger considered the receivables problem so important that he gave it his own personal attention. This required constant badgering of the contractor until payment was received. Although payments were slow, bad debts had not been significantly large. Ninety-five per cent of Canfab's business was of the contract and holdback nature. As of November 1, 1987, receivables stood as follows:

Less than 30 days	$264 000
30 to 60 days	208 000
60 to 90 days	80 000
Over 90 days	44 000
Holdbacks*	216 000
Liens and Legal*	36 000
Total	$848 000

*Information pertinent to Liens and Holdbacks may be found in Appendix 1. Legislation similar to The Builders Lien Act of Alberta is in place in other provinces.

Inventories in late 1987 stood at approximately $500,000, of which $100,000 was raw materials, $200,000 work-in-process, and $200,000 finished goods. The company produced primarily on a job basis, but also manufactured items for stock. A fairly large inventory of finished goods was required to service orders that requested immediate delivery. Because of the poor working capital position of the company, management was unable to speculate on the purchase of steel. Usually, just enough sheet steel was purchased to take advantage of quantity discounts. This practice caused inventories of raw materials to fluctuate considerably throughout the year.

The lack of scheduling and status reporting allowed work-in-process to be controlled only by visual inspection. Mr. Kruger indicated that he recognized this as a problem, and expressed a desire to improve his inventory control procedures. Previously physical inventories had been taken once per year; however, the inventory of paint had been checked three times in 1987 and Mr. Kruger was in the process of developing records which would enable him to exercise greater control over raw steel. Also planned for the near future were more detailed perpetual inventory records.

Mr. Kruger's statement, "we pay when they holler", generally reflected the company's policy in making payments to suppliers. In order to minimize the need for bank credit and to keep this line open as a future source of funds, Canfab held back payments as long as possible. In Mr. Kruger's opinion, this practice was typical of everyone in the industry. Steel mills, however, did not allow such practices. With a three month lead time, they would not even accept orders from a customer with accounts over 30 days. As a result, many of Canfab's competitors purchased from warehouses.

Land was carried on the books at $45,200; however, Mr. Kruger conservatively estimated its present value at over $500,000, since it was in downtown Edmonton in a location of historical significance to the city. On the other hand, the buildings were in poor repair.

Kruger considered factoring as a method of financing too expensive, especially since he had been able to obtain bank loans on his accounts receivable and fixed assets at a considerably lower rate of prime plus 2%.[1] Factors' rates reflected their traditional distaste for service accounts because of installation damage claims and customer refusal to release holdbacks until paint touch-up was completed satisfactorily.

Because of the poor performance of the company over the past ten years and the present questionable financial position, Mr. Kasmar realized that sale of common or preferred stock was either impractical or impossible at this time. Furthermore, Mr. Kruger in no way wanted to jeopardize his control and ownership of the firm through a stock issue. In acquiring control of the company, he had realized that the venture was a high risk. For this reason, he was unwilling to invest additional funds in the business himself. The aim of the president was to improve the profit position of the company through stricter cost control and better marketing strategy. Mr. Kruger had stated openly to Mr. Kasmar that until funds could be generated internally, he hoped to woo the bank into extending Canfab's loan and increasing it when needed.

[1] The prime rate was currently 9.75%.

EXHIBIT 1
CANFAB INC

Balance Sheet for the years ended February 28, 1984 – 1987

Assets	1987	1986	1985	1984
Current Assets				
Cash	$ 3 200	$ 1 600	$ 1 600	$ 2 700
Accounts Receivable (net)	1 114 584	672 968	871 260	791 928
Inventories	662 620	541 017	564 692	674 248
Prepaid Expenses	2 265	5 632	18 128	24 792
Deposits	0	0	1 500	1 000
Total Current Assets	1 782 669	1 221 217	1 457 180	1 494 668
Fixed Assets (net of accumulated – depreciation)				
Land	45 200	45 200	45 200	45 200
Buildings	163 060	138 408	147 744	157 620
Machinery and Dies	115 140	25 556	29 460	36 824
Trucks and Auto	884	1 264	4 864	6 948
Total Fixed Assets	324 284	210 428	227 268	246 592
TOTAL ASSETS	$2 106 953	$1 431 645	$1 684 448	$1 741 260
Liabilities				
Current Liabilities				
Bank Overdraft[1]	143 852	0	337 744	162 616
Bank Loans[1]	640 000	536 000	588 000	560 000
Accounts Payable	751 980	86 968	94 376	159 148
Accrued Expenses	0	82 388	86 952	64 556
Cheques Outstanding	0	209 040	0	0
Taxes Payable	57 744	0	0	0
TOTAL CURRENT LIABILITIES	1 593 576	914 396	1 107 072	946 320
Mortgage Payable	0	4 852	6 388	7 864
Shareholders Equity				
Preferred A (issued 5250 @ $40.00)	210 000	210 000	210 000	210 000
Common (issued 66 808 @ NPV)	34 020	34 020	34 020	34 020
Capital Surplus	13 344	13 344	13 344	13 344
Retained Earnings	256 013	255 033	313 624	529 712
TOTAL LIABILITIES & EQUITY	$2 106 953	$1 431 645	$1 684 448	$1 741 260

[1] Amounts due to the bank are secured by:
(1) Collateral mortgage on company's premises of $500 000.
(2) A general assignment of receivables.
(3) An assignment of inventories under Section 88 of the Bank Act.

EXHIBIT 2
CANFAB INC.

Statement of Profit and Loss for the years ended February 28, 1984 – 1987

	1987	1986	1985	1984
Sales	$ 4 027 852	3 205 452	3 892 168	3 401 448
Cost of Goods Sold	3 639 820	2 861 588	3 621 056	3 163 380
Gross Profit	388 032	343 864	271 112	238 068
Expenses				
Administration	190 112	235 588	269 692	243 864
Selling	145 960	114 372	161 724	181 812
Interest & Bank Charges	66 700	77 015	64 860	53 184
Total Expenses	402 772	426 975	496 276	478 860
Operating Profit (Loss)	(14 740)	(83 111)	(225 164)	(240 792)
Other Income	15 720	24 520	9 076	34 176
NET PROFIT (LOSS)	$ 980	(58 591)	(216 088)	(206 616)

EXHIBIT 3
CANFAB INC.

Financial Statistics

	1987	1986	1985	1984	1983	1982	1981	1980	1979	1978
Current Ratio	1.12	1.34	1.32	1.58	2.33	2.40	1.64	2.09	2.38	2.07
Acid Test	0.70	0.74	0.79	0.84	1.05	1.35	0.97	1.15	1.32	1.23
Inventory Turnover (days)	66	69	57	78	N.A.	N.A.	62	N.A.	52	52
Age of Receivables (days)	101	77	82	85	59	69	83	N.A.	72	81
Earnings/Share	0.015	(.88)	(3.23)	(3.09)	(1.07)	0.91	(.82)	(.62)	0.90	.99
CGS/Sales	90.4	89.3	93.0	93.0	87.1	96.0	99.5	101.0	96.0	97.0
Gross Profit/Sales	9.6	10.7	7.0	7.0	12.9	4.0	0.5	(1.0)	4.0	3.0
Admin. Exp./Sales	4.7	7.3	6.9	7.2	8.1	6.7	6.6	7.5	7.0	6.8
Selling Exp./Sales	3.6	3.6	4.2	5.3	5.9	4.8	5.0	6.5	5.3	5.1
Interest Exp./Sales	1.7	2.4	1.7	1.6	1.5	2.9	1.6	0.5	2.4	1.2
Net Profit/Sales	0.0	(1.8)	(5.6)	(6.1)	(2.3)	1.3	(1.2)	(1.2)	1.4	1.6
Equity/Assets	24.4	35.8	33.9	45.2	63.0	64.5	46.8	58.5	62.8	57.5
Debt/Assets	75.6	64.2	66.1	54.8	37.0	35.5	53.2	41.5	37.2	42.5
Sales ($000s)	4028	3205	3892	3401	3132	4800	4416	3592	4232	4184
Equity ($000s)	513	512	571	787	988	1064	1012	1072	1124	1092
Profit After Taxes ($000s)	1.0	(58.6)	(216.1)	(206.6)	(71.2)	61.2	(54.8)	(41.6)	60.4	66.4

EXHIBIT 4
CANFAB INC.

Income Statement Incorporating Fixed and Variable Expense Estimates
for the year ended February 28, 1987

Sales		$4 027 852
Variable Expenses		
Commissions	102 000	
Heat, Light and Power	70 592	
Materials	2 607 576	
Direct Labour	616 000	
Repairs and Maintenance	62 572	
Miscellaneous and General	22 408	
	3 481 148	
Less: Inventory Adjustment	21 276	3 459 872
Contribution Margin		567 980
Fixed Expenses		
Salaries	313 492	
Telephone	800	
Supplies	6 400	
Depreciation	27 560	
Heat, Light and Power	1 200	
Insurance	19 552	
Taxes	81 456	
Repairs and Maintenance	60 000	
Interest	64 060	
Miscellaneous	8 200	582 720
		(14 740)
Other Income		15 720
NET INCOME		$ 980

APPENDIX 1
Summary of Pertinent Sections of The Builders' Lien Act of Alberta

2. For the purposes of this Act, a contract or a subcontract is substantially performed

   (a) when the work under a contract or a subcontract or a substantial part of it is ready for use or is being used for the purpose intended, and

   (b) when the work to be done under the contract or subcontract is capable of completion or correction at a cost of not more than

   (i) 3% of the first $500,000 of the contract or subcontract price,

   (ii) 2% of the next $500,000 of the contract or subcontract price, and

   (iii) 1% of the balance of the contract or subcontract price.

4(1). Subject to subsection (2), a person who

   (a) does or causes to be done any work on or in respect of an improvement, or

   (b) furnishes any material to be used in or in respect of an improvement,

   for an owner, contractor or subcontractor has, for so much of the price of the work or material as remains due to him, a lien on the estate or interest of the owner in the land in respect of which the improvement is being made.

15(1). Irrespective of whether a contract provides for instalment payments or payment on completion of the contract, an owner who is liable on a contract under which a lien may arise shall, when making payment on the contract, retain an amount equal to 15% of the value of the work actually done and materials actually furnished for a period of 45 days from

   (a) the date of issue of a certificate of substantial performance of the contract, in a case where a certificate of substantial performance is issued, or

   (b) the date of completion of the contract, in a case where a certificate of substantial performance is not issued.

32(1). A lien that has been registered ceases to exist unless, within 180 days from the date it is registered,

   (a) an action is commenced under this Act

   (i) to realize on the lien or

   (ii) in which the lien may be realized,

   and

   (b) the lien claimant registers a certificate of lis pendens in respect of his lien in the appropriate land titles office.

GOURMET GADGETS INC.

Ken Lanzetta, president of Gourmet Gadgets Inc. (Gourmet), required funding to start manufacturing and marketing a new invention of his, a pasta server. He was uncertain how much funding he would need since the amount was dependent on sales. He wanted to start production in two weeks, on August 1, 1989. Since his distribution system was already arranged, he believed he could start selling as soon as the units were produced. He approached several venture capitalists after being turned down by the Confederation Bank, a Canadian chartered bank, but was reluctant to agree to what he considered excessive demands for their capital investment. He had just returned from a meeting with Arthur Cohen, a private investor from Toronto, who had expressed an interest in the firm. In order that he could evaluate his potential investment, Mr Cohen asked Lanzetta to produce projected income statements, balance sheets, and cash flow statements for Gourmet Gadgets Inc. up to July 31, 1990.

History

Gourmet Gadgets Inc., founded in May 1989, was owned jointly by Ken and Mary Lanzetta. The company was formed to design, develop, manufacture and market a unique household utensil, a pasta server. The specially curved patented plastic apparatus, to be sold retail for $3.75, could be used to stir, pick up and serve all varieties of pasta.

Ken, who was 35, had conceived the idea for the device while working for the Food Research Institute of Agriculture Canada as a research biologist. As a recent M.B.A. graduate, he was confident that he could bring his idea to fruition. He enthusiasm was echoed by his wife, Mary, aged 30, who, after having worked as a professional teacher, was to enter an M.B.A. program in September. In addition to her studies, she planned to act as vice-president and secretary of Gourmet Gadgets, while Ken would be president and treasurer.

13

The Lanzettas had already spent $10,500 before incorporation on obtaining patent approval for their invention in Canada and the United States. Patents were also being processed in Italy, Germany, France and the United Kingdom. With initial capital of $18,000 raised from personal loans of $10,500 from the Confederation Bank and $7,500 from Best Finance Ltd., the Lanzettas had established an office at their home in Kitchener and purchased production equipment. Capital expenditures consisted of $750 for office equipment, $20,250 for a single cavity production mould, $3750 for tools and dies and $3750 for a blister pack mould. Development costs incurred on the moulds were included in these amounts.

By July, Gourmet Gadgets Inc., was ready to begin production. An agreement was made with Perfect Plastics, Inc. in Cambridge to manufacture the utensil under contract, using Gourmet Gadgets moulds, at a cost of $.60 per unit. Packaging arrangements were concluded with B. Crawford & Sons Lithographic Ltd. of Kitchener to package the products the same month as produced. Distribution agreements were made with Household Ware Sales, Inc., Cooker Ltd., and Firenzo Sales Ltd.

Unfortunately, by this time, initial funds had been exhausted on capital expenditures and $10,500 was due in August on the production mould. Cash was also required for monthly administrative expenses of $3,750 for salaries, office expenses, insurance, telephone, utilities, automobile expenses, and miscellaneous supplies once production started. Perfect Plastics would not begin production without a 50 percent deposit and the remainder was due before any units would be released for sale. The packaging company also required cash payments on delivery. Without additional funding, the Lanzettas could not start production or distribution.

Production

The pasta server would be manufactured by an injection moulding process. The process made possible the rapid production of highly finished and detailed plastic units. Plastic was melted and then injected under thousands of kilograms of pressure into a mould which was held closed by a clamping mechanism. The devices were formed into a cavity, the two halves of the mould separated allowing the formed part to fall free. In injection moulding, parts could be formed in either single or multiple cavity moulds, depending on total production, production rate, size and weight of the part, size of machine available and the mould cost. Gourmet Gadgets Inc. initially planned to use a single cavity production mould (one device per cycle). Since four cycles could be completed per minute, monthly production capacity was about 40,000 units.

Ken feared a stock-out and planned an initial production run of 40,000 units. His production strategy was to order sufficient units to replace units sold, and to maintain a minimum of 10,000 units inventory. Perfect Plastics required production runs of at least 5,000 units. Ken planned initially to store inventory in the basement and garage of his home, but if inventory exceeded 10,000 units he would have to rent warehouse space at a cost of $200 per month. The warehouse space, with a capacity of 35,000 units, could be leased on a monthly basis and no annual lease was required. Lease payments were due the month following the actual lease.

Ken had also discussed with his accountant the problem of depreciation of the production mould. The life of a mould depended on the type of steel used, the number of cycles, the type of material to be moulded and the complexity of the part to be manufactured. Handled properly, moulds used to manufacture devices similar to the pasta server lasted for millions of units. However, from a practical viewpoint, Ken recognized that his single cavity mould could be obsolete after producing only 162,000 units if he decided to buy the new two cavity mould. His accountant suggested that a depreciation charge of $.125 per unit be used in pro-forma statements to account for wear and tear and obsolescence of the mould. A combined depreciation charge of $.015 per unit was recommended for the package mould and tool and dies. In addition, ten dollars per month was allowed for depreciation of office equipment, which was to be considered as an administrative expense.

The products would be blistered packaged on an attractive backing which would clearly show the consumer various applications for the device. Products would be packaged the same month as they were produced. Packaging costs for the product were $.0375 per unit. Material costs were included in these prices. Gourmet Gadgets Inc. would pay for shipping expenses of $.075 per unit, incurred when units were sold.

Marketing

The Lanzettas suggested that every family in North America was a potential purchaser, since they believed all families ate some variety of pasta. The Canadian population consisted of 8.99 million families (1986 Census data, Exhibit 1). Similar data is provided for Ontario, Toronto and Kitchener. The United States market was about ten times larger.

Household Wares, Inc. would handle the accounts of the Hudson's Bay Company, Woolco and Safeway. Cooker Ltd. was to handle Eaton's, Sears and independent boutiques. Firenzo Sales Ltd. would handle grocery outlets such as I.G.A., Loblaws and A & P.

The wholesale price by Gourmet Gadgets to the distributors was $1.58 per unit, net 30 days. Ken believed 50 percent of receipts would be paid the month following the sale and the remainder within the second month. Wholesalers would sell the product to retail outlets for $1.88. Gourmet Gadgets Inc. was also considering expanding distribution to the United States and, once patents were approved, to Europe.

Although no identical products used specifically for pasta were on the market, similar plastic kitchen utensils were occasionally used for pasta serving. These devices sold for $2.98 to $4.49, with retailers generally receiving a 100 percent markup.

Promotion by Gourmet Gadgets would consist of an attractive blister package for the product and free guest appearances on television talk and cooking shows such as *Canada A.M.* and *Celebrity Cooks*. Free press exposure was anticipated through editorial statements and consumer goods articles. Retail stores would be encouraged to conduct in-store promotions and display the device with pasta products. Consumer questionnaires would be made available to ascertain public reaction.

Considerable reliance was placed on the distributors to promote the product. The Lanzettas anticipated that 500 units would be given away monthly for the first four months for promotional purposes. Ken's accountant suggested that these should be counted as sales expenses at their cost of $1.115 per unit ($.60 for mould manufacturing, $.375 for packaging, plus $.14 for depreciation), the same amount as would be used to value inventory. The other suggestion was to delay amortization of the patent until Gourmet Gadgets had two profitable years.

Financial Implications

Exhibit 2 shows the balance sheet for Gourmet Gadgets as of July 15, 1989. Arthur Cohen was considering investing up to $75,000 for a fifty percent share of the equity and profits of the new company. Cohen stated that he may be willing to settle for a smaller ownership stake but his investment would be disproportionately lower. He would not consider investing an amount greater than $75,000 unless the Lanzettas increased their investment in the company significantly. However before he made any commitments, he wanted to examine very carefully a set of pro-forma statements for the venture.

The Lanzettas did not believe that they could invest any more personal funds in the company since their personal assets of $39,300 were tied up in their home and personal possessions (Exhibit 3). Cohen suggested that the Lanzettas calculate the amount of financing required each month and from those calculations determine the total amount of financing that he would need to invest.

Monthly sales of the pasta serving devices were difficult to project. Ken's reasonable expectation was 10,000 units and he had prepared a production schedule based on this sales level (Exhibit 4). His most pessimistic and optimistic monthly sales forecasts were 5000 units and 30,000 units respectively. If sales were 30,000 units or more per month, for two consecutive months, he planned to order a larger two-cavity production mould (two devices per cycle). The capital cost, including development, would be $54,000, payable in three monthly installments, starting the month the equipment was ordered. A three month lead time, from the time of ordering, was required before this mould would be operational. When operational, the mould would not only double production capacity, but also cut costs in half to $.30 per unit. Ken's accountant suggested a depreciation allowance of $.054 per unit for the two-cavity mould. With the reduction in material and depreciation costs, inventory would be costed at $0.744 per unit.

Ken believed that the first twelve months of sales were critical for the success of Gourmet Gadgets. He required forecasted cash flow, income statements, and balance sheets for his three different sales projections. Ken planned to use a 20 percent tax rate. If taxes were payable, they would be due 45 days after Gourmet Gadgets' year end of July 31, 1990.

The Lanzettas wished to limit the amount of money required from Mr. Cohen. They wanted to retain as much control over the business as possible. However they recognized the danger of being under-financed. Once they decided what amount they would request from Mr. Cohen, they would complete a formal information package and drop in to see Mr. Cohen with their completed pro-forma financial statements.

EXHIBIT 1
GOURMET GADGETS INC.

Composition of Canadian Households
(1986 Census Data)

Area	Number of Members					Mother Tongue			
	1	2	3	4-5	6+	English	French	Italian	German
Canada 8 991 675 households	1 934 710 (21.5%)	2 701 175 (30.5%)	1 599 320 (17.8%)	2 409 800 (26.8%)	346 660 (3.9%)	15 334 085 (63.0%)	6 159 740 (25.3%)	455 820 (2.0%)	438 675 (1.8%)
Avg. Number of People per household = 2.8									
Ontario 3 221 725 households	679 645 (21.1%)	964 400 (29.9%)	570 070 (17.7%)	883 060 (27.4%)	124 550 (3.9%)	6 941 930 (79.6%)	424 720 (4.9%)	289 770 (3.3%)	150 150 (1.7%)
Avg. Number of People per household = 2.8									
Toronto 1 199 805 households	257 195 (21.4%)	340 245 (28.4%)	214 490 (17.9%)	331 900 (27.7%)	55 970 (4.7%)	2 395 150 (73.6%)	43 845 (1.4%)	193 210 (5.9%)	52 785 (1.6%)
Avg. Number of People per household = 2.8									
Kitchener 110 155 households	22 040 (20.0%)	33 230 (30.2%)	19 975 (18.1%)	31 135 (28.3%)	3 770 (3.4%)	249 155 (83.1%)	3 710 (1.2%)	1 565 (0.5%)	16 775 (5.6%)
Avg. Number of People per household = 2.8									

EXHIBIT 2
GOURMET GADGETS INC.

Balance Sheet as of July 15, 1989

Assets		Liabilities	
Current	$ 0	Current Accounts Payable	$10 500
Total Current Assets	0		
Equipment			
Single Cavity Mould	20 250		
Tools and Dies	3 750	Equity	
Blister Package Mould	3 750		
Office Equipment	750	Common Stock	28 500
	28 500		
Other			
Patent	10 500		
	$ 39 000		$39 000

EXHIBIT 3
GOURMET GADGETS INC.

Lanzetta's Personal Balance Sheet
as of July 15, 1989

Assets		Liabilities	
Cash	$ 300	Bank Loans	$ 18 000
Real Estate	60 000	Mortgages	45 000
Automobile	10 500	Other Liabilities	6 000
Stocks, Bonds, Etc.	0		
Household & Personal Effects	37 500	Total Liabilities	69 000
		Net Worth	39 300
TOTAL ASSETS	$108 300	TOTAL LIABILITIES & NET WORTH	$108 300

EXHIBIT 4
GOURMET GADGETS INC.

Production Schedule (in units)
(10 000 units/month sales)

Month	Production		Sales	Promotion	Inventory	
	Moulded	Packaged			Home	Warehouse
August	40 000	40 000	10 000	500	10 000	19 500
September	0	0	10 000	500	10 000	9 000
October	5 000	5 000	10 000	500	10 000	3 500
November	7 000	7 000	10 000	500	10 000	0
December	10 000	10 000	10 000	0	10 000	0
January	10 000	10 000	10 000	0	10 000	0
February	10 000	10 000	10 000	0	10 000	0
March	10 000	10 000	10 000	0	10 000	0
April	10 000	10 000	10 000	0	10 000	0
May	10 000	10 000	10 000	0	10 000	0
June	10 000	10 000	10 000	0	10 000	0
July	10 000	10 000	10 000	0	10 000	0

LAPLANDER LIMITED

In late March, 1977, James Goodwin was preparing an application for an operating loan from the Confederation Bank. As President of Laplander Limited (Laplander), a recently incorporated company, Goodwin was anxious to determine the credit needs for the firm over the first two years of operation. He wished to present his case for these funds positively to the bank in order to obtain financing for his proposed production start in October.

The Company

A month before approaching the bank, Goodwin had resigned from his position as the general manager of a large sporting goods store in Montreal. During his fifteen years with the store, he had observed the increasing popularity of cross-country skiing. Exhibit 1 indicates that the surge in demand for cross-country skis had largely been satisfied from imports. Although Canada had for years been a major importer of cross-country skis, the rapid growth in the popularity of skiing in recent years had made domestic manufacture more attractive. Over the years, there had been several attempts to manufacture skis in Canada, but this was difficult given the competition from well-known brand names and the problems associated with providing a quality product with a complex technology.

At a 1976 trade show, Goodwin met and later formed a close business relationship with the representatives of a large cross-country ski manufacturer, Sweden Ski AB. Due to production constraints at its European plant, Sweden Ski had never been able to satisfy all of its Canadian orders. As a result, it had, for the past two years, been seeking a production licensing agreement with a North American firm to produce and distribute the company's full line of cross-country skis, which were now subject to a Canadian import tariff of 15 percent. When Goodwin heard of this opportunity, he brought together several Canadian investors and began negotiations for the North American production rights.

In February 1977, a joint venture agreement was finalized by which Laplander would receive exclusive North American production and marketing rights to the full line of Sweden Ski's cross-country skis. In order to prepare for production, Laplander agreed to pay Sweden Ski an amount totalling $120 000 for the initial start-up costs, covering the technical, sales and advertising assistance that Sweden Ski would provide over the six months from April to September of 1977. Laplander planned to pay this amount in monthly installments of $10 000 commencing at the end of October 1977. Also, the terms of the agreement specified a royalty of four percent of net sales, payable at the end of each selling season (January). Sweden Ski would also supply Laplander with the necessary raw materials to ensure that its high quality standards were maintained.

In order to finance Laplander, Goodwin persuaded several prominent Montreal businessmen to join with him and invest a total of $200 000 among them. Two of these investors had extensive business and personal links to the Confederation Bank and one was a major sporting goods distributor. Since the businessmen were deeply involved in other business activities, their involvement in Laplander would be passive. This would leave Goodwin with the brunt of the management and operating duties. Goodwin believed that the ownership group could provide the financial support that the new business would require, since all of his partners had substantial personal assets, and he himself was financially comfortable. Sweden Ski would contribute $135 000 of equity financing for 40 percent of the common shares. Goodwin's group obtained 60 percent of the common shares, while Goodwin himself had 25 percent.

Goodwin also sought out various government assistance programs to finance the new venture, and in February 1977 received support from the Atlantic Provinces Development Corporation (APDC). In return for locating the plant in the Atlantic Provinces, the APDC agreed to lend Laplander $285 000 to cover machinery purchase and some start-up costs. The loan was to be secured by the company's production machinery and a floating charge on other assets except inventory and accounts receivable. Interest payments were due the first of each October in arrears; however, the principal repayments were deferred until October 1st, 1982, at which time blended interest and principal payments would begin and continue for 15 years until 1990. The interest rate would be 11.25 percent, and the blended interest and principal payments were scheduled at $53 067 annually. Other provisions of the loan agreement stipulated that the loan would not be advanced until Laplander had secured a $1 million operating line of credit with a financial institution and the plant had started production.

With the joint-venture agreement and APDC financing in hand, Laplander searched the Atlantic Provinces for a suitable plant and subsequently located a developer in New Brunswick willing to build the facility according to Laplander's specifications. A new single-storey building was to be constructed on a leaseback basis, and would be 19 000 square feet in size with the potential for expansion, if needed. The layout of the plant would accommodate 16 720 feet of production space with the remaining footage to be used as office space. The rental agreement covered four years and specified rentals of $4700 per month. The installed cost of the production equipment was $250 000, and was to be paid for when installation was complete.

The developer indicated that the plant facility should be completed by the end of September, and that production would be ready to commence at the beginning of October. The technical expert on loan from Sweden Ski speculated that the production equipment could also be installed and operating by the beginning of October, dependent upon the progress of the plant construction. The developer refused to provide a guaranteed completion date, however, claiming that labour difficulties were always an unpredictable problem that could delay construction.

Laplander's Sales Plan

Industry analysts had forecasted sales growth of cross-country skis to be at least 20 percent per annum over the four years following 1975. Based on the increased demand and the past orders that Sweden Ski had received, Goodwin estimated that he could sell 47 500 pairs of skis in the 1978 selling season (June 1978 to November 1978), and 60 800 pairs of skis the following year. Although Sweden Ski had sold only 20 000 pairs in the previous sales season, the distributors they served thought that sales of 47 500 pairs were achievable. The sales estimates, which included an 11 percent federal sales tax payable by the manufacturer 30 days after the sale, were forecasted as follows:

	1978	1979
June	$ 292 500	$ 556 000
July	585 000	585 000
August	439 000	439 000
September	146 500	146 500
October	146 500	146 500
November	175 500	175 500
Total	$1 785 000	$2 048 500

Because of the anticipated growth in North American demand for cross-country skis, Goodwin speculated that "the production of the new plant for the first two years would probably not be sufficient to supply the North American market." He also believed that the heaviest orders could be expected in the early selling months, since the majority of orders were received from distributors at the spring trade shows, and many distributors took advantage of the lenient credit terms that manufacturers offered for buying early.

Goodwin thought that the majority of Laplander ski sales would be to the knowledgeable cross-country skier who was trading up to a more expensive and higher quality ski. In order to market the Laplander line successfully, Goodwin planned to personally attend all the ski trade shows in the spring of 1978. The following year, in January 1979, Laplander would kick off a three month promotion campaign in ski magazines costing $6500 per month and designed to stimulate further interest in Laplander skis for the upcoming trade shows. Goodwin believed that this promotion would be sufficient, since there was only one other major Canadian manufacturer of cross-country skis, which began operations under license in 1975. Its main ski line was also of high quality; but the Laplander was less expensive. Goodwin was aware that several other leading European cross-country ski manufacturers were making plans to license North American production rights. This added to his desire to get started as soon as possible on production of the Laplander ski in Canada.

Goodwin assumed he would offer dealers the same credit terms as most of his competitors. Common practice required payment of 30 percent of the invoiced amount in the month following delivery, with the balance (70 percent) payable in January. These terms were designed to encourage early orders since distributors could enjoy the benefits of a maximum of seven months' credit. Although the majority of retail sales occurred in November and December, most distributors usually did not receive payments from retailers until January. Laplander would accept returns of defective skis, but not returns of unsold skis.

One of the major worries facing retailers was cited by a member of the Ski Industries Association:

> The cross-country ski industry is especially vulnerable to the whims of nature. People tend to buy downhill equipment in the fall. But with cross-country, they wait for snow. When there is no snow, or little snow, it could be very bad.

In 1975, sales of imported cross-country skis were concentrated in Eastern Canada, with Quebec and the Atlantic Provinces accounting for approximately 72 percent of the cross-country ski market, and Ontario sales comprising 22 percent of the national totals.

Cross-country skis were sold through two distribution channels, either department and chain stores (40 percent of market), or sporting goods and specialty stores (60 percent). Goodwin planned to sell his skis through five major Canadian distributors, who would then market the skis to Canada's estimated 2800 sporting goods dealers. He had investigated each distributor personally, and judged them to be capable distributors as well as safe credit risks. One of the five distributors was also an investor in Laplander, and his company planned to distribute roughly one quarter of Laplander's planned production. Goodwin had also made plans to sell in the U.S., and had reached a tentative agreement with a U.S. distributor. This prospect excited him because studies had shown that Americans had not yet adopted cross-country skiing to the degree Canadians had. Therefore, the huge American market seemed to hold enormous potential. In addition, a low U.S. import duty (eight percent) and favourable exchange rates on the Canadian dollar would make Canadian exports very competitive with U.S. manufactured skis.

Laplander's Production

The production of cross-country skis would commence in October 1977, and for the first six months Laplander's employees would be trained by Sweden Ski craftsmen. Goodwin hired an experienced production manager whose previous experience was in the manufacture of hockey sticks. Goodwin was confident that the new plant manager's experience with cost control and plant management would make Laplander's production process smooth and efficient.

The production process consisted of the pressing together, cutting and finishing of materials such as fiberglass, epoxy, birch, ash and poplar. Although this process was labour-intensive, the use of wood materials produced a superior-quality ski since the solidity of the ski could be assured. Recent technological trends had led other manufacturers to use foam in the core of their cross-country skis. This foam could be mould-injected at enormous cost savings since the materials were cheaper and less labour was required. However, Goodwin believed that sophisticated ski purchasers would recognize the Laplander quality and not be attracted to cheaper, inferior foam-core skis. One problem particular to foam injected skis was their tendency to suffer broken tips more often than sandwich wood models.

Skis were manufactured in lengths ranging from 170 to 225 centimeters (at five cm intervals), and widths ranging from "racers" (35 millimeters) to "citizen-racers" (45 mm) to "tourers" (55 mm). Since there was a wide range of sizes, and production runs could only accommodate one length and width at a time, Goodwin figured that a minimum of seven to eight months of steady production would be required to produce the full range of ski lengths in all models. Twelve months of steady production would ensure that the sales targets in the company's 1978-79 season could be readily achieved.

Goodwin estimated that the labour costs would be $13 500 in October and November 1977, $15 200 in December, and $17 100 in each subsequent month. Employee benefits would be a constant $2700 per month.

Raw materials could be either European (from Sweden Ski) or locally sourced. The European materials, which included a 12.5 percent tariff paid by the seller, were purchased on net 90 day terms, while the local materials were purchased on net 30 day terms. Goodwin had decided to import European raw materials in order to maintain visual comparability with existing

Laplander skis in the stores, and to attempt to achieve the same high quality as Sweden Ski. The estimated material purchases were:

	European Sourced	Canadian Sourced
September 1977	$100 500	$4 100
October 1977	66 000	4 100
November 1977	66 000	5 500
December 1977	66 000	5 500
January 1978	52 000	8 300
February 1978	66 000	4 100
March 1978	66 000	8 300
April 1978	66 000	6 900
May 1978	66 000	8 300
June 1978	66 000	6 900
July 1978	66 000	8 300
August 1978 to September 1979	66 000	8 300

Goodwin thought that over the next two years Laplander's production efficiency would improve, resulting in lower cost of goods sold. In the first year ending September 30, 1978, cost of goods sold would be roughly 86 percent of net sales (after federal sales taxes had been deducted), and in the second year 75 percent of net sales.

The other costs that Laplander would face beginning in October 1977 were $12 500 per month for factory overhead (rising to $13 000 in the second year of operations), $6300 per month for administrative wages, and $1900 per month for office overhead (falling to $1500 in the second year of operations). Laplander's production machinery and start-up costs of $120 000 were depreciable for tax purposes at the CCA rate of 20 percent but these amounts were not included in the estimates of overheads. Also, Goodwin knew that federal corporate income taxes at a rate of 48 percent (a 25 percent rate was allowed for small businesses earning less than $50 000) should be included in his cash flow estimates. Corporate income taxes for Laplander's first year of operation ended September 30, 1978 would be payable on November 30 of that year. In the following years of operation, estimated taxes based on the previous year's income would be due on an equal monthly installment basis.

Developing a Cash Budget

With Laplander's estimated September 30, 1977 balance sheet (Exhibit 2) in hand, Goodwin started working out a two year monthly cash budget that would be used to support his application for credit to the Confederation Bank. The branch manager at the Confederation Bank indicated that the rate of interest charged on operating loans would be prime plus 1-3/4 percent; the Confederation Bank prime currently stood at 8-1/4 percent.

Goodwin believed that his cash needs should be projected carefully since the branch manager had raised several questions about Laplander's ability to repay its loans, the available collateral, and whether the company needed temporary or permanent financing. Future discussions with the bank would undoubtedly focus on the viability of the new venture and Goodwin knew that he should be prepared to discuss any concerns or doubts that would arise in the bank's analysis of Laplander's loan request.

EXHIBIT 1
LAPLANDER LIMITED

**Canadian Ski Industry
Cross Country Ski Imports vs Domestic Production
1970-1976**

	Domestic Production		Imports	
	Pairs	Wholesale Value	Pairs	Wholesale Value
1970	4 000	$ 56 000	27 792	$ 338 000
1971	6 000	53 000	49 868	549 000
1972	10 000	142 000	114 385	1 332 000
1973	12 000	154 000	351 471	3 416 000
1974	39 000	575 000	414 018	5 094 000
1975	40 000	600 000	405 812	6 125 000
1976[1]	100 000[2]	n.a.	695 000	n.a.

[1] Estimates
[2] Canadian exports in 1976 totalled 10 000 pairs

Source: Statistics Canada

EXHIBIT 2

LAPLANDER LIMITED

**Pro Forma Start-up Balance Sheet
as of September 30, 1977**

Assets

Current Assets	
Cash	$370 000
Inventory	104 600
Total Current Assets	474 600
Fixed Assets	
Plant Machinery & Office Equipment	250 000
Start-up Costs	120 000
Total Fixed Assets	370 000
TOTAL ASSETS	$844 600

Liabilities & Shareholders' Equity

Current Liabilities	
Accounts Payable	$104 600
Start-up Costs payable to Sweden Ski AB	120 000
Loan Payable, APDC	285 000
	509 600
Shareholders' Capital	335 000
TOTAL LIABILITIES AND SHAREHOLDERS' EQUITY	$844 600

PERREAULT BROTHERS LIMITED

Ms. Nancy Harris, the accountant for Perreault Brothers Limited (PBL), a commercial and industrial mechanical building contractor in Saskatoon, received an urgent request from Michel Perreault on January 6, 1989, to prepare cash-flow projections for the firm. The two Perreault brothers had just emerged from discussions with Mr. Bill Melnyk, the branch manager of the Confederation Bank. Mr. Melnyk had expressed grave concern over the bank's growing commitment to PBL, currently $357,000, and the firm's ability to repay the loan. He had requested that PBL prepare a cash forecast outlining a plan for reduction of the bank loan, and financial statements as of December 31, 1988.

In its past association with the bank, PBL had negotiated its loan needs by outlining the cash requirements of specific contracts and by posting collateral as requested. The total collateral posted as of January 6, 1989, consisted of a general assignment of the accounts receivable and inventory under Section 178 of the Bank Act, and a mortgage against all fixed assets of PBL, plus the Perreault brothers' personal guarantees for the company's loans. A recent schedule of net worth that the brothers had completed for the bank valued their net personal assets, excluding the business, at $162,500. This amount consisted almost entirely of the brothers' homes and personal effects after deducting $200,000 in outstanding mortgage loans obtained from the Confederation Bank.

Their discussions with Mr. Melnyk now made it clear to the Perreault brothers that they would have to accurately assess financial needs to maintain the bank's continued support. As a starting point, they visited Ms. Harris to talk about preparation of the financial reports and the cash-flow projection.

Company History

PBL was founded by Michel and Andre Perreault in 1976. Before creating the firm, both Michel and Andre had studied metal working in technical school and worked for several years as journeymen. Using their accumulated savings of $25,000, they decided to go into business for themselves. Since neither brother had any experience in running a business at the time of incorporation, they decided to undertake only small construction contract jobs.

Initially, PBL specialized in sheet-metal work. As business proved profitable, they expanded activities to include contracts for the installation of plumbing and heating. PBL grew rapidly along with the Saskatchewan economy, which was fueled by the oil boom in the late 1970's. However, with the introduction of the National Energy Program in the fall of 1980, the oil industry crashed and with it the economies of the prairie provinces. Problems in the Saskatchewan economy were compounded by the Canada-wide recession of 1981-1982. With some belt-tightening and careful management, PBL was able to survive the recession. By 1988, the firm had expanded to 32 production employees (10 in the metal shop and 22 in the field), plus two administrative personnel in addition to the brothers. This expansion necessitated a new plant, which PBL leased, with a floor area of 10,000 square feet – 9,500 square feet for the manufacturing operation and storage, and 500 square feet for the office. The major fixed asset investments of the company were the basic tools of the manufacturing operation (small tools, welding equipment, and an immovable metal-bending press), three trucks, and the two cars used by the Perreault brothers.

Michel Perreault, 46 years old, and Andre Perreault, 49, believed that with hard work the company would continue to be the success it had always been. Both brothers were considered workaholics by their business associates. As PBL's business expanded, the Perreault brothers spent more time administering the company and less time working at their trades. In 1988, with rare exceptions, they spent all of their time in administration. Michel Perreault supervised the manufacturing operations and a small portion of the outside work, while Andre quoted on jobs and supervised the major portion of the outside work. This re-organization, a larger equity base, and an expanded workforce enabled the company to undertake larger contracts. The first major contract, begun in late 1986, and worth approximately $1.6 million, involved 18-20 months of work on a large commercial development. Such a large contract was a substantial departure for the company, and it had been a major factor in gaining the increased financial support from the Confederation Bank.

Billings and Collection Procedure

Most of PBL's revenue came from acting as a subcontractor on construction projects. This typically involved the submission of a bid for the plumbing, heating, and sheet metal work in a commercial or industrial construction project being undertaken by a contractor. If the PBL bid was successful, PBL would do the bulk of the work but would subcontract parts of the job such as the installation of control devices. In the construction trade, once a bid has been accepted, the contractor and subcontractor are expected to meet all specifications for the price quoted. If the materials, labour or overhead costs vary, the contractor or subcontractors bear the loss or enjoy the extra profit. Each subcontractor submits monthly billings to the contractor, outlining materials, labour and overhead allocated to the construction project in the past month. The general contractor in turn submits an estimate of total costs to the client. The architect, in consultation with the general contractor, approves, varies, or disapproves the billings, based on his estimate of the work done to date. The architect then submits the vetted billings to the client, who then pays the general contractor the amount of the approved monthly billings, less a statutory holdback (10 percent in the case of all contracts undertaken by PBL in 1988). The purpose of such holdbacks is to protect the client against mechanics' liens which could be applied against the job by subcontractors and tradesmen. Once the general contractor receives its billings (less the holdback), the subcontractors are each paid subject to the same 10 percent holdback provision. PBL expected each month's billings to be paid after about 30 days, while holdbacks were expected to be paid three to six months after the mechanical work was substantially completed.

Competitive Conditions

The city of Saskatoon acted as a transportation and servicing hub for a variety of industries in northern Saskatchewan, including government, farming, oil, potash, uranium and light manufacturing. The Saskatoon economy was closely tied to the resource sector. As a result, building activity in Saskatoon varied greatly from year to year (see Exhibit 1). Residential construction in 1988 was down modestly from 1987 levels, but was forecasted to decline a further 29 percent in 1989. Commercial construction was down 48 percent from 1987. Economists had been predicting that the preceding summer's severe drought, the September plunge in world oil prices, and a troubled potash industry could put all of Saskatchewan into a major recession. There was also growing concern about the federal government's debt and what action the government would take to combat the problem.

On the positive side, world oil prices were showing signs of recovery and Saskatoon firms were well positioned to participate in the recently announced heavy oil upgrader facility at Lloydminster. In December, the Saskatoon area had a heavy snowfall, making farmers more optimistic about the coming farm season.

In order to gain a foothold in the mechanical contracting business, PBL had bid aggressively for jobs in 1986. The net result of this aggressive bidding was that gross margins previously averaging 20 percent were reduced. Flat business activity and a decline in house construction were causing the chartered banks to carefully review all of their construction loans.

Current Financial Position

At their meeting, Ms. Harris and the Perreault brothers discussed business prospects and future plans for the firm. Ms. Harris presented the Perreault brothers with preliminary financial statements for the fiscal year ending December 31, 1988, as well as comparative statements for 1983 to 1987 (see Exhibits 2 and 3).

All three were especially bothered by the extraordinary expenses of $164,200. Of this amount, $44,600 arose from a 1985 investment in Blue Water Limited, a family business that retailed boats and motors. The company declared bankruptcy in the fall of 1987, and the investment was written off. Another $111,800 resulted from the bankruptcy of a major customer. And the remaining $7,800 arose from other minor bad debt losses.

Forecasting for 1989

Ms. Harris noted that she had no information regarding future manufacturing overhead or selling and administrative expenses. The brothers told Ms. Harris that manufacturing overhead included shop supplies, rent, utilities, vehicle expenses, business and unemployment insurance, maintenance and fringe benefits. Their selling and administrative expenses encompassed owners' compensation, life insurance, office salaries, car expenses, legal and audit expenses, stationery, telephone, fax, courier, and interest. Over the next twelve months, they forecasted their expenses as follows:

Monthly Forecasts of Manufacturing Overhead and Selling & Administrative Expenses

Month	Manufacturing Overhead	Selling/ Administrative Expenses	TOTAL
January 1989	$13 650	$19 500	$33 150
February	9 100	22 425	31 525
March	8 775	18 850	27 625
April	13 365	17 060	30 425
May	8 240	18 200	26 440
June	12 500	16 770	29 270
July	6 825	16 770	23 595
August	6 825	21 890	28 715
September	6 825	16 495	23 320
October	6 260	17 055	23 315
November	6 260	18 200	24 460
December	11 660	19 900	31 560

Ms. Harris next moved to a review of PBL's current contracts (see Exhibits 4 to 6). The brothers noted that their estimates were highly speculative since there were many uncertainties in their line of business. For example, they pointed out that in the case of Contract Number 4, all the firms involved had incurred costs higher than expected in meeting the original specifications, because of insufficient detail in the architect's original drawings. In addition, all the large jobs currently in process would likely be over budget since inflation had caused both raw materials costs and wage rates to rise higher than expected. The variance in actual materials and labour costs from budgeted costs for all four contracts would be, at most, 33 percent. Michel Perreault estimated that $97,000 of the budgeted material expenses for January would likely be supplied by drawing down the available raw material inventories.

The conversation turned to consideration of future prospects for the firm. Ms. Harris observed that their current contracts would be substantially completed by the end of March 1989 and asked about the type of business that could be expected in the coming year, especially in light of the uncertain local economy. Andre responded that the firm expected to return to smaller contracts with a greater emphasis on metal working and higher profit margins. He also anticipated substantial cuts in their workforce, probably down to a crew of 12 to 20. While the volume of such contracts was uncertain, they expected to generate $100,000 to $130,000 of billings per month, starting in April. It was difficult to estimate labour and material expenses for the new jobs; however, the brothers expected that material and labour costs would be similar and in total should not exceed 75 percent of billings. Ms. Harris asked about their billings expectations with this new business. Michel Perreault replied that future billings would be made when their part of the contract was essentially complete, and that the normal trade terms were net 30 days. Holdbacks on this new business were expected to be collected in two to four months. Reviewing their past experience, neither brother expected to return to the large contract field unless they could obtain a substantial gross margin, in the area of 20 percent. They did not expect this to happen in the near future, but were interested in Ms. Harris' opinion. Although the firm expected to earn profits in the coming year, there would be no tax payments due to tax loss carry forwards from previous years.

The brothers closed the discussion by asking Ms. Harris to review their financial situation and to make recommendations. They expected her to have the financial projections for the bank and the recommendations ready by the end of the week. Getting up to leave, Michel said:

> I don't understand why the bank is concerned. We've given them over $1 million in collateral from the company and our homes—what more do they want?

EXHIBIT 1
PERREAULT BROTHERS LIMITED

Building Permits Issued in Saskatoon
1984 – 1988
($000)

	1988 (preliminary)	1987	1986	1985	1984
Residential	98 718	100 244	126 282	102 735	96 775
Industrial	8 512	8 448	17 902	3 911	4 184
Commercial	43 489	83 983	34 733	49 635	44 683
Institutional & Government	68 888	37 876	80 850	29 329	56 111
Total Building Permits	219 607	230 551	259 767	185 610	201 753

Source: Statistics Canada

EXHIBIT 2
PERREAULT BROTHERS LIMITED

Balance Sheets for years ending December 31
($000)

	1988 (preliminary)	1987	1986	1985	1984	1983
Assets						
Cash	$ 0.0	$ 0.0	$ 106.3	$ 0.0	$ 16.3	$ 2.0
Accounts Receivable, Net	544.7	349.7	715.0	314.3	189.2	401.7
Inventory — Raw Materials	109.2	11.7	14.3	32.5	25.1	14.7
— Work in Process	32.5	39.0	89.1	4.2	0.0	2.2
Prepaid Expenses	58.5	87.8	40.3	14.3	20.4	6.4
Total Current Assets	744.9	488.2	965.0	365.3	251.0	427.0
Investments	7.8	55.0	48.1	42.9	30.9	26.9
Life Insurance (Cash Surrender Value)	14.3	10.4	6.8	5.2	4.2	2.6
Fixed Assets, Net	204.5	210.6	144.0	78.7	83.6	77.7
Other Assets	1.6	1.6	1.6	1.7	1.6	1.6
TOTAL ASSETS	973.1	765.8	1 165.5	493.8	371.3	535.8
Liabilities & Equity						
Bank Overdraft	11.1	17.3	0.0	4.6	0.0	0.0
Bank Loan	357.5	182.0	286.0	91.0	65.0	97.5
Accounts Payable	314.6	253.5	487.2	148.2	103.9	257.4
Other Current Liabilities	89.1	81.1	113.8	60.8	59.3	50.7
Total Current Liabilities	772.3	533.9	887.0	304.6	228.2	405.6
Long Term Debt Due to Officers	87.1	9.1	4.8	0.0	7.8	30.3
Total Liabilities	859.4	543.0	891.8	304.6	236.0	435.9
Preferred Stock	39.0	39.0	39.0	39.0	39.0	39.0
Common Stock	8.1	8.1	8.1	8.1	8.1	8.1
Retained Earnings	66.6	175.7	226.6	142.1	88.2	52.8
Total Equity	113.7	222.8	273.7	189.2	135.3	99.9
TOTAL LIABILITIES & EQUITY	$973.1	$765.8	$1 165.5	$493.8	$371.3	$535.8

EXHIBIT 3
PERREAULT BROTHERS LIMITED

Income Statements for the years ended December 31
($000)

	1988 (preliminary)	1987	1986	1985	1984	1983
Sales	$2 427.1	$1 822.6	$1 735.2	$1 404.4	$1 136.9	$1 211.0
Cost of Goods Sold						
Materials	1 043.0	770.0	522.3	351.0	363.7	492.7
Labour	987.0	759.0	806.9	666.9	433.2	399.8
Depreciation	24.1	27.6	24.4	12.4	13.3	9.8
Overhead (Manufacturing)	32.5	39.0	35.8	118.3	117.7	78.7
Total Cost of Goods Sold	2 086.6	1 595.6	1 389.4	1 148.6	927.9	981.0
Gross Margin	340.5	227.0	345.8	255.8	209.0	230.0
Selling and Administrative Expenses						
Management — Compensation	153.4	164.1	134.9	102.4	75.0	78.7
Other	132.0	118.3	105.6	84.9	88.1	72.8
Total Selling and Administrative Expenses	285.4	282.4	240.5	187.3	163.1	151.5
Net Operating Income	55.1	(55.4)	105.3	68.5	45.9	78.5
Other Income	0.0	0.0	5.2	1.7	0.4	0.0
Other Expenses	164.2	11.1	0.0	0.0	0.0	44.9
Net Income Before Taxes	(109.1)	(66.5)	110.5	70.2	46.3	33.6
Taxes	0.0	(15.6)	26.0	16.3	10.9	7.8
Net Income After Taxes	$ (109.1)	$ (50.9)	$ 84.5	$ 53.9	$ 35.4	$ 25.8

EXHIBIT 4

PERREAULT BROTHERS LIMITED

Current Contracts Position as of December 31, 1988 and Expected Billings to June 30, 1989
($000)

	Contract Number				
	1	*2*	*3*	*4*	*Totals*
Contract Position as of December 31, 1988					
Amount Billed as of Dec. 31, 1988	$113.4	$ 68.0	$294.8	$1 312.1	$1 788.3
Amount Unbilled as of Dec. 31, 1988	254.6	267.5	209.5	290.8	1 022.2
Total Bid	368.0	335.5	504.3	1 602.9	2 810.5
Past Billings					
Collection to Date	34.1	27.3	190.5	991.6	1 243.5
Holdback	11.3	6.8	29.5	131.2	178.8
Collections Due in January 1989	68.0	33.9	74.8	189.3	366.0
Amount Billed as of Dec. 31, 1988	113.4	68.0	294.8	1 312.1	1 788.3
Expected Billings					
January 1989	57.9	167.4	25.4	185.9	436.6
February 1989	88.8	63.7	58.5	97.5	308.5
March 1989	107.9	36.4	33.2	7.4	184.9
April 1989	0.0	0.0	33.2	0.0	33.2
May 1989	0.0	0.0	33.2	0.0	33.2
June 1989	0.0	0.0	26.0	0.0	26.0
Amount Unbilled as of December 31, 1988	$254.6	$267.5	$209.5	$ 290.8	$1 022.4

EXHIBIT 5
PERREAULT BROTHERS LIMITED

Accounts Payable Aging
as of December 31, 1988
($000)

Month of Purchase	Amount	% of Total Accounts Payable
December 1988	$ 69.3	22
November 1988	44.5	14
October 1988	86.5	27
September 1988	21.5	7
August 1988	37.1	12
July 1988	53.0	17
All Others	2.9	1
Total Accounts Payable December 31, 1988	$314.8	100

EXHIBIT 6
PERREAULT BROTHERS LIMITED

Budgeted Materials and Labour Expenses
for Completion of Current Contracts
($000)

	Contract Number				
	1	2	3	4	Totals
Budgeted Material Expenses					
January 1989	$37.7	$61.5	$ 0.0	$ 90.6	$189.8
February 1989	32.2	13.0	19.5	39.0	103.7
Total	69.9	74.5	19.5	129.6	293.5
Budgeted Labour Expenses					
January 1989	23.8	27.3	31.2	59.8	142.1
February 1989	16.9	27.3	16.9	17.6	78.7
March 1989	15.6	13.7	40.3	2.6	72.2
Total	$56.3	$68.3	$88.4	$ 80.0	$293.0

FISHER ELECTRIC INC.

On February 5, 1989, Gerry Wilson, the manager of the main Vancouver branch of the Confederation Bank, was considering an application for a $10.0 million line of credit from Fisher Electric Inc. (Fisher). Fisher currently conducted all of its banking activities with Pacific Bank of Canada (Pacific), a major competitor of Confederation's and acquiring the account would be a coup for Wilson.

Michael Murray, the President of Fisher, initiated the discussions with Wilson because he believed that the credit limit of $8.5 million imposed on Fisher by Pacific was restricting to the company's existing operations and its plans for continued growth and expansion. Pacific's credit manager maintained that Fisher's loan amount should stabilize in 1989 after a rapid buildup over the past five years to its current level, and he advised Murray that the maximum loan he would consider at this time was $8.5 million.

Murray had started with Fisher in 1983 as the manager of its highly successful Vancouver branch. His uncle, who had founded the company, sold all of his shares to Murray in 1985. In 1989, 72 percent of Fisher common stock was owned by Murray and 28 percent by the four branch managers and three other key employees. Murray initiated a stock purchase plan in 1986 to keep his key people and to focus their attention on the profitability of the business.

Fisher had been a Pacific Bank customer for over 35 years, and had a record of growth and profitability over the past four years which impressed Wilson. The company's recent financial statements are presented in Exhibits 1 and 2.

Fisher operated as a wholesaler of electrical supplies, selling to contractors of single family and multiple dwelling units, as well as to retailers of electrical products such as hardware stores and building supply outlets. The firm's branches were located in the western Canadian cities of Saskatoon, Edmonton, Calgary and Vancouver. The head office was located in Vancouver.

Fisher's products consisted of a large variety of electrical supplies and materials generally used in residential construction. Principal items sold were wiring, all types of fixtures, breaker panels, fuse panels, switch and receptacle boxes, electric baseboard heaters and ground floor receptacles. Fisher was gradually expanding its line into related products such as security systems.

Each branch purchased independently from an established product list and dealt directly with approved suppliers. Murray instituted monthly meetings with the individual branch managers, during which inventory control was stressed. Each branch manager received separate financial statements for his operations with key ratios such as inventory turnover, gross profit percentages and net profit to sales highlighted. Each branch's results were discussed at each meeting.

Most manufacturers of electrical products offered volume discounts and early payment incentives. Manufacturers typically offered a 2% discount for payment within 20 days. On large orders Fisher would attempt to take advantage of these discounts. Usually, however, Fisher paid its accounts in about 60 days, which was the industry standard, although the bank loan limit sometimes forced Fisher to take a longer time to pay. All payments to creditors were made from head office on the basis of approved invoices from the branches.

Fisher management believed that high inventory levels provided clients with the best service and sheltered the company somewhat from price increases. The wholesale electrical supply business was highly competitive and Murray was convinced that Fisher would lose business to its competitors if it was caught in stock outs. Contractors wanted supplies on demand and they counted on Fisher to supply them. Tomorrow was too late. Electrical products had experienced inflationary price increases of roughly 3 to 4 percent in each of the last three years.

Fisher's sales were relatively stable throughout the year. Trade credit was granted to contractors and retail hardware and building supply stores by the individual branch managers who obtained credit reports on all new accounts and regularly updated reports on existing customers. When an account receivable exceeded 90 days outstanding and $20,000, Fisher's credit manager at head office became involved. The credit manager met with the branch managers quarterly to review all receivables. One of Fisher's major customers went bankrupt in 1987, with the company recovering approximately $200,000 of $800,000 owing. Normal bad debt losses, which were included in general expenses, amounted to about $100,000 per year.

Most of Fisher's recent sales growth could be attributed to the recovery in residential construction activity in the cities and surrounding suburban areas where the company operated. Exhibit 3 presents the actual levels of housing starts in each city over the past ten years and compares them with the national level; and provides projected levels of housing starts for 1989. Fisher's sales dropped with the level of new housing starts in 1982, 1983, and 1984 and the company incurred small losses in each of these years.

Fisher's sales and profits increased each year for the past four years. Murray predicted that net sales for fiscal 1989 would be $56 million.

The existing branches in the chain varied considerably in sales and earning performance. Vancouver had consistently outperformed expectations and contributed 40 percent of the total profits in 1988, while Saskatoon had been a major disappointment over the last three years and barely reached break-even in 1988.

Fisher had undertaken an aggressive sales approach to residential electrical contractors in western Canada. The objective was to increase Fisher's market share and customer loyalty. In 1988, 55% of Fisher's sales were to new housing contractors with the remaining 45% of sales going to retail outlets.

Frank Scully, sales manager, estimated that sales volume in 1989 would be 10% greater than in 1988 and 10% greater again in 1990 over 1989 because of the sales effort and the steadily increasing new housing market. He forecast selling prices would increase an average of four percent in each year.

Murray proposed that Confederation Bank take as security for its $10.0 million line of credit both a demand debenture against Fisher which would include a first floating charge against inventory and a general assignment of accounts receivable. In Wilson's opinion, the realizable value of the inventory was high since it consisted of staple merchandise. Although a distress sale would probably not realize book value, Wilson estimated that there was sufficient value to recover at least 50 percent of cost in a reasonably short time period.

For similar accounts, the Confederation Bank charged prime plus $1\frac{1}{2}\%$ on loan balances. Prime was currently at $12\frac{3}{4}$ percent. In addition, the bank usually set a margin formula that in effect limited borrowings to 75 percent of current (less than 90 days) receivables and 50 percent of inventory.

Gerry Wilson wondered whether he should accept the account. If he did take it, was $10 million a sufficient amount? What would Fisher's future credit needs be? Was the collateral package proposed by Murray satisfactory?

EXHIBIT 1
FISHER ELECTRIC INC.

Income Statement
for the years ended December 31, 1986 – 1988
($000)

	1988	1987	1986
Gross Sales	$49 620	$43 104	$38 254
Less Discounts Allowed	762	654	598
Net Sales	48 858	42 450	37 656
Cost of Goods Sold	38 877	33 466	29 828
Gross Profit	9 981	8 984	7 828
Operating Expenses			
Administrative	3 114	3 144	2 706
Selling	1 730	1 130	1 028
Warehouse	2 342	2 078	1 826
Total Operating Expenses	7 186	6 352	5 560
Operating Income	2 795	2 632	2 268
Interest Expense	1 460	912	753
Income Before Taxes	1 335	1 720	1 515
Income Tax	614	791	697
Income After Taxes	721	929	818
Dividends	$ 0	$ 0	$ 640

EXHIBIT 2
FISHER ELECTRIC INC.

Balance Sheet as at December 31,
1986 – 1988
($000)

	1988	1987	1986
Assets			
Current Assets			
Cash	$ 94	$ 100	$ 0
Accounts Receivable	9 104	7 582	6 212
Inventory	14 716	12 372	10 348
Prepaid Expenses	640	1 082	490
Total Current Assets	24 554	21 136	17 050
Land	494	494	442
Building & Property Net	1 402	1 314	1 056
Equipment & Other Fixed Assets Net	1 446	1 552	1 038
TOTAL ASSETS	27 896	24 496	19 586
Liabilities			
Current Liabilities			
Bank Loan	8 200	6 995	6 550
Trade Payables	7 662	7 284	5 292
Long Term Debt, Current Portion	549	234	12
Income Taxes Payable	370	505	348
Total Current Liabilities	16 781	15 018	12 202
Five Year Term Loan Secured By Fixed Assets – 14%	2 831	1 971	862
Total Liabilities	19 612	16 989	13 064
Shareholders' Equity			
Equity	406	350	294
Retained Earnings	7 878	7 157	6 228
Total Shareholders Equity	8 284	7 507	6 522
TOTAL LIABILITIES AND SHAREHOLDERS' EQUITY	$27 896	$24 496	$19 586

EXHIBIT 3
FISHER ELECTRIC INC.

Residential Housing Starts in Canada and Selected Cities

Housing Starts	1989 (projected)	1988	1987	1986	1985	1984	1983	1982	1981	1980	1979	1978
All Canada	185 000	189 635	215 340	199 785	165 826	110 874	134 207	104 792	142 441	125 013	151 717	178 678
Saskatoon	1 800	1 426	1 746	1 963	2 002	1 462	2 529	3 481	2 076	1 880	4 259	3 250
Calgary	4 200	3 800	3 466	2 679	2 318	1 803	4 882	9 599	15 172	11 104	12 383	15 382
Edmonton	4 500	4 133	3 608	2 561	2 528	2 384	6 543	9 738	11 999	9 967	12 298	17 065
Vancouver	18 800	17 901	17 860	13 578	11 315	9 683	12 302	9 247	15 227	16 780	12 827	12 183
Total 4 cities	29 300	27 260	26 680	20 781	18 163	15 332	26 256	32 065	44 474	39 731	41 767	47 880
Growth	0.07	0.02	0.28	0.14	0.18	−0.42	−0.18	−0.28	0.12	−0.05	−0.13	

Sources:
1. Canada Mortgage and Housing Corporation
2. Statistics Canada; Canadian Economic Observer

CHESTER FRANCHISORS LIMITED

In January 1987, Christine McNab, a Senior Account Manager with the Confederation Bank, was preparing a credit application. A Confederation client, Chester Franchisors Limited, which in turn owned the DDDelicious DDDonuts and Jedida Cookies (pronounced Joh-dee-dah) master franchisor companies, had applied for a new $335,000 operating loan. This loan would replace existing operating loans of $165,000 and the increased credit would be used to finance the opening of two new company owned Jedida Cookies franchise outlets in Vancouver.

Franchising in Canada

Franchising was an increasingly popular method of distributing goods and services in Canada, and accounted for over one third of all retail sales. Franchised businesses had developed a reputation for success with both lenders and investors. Christine McNab had read that fewer than 10% of new franchises failed in their first five years of business, relative to a comparable new independent business failure rate of 70%. The bulk of the growth in franchising had occurred in the service sector and more specifically in the retailing of fast foods such as hamburgers, ice creams, and baked products. In the baked products franchising field, the market was divided into three categories: cookies, donuts, and gourmet bakery shops. The competitors in each of the categories are listed in Exhibit 1.

Confederation Bank Franchise Plan

Christine McNab knew that the Confederation Bank had designed a special financing package that was tailored to the needs of franchisors and franchisees. The Confederation Bank's Franchise Plan, which is outlined in Exhibit 2, was designed to standardize financing packages for all franchisors. Once a franchisor was approved by the Confederation Bank, a Franchisee

45

Assistance Program was set up to handle the specific banking needs of franchisees. For instance, Chester Franchisors' subsidiary, DDDelicious DDDonuts Ltd., had a Franchisee Assistance Program with the Confederation Bank, and many of its individual franchisees had loans with Confederation.

Chester Franchisors Limited

Chester Franchisors Limited was incorporated in 1981 to act as a holding corporation. The company founders, Henry Dillman and Charlie Driggs, had established track records through their involvement with various franchised outlets concentrated in the hospitality industry. Dillman had worked for a time with a large accounting firm which serviced the franchising industry, and then had invested in and managed a pizza franchise. During his ownership of the franchise, which he had sold in 1981, he had met Driggs who had been hired as an assistant manager. Driven by a desire to build upon their experience, they had created Chester Franchisors as a vehicle for investing in franchising operations that offered high growth potential and low investment requirements. Non-consolidated financial statements for Chester Franchisors are reproduced as Exhibits 3 and 4.

Chester Franchisors was headquartered in Toronto's Spadina and Queen Street district, in leased premises located above their flagship, a company owned DDDelicious DDDonuts outlet. Their business interests were focussed exclusively on franchising, and they held major ownership positions in two franchisor companies as outlined in Exhibit 5. Chester Franchisors owned 100% of the shares of DDDelicious DDDonuts Ltd., which was the franchising parent for a chain of 22 donut shop outlets. Chester Franchisors also owned a 75% ownership share in Jedida Cookies Ltd., which was the franchising parent of a successful and expanding chain of gourmet cookie shops. A summary of financial data on these two firms can be found in Exhibit 6, and a comparison of the average performance of company owned outlets is found in Exhibit 7.

Chester Franchisors had been a Confederation Bank client since establishing operations in 1981. In 1983, when Chester purchased a 75% share of Jedida Cookies for $300,000, the Confederation had extended a $150,000 operating loan to finance the purchase and Dillman and Driggs had put up a total of $150,000 in shareholders' loans.

DDDelicious DDDonuts Ltd.

DDDelicious DDDonuts Ltd. had been established by Dillman and Driggs in 1981 to compete in the donut retail market. The first outlet was opened at Spadina and Queen in downtown Toronto and had been very successful, and by January 1987, DDDelicious DDDonuts had grown to 22 outlets located in major southwestern Ontario cities. The success in expanding the DDDelicious DDDonuts franchise concept had been aided by a profile article on DDDelicious DDDonuts and its founders that had been written for a Toronto newspaper with Ontario-wide distribution. Dillman and Driggs' knack for self promotion had managed to turn a reporter's background industry research interview into a profile article on DDDelicious DDDonuts that had led to numerous inquiries regarding franchise rights.

In 1982, Dillman and Driggs began to franchise their donut shop concept across southwestern Ontario. They drew up an application form which asked franchisee applicants questions on their work experience, education, income levels and assets. In addition, their decision on new franchisees was based on their sense of the applicant's motivation. Presently, there were 16 pending applicants for DDDelicious DDDonuts franchise rights, but these applicants were not viewed as ideal candidates. Dillman and Driggs were considering running another national advertisement in *The Globe and Mail* to generate new applicants.

Once the franchisee applicant was accepted, the franchisee was responsible for paying the franchise fee and raising the required investment funds. The franchise fee was $20,000 per outlet plus a required $100,000 startup investment. DDDelicious DDDonuts Ltd. required that each new franchisee finance at least the $20,000 franchise fee from personal resources, although in three cases, Dillman and Driggs had accepted a one-year note for part of the franchise fee. The franchise fee went into the parent franchisor's general revenues, while the $100,000 startup investment was required for equipment purchases ($70,000) and leasehold improvements and exterior/interior furnishings ($30,000) as arranged by DDDelicious DDDonuts Ltd. The franchisee was responsible for raising the $100,000 startup investment from a bank, trade creditor or their own personal resources.

Once the franchisee outlet was opened, royalties payable to the franchisor parent were set at 4% of sales plus a 1% of sales contribution to a pooled advertising fund. In addition, each franchised outlet agreed to purchase its product materials from DDDelicious DDDonuts. The product materials included coffee, sugar, flour, flavourings, napkins, and cups, and these products were delivered to franchisees once a week on a net 30 day basis. DDDelicious DDDonuts had succeeded in obtaining significant volume discounts from suppliers of these items and was able to pass these savings along to its franchisees.

The DDDelicious DDDonuts approach to donut retailing was very straight-forward, with all donuts prepared at the shop from a selection of basic core ingredients. The shops had counter seating for 22 and table seating for 12 and were open for 24 hours, seven days a week. The menu featured 22 different varieties of donuts. Sales of coffee and tea accounted for roughly 50% of the sales revenues in a typical outlet and the price charged for coffee and donut averaged $1.25.

The performance of the 22 DDDelicious DDDonuts outlets was uneven. Annual sales ranged from a high of $275,000 at one company owned outlet to a low of $195,00 at an outlet in suburban Toronto. Dillman and Driggs had the right to spot audit any franchisee accounts at any time, but rarely did so. Nevertheless, they were suspicious that some franchisees were not accurately reporting sales since they did not perform as well as the two company owned outlets. This suspicion had been confirmed when Chester Franchisors had been forced to temporarily take over two franchisee outlets when the owner of the two outlets had experienced financial difficulties.

An examination of the accounts showed that not only had sales been under-reported, but certain ingredients had been sourced from outside suppliers. After a two month period, both franchisee outlets had been sold to new owners. Dillman and Driggs had experienced great difficulty in hiring reliable management and staff for this two month period, as the former owner had largely staffed both outlets with relatives and friends.

The top three donut franchisors in Ontario by sales volume were Tim Horton, Country Style and Mr. Donuts. All three were well established and had located outlets in the prime malls and store front locations. Each of the three was able to mount expensive advertising and promotional support campaigns featuring giveaway coffee mugs and special donut deals. DDDelicious DDDonuts, given its relative size, was not able to mount advertising and promotional campaigns to match this and instead used most of the advertising/promotional money to recruit new franchisees and assist in promoting newly opened outlets.

DDDelicious DDDonuts had its franchisor and much of its franchisee business with the Confederation Bank. The franchisor parent had a $100,000 operating loan authorization with $89,000 outstanding, and 15 of the 22 franchisees had a total of $1,500,000 in small business ($650,000) and operating ($850,000) loans outstanding which were operating satisfactorily. In addition, all of the DDDelicious DDDonuts franchisees had arrangements with nearby Confederation branches to handle their daily cash deposits.

Jedida Cookies Ltd.

Jedida Cookies was founded in 1981 when Laurie McPherson and Linda Nelles had opened their first outlet in Toronto's fashionable Yorkville district. In 1983, when Jedida Cookies Ltd. was still a small Toronto-based chain numbering only two outlets, Dillman and Driggs had approached McPherson and Nelles to investigate franchising possibilities. Once they had a chance to assess the Jedida Cookie business, they were highly impressed and had tendered a proposal to purchase a 100% ownership interest in the Jedida Cookies franchise concept and its two Toronto-based, owned and operated outlets. At first, McPherson and Nelles had been reluctant to sell off even a piece of their business, let along a 100% equity position. However, they had eventually reached agreement and a 75% position was purchased by Chester Franchisors Ltd. for $300,000. Chester Franchisors owned 7,500 shares, while McPherson and Nelles retained the remaining 2,500 shares outstanding. The Jedida Cookie franchise chain had since grown to ten outlets located in Ontario and Quebec by 1987.

The Jedida Cookie business concept was to sell "hot from the oven" cookies. In the opinion of the founders, Jedida Cookies' formula for success was ensured by their fresh, high quality, soft and chewy cookies, by their delectable aroma aided by an open baking concept, and by the wide selection of chocolate cookies available. The outlets were geared toward takeout service and therefore, no seating space was provided. Most of the outlets were storefront locations on main street settings, although there were a few mall locations.

A Jedida Cookies outlet required limited space given the takeout concept. Therefore, the Jedida outlets featured high sales turnover with a sales per square foot ratio of $600 to $2,000 per year versus the average mall standard of $230. Christine noted that Jedida Cookies offered 70% gross margins compared to gross margins of 45% to 55% earned by most food retailers. She thought that the cookies probably served a wide market and the product had appeal to all age groups. The cookie itself was of high quality and sold for less than one dollar.

Jedida Cookies presently sold two different types of franchises – a regional franchise or a store franchise. Regional franchises sold for a negotiated lump sum fee, which depended upon the size of market granted, and then 2% of sales thereafter. Regional franchise holders were then free to sub-franchise outlets. The only regional franchise sold so far had been for the province of Quebec, and Jedida Cookies had obtained $100,000. A store franchise sold for a $25,000 fee plus $60,000 investment in startup costs, and then 6% of sales in royalty fees and 2% of sales in advertising contributions. Based on the average performance from existing outlets, each outlet's sales would be roughly $300,000 per annum with a net profit before taxes of $60,000 (20% of sales). At the insistence of McPherson and Nelles, Jedida Cookies Ltd. had hired a full-time accountant whose responsibility was to conduct spot audits of all Jedida franchisees for both financial and operational compliance.

After Dillman and Driggs' involvement, Jedida Cookies had expanded rapidly through 8 newly franchised outlets which brought the chain to a total of 10 outlets. Dillman and Driggs used the same screening approach to select franchisees for Jedida as they used for DDDelicious DDDonuts, except that McPherson and Nelles insisted on thorough financial investigations of participants, and also that all their outlets be owner-managed. It had been easier to select new franchisees because Jedida Cookies had a lengthy waiting list of 75 applicants wanting franchise rights. Jedida's rapid expansion had attracted the interest of other franchisors and Jedida Cookies had been approached frequently concerning the licensing of rights to the

United States and other countries around-the-world. A flour supplier had offered Jedida Cookies Ltd. $1,000,000 for the exclusive rights to franchise the concept world-wide outside Canada. Dillman and Driggs had seriously entertained the offer; however, for the present time they wanted to concentrate on growth inside Canada.

The banking business of the Jedida Cookies parent and franchisees was presently lodged with a competitor bank; however, Jedida's management was somewhat dissatisfied with the level of service and were looking for a new bank to look after their needs. Jedida had no bank loans outstanding and its 10 franchised outlets had a total of $400,00 in operating and small business loans outstanding.

Franchise Relationship

Christine McNab looked over the lists of franchisees for both DDDelicious DDDonuts and Jedida Cookies. She thought it would be useful to telephone a few outlets and speak to the managers about their particular outlets. The DDDelicious DDDonuts outlet she phoned was owned by an absentee investor. The employee who answered the telephone answered her questions as best he could:

> Most of our business is concentrated in either the early morning or late evening hours. Daytimes are usually pretty slow, so we don't need much staff. The owner drops in every once and a while to make sure things are okay, and to look at receipts and stuff like that.

Next, Christine McNab telephoned a Jedida outlet located in a busy downtown Toronto location. The owner/manager gave Christine some quick impressions:

> My business just doesn't stop until after dinner. All day long. Our 'choco-nut' cookies are the most popular. My biggest problem is keeping staff. We turn over our cook and sales positions about three times per year. There just aren't many kids these days, you know.

The Expansion to Vancouver

In December 1986, Dillman and Driggs had made a trip to Vancouver to interview several interested franchisee applicants for Jedida Cookie outlets. While they had not been overly impressed with the franchisee applicants per se, they were very impressed with Vancouver as a market into which to expand the Jedida Cookies chain. They had selected two locations with high pedestrian traffic, one on Robson Street and another on Denman Street, near the Stanley Park area. Their plan was to open two company owned outlets in these locations to serve as flagship outlets for further franchisee development in British Columbia. In order to start up these company owned outlets, they required an additional $170,000 in operating loans, which would increase the total operating loans to $335,000.

Financing Needs

Chester Franchisors planned to use the Confederation Bank operating loans of $335,000 as bridge financing until a future planned private offering of Chester Franchisors non-voting preferred stock could raise $400,000 in new equity. The loans would be supported by a charge against all of the company assets, a guarantee and postponement of claim for the full loan amount by DDDelicious DDDonuts Ltd., and the hypothecation of 7,500 shares of Jedida Cookies. Dillman and Driggs had emphasized that they viewed this loan as temporary bridge financing until new equity could be raised to fund their further development plans. While they were prepared to offer a full corporate guarantee from DDDelicious DDDonuts, the terms of the share-holders' agreement with Nelles/McPherson prevented the extension of a corporate guarantee from Jedida Cookies.

Decision to be Made

Christine McNab opened a courtesy package of Jedida Cookies that had been sent to her branch. She had also been sent a courtesy box of a dozen DDDelicious DDDonuts donuts, which she had distributed among the branch staff. Jedida Cookies seemed poised for big growth potential but DDDelicious DDDonuts was operating in a very competitive market seg-ment. While the parent, Chester Franchisors, needed bridge financing, Christine McNab was also mindful that the Confederation Bank wanted to increase its franchising industry loans.

EXHIBIT 1
CHESTER FRANCHISORS LIMITED

Franchising in Canada
January 1987

Market Competitor's	When Established	# of Units Owned	Franchised	Franchise Fee (in 000s)	Req'd Total Inv.	Royalty
Cookies						
Bel Gaufre	1978	2	11	15	50	6.0%
Brian's Cookies	1983	1	3	75	100	N/A
Famous Amos Choc. Chip	1984	1	0	10	N/A	5.0%
Jedida's Cookies	1981	2	8	25	85	8.0%
Munchies Cookie Empor.	1981	1	6	15	N/A	5.0%
Mrs. Field's Cookies	Planning Expansion Into Canada					
Sweet Rosie's Cookies	1984	4	0	N/A	75	5.0%
Donuts						
Country Style Donuts	1962	5	95	35	160	4.5%
DDDelicious DDDonuts	1981	2	20	20	120	5.0%
Donut Delite Cafe Inc.	1984	1	10	20	127	5.0%
Donut World Inc.	1978	6	0	N/A	N/A	6.0%
Donut & Things International	1986	0	6	25	195	5.0%
Dunkin Donuts (Canada) Inc.	1950	0	77	40	200	10.9%
Dutch Master Donuts Ltd.	1979	2	5	N/A	N/A	5.0%
Hart to Hart Donuts	1986	1	2	5	N/A	3.0%
Hol'n One Donut House	1978	4	6	5	40	3.0%
King Donuts	1976	2	2	75	150	N/A
Lil' Orbit Donuts	1972	0	20	20	N/A	N/A
Mr. Donut	1958	0	48	15	106	N/A
Nuffy's Donuts	1982	5	3	20	N/A	5.0%
O'Donuts Coffee Shops	1969	1	18	35	200	6.5%
Robin's Donuts	1975	10	78	35	156	4.0%
Tim Horton Donuts	1965	0	300	70	200	7.0%
Gourmet Bakery Shops						
Carole's Cheesecake Co. Ltd.	1979	2	7	35	90	N/A
Croissant + Plus	1980	10	20	40	135	4.5%
Heavenly Muffins	1985	0	10	20	75	8.0%
Hunts Bakeries	1904	0	20	15	N/A	5.0%
MMarvellous MMuffins	1979	3	61	25	118	6.0%
Treats	1977	4	70	25	90	8.0%

Source: 1987 Franchise Annual

EXHIBIT 2
CHESTER FRANCHISORS LIMITED

Confederation Bank Franchise Plan
(A Custom-tailored Program of Financial Services for Franchise Operations)

Credit Services

Operating Loans	— inventory, accounts receivable, operating expenses
Letters of Guarantee	— utility payments
Term Loans	— franchisors: development and startup costs
	franchisees: equipment and leasehold
Small Business Loans	— franchisors: company owned outlets only
	franchisees: equipment and leasehold

Deposit Services

Cash Management	— current accounts
	— centralized banking
	— payment distribution
	— night and day deposit

Other Banking Services

Payroll	— automated payroll
Insurance	— business loan insurance coverage up to $500 000
Credit Cards	— Corporate and Merchant (franchisees) VISA

EXHIBIT 3

CHESTER FRANCHISORS LIMITED

Non-Consolidated Income Statement for the years ended December 31, 1984 – 1986

	1984	1985	1986
Revenue			
Management Fees from DDDelicious DDDonuts	$125 000	$125 000	$100 000
Management Fees from Jedida Cookies	20 000	20 000	20 000
Dividends from DDDelicious DDDonuts*	0	0	0
Dividends from Jedida Cookies*	15 000	20 000	50 000
	$160 000	$165 000	$170 000
Expenses			
Salaries & Bonuses	$ 84 321	$ 93 866	$108 206
Rent	11 852	12 001	12 356
Travel & Entertainment	7 981	8 155	8 929
Telephone	2 984	6 092	10 721
Office Supplies	2 215	3 866	4 543
Professional Fees	15 250	19 600	25 300
Bank Interest	11 655	12 161	11 254
Other	1 190	984	1 003
	$137 448	$156 725	$182 312
Profits Before Taxes	22 552	8 275	(12 312)
Taxes	1 888	0	0
PROFIT AFTER TAXES	$ 20 664	$ 8 275	$(12 312)

*Dividends from tax paying Canadian corporations were non-taxable.

EXHIBIT 4
CHESTER FRANCHISORS LIMITED

Non-Consolidated Balance Sheet
as at December 31, 1984 – 1986

	1984	1985	1986
Assets			
Cash	$ 16 774	$ 5 492	$ 7 532
Loans Receivable from DDDelicious DDDonuts Ltd.	75 833	101 026	106 419
Investment, at cost, in Jedida Cookies Ltd.	300 000	300 000	300 000
Fixed Assets, net	942	1 068	1 258
	$393 549	$407 586	$415 209
Liabilities and Shareholders' Equity			
Bank Loan	$131 912	$153 951	$158 961
Accounts Payable	9 161	12 371	12 005
Deferred wages + Bonuses Payable	30 500	11 013	26 304
Shareholder Loans	157 075	157 075	157 075
Net Worth	64 901	73 176	60 864
	$393 549	$407 586	$415 209

55

*Case 6
Chester
Franchisors
Limited*

EXHIBIT 5
CHESTER FRANCHISORS LIMITED

Corporate Structure

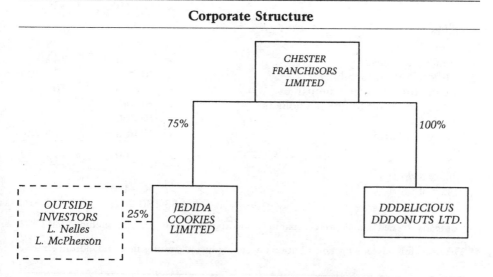

EXHIBIT 6

CHESTER FRANCHISORS LIMITED

Financial Performance of Jedida Cookies Ltd.
and DDDelicious DDDonuts Ltd. in 1986

Income Statement – 1986*	Jedida Cookies	DDDelicious DDDonuts
Income		
Franchise Fees	$ 50 000	$ 80 000
Royalties**	187 857	150 112
Interest and Dividends	12 433	0
Product Sales	N/A	987 024
	250 291	1 217 136
Expenses		
Administrative & Sales Expenses**	92 953	344 232
Product Costs	N/A	859 640
	92 953	1 203 872
Earnings	157 337	13 264
Taxes	27 202	601
Net Earnings	$ 130 135	$ 12 663
Dividends	$ 66 666	$ 0
Balance Sheet as at December 31, 1986		
Assets		
Cash	$ 59 879	$ 0
Inventory	0	162 517
Accounts Receivable	56 348	170 643
Other Current Assets	0	16 252
Development Costs and Fixed Assets	101 433	130 120
	$ 217 660	$ 479 532
Liabilities		
Bank Loans	0	88 825
Trade Payables	0	242 151
Other Current Liabilities	40 709	25 208
Loans from Related Companies	0	106 419
Loans from Minority Shareholders	24 946	0
Capital	10 000	1
Retained Earnings	142 005	16 928
	$ 217 660	$ 479 532
Summary Statistics		
Number of Outlets	10	22
Retail Sales	$3 130 962	$3 752 800

* Company owned stores were separately incorporated and are not included in these statements.

** The fees for advertising contributions were deducted from sales and administrative expenses.

EXHIBIT 7

CHESTER FRANCHISORS LIMITED

Average Profit and Loss Performance of Company Owned Outlets for year ended December 31, 1986

	Jedida Cookies	DDDelicious DDDonuts
Sales	$ 310 000	$260 000
Cost of Sales	94 500	70 000
Gross Profit	215 500	190 000
Expenses		
Management	30 000	28 000
Baker & Counter Help	43 000	55 000
Rent	20 000	45 000
Depreciation & Amortization	10 500	7 000
Gas & Hydro	2 000	6 000
Promotion	4 000	0
Telephone	2 000	500
Insurance	1 000	1 000
Maintenance	1 000	1 000
Accounting & Legal	4 000	2 500
Loan Interest & Bank Charges	3 500	12 000
Miscellaneous	8 000	8 000
Royalties	24 800	13 000
Total Expenses	$153 800	$179 000
Net Profit Before Taxes	$ 61 700	$ 11 000
Number of Company Owned Outlets	2	2

Case 6
Chester
Franchisors
Limited

Accounts Receivable Management

WARNER-LAMBERT CANADA INC.

On September 17, 1982, Bob Serenbetz, President of Warner-Lambert Canada Inc. (Warner-Lambert) emerged from a meeting with his credit manager, Joe Champagne, and the principals of Coast Distributors Limited (Coast), Warner-Lambert's exclusive wholesale distributor for Vancouver Island. The meeting was called to review Coast's most recent financial statements in light of Warner-Lambert's outstanding account receivable of $1.2 million. Coast's profits and equity had fallen to the point where both were now negative. Champagne recommended in August that shipments to Coast be discontinued, but Serenbetz had decided against such drastic action, pending the review of financial statements and Coast's operating plan. Serenbetz now had to decide what action to take regarding the account and the sales of products in the region.

Warner-Lambert Canada Inc.

Warner-Lambert Canada Inc., a wholly-owned subsidiary of Warner-Lambert Company in the United States, marketed a wide range of consumer and health care products. These products were distributed nationally through all the major food and drug chains, department stores, wholesalers, hospitals and laboratories. The company was organized in five divisions consisting of Adams Brands, Parke-Davis, Personal Products, Diagnostics, and Deseret (Exhibit 1). Sales for all divisions were approximately $190 million in 1982. Competition came from other large firms such as Wrigley Canada Inc., Gillette of Canada Limited, and Hoechst Canada, which sold similar products through the same distribution channels. Management believed stable growth was important to the continued success of the company. Emphasis was placed on marketing and distribution functions to achieve a strong market position in all product lines. Product research and development was considered necessary for sustained future growth.

Coast Distributors Limited

Coast Distributors Limited acted as a manufacturer's agent and distributor for wholesale and retail distribution in patent medicines, confectionery, and grocery products. The company acted for over 50 firms including Warner-Lambert. Sales of approximately $11 million in 1981 were handled through one major warehouse location and a smaller branch warehouse in the region. Coast employed 55 people. Credit sales accounted for 95 percent of the total on terms of net 30 days. During its years in business, the company had built and maintained a large and loyal customer base throughout the island.

Coast's common stock had been acquired by David Campbell Limited from the original Bromley family interests in 1978. David Campbell Limited was a holding company owned by David Campbell, a prominent lawyer in Nanaimo, and his family. Campbell had acted for the estate of Charles Bromley, the founder of Coast, who had died in 1975. David Campbell was well regarded in the community as a lawyer and businessman.

The acquisition of Coast by David Campbell Limited had been financed by bank borrowings. In 1980, the two companies were merged under the Coast Distributors name. At this time Campbell named Earl Keith as President and Chief Executive Officer. Keith had run Coast for over 20 years and had extensive experience in the distribution business on Vancouver Island. David Campbell became a Director and Chairman of the Board of Coast Distributors.

Coast had distributed Warner-Lambert products for 56 years, acting as a distribution centre by taking title to the merchandise and carrying a full product line. Good relations evolved because of the quality of service provided by Coast in distribution, credit management, and credit risk assumption. Coast kept its own account with Warner-Lambert current.

The current exclusive agency agreement between Coast and Warner-Lambert for the region of Vancouver Island was negotiated in 1966. Under this arrangement, all Warner-Lambert Divisions sold to Coast at list price less any discounts specific to a particular division. This was termed the best wholesale price. Warner-Lambert would then pay Coast ten percent of the best wholesale price for the distribution and warehousing services it provided. The payments were made quarterly by cheque to Coast. Shipments were made once per week F.O.B. destination with payment terms of net 60 days. However, the agreement also granted an extended dating program because of the logistical problems of selling in this market (i.e. isolated towns) that went as follows:

Adams and Parke Davis Divisions

| May 1 — Oct. 31 | 60 days |
| Nov 1 — Apr. 30 | 120 days |

Personal Products Divisions

| May 1 — Oct. 31 | 1% 75, net 120 |
| Nov 1 — Apr. 30 | 1% 135, net 180 |

These terms were effective from the due date of the original invoice and additional dating might be allowed for special promotions. Coast was encouraged to submit tenders for government and hospital contracts at prices quoted by Warner-Lambert. However, no allowance would be paid on these orders.

The credit limit granted to Coast had risen to $1.2 million by 1981. This credit limit was reviewed and adjusted annually, based on information from financial statements submitted as requested by Warner-Lambert's credit manager. The determination of the credit limit was based on a formula tested extensively by major corporations. The formula incorporates the overall financial condition of the firm, including working capital and long term viability. Credit limits were built up under the formula by adding assigned percentages of the amount of a customer's working capital, net income, and net worth, while reductions were made under the same system of assigned percentages for long term debt and net losses. The formula was modified for quick and pledged assets. A discretionary assignment by the credit manager accounted for past performance and future prospects, trade and bank references, general reputation, or any other factors which may have been unique to the business. This discretionary factor could adjust the credit limit by plus or minus 25 percent, or possibly suspend credit altogether. A table of company statistics included in the evaluation provided client history and the degree of exposure the creditor faced. The purpose of the formula was to have a structure from which consistent decisions could be made. At Warner-Lambert, the level of authority required for approval of credit limits depended on the amount requested. The Credit Manager had authority up to $100 000, the Treasurer to $300 000, the V.P. Finance to $500 000, while the President had unlimited discretion. The credit limits established for Coast and the calculations based on the formula are presented in Exhibit 4.

Events Leading to the Meeting

Relations between the two companies had been good in the past, with Coast generally supplying an appropriate level of service for the compensation it received. However, in April 1981, Champagne requested audited financial statements for the year ended December 31, 1980, but received one for the year ended March 31, 1980. After reviewing this statement, he found several items of concern. Directors' remuneration had increased $123 000 in 1979, following the appointment of two additional directors; namely, the wives of David Campbell and Earl Keith. At the same time, dividends to shareholders were substantial at $94 000 in cash and $400 000 in stock. Coast's bank loan increased during this period by $400 000. From March 1979 to 1980, net profit after tax was halved. With rising interest rates and bank loans and falling profits, Champagne recommended a reduction of Coast's credit limit until he could get answers for recent organizational changes and company behaviour. He suggested lowering the amount to correspond with Warner-Lambert's credit criteria of about $194 000 (Exhibit 4) using 1980 data. Several requests for more current financial information followed over the next few months but were refused by Coast. A personal visit by a member of the credit department was made in September, 1981 to examine Coast's operations and find out what was happening within the company. The company restructuring was explained, as was the recent expansion and increased bank debt. The Warner-Lambert representative felt positive about the future of Coast. Current financial statements were to have been forwarded to Warner-Lambert. The statements never arrived.

In August of 1982, Champagne again tried to secure recent audited statements and once again was refused. Concerned about a significant deterioration in the financial position of Coast and the considerable risk exposure confronting Warner-Lambert, he recommended suspension of credit as a means of acquiring the information requested.

A profitability analysis of the account to Warner-Lambert was prepared as part of the annual credit review. The last profitability standing of the Coast account occurred at the end of November 1981. The results are presented in Exhibit 5. The study compared Coast's account to Warner-Lambert's average. Average days sales outstanding (DSO) of Warner-Lambert accounts receivable was 59 days, excluding Coast sales. Coast's account was 125 DSO, but was not past due. Coast's own accounts receivable DSO was only 68 days which suggested that Warner-Lambert was contributing substantially to the short term financing requirements of Coast. Warner-Lambert products amounted to 25 percent of Coast's sales but represented 50 percent of Coast's accounts payable. Warner-Lambert's cost of carrying the excess receivables over the average was estimated at $58 000 annually, using a 15 percent interest rate. At that time, the excess in receivables above the average was $43 000 for Parke-Davis, $322 000 for Adams Brands, and $31 000 for Personal Products. These varied with interest rates. This coincided with the fact that Warner-Lambert's own credit limit evaluation indicated that Coast did not deserve any credit. The results of this analysis suggested several things to Warner-Lambert. There was a need to review both the size of Coast's credit line and the payment terms which were negotiated 16 years previously.

Coast management finally agreed to a meeting with Warner-Lambert in September 1982. At the meeting Coast supplied audited financial statements for the year ended December 31, 1981 and unaudited results for the first eight months of 1982. These statements are presented in Exhibits 2 and 3.

Serenbetz now had several alternatives to consider. With Coast's actual financial position much worse than anyone at Warner-Lambert anticipated, and with the credit limit formula showing a negative amount, Serenbetz knew that a tough decision concerning Coast was a real possibility. He would have to develop options and consider each one carefully.

The first option was to restructure the present credit arrangements with Coast and work with the firm to improve the business. The major advantage would be to use Coast's well established distribution network and client base. This would eliminate the time and cost incurred to set-up alternate distribution channels, should the Coast account be suspended. At the same time, by reducing Coast's credit terms and limit, Warner-Lambert's risk exposure would be reduced.

Serenbetz wondered if improving the efficiency of Coast's inventory of Warner-Lambert products would help to solve the problem. Inventory would turn over faster if shipments were smaller and more frequent. Merchandise would always be current and no slow-moving stock would accumulate. Although higher shipping costs would be incurred by Warner-Lambert, a lower inventory amount for Coast would reduce the investment in the account by Warner-Lambert. Currently, Coast carried $300 000 of Warner-Lambert products in inventory. In addition, reducing the credit terms to Coast, possibly through cash discount offerings, would further reduce exposure. A proposal to establish a bonded warehouse and place Coast on a consignment basis with separate inventories was discussed. Coast's collections on these products, when sold, would be kept in a separate account. Frequent audits would have to be conducted to verify the records. However, with the availability of such records, the movement of products and funds could be closely supervised. If more sales representatives were employed by Warner-Lambert on the Island, they would be able to conduct the audits in addition to their duties of product promotion.

A second alternative would be to suspend all credit to Coast and attempt to collect the present outstanding balance. The account represented a substantial amount of business for Warner-Lambert. The exclusive agreement left Warner-Lambert totally dependent on Coast for sales on Vancouver Island and susceptible to Coast's credit problem. If Warner-Lambert's credit to Coast was suspended, an alternate means of distribution had to be found for the region.

About 60 wholesalers operated in the area; however, most were small jobbers — only eight to ten could replace Coast. Merchandise could be sold to them on regular credit terms and with existing compensation rates. Upon further investigation, it became apparent that these firms were smaller than Coast and were not so centrally located. The number of shipments to the alternate distributors would increase. Supplies were shipped by sea once per week from the Vancouver distribution centre. Increasing the number of shipments would raise freight costs to Warner-Lambert. Merchandise was currently shipped in container loads. If smaller wholesalers could not purchase full loads, Warner-Lambert would lose the cost efficiencies container lots provided. Poorer service and lost sales could also result from reduced coverage and the loss of a loyal customer base.

Although additional credit accounts would also have to be supervised because of an increased number of distributors, the risk would be spread around, reducing Warner-Lambert's exposure. Serenbetz thought that sales might drop by as much as ten percent on the island if other wholesalers were used, because of the strong relationship established between Coast and its customers. But he was uncertain whether the sales decline would be permanent or temporary. More frequent shipments to Vancouver Island and servicing more wholesale accounts might push Warner-Lambert's costs up by two percent.

Warner-Lambert could also set up its own distribution centre on Vancouver Island and sell directly to wholesalers and retailers. This would entail a large capital outlay and take time to establish. As well, many more credit accounts would have to be serviced and more salesmen hired. But the control gained over these functions might contribute to a more efficient operation.

A third alternative was to leave the account as it was and continue the extended dating terms for all divisions. Though the Coast account was over the acceptable line of credit, the firm still abided by the terms of the credit agreement. According to a recent Dun and Bradstreet report, Coast's payment record varied from prompt to 30 days slow, which was acceptable performance in this industry. Apparently the other suppliers were not concerned with Coast's account and, in all likelihood, had not received the 1981 statements. Coast's financial position had not affected its sales performance — Coast sold $2.3 million of Warner-Lambert merchandise in 1981.

Serenbetz knew that a good distribution system was the key to achieving and maintaining market share. But increased risk exposure due to Coast's deteriorating financial position could put Warner-Lambert in a high loss situation. Although Coast's operating profit for the first eight months of 1982 was better than 1981, interest costs had offset this — causing a net loss which further reduced the company's net worth. Serenbetz knew he must make a decision soon and communicated this to the departments concerned.

EXHIBIT 1
WARNER-LAMBERT CANADA INC.

Major Brands

ADAMS BRANDS	— Chiclets, Dentyne, Certs, Clorets, Trident Sugarless Gum, Halls, Rolaids, Dynamints, Bubbaloo, Bubbilicious, Freshen-Up Gum, Blue Diamond Almonds
PARKE-DAVIS	— Agarol, Anusol, Benylin, Benadryl, Caladryl, Gelusil, Sinutab, Strepsils, Pardec, Chloromycetin, Coly-Mycin, Choledyl, Dilantin, Peritrate, Pyridium, Mandelamine, LoEstrin
PERSONAL PRODUCTS	— Listerine Antiseptic, Listermint with Fluoride, Listerine Lozenges, Bromo-Seltzer, Efferdent, Schick, Topol Tooth Polish, Porcelana Medicated Cream, Softsoap
DIAGNOSTICS	— Simplastin, Verify, Coag-A-Mates, Sure-Sep, Blood G.A.S., Wellcome Reagents, Blood Bank Reagents, Micro I.D., Radioimmuno-Assay Reagents, Chemistry Reagents, Reagants, Microbiology Reagents, Chemistry Quality Control Products, Antimicrobial Disks
DESERET	— Angiocath, E-Z Serubs, Filter Masks, Ground-It, Hemodialysis E.Z. Sets, Minicaths, Unigard, E.K.G.

EXHIBIT 2
WARNER-LAMBERT CANADA INC.

Coast Distributors Limited
Income Statement
for the periods described
($000)

	8 Months to August 31 1982	Year Ended December 31 1981	9 Months Ended December 31 1980[1]	Year Ended March 31 1980
Net Sales	$7 308	$11 020	$8 166	$9 545
Less				
Cost of Goods Sold	6 079	9 169	6 757	7 807
Gross Profit	1 229	1 851	1 409	1 738
Deduct Expenses				
Selling, Warehouse & Delivery	416	899	697	647
Admin. and General	521	817	620	782
Subtotal	937	1 716	1 317	1 429
Operating Profit	292	135	92	309
Excess (Deficiency) of Other Income Over Charges[2]	(311)	(547)	(70)	4
Net Income Before Tax	(19)	(412)	22	313
Current Tax	—	(20)	5	(150)
Net Income	$ (19)	$ (392)	$ 17	$ 163

[1] Fiscal year end December 31, 1980 was only nine months long due to amalgamation of Coast Distributors Limited and David Campbell Ltd.
[2] Other Income includes: net cash discounts, gain on disposal of property and equipment, rent, and miscellaneous. Other charges include: long term interest and other interest charges of $337 000 August 31, 1982, $555 573 December 31, 1981, $11 968 December 31, 1980, $69 962 March 31, 1980 and excess of premiums paid over increase in cash surrender value of life insurance.

Ratios (Percentage of Net Sales)

	1982	1981	1980	1980
Gross Profit	16.81	16.79	17.26	18.21
Operating Profit	3.99	1.21	1.13	3.24
Net Income	(.25)	(3.57)	.21	1.71

EXHIBIT 3
WARNER-LAMBERT CANADA INC.

Coast Distributors Limited Balance Sheet
December 31, 1980, 1981 and August 31, 1982
($000)

	Aug. 31 1982	Dec. 31 1981	Dec. 31 1980
Assets			
Current Assets			
Cash	$ 1	$ 1	$ 4
Receivables (Net)	1 627	1 644	1 982
Inventories at Lower of Cost or Replacement Cost	2 322	2 136	2 456
Prepaid Expenses	81	22	19
Total Current Assets	4 031	3 803	4 462
Investments, Loans and Advances	142	113	106
Property, Plant and Equipment	1 240	1 204	1 238
Less: Accumulated Depreciation	519	453	387
	721	751	851
Land	184	146	146
Net Property, Plant, and Equipment	905	897	997
TOTAL ASSETS	$5 078	$4 813	$5 565
Liabilities and Equity			
Current Liabilities			
Outstanding Cheques Less Cash	228	59	382
Demand Loan	1 103	1 250	800
Current Portion of Long Term Debt	32	96	72
Subtotal	1 363	1 405	1 254
Accounts Payable	2 216	1 912	2 163
Income Taxes Payable	0	0	29
Total Current Liabilities	3 579	3 317	3 446
Long Term Debt	1 629	1 608	1 722
Deferred Income Taxes	0	0	20
Shareholders' Equity			
Class A Preferreds	36	36	36
Class B Preferreds	47	47	142
Common Shares	5	5	5
Retained (Deficit) Earnings Beginning	(199)	194	1 246
Add: Net Income	(19)	(392)	17
Adjustment (Note 1)	—	—	1 069
Retained (Deficit) Earnings Ending	(218)	(199)	194
TOTAL LIABILITIES AND EQUITY	$5 078	$4 813	$5 565

Exhibit 3 (continued)

Note 1:   During 1980 Coast Distributors Ltd., and David Campbell Limited were merged. The new company Coast Distributors Limited has adopted a December 31 year end whereas the company previously had a March 31 year end. As a result, the financial statements for the year ended December 31, 1980 only represent nine months operations. When the accounts of the two companies were consolidated, the purchase price of the equity on David Campbell Limited's accounts was offset against the book value of the equity in Coast Distributors Limited's accounts resulting in a write-down of $1 069 thousand.

EXHIBIT 4
WARNER-LAMBERT CANADA INC.

Coast Distributors Limited
Credit Line Evaluation

Item	Allowance	1979	1980	1981
Working Capital	10%	113	115	49
Quick Assets	Max 5% (50% of W/C Credit)	56	57	25
Pledged Rec/Inv.	(10%)	(28)	(33)	(37)
Long Term Debt	(3%)	(2)	(11)	(48)
Net Worth	2%	34	35	(22)
Net Income	10% or (20%)	50	31	(78)
Other*				
Credit Line		223	194	(111)
Cr. Line Requested		1000	1000	1200
Cr. Line Approved				
Date				

*Comment: _____

Approval					
	MGR./SUPER.	CR. MGR.	TREAS.	V.P. FIN.	PRES.
Date					

Statistics				
Working Capital Ratio		1.68	1.54	1.15
Quick Asset Ratio		.73	.71	.50
L/T Debt % Wkg. Cap.		5.30	31.48	331.34
L/T Debt % Net Worth		3.54	20.44	1434.82
*Cr. Line % Wkg. Cap.		88.26	86.96	247.42
*Cr. Line % Net Worth		59.07	56.47	1071.43
*Cr. Line % Curr. Debt		60.39	47.30	36.16

EXHIBIT 5
WARNER-LAMBERT CANADA INC.

Accounts Receivable Data
($000)

	Parke Davis	Adams	Personal Products	Total
Coast Accounts Receivable Balance Outstanding at 30/11/81	$243	$ 467	$64	$ 744
Coast Days Sales Outstanding	120 days	129 days	119 days	125 days
Warner-Lambert D.S.O. excluding Coast at 30/11/81	99 days	40 days	60 days	59 days
D.S.O. difference converted to dollars	$ 43	$ 322	$ 31	$ 396
Cost of carrying excess Coast Receivables at 15% per annum	$ 6	$ 48	$ 4	$ 58
Sales of Warner-Lambert products to Coast, 1981	$738	$1322	$197	$2257
Commissions paid to Coast	$ 74	$ 132	$ 20	$ 226
Contribution to Warner-Lambert from sales to Coast	$297	$ 592	$ 65	$ 954

ALFRED BROOKS MENSWEAR LIMITED

In early February 1989, Harry Lagerfeld, the Treasurer of Alfred Brooks Menswear Limited (known as ABM in the trade), was preparing for an introductory meeting with an account manager from the Confederation Bank. ABM had been dealing for several years with the Metropolitan Bank, but when Lagerfeld told Metropolitan about ABM's plans for a large expansion over the next year, he had been met by a noncommittal response. Lagerfeld was surprised at Metropolitan's hesitancy and felt it was an appropriate time to reassess ABM's banking relationship.

Up to now ABM's products had largely been produced and sold in Canada. However, in the past year, Alfred Brooks had personally spearheaded a concerted selling effort to Sutton's, a large national department store in the United States, and this effort had led to a major order. The order would cause fiscal 1989 sales to increase 80% over the sales for fiscal 1988 and Lagerfeld knew that additional working capital would be needed.

At the same time, Lagerfeld and the company buyer were nearing completion of an agreement with a Hong Kong supplier called Leung Manufacturing, for the contract production of the new line of suits. Preliminary manufacturing of "unfinished" suits was to take place in Hong Kong before shipment to Toronto for "finishing". ABM had purchased fabric from abroad in the past, but in order to meet the tight cost targets on this new order, ABM had been forced to follow the strategy of other North American garment manufacturers and source more value-added production from the Far East. By importing the clothing in "unfinished" form, ABM would minimize punitive duties and be able to claim Canadian content in the garments subsequently exported to the United States. The rule of origin interpretation for men's suits required that 50% of the cost be Canadian value-added.

The Clothing Industry

Menswear was a major segment within the clothing manufacturing industry, and suits/sports coats made up 12% of the menswear share of wardrobe dollars. Menswear had enjoyed reasonably healthy growth in the 1980's as the numbers of men in their 30's and 40's, who were the prime suit purchasing market, increased. At the same time imports took on an increasing share of the market, as seen in Exhibit 1.

Competition in both Canada and the U.S. within the suit/jacket manufacturers segment was intense. The industry was heavily dependent upon sales of branded and private label menswear to discounters, general merchandise stores (Sears, Ward's, Sutton's), department stores and men's specialty retailers. Additionally, a few manufacturers had set up their own retail outlets.

In 1987, the U.S. and Canada signed a comprehensive Free Trade Agreement (FTA). The clothing manufacturing industry had historically received a high degree of government protection in both countries because of the significant employment the industry generated. Government protection policies included duties/taxes, import quotas and subsidies. As a result of the FTA, the duties on domestically produced clothing traded across the border were to be reduced. However, the duty reduction would not be applied to clothing manufactured abroad and imported into Canada or the U.S. for re-export, unless the finished garments had a significant domestic value-added component (minimum of 50% content). The present U.S. duty on men's suits was 77.2 cents/kilogram plus 20%, and this was to be reduced to 0 over a ten-year period in ten equal reductions of 10%.

Lagerfeld was concerned about the impact of the recently passed Free Trade Agreement. Although ABM would benefit under the FTA through lower duties on cross-border shipments of Canadian-made garments into the U.S., Lagerfeld worried that competing U.S. manufacturers who possessed greater resources would soon be making significant inroads into the Canadian market. The larger American competitors were approximately twenty times the size of ABM in terms of sales.

Alfred Brooks Menswear

Company Background

Established in 1978 by Alfred Brooks, ABM manufactured men's suits and jackets for wholesale distribution in Canada; a small portion was also wholesaled in the U.S. and Italy. Alfred Brooks, now 55, had started work as a tailor when he was 15 and had spent his life in the industry. Before starting ABM with the proceeds of an inheritance, he had worked for eight years as the general manager of a major Canadian men's clothier.

Alfred Brooks acted as Chairman and President of the company. The senior management group included Ben Bulmer, who was the Marketing Manager, Denham Crawford, who was Operations Manager, and Harry

Lagerfeld, who acted as Treasurer. All three senior managers had been with ABM since its inception and had varied backgrounds in the industry prior to joining the company. Alfred Brooks had designed generous compensation packages for each of his senior managers to keep them motivated and loyal to the company.

ABM employed 25 full-time employees including 4 managers (including Brooks), 2 office support staff, 2 buyers, 2 designers, 5 pattern makers/cutters, 3 sales people, 2 shippers and 5 warehouse workers/inspectors.

Garments were manufactured by casual employees, primarily new immigrants to Canada, who were paid on a piecework basis. Anywhere from 10 to 200 such workers were employed at any particular time and these workers were not unionized.

Manufacturing and Warehousing Facilities

ABM was located in Toronto's Spadina garment district operating out of premises rented under a 15-year lease, and was into the second year of the first five-year term with two renewal options remaining. ABM's administrative, selling, manufacturing and warehousing operations were all located at the leased Spadina facility, although it occasionally rented temporary warehousing space when needed.

Suit Design and Development

Alfred Brooks personally supervised all aspects of suit and jacket design and development. The preliminary design process was spearheaded by two highly experienced designers. Suit patterns were then laid out by pattern-makers who were hired on freelance contracts. Cloth bolts were cut in substantial quantities and the cloth pieces were then sewn together by seamsters working on a piecework basis. ABM occasionally contracted some manufacturing to other Toronto clothiers.

In Alfred Brook's opinion, ABM had cultivated a quality reputation. ABM was very careful about the materials it chose, picking classic patterns and colours in fabrics with a lasting feel. Brooks instinctively steered away from faddish colours or finishes. ABM also produced sophisticated looking end products, with much handwork involved in the sewing, assembly and pressing of the suit. As a result, ABM's finished product had a sophisticated look to it, resembling European styled suits more than American.

Markets

Over the years, Alfred Brooks had developed a good sense of who wore his suits and jackets. In his opinion, ABM's target customer was a white collar male who wanted top-of-the-line quality but at reasonable prices. ABM's suits typically retailed in the $250 to $300 price range, which was below the top-end quality suits at $400 plus (Holt Renfrew, Harry Rosen), but above the mass market suits at the $150–$200 range (Tip Top, Moores).

ABM sold most of its suits to a client list of 48 Canadian retailers such as large department stores and menswear chains but roughly 10% of annual sales were to a mix of 11 retailers in the United States. ABM also sold a small number of suits (less than 1% of sales) to an Italian retailer who had been a customer for several years and Brooks was anxious to expand his sales to other Italian retailers. Lagerfeld provided the Bank with a monthly list of accounts receivable outstanding, which is attached as Exhibit 2, and a listing of inventory on hand. Both were pledged as security for the company's loans but Lagerfeld was annoyed that the Bank excluded ABM's accounts receivable from American and Italian retailers when calculating the amount of operating funds available to the company. Accounts receivable in the U.S. (and a few in Canada) were protected with insurance from American Credit Indemnity (ACI).

ACI was a commercial credit insurer that established credit limits for an approved list of accounts and insured accounts receivable up to that limit. The insurance fee charged was based on the Dunn and Bradstreet ratings for the buyer firms. Although ABM had never had to make a claim under its policy, Lagerfeld had heard that obtaining a claim was difficult in certain circumstances. The insurance did not apply to trade disputes; there was a $100,000 deductible.

All sales were made on an open account basis. Most invoices stated terms of 2%, 10; net 30 days, although some of ABM's retailers stretched these terms. The larger Canadian clients typically took between 45 and 60 days to pay and some were offered extended terms of up to 90 days. Additional discount terms were selectively offered to ABM's larger customers. Typically, a discount/warehousing allowance ranging between 2% and 6% was offered depending on the size of the client and was given in exchange for prompt payment (within 10 days). Discounts were not deducted from the monthly accounts receivable listing, but were allowed only when payment was received. Returns were not allowed, except under special agreement.

Expansion: The Big Order

Late in 1988 Ben Bulmer of ABM had visited the menswear buyer for Sutton's in Dallas to show him the new "swatch books"[1] for the upcoming 1989 fall season. Sutton's was a potentially very important account. The company was a very profitable, large national department store with over 1,000 branches and sales exceeding $9 billion. One of the company's key product lines was clothing.

[1] "Swatch books" were similar to catalogues and indicated different fabric textures, finishes, patterns and colours.

Sutton's had always received positive customer feedback about the Alfred Brooks line of suits. In particular, their American clientele liked the distinctive European style cuts of the Alfred Brooks suits together with their reasonable prices. Alfred Brooks thought that with a little hard sell they might be able to get Sutton's to double their previous years purchases of C$800,000.

The ABM team learned that Sutton's planned to feature the ABM suits more widely than ever before. The buyer verbally committed Sutton's to a huge order, saying it would be for at least 70,000 suits. Alfred Brooks was flabbergasted!

On Friday, February 3, 1989, ABM received the purchase order: Sutton's total order would amount to 71,130 suits at US$137.50 each for a total sale price of US$9,780,375. The exchange rate that day was C$1.1858/US$1.00, which worked out to a total order of C$11,597,568. The order was denominated in U.S. dollars.

The purchase order stated that the suits were to be delivered to specified U.S. warehouses in five tranches to be received as follows: on the 15th of July, August, September and October – 15,000 suits, and on the 15th of November – 11,130 suits. The order specified quantities by fabrics, colours and sizes. The agreed terms of sale were 60 days with an offered discount of 6%, 10; E.O.M. (end of month). There was no provision for returns, but Sutton's reserved the right to refuse shipments if the quality did not match the samples. No backorders or substitutions were allowed. Freight and duties were to be paid by ABM F.O.B. to the specified warehouse.

The Sutton's order, taken together with the orders already on hand from other retailers, would mean a huge leap in sales from C$20.9 million in 1988 to C$37.3 million in 1989. Lagerfeld estimated that monthly sales would be as follows:

**Monthly Sales
December 1988 – November 1989**
($000)

Month		Month	
Dec. 88	$2 993	Jun.	$2 742
Jan. 89	1 292	Jul.	3 728
Feb.	2 393	Aug.	5 903
Mar.	1 860	Sep.	5 644
Apr.	308	Oct.	4 547
May	512	Nov.	5 378
		TOTAL	$37 300

Financial Implications

Lagerfeld knew that he would require financial assistance to meet the cash flow demands of the new order. In an attempt to quantify the needs he drew up the annual pro forma financial statements and monthly cash flow forecasts seen in Exhibit 3. Since banks typically require a margining of inventories and accounts receivable, he drew up the schedule seen in Exhibit 4, which indicates the monthly margin position.

Key Suppliers

ABM's suppliers of fabric (primarily wool knit cloth bolts), buttons, zippers, and thread were Canadian and these raw materials were purchased on an open account basis. Terms varied from 2%, 10; net 30 to one supplier who extended 180-day terms. Ninety percent of ABM's accounts payable were owed to trade accounts, with the remaining 10% being sundry payables such as deductions from source and vacation pay. ABM maintained very good relations with trade creditors and always kept payments in line with the terms outlined. A schedule of outstanding accounts payable can be found in Exhibit 5.

The fabric and preliminary manufacturing for the Sutton's sale would be sourced from Leung Manufacturing in Hong Kong in order to meet the cost targets for the order. ABM planned a gross margin of C$30 per suit, and had based this on a US$43/suit raw material and labour (cutting and preliminary assembly) component from Hong Kong. The unfinished suits would then be shipped to Canada for finishing: pressing, sewing on zippers, belt loops, buttonholes and buttons, and the final tailoring of pleats and pockets.

The fixed price contract for the Hong Kong production was denominated in US$. It specified delivery to Canada in five tranches of 15,000 suits on the 1st of May, June, July, August and September. ABM had ordered a larger number of unfinished suits than needed for the Sutton's order and planned to sell the excess suits in Canada. Leung Manufacturing was responsible for delivering the unfinished suits to dockside in Hong Kong, and thereafter the costs of freight, insurance and duty were to be paid by ABM.

Leung Manufacturing had been suggested to Alfred Brooks by a close friend who owned a womens' outerwear manufacturing company and had used Leung previously. Brooks had made some independent enquiries and found out that Leung had been in business since 1947 and had been managed by two generations of the Leung family. Annual sales were in the US$50 million range and Leung had always been profitable. Mr. Leung had never heard of ABM and wanted some assurance of ABM's ability to pay before he would set the production in motion. Moreover, Leung wanted to be paid within 30 days of delivery and production would not start until the method of payment was confirmed.

Financial Status

The financial statements for the fiscal year ending November 30, 1988 had just been received from the accountants and are shown in Exhibit 6. Lagerfeld was proud of the rebound in profitability from the depressed levels of 1987 when an aggressive effort to expand in the U.S. had been initiated with low introductory prices, which had significantly reduced the overall gross margin that year. Lagerfeld knew that ABM performed well in comparison to the industry and he had put together some of the key industry averages, which are shown in Exhibit 7.

In February 1989, the prime interest rate charged by Canadian financial institutions was set at 12.75%. The prime rate in the United States was 11.0% while the Confederation Bank set a base rate on U.S. dollar loans of 11.5%. Canadian prime rates had increased from the levels of late 1987 when the rate had been set at 9.75%. Further increases in the prime rate were expected, as the Bank of Canada continued its policy of fighting inflation (which was exceeding 5%) through increases in the Bank of Canada rate. This made-in-Canada interest rate strategy continued to keep the Canadian dollar strong relative to the U.S. dollar in spite of a worsening Canadian balance of payments. The U.S. dollar was currently trading at C$1.1858. The U.S. dollar had weakened steadily since 1987 at which time it was trading at approximately C$1.3200. During the past twelve months the value of the U.S. dollar had been quite erratic relative to the Canadian dollar, fluctuating between C$1.2400 and C$1.1700. The forward rate for Canadian dollars for three months was $1.1883, for six months was $1.1940 and for one year was $1.2032.

Decision at Hand

ABM had been a Metropolitan Bank client since inception. Lagerfeld knew that ABM lacked sufficient working capital and he wanted an expansion in its operating loan to help accommodate increased sales. Lagerfeld estimated that ABM would require an increase in its operating loan ceiling from $8,250,000 to $12,000,000 in order to finance its expanded production and sales resulting from the Sutton's order. However, the Metropolitan Bank had been hesitant in committing to an increase in the company's operating loans, and Lagerfeld hoped that the Confederation Bank would react more positively. He had also arranged a meeting with a representative from Irving Trust.

EXHIBIT 1
ALFRED BROOKS MENSWEAR LIMITED

Canadian Garment Shipments
1981–1985
(000s of garments)

	1981	1982	1983	1984	1985
Domestic	372 876	336 112	338 500	339 724	338 706
Less Exports	4 383	4 606	4 426	4 998	5 137
Net Domestic	368 493	331 506	334 074	334 726	333 569
Plus Imports	165 489	166 402	202 453	237 277	247 539
Total Canadian Market	533 982	497 908	536 527	572 003	581 108
Imports/Total	31.0%	33.4%	37.7%	41.5%	42.6%

Source: Government of Canada Report on Apparent Markets for Textiles
and Clothing, *Financial Post*, April 20, 1987.

EXHIBIT 2
ALFRED BROOKS MENSWEAR LIMITED

Accounts Receivable
as of January 31, 1989
(in $000s)

	Days Outstanding				
	0–30	*31–60*	*61–90*	*Over 90*	*Total*
Canada					
Large Diversified Clothing Retailer	$ 144	$ 580	$ 241	—	$ 965
Large National Department Store	—	222	395	—	617
Large National Department Store	—	355	—	—	355
Regional Department Store	—	—	292	—	292
Large Mens Clothing Chain	—	145	—	—	145
Other retailers	62	175	220	201	658
					3 032
United States					
Sutton's	—	145	—	—	145
Northeast Department Store	125	—	—	—	125
Midwest Department Store	—	—	60	—	60
Other retailers	—	65	39	43	147
					477
Italy					
Northern Menswear Chain	—	58	—	—	58
TOTAL	$ 331	$1 745	$1 247	$ 244	$3 567

EXHIBIT 3

ALFRED BROOKS MENSWEAR LIMITED

**Pro Forma Balance Sheet
as of November 30, 1989**

Assets

Accounts Receivable	$ 9 925
Directors' Advances	86
Inventory	4 655
Deposits	2
Prepaid Expenses	55
	14 723
Net Fixed Assets	214
TOTAL ASSETS	$14 937

Liabilities

Bank Loans	$ 6 443
Account Payable	2 596
Income Taxes Payable	995
	10 034
Shareholder Loan	1 487
TOTAL LIABILITIES	$11 521

Shareholders' Equity

Capital Stock	339
Retained Earnings	3 077
	3 416
TOTAL LIABILITIES & EQUITY	$14 937

EXHIBIT 3 (continued)

Pro Forma Income Statement
for the year ending November 30, 1989

Sales		$37 300
Cost of Goods Sold		
Beginning Inventory	4 558	
Purchases & Labour	30 459	
Available for Sale	35 017	
Less Ending Inventory	4 655	30 362
Gross Profit		6 938
Expenses		
Selling & Administrative	3 240	
Interest	1 239	
Depreciation	61	
		4 540
Earnings Before Taxes		2 398
Taxes		995
Net Income		$ 1 403

81

*Case 8
Alfred Brooks
Menswear
Limited*

EXHIBIT 3 (continued)

Monthly Cash Budget for December 1988–November 1989
(in Canadian $000s)

	Dec	Jan	Feb	Mar	Apr	May	Jun	Jul	Aug	Sep	Oct	Nov	Total
Sales													
Sutton's[1]	$ 0	$ 0	$ 0	$ 0	$ 0	$ 0	0	$ 2 446	$ 2 446	$ 2 446	$ 2 446	$ 1 814	$11 598
Other	2 993	1 292	2 393	1 860	308	512	2 742	1 282	3 457	3 198	2 101	3 564	25 702
Total Sales	2 993	1 292	2 393	1 860	308	512	2 742	3 728	5 903	5 644	4 547	5 378	37 300
Opening Loan Balance	-3 901	-4 310	-4 709	-4 010	-5 235	-5 507	-7 125	-9 260	-11 769	-12 076	-11 978	-9 347	-3 901
Cash Inflows:													
Collections[2]													
Sutton's	0	0	0	0	0	0	0	0	0	2 446	2 446	2 446	7 338
Other	2 539	2 634	2 993	1 292	2 393	1 860	308	512	2 742	1 282	3 457	3 198	25 210
TOTAL AVAILABLE	2 539	2 634	2 993	1 292	2 393	1 860	308	512	2 742	3 728	5 903	5 644	32 548
Cash Outflows													
Leung Purchase[3]	0	0	0	0	0	0	765	765	765	765	765	0	3 825
Labour	530	530	530	530	530	530	530	530	530	530	530	530	6 360
Material	2 082	2 163	1 371	1 641	1 786	2 580	756	1 306	1 331	1 913	1 585	1 851	20 365
Admin. & Selling	270	270	270	270	270	270	270	270	270	270	270	270	3 240
Interest: Al Brooks[4]	17	17	17	17	17	17	17	17	17	17	17	17	204
Taxes	0	0	61	0	0	0	0	0	0	0	0	0	61
TOTAL OUTFLOWS	2 899	2 980	2 249	2 458	2 603	3 397	2 338	2 888	2 913	3 495	3 167	2 668	34 055
Preliminary Balance	-4 261	-4 656	-3 965	-5 176	-5 445	-7 044	-9 155	-11 636	-11 940	-11 843	-9 242	-6 371	-6 371
Loan Interest[4]	-49	-53	-45	-59	-62	-81	-105	-133	-136	-135	-105	-72	-1 035
Ending Balance	$-4 310	$-4 709	$-4 010	$-5 235	$-5 507	$-7 125	$-9 260	$-11 769	$-12 076	$-11 978	$-9 347	$-6 443	$-6 443

Assumptions
[1] C$1.1858/US$1.00
[2] 60 days.
[3] 30 days.
[4] Prime rate at 12.75% + 1% = 13.75%

EXHIBIT 4

ALFRED BROOKS MENSWEAR LIMITED

Loan Margin Calculation for December 1988–November 1989

(in Canadian $000s)

	Dec	Jan	Feb	Mar	Apr	May	Jun	Jul	Aug	Sep	Oct	Nov
Accounts Receivable	$ 5 627	$ 4 285	$ 3 685	$ 4 253	$ 2 168	$ 820	$ 3 254	$ 6 470	$ 9 631	$11 547	$10 191	$ 9 925
Inventory	4 734	6 375	6 328	6 985	9 051	11 744	11 563	11 129	8 950	7 564	6 743	4 746
Margin[1]	6 587	6 401	5 928	6 682	6 152	6 487	8 222	10 417	11 698	12 442	11 015	9 817
Operating Loans	−4 310	−4 709	−4 010	−5 235	−5 507	−7 125	−9 260	−11 769	−12 076	−11 978	−9 347	−6 443
Surplus/(Deficit)	$ 2 277	$ 1 692	$ 1 918	$ 1 447	$ 645	$ −638	$ −1 038	$ −1 352	$ −378	$ 464	$ 1 668	$ 3 374

Assumptions
[1] Accounts Receivable @ 75%
Inventory @ 50%

EXHIBIT 5
ALFRED BROOKS MENSWEAR LIMITED

Accounts Payable
as at January 31, 1989
(in $000s)

Supplier (month of invoice)	
Textile Supplies Inc. (various)	$ 195
Canadian Worsted Knit Products Ltd. (Dec/88)	262
Texfab Manufacturers Ltd. (Nov/88)	542
Toronto Garment Centre Inc. (Oct/88)	606
Sundry payables	217
TOTAL	$1 605

EXHIBIT 6
ALFRED BROOKS MENSWEAR LIMITED

Financial Statements

AUDITORS' REPORT

We have examined the balance sheet of Alfred Brooks Menswear (Canada) Ltd. as at November 30, 1988 and the statements of income and retained earnings for the year then ended. Our examination was made in accordance with generally accepted auditing standards, and accordingly included such tests and other procedures as we considered necessary in the circumstances.

WATERHOUSE ROSS
CHARTERED ACCOUNTANTS

Toronto, Ontario
January 29, 1989

EXHIBIT 6 (continued)

Balance Sheet
as at November 30, 1988
(in $000s)

	1988	1987	1986	1985
Assets				
Current Assets				
Accounts Receivable	$ 5 173	$ 7 860	$4 079	$3 780
Loans Receivable – Director	86	55	7	40
Inventory (note 2)	4 558	4 139	3 646	2 762
Deposits	2	2	2	5
Prepaid Expenses	55	39	44	21
Income Taxes Refundable	0	97	0	0
	9 874	12 192	7 778	6 608
Net Fixed Assets (note 3)	275	168	118	110
TOTAL ASSETS	$10 149	$12 360	$7 896	$6 718
Liabilities & Shareholders' Equity				
Liabilities				
Current Liabilities				
Bank Loan (note 4)	$ 3 901	$ 6 834	$2 638	$1 518
Accounts Payable	2 687	2 339	1 980	2 395
Income Taxes Payable	61	0	96	61
	6 649	9 173	4 714	3 974
Long Term Debt (note 5)	1 487	1 487	1 487	1 487
	8 136	10 660	6 201	5 461
Shareholders' Equity				
Capital Stock	339	339	339	339
Retained Earnings	1 674	1 361	1 356	918
	2 013	1 700	1 695	1 257
TOTAL LIABILITIES & SHAREHOLDERS' EQUITY	$10 149	$12 360	$7 896	$6 718

EXHIBIT 6 (continued)

Income Statement
for the Year Ended November 30, 1988
(in $000s)

	1988	1987	1986	1985
Sales	$20 965	$21 570	$18 763	$18 144
Cost of Sales				
Inventory, Beginning Year	4 139	3 644	2 762	901
Purchases	13 249	13 985	12 315	12 831
Labour	4 151	4 808	4 195	4 013
Styling & Designing	68	74	35	233
	21 607	22 513	19 307	17 978
Inventory, End of Year	4 558	4 139	3 644	2 762
	17 050	18 374	15 663	15 216
Gross Profit	3 915	3 196	3 100	2 928
Expenses				
Selling (note 6)	1 400	1 314	1 050	1 015
Administrative (note 6)	1 193	965	785	780
Depreciation and Amortization	61	38	31	28
Interest	873	873	687	544
	3 527	3 190	2 553	2 367
Income Before Income Taxes	388	6	547	561
Income Taxes	75	1	109	115
NET INCOME	$ 313	$ 5	$ 438	$ 446

See accompanying notes.

EXHIBIT 6 (continued)

Notes to Financial Statements
as at November 30, 1988

1. *Accounting Policies*

   Inventory

   Inventory is valued at the lower of cost (first-in, first-out basis) and net realizable value.

   Depreciation and Amortization

   The company depreciates its fixed assets by the declining balance method at the following rates per annum:

Machinery and Equipment	20%
Furniture and Fixtures	20%
Truck	30%
Computer Equipment	30%

   Leasehold improvements are amortized by the straight-line method over the term of the lease for a period of 5 years.

2. *Inventory*

   Inventory consists of the following:

	1988	1987
Raw Materials	$ 628 127	$2 069 144
Work in Process	937 272	491 136
Finished Goods	1 790 542	1 435 504
Goods in Transit	1 201 631	143 462
	$4 557 572	$4 139 246

3. *Fixed Assets*

	Cost	Accum. Depr.	Net 1988	Net 1987
Machinery and Equipment	$140 784	$ 51 066	$ 89 718	$ 64 448
Furniture and Fixtures	91 410	29 564	61 846	25 995
Truck	15 954	4 786	11 168	15 954
Computer	81 202	41 730	39 472	24 037
Leasehold Improvements	120 050	47 383	72 667	37 670
	$449 400	$174 529	$274 871	$168 104

EXHIBIT 6 (continued)

Notes to Financial Statements
as at November 30, 1988

4. *Bank Loan*

Bank loans are secured by a registered general security agreement covering accounts receivable and inventory to the extent of $8 250 000, and by the issuance of a $5 500 000 debenture which provides for a fixed and floating charge on all assets of the company.

5. *Long Term Debt*

Long term debt is payable to the shareholder, bearing interest at bank prime plus 1% per annum with no specific terms of repayment.

6. *Selling & Administrative Expenses*

Selling	1988	1987
Delivery, Freight, Shipping	$ 731 564	$ 633 465
Rent/Warehousing	227 146	157 518
Travel/Entertainment/Promotion	441 059	523 480
	$1 399 769	$1 314 463
Administrative		
Bad Debts	$ 33 190	$ 29 419
Charitable Donations	5 087	34 965
Computer	55 353	46 001
Insurance	68 063	89 550
Management Salaries	208 845	185 644
Professional Fees	113 540	39 831
Rent	45 966	7 956
Repairs & Maintenance	90 852	43 920
Salaries	400 981	353 991
Taxes	67 538	63 535
Telephone	103 391	69 882
	$1 192 806	$ 964 694

EXHIBIT 7

ALFRED BROOKS MENSWEAR LIMITED

Key Industry Ratios — Men's and Boys' Clothing
(Asset Size US $1–10 million)

	Upper Quartile	Median	Lower Quartile
Gross Margin		25.8%	
Operating Expenses		19.5%	
Profit Before Taxes		5.2%	
Current Ratio	2.2	1.9	1.5
Quick Ratio	1.6	.9	.6
Days Receivable	33	51	83
Days Inventory	39	91	122
Days Payable	13	25	36
Sales/Working Capital	2.9	6.2	10.0
EBIT/Interest	9.3	3.0	1.2
Debt/Equity	.8	1.5	2.4
Profit Before Taxes/Equity	42.6%	15.3%	2.5%
Sales/Assets	3.1	2.0	1.4

Source: Robert Morris Associates, 1988

89

*Case 8
Alfred Brooks
Menswear
Limited*

Capital Structure
Decisions

BELLEVIEW HOTEL LIMITED

In October, 1988, Ms. Linda Park, president of Belleview Hotel Limited (BHL), had just returned from a meeting with other directors of BHL. They had discussed three financing proposals to raise $1,560,000 for BHL. Ms. Park was uncertain as to the impact of the three proposals on the financial viability of BHL, the returns to herself, and to other investors. The meeting ended with the rest of the directors turning the decision over to her.

History

After several years as a hotel manager for a national chain, Park had established herself in the tourist accommodation business close to a medium-sized Ontario city along the St. Lawrence River. Park chose this location because the route was heavily travelled by tourists during the spring and summer months. In 1981, she formed a company known as St. Lawrence Motor Courts, Limited, and erected an elaborate, modern motel on this site. The buildings provided complete tourist accommodation, shelter for automobiles, and spacious dining facilities with entertainment for guests. Park considered St. Lawrence Motor Courts, Limited, a very successful venture.

In the following years, there sprang up in the area surrounding Park's establishment many new industries which had been attracted by easily accessible railway and shipping facilities, and by the proximity of a large market area. These industries were not along the main tourist route on which St. Lawrence Motor Courts was situated; consequently, they did not in any way adversely affect the attractiveness of the site as a potential tourist stop-over. However, the general expansion in the area, which soon became known as "the golden mile", attracted many business people who, not infrequently, found it necessary to remain in the city overnight in order to complete their business.

The BHL Project

With these developments in mind, Park approached a number of large industries in the vicinity in the summer of 1988 with a proposal regarding accommodation for visiting business people. Her suggestion was well-received, and several manufacturing concerns expressed an interest in maintaining permanent accommodation for visitors on business. With this encouragement, and in view of the overflow of visitors experienced to date, Park conceived the idea of constructing a modern hotel on an immediately adjacent property. Park hoped that part of this development would provide steady, year-round business by arrangement with the local industries, while the remainder would be used to catch the overflow from the St. Lawrence Motor Court during the tourist season.

Park then considered the type and size of hotel that would be desirable, and tried to estimate the costs of such a project. The property adjacent to the St. Lawrence Motor Courts, which Park owned, was 75 feet wide and 235 feet in length, and was appraised at $400,000. After consultation with a local architect, Park developed a plan for a hotel building which fulfilled the apparent prerequisites. The plan called for a three-storey structure, containing four suites of two rooms each, 24 twin bedrooms, 23 double bedrooms, a large front store, seven smaller stores, and other facilities which Park felt might eventually accommodate a barber, hairdresser, and a doctor's office and apartment.

Ms. Park then attempted to estimate the profitability of such an establishment. She felt that, based on her experience with the Motor Court business, the income from the four suites and the bedrooms should be in the neighborhood of $4000 per day, presuming that all accommodation was occupied. The income from leases of other parts of the building she estimated at $8000 per month, with 100 percent occupancy. Rent would be charged as a percent of sales and was expected to vary with occupancy. Other income eventually would be derived from gift counters, papers, display space, and from a large central area, 100 feet by 20 feet in the basement, for which a purpose had not yet been planned.

Apart from the incorporation expenses, which were expected to be about $30,000, Ms. Park estimated her yearly operating expenses, again based on 100 percent occupancy (see Exhibit 1).

Park felt that in estimating the profitability of the hotel, an estimate of 75 percent average occupancy over a year was realistic, and 50 percent occupancy the lowest possibility. All store and office spaces were to be leased on a yearly basis. Income taxes were estimated at 46 percent.

The estimated cost of erecting a brick, concrete and steel hotel such as the one proposed was set at $1,300,000. After considerable investigation, Ms. Park set the estimated cost of furnishing the hotel at $720,000. She judged that working capital of $50,000 would be required in order to operate the business. Further, since her estimate of the profitability of the new hotel seemed to warrant a venture into this expanded field of business activity, she was certain that the required capital could be raised.

Accordingly, Ms Park met with a few of her associates, two lawyers and three local businessmen, to discuss the establishment of the new business. It was decided, in view of the degree of speculation involved in a new venture of this kind, and also because of the possibility of future expansion in the hotel business, that the business should be established as an independent corporate body with no financial connection whatsoever to St. Lawrence Motor Courts, Limited.

Thus, the new company, to be known as the Belleview Hotel, Limited, was to be incorporated as a company to operate hotels and automobile tourist homes. The head office would be established on the property of St. Lawrence Motor Courts, Limited. Ms. Park would become the president and chairman of the board of directors. The original patent would have a share capital of 200,000 – eight percent preference shares with a par value of $25 each, and 500,000 common shares without nominal or par value.

BHL Financing Proposals

Park foresaw the desirability of getting construction underway as quickly as possible, so that sufficient headway would be made by winter for the work to be continued indoors. It was anticipated that the new structure would be completed in time for the 1989 peak season. Since considerable time would be required to raise the necessary capital, Park decided to provide the funds required to begin construction immediately from her personal savings. Such amounts were to be repaid by the company. The necessary arrangements were completed, and construction of the new hotel commenced in September 1988.

In August, considerable progress had been made in planning operations. Park felt that attention must be turned now to the matter of providing the permanent capital, which had been previously estimated at $2.5 million: working capital, $50,000; land, $400,000; building, $1,300,000; furnishings, $720,000; and organization costs, $30,000.

As the first step in the financing plan, BHL would enter into an agreement with Park to purchase the land on which the hotel was to be built for $400,000. Under the purchase agreement, BHL contracted to give Park 80,000 shares of common stock in consideration for this land.

The second step, to aid in the financing of the furnishings, had BHL negotiate a tentative ten percent , 5-year term loan of $540,000 with the suppliers. Blended annual payments of $142,450 were due starting at the end of the first fiscal year.

With $1,560,000 still required, Park arranged preliminary discussions with her associates to decide the most feasible method of raising the capital. She had entertained the thought of a first mortgage on the company's real estate. The mortgage would be for $1,560,000, 10-year term, at 12 percent. The annual principal and interest payments would be $276,000, with payments due at the end of BHL's fiscal year. However, Park was concerned that the fixed interest charges might prove too great a risk at the present, with future earning prospects uncertain.

In response, Park's associates made a second proposal: the sale of common shares in units of 10,000 shares at five dollars per share, total unit value, $50,000. Legal expenses for the issue were expected to be $50,000. To promote sales, sellers of the units would be given a 15 percent commission. The number of units would be limited to 38, to avoid many of the new issue requirements of the Ontario Securities Commission. Ms. Park objected to the common stock proposal, as her proportion of the profits would be substantially reduced.

A third proposal was raised: 76,000 shares of eight percent, $25 par value preferred shares in units of 2,000 preferred shares. The preferred shares would be redeemable at $26, and the dividends would be cumulative. If dividends were passed for two consecutive years, the preferred shares could elect a majority of the board of directors. Legal costs of issue were expected to be $50,000 and a 15 percent selling commission would be instituted to promote their sale. In addition, the unit purchaser would be entitled to subscribe to one common share at five dollars per common share for each preferred share purchased.

After the development of the last proposal, the discussions adjourned. The directors stated that the final decision rested with Park.

EXHIBIT 1
BELLEVIEW HOTEL LIMITED

Annual Operating Expenses at 100% Occupancy

	Total Variable Cost	Fixed Cost	Total Cost
Advertising	$	$ 10 000	$ 10 000
Heat, light, water	32 000	32 000	64 000
House supplies	32 000		32 000
House wages	144 000		144 000
Repairs & maintenance	24 000	24 000	48 000
Insurance		8 000	8 000
Salaries		80 000	80 000
Laundry	40 000		40 000
Office expenses		16 000	16 000
Miscellaneous		6 000	6 000
Linen	15 000		15 000
Telephone		8 000	8 000
Automobile & travel		12 000	12 000
Municipal taxes		30 000	30 000
Depreciation		180 000	180 000
	$287 000	$406 000	$693 000

HIGHLAND DAIRIES LIMITED

In early August, 1989, Nancy Clark, Treasurer of Highland Dairies Limited (Highland) was examining alternatives for financing the proposed $12.75 million acquisition of Densmore Creamery Ltd. (Densmore). The acquisition was expected to be completed by November 31st. The Directors of Highland were scheduled to meet in two weeks to approve the acquisition of Densmore and decide on a financing plan for the purchase and the on-going operations of the combined business. Highland was a private company which had relied primarily on bank credit and retained earnings to finance its past growth. Clark knew that her report to the Board would have to be particularly well presented since several of the Board members had no previous experience with a public security issue, which was one of her options for Board consideration.

John Ingalls, President of Highland, saw this acquisition as an opportunity to extend the company's market, expand production capacity and achieve economies of scale. The dairy industry in Canada was subject to a variety of government regulations and was very competitive. In Ontario alone there were about 150 dairies and industrial milk processors. Ingalls believed that corporate size was a key success factor in the industry and that acquiring Densmore would enable Highland to almost double its operations. He had negotiated a purchase price for Densmore which he thought was a "steal" and now it was up to Clark to figure out how the funds could best be raised.

The Dairy Industry

Raw milk could be sold to either dairies or processors. Approximately forty percent of all milk produced went to dairies while the remainder went to industrial milk processors. Dairies pasteurized and packaged raw milk into cream or table milk products such as homogenized, two percent, skim and buttermilk. Processors converted milk into by-products such as butter, yogurt and cheese, or into component substances that could be further used by other processors to produce ice cream, puddings or cake mixes.

Worldwide the dairy processing industry was subject to restrictive government regulation. In Canada, the supply and pricing of milk was controlled by two regulatory bodies, the provincially run Milk Marketing Boards (MMBS) and the Canadian Dairy Commission (CDC).

The MMBS were controlled by the milk producers (dairy farmers). Their marketing responsibilities involved control over production quotas, pricing, supply allocation and the final sale of fluid milk and cream destined for the consumer market.

The CDC was administered by the federal government. The two main objectives of the CDC were: i) to provide efficient producers of milk and cream with the opportunity of obtaining a fair return for their labour and investment; ii) to provide consumers of dairy products with a continuous and adequate supply of dairy products of high quality. The activities which the CDC undertook to meet these objectives included advising the government on dairy policy, determining requirements for industrial milk and cream for the purpose of establishing market sharing quotas, calculating the target price for industrial milk, and chairing the Canadian Milk Supply Management Committee which coordinated the management of industrial milk and cream supplies in Canada.

The MMBS and CDC established varying prices for milk, depending upon its end use (Exhibit 1). The highest price was set for milk sold to consumers, and the supply of this milk was controlled by farm production quotas. Prices for industrial milk were calculated using a cost index that allowed efficient producers to make a reasonable profit. To determine the index, cost data were collected from about 300 farms. A random sample of farms was selected, costs analyzed and the farms rank-ordered by costs. The average cost of the bottom 70 percent of this sample was used as a base price for fluid milk after allowing for a reasonable return for the farmer. This price was set yearly and was reviewed mid-year. As shown in Exhibit 1, the price of industrial milk was set below that of fluid milk. In addition, the CDC offered price supports and subsidy payments for some milk products to further encourage their production.

Milk supplies for classes 1 to 4c were given priority in distribution. Milk demand for classes 1 to 4c was satisfied by allocating proportional shares of each producer's milk deliveries, and the residual was distributed on a quota basis to class 5 and 6 processors. Farmers attempted to target their production volumes to fill the need of classes 1 to 4 milk only. Thus, there were often seasonal shortages to meet the demands for classes 5 and 6 milk. The CDC had instituted a processor-quota system to equitably distribute these classes of lower priced milk. In an effort to increase their quota shares, some processors acquired smaller processors, and this resulted in industry rationalization and consolidation.

Highland Dairies

Founded in the late 1920's, Highland had grown steadily over the past 60 years. Originally Highland had produced only milk, butter and cream; however, by the late 1940s, it had entered into the production of specialized dairy and dairy substitute products. By 1989, Highland had grown to become one of Canada's largest dairy processors, as well as a major producer of vegetable fat based dairy product substitutes. Highland was organized into two divisions, Flavours, and Protein Supplements and Replacements. The Flavours division enjoyed significantly higher margins. One of the Flavour products, hydrolized protein, was used extensively in soups as a broth protein agent. The Protein Supplements and Replacements division consisted of products that were sold to manufacturers of such food products as baked goods, candies, processed meats, pharmaceuticals, sauces, artificial creamers, whipped toppings and baby food.

Highland's products were manufactured in Woodstock Ontario. The company was a major employer (240 employees) and tax payer in the community. Highland's processing equipment included precipitators, pasteurizers, homogenizers, agglomerators, dryers, cookers and condensors. Considerable skill was required to operate this complex, technical machinery and operations were carried on round-the-clock with three eight-hour shifts per day. Because of the relatively instantaneous processing of products, there was modest work-in-process inventory.

Financing Needs in the Past

The president and principal shareholder in Highland, John Ingalls, had acquired the company in the early 1970s with a group of investors. The financial statements in Exhibits 2 and 3 show that to this point in time Highland relied exclusively on the Confederation Bank for financing beyond its retained earnings and new share capital issued through employee stock options.

As of August 10, 1989, the Confederation's term and operating credit to Highland totalled $8.4 million, down slightly from a mid-June all-time peak of $8.7 million.

Highland's term loan of roughly $2.7 million had recently been negotiated with a term of twelve years and an interest rate of prime plus one and a half percent. Annual principal payments amounted to $180,000. The loan was secured by a debenture which imposed limits on dividends and capital expenditures. The collateral consisted of Highland's fixed assets.

The operating line of credit amounted to $6.0 million and was secured by a pledge of accounts receivable and inventory. The interest rate on the operating credit was prime plus one half percent (prime + ½).

The Acquisition Opportunity

The formal acquisition proposal that was put forward by Highland on August 10, 1989, offered to purchase all of the Densmore Creamery Limited common shares for $12.75 million. The acquisition offer had been discussed with Densmore's management group, who seemed receptive. The management group held thirty percent of Densmore's shares, with the remaining seventy percent widely held by individual farmers. From discussions with Densmore's senior managers, Ingalls knew that they were discouraged about the company's future prospects. While the Densmore managers had confidence in the facilities and products, they realized that they were not taking full advantage of their equipment. Densmore's modern facility in Sherbrooke, Quebec utilized the latest milk processing equipment; however unless its utilization and efficiency rates increased, it would lose money. The management group did not believe that the company could achieve the additional volume to accomplish these cost savings.

Ingalls thought that the acquisition was ideal, since Densmore and Highland made the same basic dairy products and serviced similar markets. The acquisition would allow Highland to purchase additional capacity very inexpensively. This capacity was needed since the present Highland manufacturing facilities at Woodstock were taxed to their limits, especially the dryer facilities. Densmore had superior drying facilities that were being significantly underutilized at the present volume of business.

An amalgamation of the two operations would result in the transfer of the majority of Highland's manufacturing facility to Sherbrooke, close to the major Quebec markets. It was Ingalls' opinion that the Sherbrooke operation, which employed 180 people, would have improved efficiency once Highland's volume of business was transferred and its expertise and proven technologies were introduced.

Ingalls planned to transfer the major portion of Highland's protein substitute production, which required the use of dryers, to Sherbrooke, thus optimizing the use of Sherbrooke's larger drying units. This move would then leave the Woodstock facility open to expand Highland's Flavours division, which at this point was operating at capacity and required expansion within the next few years.

Densmore's most recent balance sheet indicated total assets of nearly $17.7 million but, in Ingalls' estimation, these assets had a replacement value of $22.5 million. Densmore's income statements are presented in Exhibit 4. Preliminary estimates for 1989 indicated sales of $87.42 million and profits of $2.26 million, most of which would be earned in the first six months of the year. The Densmore management group indicated that earnings of $3.3 million could reasonably be expected in future years, if the level of operations approached capacity.

Financing Options

Clark had carefully explored several options in preparing for the Board meeting. Interest costs were at what many economists considered to be a high level, and some thought that interest rates would fall in the near future. Exhibit 9 presents current interest rate information.

Clark talked to officers in several financial institutions and securities firms and narrowed her options to three choices. These are individually discussed in the following paragraphs.

Bank Financing

Confederation Bank proposed a financing arrangement which would enable Highland to proceed with the acquisition and, as well, to finance the combined operations. Confederation proposed: A $9.0 million operating loan at an interest rate of prime plus one-half percent (prime at $\frac{1}{2}$) secured by the combined receivables and inventories of Highland and Densmore.

A $12.75 million term loan at prime plus two percent (prime + 2) repayable over a 12 year period beginning January 1, 1990, with monthly interest and principal payments secured by a first mortgage on land and buildings of Densmore and a floating charge on all other Densmore assets. Confederation would handle all of the banking activities for the combined operation. The loan would restrict annual capital expenditures to $750,000 and dividends to not more than 50 percent of yearly earnings.

The existing term loan to Highland ($2.7 million), secured by Highland's fixed assets, would be retained.

Pension Fund Private Placement

Clark approached Charles Belyea, the manager of a large Ontario corporate pension fund about the possibility of a term loan. This pension fund, with assets of over $2 billion, was known to invest up to five percent of the fund in smaller companies operating within the province. Belyea called her back after three days and offered financing as follows:

> A $12.75 million debenture at 11.25 percent for 15 years secured by a first mortgage on Densmore's real estate and a floating charge on the other assets of Densmore, subject to the assignment of receivables and inventory for the bank operating loan. This loan would require an annual sinking fund payment of $750,000 beginning on December 31, 1990. The pension fund would also receive 50,000 common shares of Highland for making the loan.

Public Offering of Securities

The final major option involved "going public" with an issue of common shares. Clark discussed this possibility with Mitch Kaplan, Vice-President, Underwriting, at National Securities in Toronto. Kaplan explained that since October 1987 there had been few initial public offerings of shares in Canada. Recently, however confidence was gaining in the stock markets as the TSE 300 index reached new highs and going public was again considered a viable alternative. Clark knew that, in going public, Highland would have to undergo a rigorous examination of its operations, financial records, and legal situation both by the underwriter and the Ontario Securities Commission (OSC). Kaplan estimated that the process would take four to six months.

During a second visit, after Kaplan had reviewed the company, he pointed out that Highland would have to bear the legal and audit costs of the examination, amounting to about $250,000, as well as pay an underwriting fee of six percent of gross proceeds. In return, National would underwrite the issue, setting the price just prior to the public offering.

Kaplan indicated that under current market conditions, and assuming no problems with the OSC, National would underwrite the shares at a price of about $14.00 to the public. He suggested that the offer should be for one million shares to assure a reasonable market and meet stock exchange listing requirements.

Kaplan also discussed a possible placement of preferred stock. Recent preferred issues indicated that Highland could float $13.5 million of preferred stock with a dividend rate of 10.25 percent, which would provide net proceeds of $12.75 million for the company. However because of interest rate uncertainty, investors were currently reluctant to lock-into fixed rate securities for long terms and the investment banker indicated that the Highland issue might have to carry a "retraction" option that would permit investors to cash in on the preferred stock within seven to ten years.

Further Conversations

Clark returned to the Confederation Bank after her discussions with Belyea and Kaplan. The bank indicated that it would provide bridge financing for Highland between the date of the acquisition and that of a public stock offering at a rate of prime plus two percent. In addition, the bank agreed to grant the operating loan of $9.0 million under any option, provided that Highland used the Confederation Bank for all its banking activities.

At this point, Clark began her analysis of the financing options. The first step was to prepare a projected consolidated income statement for Highland and Densmore for the next three years (Exhibit 5), and a pro forma balance sheet at December 31, 1989 (Exhibit 6). She took from her files a recent Statistics Canada publication showing average ratios for the dairy industry

(Exhibit 7) to use as a basis for comparison. Clark also compiled a share-holder list and included the proposed additions (Exhibit 8) before preparing a·summary of all the financial market information she had accumulated (Exhibit 9). "Now the fun begins", she said aloud to the empty office as she began her deliberations over the various options.

EXHIBIT 1
HIGHLAND DAIRIES LIMITED

Milk Classification and Pricing

Class of Milk	Types of Product	Price Determination	Availability of Milk
1 & 2	Fluid Milk Sold to Consumers	Determined by Milk Marketing Board	Unlimited
3	Fluid Creams Cottage Cheese Yogurt Egg Nog	81% of Class 1 Milk	Unlimited
4	Ice Cream Mixes Confectionary Prod. Milk Shake Yogurt Ice Cream Frozen Yogurt Puddings Infant Products	81% of Class 1 Milk	Unlimited
4 (a)	Speciality Cheese	77% of Class 1 Milk	Unlimited
4 (b)	Brick Cheese Colby Cheese	77% of Class 1 Milk	Unlimited
4 (c)	Sterilized Milk For Export	81% of Class 1 Milk	Unlimited
5	Butter, Casein Condensed and Evaporated Milk Skim and Whole Milk Powder	74% of Class 1 Milk	Milk Supplies Sometimes Limited. Quotas on Supply
5 (a)	Cheddar Cheese	74% of Class 1 Milk	Milk Supplies Sometimes Limited. Quotas on Supply
6	New products	74% of Class 1 Milk	

EXHIBIT 2
HIGHLAND DAIRIES LIMITED

Income Statement
for the years ended June 30, 1986 – 1989
($000)

	1989	1988	1987	1986
Sales	$91 044	85 341	69 909	50 274
Cost of Sales	74 664	69 807	57 885	41 409
Selling & Admin. Expenses	8 010	7 863	6 735	4 569
Earnings Before Int. & Tax	8 370	7 671	5 289	4 296
Interest Expense	960	555	390	384
Income Tax	3 258	3 129	2 154	1 722
Net Earnings	4 152	3 987	2 745	2 190
Dividends	1 350	1 200	825	750

EXHIBIT 3
HIGHLAND DAIRIES LIMITED

Balance Sheet as at June 30, 1986 – 1989
($000)

	1989	1988	1987	1986
Assets				
Current Assets				
Accounts Receivable	$ 6 180	$ 5 235	$ 4 803	$ 2 664
Inventory	10 695	5 754	4 608	4 827
Total Current Assets	16 875	10 989	9 411	7 491
Fixed Assets				
Plant & Equipment (net)	10 986	6 798	5 277	4 209
Goodwill	1 248	1 350	1 428	1 560
Total Fixed Assets	12 234	8 148	6 705	5 769
TOTAL ASSETS	29 109	19 137	16 116	13 260
Liabilities and Shareholders' Equity				
Current Liabilities				
Bank Loan	5 652	3 249	2 895	1 320
Accounts & Other Payables	4 050	3 552	3 429	2 502
Total Current Liabilities	9 702	6 801	6 324	3 822
Long Term Bank Debt	2 829	1 113	1 284	2 667
Shareholders' Equity	16 578	11 223	8 508	6 771
TOTAL LIABILITIES	29 109	19 137	16 116	13 260

EXHIBIT 4
HIGHLAND DAIRIES LIMITED

Densmore Creamery Ltd.
Income Statement
for the years ended December 31, 1985 – 1988
($000)

	1988	1987	1986	1985
Sales	$69 585	$64 497	$59 322	$52 629
EBIT	1 821	3 252	1 818	2 058
Interest	66	102	246	252
Income Taxes	720	1 035	603	705
Net Earnings	1 035	2 115	969	1 101
Dividends	141	138	126	126

EXHIBIT 5
HIGHLAND DAIRIES LIMITED

**Pro Forma Income Statements
for Highland and Densmore
for the years ended December 31, 1990 – 1992**
($000)

Without consideration of financing costs on $12.75 million

	1990	1991	1992
Sales	$181 200	$209 100	$223 800
EBIT	13 770	16 200	17 400
Interest on Existing Highland Debt			
Operating Loan	1 230	1 230	1 230
Term Loan	555	495	435
	1 785	1 725	1 665
Tax (46%)	5 514	6 660	7 239
Net Earnings After Tax But Before New Financing	6 471	7 815	8 496

EXHIBIT 6
HIGHLAND DAIRIES LIMITED

**Pro Forma Balance Sheet for Highland and
Densmore as of December 31, 1989**
($000)

Assets	
Current Assets	$26 700
Property & Equipment (net)	16 500
Goodwill	3 300
TOTAL ASSETS	46 500

Liabilities and Shareholders' Equity	
Current Liabilities	
Bank Loan – Operating	5 775
Accounts Payable and Accruals	6 300
Total Current Liabilities	12 075
Long Term Bank Debt	2 700
Shareholders' Equity	18 975
Financing – to be arranged	12 750
TOTAL LIABILITIES	$46 500

EXHIBIT 7
HIGHLAND DAIRIES LIMITED

Dairy Products Industry Ratios

Fixed Assets/Equity	66.6%
LTD/Equity	15.0
Cost of Sales/Sales	82.7
Sales to Inventory	13.5
Collection Period (days)	23.3
Current Ratio	1.7
Profit After Tax on Capital Employed	11.4
Profits After Tax on Total Income	2.4

Source: Statistics Canada

EXHIBIT 8
HIGHLAND DAIRIES LIMITED

Existing Shareholders and Proposed Financing Plans

	Shares
Existing Shares	
John Ingalls	410 000
Jeff Fowler	250 000
Steve McLinden	100 000
Steven Belyea	100 000
Andy Marcolin	50 000
Joyce Simpson	50 000
5 Key Employees	270 000
	1 230 000
New Shares	
Shares to Pension Fund	50 000
Shares for Stock Offering	1 000 000

EXHIBIT 9
HIGHLAND DAIRIES LIMITED

Financial Data

	Aug. 1989	Aug. 1988	Aug. 1987
Interest Rates			
Prime Commercial Bank Rate	13.50	11.25	10.00
Corporate Long Term Bond Rate — Scotia McLeod Bond Index	10.66	11.34	11.08

TSE 300 Stock Index

Index Level on Aug. 9, 1989	4 004
High for Year	4 022
Low for Year	3 348
P/E Multiple TSE 300 Companies	12.36
P/E Food Processing Companies	18.56

Preferred Stock Yields

Yield	Coupon Rate	Dividend	Price	
Canadian Utilities	6%	$6.00	67.00	9.0
National Bank	8%	2.00	21.50	9.3
Slater Steel	7½%	1.00	16.00	9.4
Trans Alta	9%	2.25	25.75	8.7

BRALORNE RESOURCES
LIMITED

In July, 1980 Bralorne Resources Limited of Calgary, Alberta, planned to raise $40 million of long-term financing. The $40 million would be used to finance acquisitions, exploration activities, and the retirement of variable rate debts. Interest rates on the variable rate debts had been fluctuating over the past year (see Exhibit 1). McLeod Young Weir Ltd., Bralorne's investment dealers, had presented Bralorne with an option to issue a $12\frac{7}{8}$ percent, 15-year secured term debenture which would be placed privately.

History

Bralorne was a diversified North American energy resource company. In addition to energy exploration, Bralorne was a manufacturer and supplier of products and services to energy-related industries. Its corporate structure and strategy had altered considerably since its origin in 1931 as the largest gold-mining company in British Columbia. Its gold reserves were considered depleted in 1971, although in 1980 the reserves were being re-examined by a joint venture with E & B Exploration of Calgary, Alberta.

In 1971, Bralorne appointed a new president, Mr. Bill Fitzpatrick, formerly corporate vice-president of Celanese Canada Ltd. His strategy was to convert Bralorne into an energy company. This strategy was based on the premise that energy, especially oil and natural gas exploration and production, would be the fastest growing area in the North American economy in the 1970s and 1980s. Bralorne set out to become not only a petroleum explorer and producer, but also a supplier of petroleum exploration and development products and services. Cash flows developed through product and supply investments would be reinvested in an oil and gas exploration program.

During the 1970s Bralorne acquired numerous companies in Alberta and Texas which specialized in producing equipment for oil exploration and development. The producing gas and exploratory leases of Buttes Resources Canada Ltd., near Medicine Hat, Alberta, were obtained in 1976.

Operating Groups

Bralorne was organized into three operating groups. Exhibit 2 outlines Bralorne's operating structure; Exhibits 3 and 4, its income statements and balance sheets.

The Oil and Gas Division, headquartered in Calgary, was engaged in development drilling of the gas reserves near Medicine Hat. Trans-Canada Pipeline was obligated to purchase all the gas from the tract although, because of a gas surplus, it was attempting to renegotiate the contract. Exploratory drilling was also carried out in other areas of Canada and in the Texas-Lousiana area of the United States. Production in 1979 was 100 million cubic meters of natural gas and 71 000 barrels of oil. Proven and probable reserves were 1.027 million barrels of oil and 3 billion cubic meters of gas. The present worth of these reserves before taxes or operating costs was estimated at $99 million (discounted at 12 percent), although they were carried on the balance sheet at cost. About five percent of Bralorne's $141 million gross revenues in 1979 was derived from oil and gas production.

The Manufacturing Group contributed about 55 percent of Bralorne's 1979 gross revenue. Barber Industries manufactured petroleum drilling equipment at plants in Calgary and Edmonton. OMSCO Industries of Houston, Texas manufactured oil field equipment, specializing in drill collars. Mark Products, Inc., and its subsidiaries, also in Houston, were leading international suppliers of equipment used to gather geophysical data for the petroleum industry. A third Houston company, Triangle Grinding, specialized in cutting and threading tools.

The Supply and Service Group consisted of Jarco Service Ltd. of Calgary, which supplied downhole tools for the drilling industry, ENOCO in Edmonton and Calgary, which produced safety control devices for the petroleum industry, and Polesystem of Calgary and Winnipeg, which manufactured light standards and ordered traffic structures. Bralorne also provided camp leasing and servicing operations for petroleum exploration crews in remote areas of Canada through Crown Caterers and Custom Structures of Edmonton. Mobile housing was supplied to the Middle East and North African oil fields through Mobile Homes Ltd., of Malta. The Supply and Service Group contributed 40 percent of Bralorne's gross revenue in 1979.

Performance

Bralorne's gross revenues rose sharply from $1.5 million in 1971 to $141 million by 1979 because of manufacturing acquisitions and expansion and continued development of natural gas reserves near Medicine Hat, Alberta. Income rose steadily from $151 000 to $10.7 million during the same period as the demand for products used in petroleum exploration and development accelerated. The future looked similarly promising, since Bralorne was in the position of being able to draw upon income from its manufacturing and service operations for use in petroleum exploration and development, and since Bralorne was diversified geographically.

Bralorne's reserves were mainly natural gas located in Canada, which had natural gas export restrictions. Although the gas was being purchased by Trans-Canada Pipelines, there were rumours that Bralorne might have to re-negotiate the contract. Other rumours persisted of a new federal energy policy for Canada and its ramifications in the petroleum industry. (See Appendix A for an outline of the taxation and exploration activities of the Canadian industry.) The United States was becoming increasingly defensive about Canadian investment in the American petroleum industry. The world economic climate, characterized by fluctuating, erratic interest rates and currency valuations, was another factor. Most of Bralorne's debts, although considered long-term, were at variable rates equal to prime plus 0.5 to one percent.

Bralorne's stock had split three for one on April 25, 1980. Currently 20.2 million shares represented the fully diluted outstanding shares either in issued shares or unexercised options and warrants. After adjusting for the three for one stock split, Bralorne's share price rose from a low of $0.32 in 1974 to a high of $12.75 in June, 1980 (Exhibit 5). The stock had traded as low as $2.67 a share as recently as January, 1978. Price-earnings ratios were at an historic high of 16.5 in June, 1980, possibly caused by the investor perception of Bralorne as an energy company rather than a manufacturing service company. To enhance the stock price, Bralorne had introduced an annual dividend of $0.07 a share in mid-1978, payable semi-annually. This dividend was to be increased to $.10 in 1980.

Expected Growth

Some industry analysts expected Bralorne's gross revenue to increase 50 percent and net income 75 percent annually for the next five years if the petroleum exploration boom continued and Bralorne continued development and acquisitions. Some security analysts had issued a strong buy recommendation, believing the stock would hit $20 a share by the fall. Other security analysts were not as optimistic and were suggesting that investors "cool their heels" for a time because of the recent dramatic increase in the share price and the historically high price earnings multiples.

The Versatile-Cornat Corporation

In August, 1976, Cornat Industries Limited of Vancouver, British Columbia acquired 50.05 percent of Bralorne's common stock for $1.42 a share (adjusted for the three to one stock split). Cornat Industries Limited had been incorporated in 1969 as a commercial credit and real estate company. The company expanded into the ship-building industry by acquiring Burrard Dry

Dock Co. Ltd., of Vancouver, the third largest such facility in Canada. Subsequent acquisitions were a manufacturer of aluminum doors and windows, moving and storage companies, a pollution control firm, and a leasing firm.

In January, 1977, Cornat Industries Ltd. acquired 52 percent of the voting shares of Versatile Industries Ltd., of Winnipeg, Manitoba, a large manufacturer of farm equipment. In July, 1978 the two companies amalgamated, resulting in the Versatile-Cornat Corporation. Several subsidiaries were sold as the new corporate strategy was to be a manufacturer of heavy industrial equipment and parts, primarily in the agricultural, marine, and petroleum sectors.

By 1980, Versatile-Cornat Corporation had increased its holdings in Bralorne to 58.6 percent. In 1979, Bralorne contributed 34 percent of Versatile's gross revenue and 40 percent of its earnings before minority interests. Bralorne assets of $149 million represented 42 percent of Versatile's total assets. Bralorne's financial data were included in Versatile's financial statements (Exhibits 6 and 7).

The operation of Bralorne was independent of Versatile. Mr. Fitzpatrick had worked hard at the development of the organization and the promotion of Bralorne as an independent energy enterprise. The only constraint on decisions was Versatile's concern about maintaining its current control position.

Possible Financing Alternatives

To raise $40 million in 1980, McLeod Young Weir, the company's investment dealers, had suggested a privately-placed debenture. Other possibilities included common stock or convertible issues.

A $40 million common stock issue could involve issuing 3.2 million shares at $12.50 per share. There was some concern about the dilution of earnings per share and the effect on stock prices.

A $40 million, 8 percent, $25 par value 20-year convertible, cummulative, redeemable preferred was another possibility. The issue would have a conversion price of $20.00 or a conversion ratio of 1.25 common shares per preferred share. Without conversion, an investment analyst believed, the coupon rate would have to be 9-1/2 percent. The preferred shares would not be redeemable until 1985, unless the common stock for 30 consecutive days was 140 percent of the conversion price. Starting five years after the issue date, the shares could be redeemed at $27.50. The call price would be reduced by $0.50 per year until the issue was callable at par in 1990. In addition, Bralorne would have to purchase one percent of the issue quarterly on the open market starting in 1985.

A third alternative was a privately-placed 15-year 12-7/8 percent debenture issue, secured by the petroleum and natural gas assets of Bralorne. The debentures would not be redeemable prior to 1990, except for sinking fund purposes. Annual sinking fund redemption would be $3 million from 1983 through to 1994. Available security at all times had to be 175 percent of the principal amount outstanding and net revenues from the reserves have to be at least 120 percent of the principal plus interest payable each year.

Any decision made regarding Bralorne's financing would directly affect its parent company, Versatile. Bralorne's debt/equity ratio was now 50/50, average for a firm in the petroleum exploration business (Exhibit 8). Versatile's ratio was 45/55, primarily because of Bralorne, and was considerably higher than other industrial manufacturers (Exhibit 9). A decision would have to be made shortly: interest rates were at their 1980 lows and inflation as reported by Statistics Canada was increasing monthly.

Mr. Fitzpatrick asked his finance staff to prepare four year projections of funding needs for both Bralorne and Versatile. On completion of the projections, the staff was to prepare a financing plan that would include a recommendation for raising $40 million immediately and needed amounts thereafter.

EXHIBIT 1
BRALORNE RESOURCES LIMITED

Market Rate Information
annual year ends to 1980, then month ends

	3 Month Treasury Bills	C.P.I.	Bank Prime	Govt. of Canada over 10 years	MYW Industrials
1970	4.44	3.3	7.50	6.99	8.83
1971	3.21	2.9	6.00	6.56	8.25
1972	3.65	4.8	6.00	7.12	8.15
1973	6.35	7.5	9.50	7.70	8.81
1974	7.12	10.9	11.00	8.77	10.72
1975	8.64	10.8	9.75	9.49	11.06
1976	8.14	7.5	9.25	8.47	9.83
1977	7.17	8.0	8.25	8.77	9.71
1978	10.46	9.0	11.50	9.68	10.34
1979	13.66	9.1	15.00	11.32	12.07
Jan., 1980	13.50	9.5	15.00	12.13	12.80
Feb., 1980	13.55	9.4	15.00	12.91	13.35
March, 1980	15.24	9.3	15.75	13.45	13.89
April, 1980	15.15	9.2	16.75	12.01	12.84
May, 1980	11.58	9.4	13.75	11.42	12.29
June, 1980	10.38	10.1	13.25	11.29	12.15

Source: Statistics Canada

EXHIBIT 2
BRALORNE RESOURCES LIMITED

Bralorne's Operating Structure

President
Mr. Fitzpatrick

Vice President   Vice President   Vice President   Vice President
                   Service   Supply

Manufacturing Group

1. Barber Industries Division (100%)
   Calgary & Edmonton, Alberta

2. Mark Products, Inc. (51%)
   Houston, Texas
   Calgary, Alberta

3. OMSCO Industries, Inc. (100%)
   Houston, Texas

4. Triangle Grinding Inc. (100%)
   Houston, Texas

Service & Supply Group

1. Crown Caterers Division (100%)
   Edmonton, Alberta

2. Custom Structures Division (100%)
   Calgary, Alberta

3. Mobile Homes Ltd. (51%)
   Malta

4. Jarco Services Ltd. (100%)
   Calgary, Alberta

5. ENOCO Ltd. (100%)
   Edmonton & Calgary, Alberta

6. Polysystem Ltd. (100%)
   Calgary, Alberta
   Winnipeg, Manitoba

Oil & Gas Division

Calgary, Alberta

Corpus Christi, Texas

Note: Bracketed figures represent percentage ownership.

EXHIBIT 3
BRALORNE RESOURCES LIMITED

Statement of Income and Retained Earnings
for the years ended December 31
($000)

	1975	1976	1977	1978	1979
Revenue					
Manufacturing Group	$ 22 540	33 655	38 766	52 951	95 521
Service Group	9 940	12 153	17 260	29 287	40 051
Oil & Gas Division	667	935	2 462	4 170	5 128
TOTAL	33 147	46 743	58 488	86 408	140 700
Expenses					
Cost of sales	23 723	34 165	41 070	60 645	93 847
General & administrative	3 825	4 762	6 236	7 723	14 740
Interest on long-term debt	589	984	2 428	2 455	4 238
Other interest	119	414	423	801	1 828
Depreciation & amortization	599	822	1 362	2 036	4 060
Depletion	388	388	864	1 365	1 050
Currency exchange loss (gain)	—	—	(288)	(675)	379
TOTAL EXPENSES	$ 29 243	41 535	52 095	74 350	120 142
Net income before tax	3 904	5 208	6 393	12 058	20 558[5]
Taxes — current	560	981	1 070	2 704	5 041
— deferred	1 247	1 451	1 842	2 332	3 593
Net income after tax	2 097	2 776	3 481	7 022	11 924
Less:					
Minority interest	0	0	0	214	1 198
Extraordinary items	994[1]	(89)[2]	(369)[3]	(277)[4]	—
Dividends	0	0	0	667	1 337
Addition to retained earnings	1 103	2 865	3 850	6 418	9 389
Previous retained earnings	5 375	6 478	9 343	13 193	19 611
Ending retained earnings	$ 6 478	9 343	13 193	19 611	29 000

[1] Write down of gold mine.
[2] Gain on sale of shares.
[3] Gain on sale of land.
[4] Accounting adjustment.
[5] Bralorne had taxable income only for its U.S. operations.

EXHIBIT 4

BRALORNE RESOURCES LIMITED

**Balance Sheet
as at December 31**

($000)

	1975	1976	1977	1978	1979
Assets					
Current Assets					
Cash	$ 1 160	1 597	1 299	2 316	1 864
Accounts receivable	7 740	10 740	12 973	19 028	33 204
Inventory	6 596	8 200	8 793	16 830	36 136
Prepaid Expenses	224	363	336	498	1 018
Total current assets	15 720	20 900	23 401	38 672	72 222
Other investments	826	342	386	829	974
Capital Assets					
Property plant and equipment	8 377	9 575	12 486	18 646	33 590
Oil and gas interests	5 059	18 963	21 566	22 771	29 052
Mining interests	1 281	1 110	984	886	946
Total capital assets	14 717	29 648	35 036	42 303	63 588
Intangible Assets					
Goodwill	2 294	3 306	3 194	3 488	10 401
Patents	0	0	1 723	1 616	1 509
Total intangible assets	2 294	3 306	4 917	5 104	11 910
TOTAL ASSETS	$ 33 557	54 196	63 740	86 908	148 694
Liabilities					
Current Liabilities					
Bank loans	$ 2 900	4 300	5 400	11 083	15 929
Accounts payable and accrueds	4 181	7 379	5 599	11 308	21 843
Dividends payable	0	0	0	0	677
Income taxes payable	591	615	313	1 420	1 483
Current portion, long term debt	2 067	7 640	2 107	3 035	6 415
Total current liabilities	9 739	19 934	13 419	26 846	46 347
Long Term Liabilities					
Long term debt	9 498	15 544	25 557	19 532	41 124
Deferred income taxes[1]	1 473	2 924	4 915	7 493	12 224
Other long term liabilities[2]	0	0	0	635	7 116

EXHIBIT 4 (continued)

Equity

Common stock	$ 6 369	6 451	6 656	12 791	12 883
Retained earnings	6 478	9 343	13 193	19 611	29 000
Total equity	12 847	15 794	19 849	32 402	41 883
TOTAL LIABILITIES AND EQUITY	$ 33 557	54 196	63 740	86 908	148 694

[1] Additional amounts arose because of acquisitions.
[2] Prepayment of natural gas sales and minority interest.

EXHIBIT 5
BRALORNE RESOURCES LIMITED

Per Share Data

	1980[1]	1979[2]	1978	1977	1976	1975	1974	1973	1972	1971
Earnings	.38	.54	.38	.25	.19	.14	.06	.15	.04	.01
Dividends	.05	.07	.035[3]							
Market Price[4]										
High	12.75	7.33	3.33	2.21	1.27	.87	.87	1.05	.97	.92
Low	6.00	2.67	1.71	.97	.64	.37	.32	.42	.60	.37
P/E										
High	16.8	13.7	8.7	9.6	6.7	6.0	13.7	7.0	24.3	92.0
Low	7.9	5.0	4.5	4.2	3.4	2.7	5.0	2.8	15.0	37.0
Average	13.4	9.3	6.6	6.9	5.0	4.3	9.3	4.9	19.7	64.5

[1] 6 months only — date of June 30, 1980. On June 30, shares were trading at $12.50 at a P/E ratio of 16.5.

[2] Pre-1979 share data adjusted for 3:1 stock split on April 25, 1980.

[3] Half year only.

[4] 60 month Beta for Bralorne to December 31, 1979 was 1.34. Standard deviation of annual returns was .4282.

EXHIBIT 6
BRALORNE RESOURCES LIMITED

Versatile Corporation
Income Statement
for the years ended December 31
($000)

Sales Revenues:	1978	1979
Bralorne	$ 86 408	140 700
Agricultural	125 911	182 509
Marine	77 861	76 734
Light Manufacturing & Service	12 857	14 601
Total Sales	303 037	414 544
Cost of Sales	231 085	294 047
Gross Profit	71 952	120 497
Selling, Gen., & Admin.	29 524	45 390
Interest — Long-term Debt	5 305	8 486
— Other	4 113	3 687
Depreciation, depletion, & Amortization	6 702	8 069
Total Operating Expenses	45 644	65 632
Net Operating Income	26 308	54 865
Other Income		
Equity in net earnings of other companies	1 113	(344)
Gain (loss) on foreign currency	2 516	(1 464)
Other	1 205	2 373
	4 834	565
Earnings before taxes	31 142	55 430
Income Taxes	13 544	23 880
Earnings before minority interest	17 598	31 550
Minority Interest	7 023	5 496
Net Earnings	10 575	26 054
Preferred Dividends	1 914	2 523
Net Applicable to Common	$ 8 661	23 531

EXHIBIT 6 (continued)

E.P.S. — Basic	$	0.88	$ 2.19
— Fully Diluted		0.79	1.90
Gross Margin		23.7%	29.1%
Net Margin		3.5	6.3
Tax Rate		43.5	43.1

Net Income: ($000)

Bralorne[1]	3 370	6 393
Agricultural[2]	3 690	15 500
Marine & Light Man. & Service	3 155	4 161
Total Net Income	10 575	26 054

E.P.S.:[3]		1978		1979
Bralorne	$	0.35	$	0.59
Agricultural		0.35		1.44
Marine & Light Man. & Service		0.30		0.39
	$	1.00	$	2.42
Less: Preferred Dividends		0.12		0.23
Basic	$	0.88	$	2.19

[1] Versatile-Cornat's 58.6% interest in the net income of Bralorne.

[2] During the first half of 1978 Versatile was consolidating only 38.8% of Versatile Manufacturing's net income.

[3] EPS contributions before giving effect to preferred share dividend requirements.

EXHIBIT 7
BRALORNE RESOURCES LIMITED

**Versatile Corporation
Consolidated Balance Sheet
as at December 31**
($000)

	1978	1979
Assets		
Current		
Cash, short-term deposits & in-vestments at cost	$ 4 081	25 202
Accounts receivable	75 019	96 387
Inventories	52 018	96 256
Prepaid expenses	1 011	2 290
Deferred income taxes	1 231	6 476
	133 360	226 611
Share purchase loans	905	1 820
Investments & advances, final subsidies	17 084	12 246
Other invests. & loans	680	2 472
Fixed Assets		
Oil & gas operations	53 961	79 778
Agriculture manufacturing	16 672	26 315
Marine operations	19 819	20 432
Other	14 317	14 865
Less: Accumulated depreciation	39 022	46 389
Net Fixed Assets	65 747	95 001
Financing costs	688	642
Goodwill	3 488	10 558
Patents	1 651	1 547
	$ 223 603	350 897

EXHIBIT 7 (continued)

Liabilities

Current

Bank Loans	$ 15 328	20 669
Accounts payable	42 295	82 560
Income taxes payable	4 089	20 130
Long-term debt, due 1 year	3 793	7 350
Dividends payable	1 167	1 716
Total current liabilities	66 672	132 425

Long-term debt

Bonds	4 251	5 422
Debentures	37 712	36 880
Bank loans & notes	21 413	48 869
Other	1 362	1 394
Less: Current amount	3 793	7 350
Total Long-term debt	60 945	85 215
Deferred income taxes	8 870	14 871
Minority interests	13 573	23 463

Shareholders' Equity

Capital stock

Preferred Series A	27 258	26 714
Class A and B	13 729	15 103
Retained Earnings	32 556	53 106
	$ 223 603	350 897

EXHIBIT 8
BRALORNE RESOURCES LIMITED

Debt/Equity and Interest Coverage Ratios
Medium-Sized Energy Companies (1979)
($000 000)

Company	Sales	Income	Assets	D/E	EBIT/I
Alberta Energy	97	27.4	651	60/40	14.7X
Aquitane	214	32.6	541	40/60	6.5X
Asamera Oil	171	4.4	118	30/70	3.0X
Bow Valley Industries	276	16.4	480	70/30	1.9X
Bralorne	141	20.6	149	50/50	4.3X
Canadian Occ. Petro.	124	20.8	219	25/75	40.2X
Hayes/Dana	212	8.7	143	30/70	6.1X
Intermetco	195	4.2	78	40/60	8.7X
Magna International	166	8.5	115	55/45	5.0X
Ranger Oil	70	10.9	269	75/25	3.8X
Revelstoke	206	8.1	103	35/65	2.9X

EXHIBIT 9
BRALORNE RESOURCES LIMITED

Debt/Equity and Interest Coverage Ratios
Large Industrial Companies (1979)
($000 000)

Company	Sales	Income	Assets	D/E	EBIT/I
Versatile	610	34	509	45/55	5.5X
Jannock (Manufacturing)	521	22	338	20/80	5.9X
Hawker Siddeley (Transportation)	547	25	467	25/75	7.0X
Crown Zellerbach (Forestry)	661	36	533	15/85	22.1X
Canron Inc. (Construction)	490	15	298	20/80	5.2X
Ivaco Inc. (Steel)	622	28	573	50/50	5.2X

APPENDIX A
The Canadian Oil and Gas Industry

Taxation

In 1905, Alberta and Saskatchewan were established as provinces. These two provinces were not granted control of their natural resources, guaranteed to all provinces by the British North American Act, until 1930. Owners of mineral rights are entitled to charge royalties, that is, a percentage of the value of all minerals produced on that land. After 1905, Alberta did not include mineral rights in the sale of Crown lands. As a result, the Crown holds about 95 percent of the mineral rights in Alberta at the present time and therefore may charge royalties. The current maximum royalties on new gas and oil is 35 percent; on old gas it is 50 percent; on old oil it is 65 percent. (Old gas and oil are defined as oil and gas produced from reserves discovered and exploited before January 1, 1974.)

The Federal government taxes the profits of the oil and gas companies. Ten percent of the corporate taxable income is returned to the Alberta provincial government. As well, an export tax on natural gas provides the Federal government with twice as much as the Alberta government receives. This export tax subsidizes imported oil for the Maritimes and Quebec.

Exploration

In 1980, the National Energy Board estimated that 150 companies would spend around $50 billion on development and exploratory drilling between 1980 and 1985. Exhibits A-1 to A-3 presents past data on exploration and development. Significant new discoveries of natural gas had been made in the foothills of the Rocky Mountains in both Alberta and British Columbia. In Saskatchewan, Lloydminster showed potential as a heavy oil belt. The rising price of oil had increased the profit potential of existing operations and of proven reserves. As well, the drilling costs of exploratory and development wells had increased, thus encouraging continuing exploitation of working operations.

Production

Crude oil and natural gas production had generally increased. In 1979, large gains in production of crude oil were made, to 86.9 million cubic metres from 76.3 million cubic metres in 1978 (see Exhibit A-4). The production increases in crude oil for 1980 are not expected to be as dramatic. An anticipated increase in demand for Canadian crude oil was expected to generate continuing increased production. It was expected that an increase of three to five dollars per barrel would be implemented, regardless of the results of the federal election (February 1980), in order to bring Canadian domestic crude oil prices closer to world prices.

A rapid increase in natural gas wellhead prices was expected over the next three years, 1980-83. It is hoped that the implementation of the Natural Gas Policy Act (N.G.P.A.) in the United States would increase the demand for Canadian natural gas. The N.G.P.A. encourages the use of natural gas as a fuel. Demand growth will decrease in existing domestic markets. The National Energy Board estimated that between 1979 and 1984 the average domestic growth in demand will be 3.5 percent, and for the rest of the 1980s, 2.9 percent. The price of natural gas is expected to follow that of crude oil, at 65 percent of the price of the BTU equivalent of crude oil arriving in Toronto.

EXHIBIT A-1
BRALORNE RESOURCES LIMITED

Where Drilling Money Was Spent
($000 000)

	1979		1978		1977	
Alberta	$1 275.0	58.1%	1 121.9	62.1%	745.9	61.0%
Saskatchewan	110.0	5.0%	68.2	3.8%	39.2	3.2%
British Columbia	213.2	9.7%	179.2	9.9%	108.7	8.9%
Manitoba	2.7	0.1%	1.9	0.1%	1.3	0.1%
North Canada	447.6	20.4%	339.7	18.8%	285.0	23.3%
Ontario	30.1	1.4%	19.2	1.1%	14.1	1.2%
Quebec	1.2	0.1%	6.2	0.3%	4.9	0.4%
Atlantic Provinces	2.1	0.1%	—	—	—	—
Offshore	111.4	5.1%	69.6	3.9%	23.8	1.9%
TOTAL	$2 193.3	100.0%	1 805.9	100.0%	1 222.9	100.0%

Source: Statistics Canada & CPA

EXHIBIT A-2
BRALORNE RESOURCES LIMITED

Where Wells Were Drilled

	1979		1978		1977		1969	
Alberta	5 600	74.1%	5 519	78.1%	5 063	82.9%	1 847	54.7%
Saskatchewan	1 300	17.2%	972	13.8%	530	8.7%	1 047	31.0%
British Columbia	400	5.3%	386	5.5%	305	5.0%	166	4.9%
Manitoba	20	0.3%	16	0.2%	11	0.2%	44	1.3%
North Canada	20	0.3%	17	0.2%	26	0.4%	56	1.7%
Ontario	200	2.6%	143	2.0%	165	2.7%	208	6.1%
Quebec	10	0.1%	6	0.1%	6	0.1%	3	0.1%
Atlantic Provs.	2	—	—	—	—	—	—	—
Offshore	10	0.1%	7	0.1%	2	—	7	0.2%
TOTAL	7 562	100.0%	7 066	100.0%	6 108	100.0%	3 378	100.0%

Source: CPA

EXHIBIT A-3
BRALORNE RESOURCES LIMITED

Drilling Costs in Western Canada and Offshore
1977 and 1978[1]

	Alberta		Other Western Provinces		Yukon	NWT & Arctic	Offshore	
	1978	1977	1978	1977	1978	1977	1978	1977
Expenditures ($000)								
Development drilling	477 400	351 200	115 500	71 300	22 900	7 100	—	—
Exploratory drilling	644 500	394 700	133 800	77 900	316 800	277 900	69 600	23 800
Total drilling	1 121 900	745 900	249 300	149 200	339 700	285 000	69 600	23 800
Drilling metrage								
Development metrage	3 215 794	2 889 527	663 479	497 725	19 671	23 454	—	—
Exploratory metrage	2 791 943	2 309 406	705 398	436 674	32 124	55 788	26 242	7 742
Total metrage drilled	6 007 737	5 198 933	1 368 877	934 399	51 795	79 242	26 242	7 742
Number of wells drilled								
Development wells	3 672	3 465	712	444	7	8	—	—
Exploratory wells	1 847	1 598	662	402	10	18	7	2
Total wells drilled	5 519	5 063	1 374	846	17	26	7	2
Drilling costs per metre and per well								
$ per development metre	148.45	121.54	174.08	143.25	1 164.15	302.72	—	—
$ per exploratory metre	230.84	170.91	189.68	178.39	9 861.79	4 981.36	2 652.24	3 074.14
$ per total metre	186.74	143.47	182.12	159.67	6 558.55	3 596.58	2 652.24	3 074.14
$ per development well	130 011	101 356	162 219	160 586	3 271 429	877 500	—	—
$ per exploratory well	348 944	246 996	202 115	193 781	31 680 000	15 438 889	9 942 857	11 900 000
$ per total well	203 280	147 324	181 441	176 359	16 647 706	10 961 538	9 942 857	11 900 000

[1] Includes suspended wells.

Source: Statistics Canada & CPA

Natural Gas and Crude Oil Production 1974-1979

	Natural Gas			Crude Oil		
	Value $ Million	000 m³	Average Price per m³	Value $ Million	m³	Average Price per m³
1974	723.8	86 239 137	8.39	3521.6	97 741 687	36.03
1975	1520.7	87 485 758	17.38	3763.9	83 001 380	45.35
1976	2649.2	87 649 797	30.22	4053.9	76 438 194	53.04
1977	3422.1	91 517 960	37.39	4871.5	76 578 729	63.61
1978	3923.5	88 610 000	44.28	5811.0	76 348 000	76.11
1979	4855.8	94 426 000	51.42	7451.9	86 910 000	85.74

MARKBOROUGH PROPERTIES INC.

In early November, 1985, Don Prowse, Executive Vice President of Markborough Properties Inc. (Markborough), was preparing for an upcoming Board of Directors meeting. On the agenda was the proposed use of interest rate hedging to minimize the company's interest rate exposure. John Brough, the Vice President of Finance and Treasurer, had identified several alternatives. Among the alternatives were interest rate swaps and caps, hedging techniques that Markborough had *not* used in the past. Recognizing that several Board members were unfamiliar with such financing vehicles, Don Prowse knew that his presentation needed to be clear and concise. With this in mind, he summoned John Brough and Simon Chan, the Assistant Treasurer, into his office to review the alternatives.

Background

Markborough Properties Inc. of Toronto was one of the largest and most diversified land and property development companies in North America. Incorporated in 1965, Markborough was created for the purpose of developing residential real estate in Mississauga, Ontario. The company quickly established a reputation for excellence, and by the early 1970's cabinet ministers, boards of trade and developers from as far away as China, Australia and England were arriving to learn about the community concept of residential development exhibited by Markborough's Meadowvale development in Mississauga.

Expansion in the 1970's was rapid. Land development operations commenced in the sun-belt states of the U.S., and Markborough began developing commercial and industrial income properties in Canada. In 1973, the Hudson's Bay Company acquired controlling interest in the company and five years later, in 1978, Markborough became a wholly-owned subsidiary. By the end of the 1970's Markborough had earned a reputation for excellence in the development and management of shopping centres and commercial properties in Canada.

On February 1, 1984, Markborough was amalgamated with Hudsons' Bay Company Developments Limited (HBCDL) which owned and managed the real estate assets of the Hudson's Bay Company. The amalgamation more than quadrupled the income property assets of Markborough. A large component of the assets consisted of shopping centres in Canada in which The Bay or Simpson's were anchor tenants. By the end of fiscal 1984, Markborough had assets in excess of $1.6 billion with approximately 35% of the company's portfolio located in the U.S. Exhibit 1 provides a summary of Markborough's assets by country at the end of fiscal 1984.

Markborough participated in two areas of the real estate development industry: the development of land for future residential, commercial or industrial uses and the development, ownership and management of income-producing properties. The property portfolio of land for sale and future development is presented in Exhibit 2.

One of Markborough's major strengths was the income stream from its shopping centre properties. Markborough owned 18 shopping centres outright and had equity interests (in proportions varying between 25% and 50%) in a further 25 centres, all located in Canada. The company had an interest in almost 1.4 million square metres of shopping centre space.

Markborough had office and mixed-use income property holdings of more than 170 thousand square metres. While most of the 13 properties were located in the Metropolitan Toronto area, including the Simpsons' Tower, others were located in western Canada and the southwestern United States. Office buildings under construction in Toronto, Washington, D.C., Las Vegas, Nevada and London, England would add almost 47 thousand square metres to the portfolio.

The income property portfolio also consisted of more than 100 thousand square metres of industrial space, a hotel and a 50% interest in two apartment buildings.

Markborough was continually expanding the income property portfolio. Additionally, the quality and productivity of the shopping centres was constantly being upgraded through a series of expansion, renovation and remerchandising programs.

As a land developer, Markborough serviced raw land by putting in roads, trunks and sewer systems. The land was then sold in lots to house builders who in turn sold houses to the public. (Markborough was involved in some house building, but this activity was limited to operations in Arizona.) By servicing large tracts of land, often in excess of 1,000 acres, Markborough was able to plan entire communities. Careful attention was paid to planning for facilities such as shopping centres, recreation centres, schools and churches, and amenities such as man-made lakes, hiking trails, country clubs and golf courses. Most of Markborough's planned communities in the U.S. were developed around championship golf courses.

Typically, the development of a large land project would take 10 to 15 years, or more, from the planning stages through to completion. Changes in the economic health of a region could dramatically accelerate or stall the development and sale of the land. The effects of the economy were considerable given that the land projects often cost $100 million or more. In the years immediately preceding 1985, Markborough's emphasis had been concentrated on residential community development in the sun-belt states of Florida, Arizona, Texas and California, where solid corporate reputations and excellent management teams were established. Spurred by a buoyant economy, sales in these developments had been strong.

In order to continue to service the market, Markborough had to replenish its land inventory. The company made major land purchases in Tampa, Florida and in Dallas and Houston, Texas. These purchases were to help ensure a continued substantial profit contribution from land development in future years. Markborough was also developing serviced lots in Whitby, Aurora and Mississauga, Ontario and in Calgary, Alberta.

Another area of land development was the custom design and build market for commercial and industrial properties. Over a period of nine years Markborough had developed an expertise for assembling land, and then building properties designed especially for a customer's needs. Many customers would foresake the possibility of capital appreciation on the buildings in order to effect immediate cash and tax savings through sale and leaseback arrangements with Markborough. Land holdings in Mississauga, Brampton and Vaughan, Ontario were marked for this purpose.

Markborough had earned a respected reputation for its stable and conservative financing policies. Since incorporation in 1965, the company had achieved continued steady growth. Though the recession of the early 1980's crippled several of Canada's land development companies, Markborough escaped relatively unscathed. A balance of land development activity coupled with a strong income property portfolio led Markborough to evolve as one of the major real estate developers in North America. Exhibit 3 presents a ten-year summary of financial highlights of the company.

The Industry

The real estate development industry in Canada was dominated by several large companies such as Olympia & York, Cadillac Fairview, Trizec, Bramalea, Campeau, Markborough and Marathon. While most of the large real estate developers were public companies; some, such as Olympia & York, were privately held. Exhibit 4 presents the key financial statistics for some of the companies.

The scope of activities for developers varied widely. Some developers, such as Trizec, were referred to as senior income property developers because they invested only in prime income property real estate. Other developers invested primarily in land development, for example, Nu-West and Costain. Costain's niche was in house building. By comparison, Markborough's strategy was to balance a strong income property portfolio with its land development operations.

During the early 1980's, when interest rates reached record levels, several real estate developers went bankrupt. The land developers that were heavily leveraged were hurt the most. Though the income property developers also suffered under heavy debt loads, they survived because of a steady cash flow from tenants. In contrast, the market for land sales dried up and the land developers had no income to finance the service payments. Land developers in western Canada suffered the most because the economy was also burdened with the woes of the oil industry. Daon (now BCE Development Corporation), Nu-West and Carma were all victims of the recession. Several developers had recognized that one way to hedge against a cyclical economy was to diversify. Some developers diversified within the real estate industry by acquiring income properties with steady cash flows, while others, such as Carma, diversified into oil and gas. Such diversification magnified the cash flow problems.

Markborough survived the recession relatively unscathed. Although revenue and net profit dropped in 1982, the company's low debt to equity ratio and geographic diversification prevented a serious threat to the company. Markborough's amalgamation with HBCDL early in 1984 further strengthened the stability of the company. Markborough had pursued a strategy of maintaining an appropriate balance of land and income property operations. Continued growth in both areas was a stated long-term objective of the company. By balancing these operations, Markborough was able to use its steady cash flow from income property revenues to help finance expanding land development operations.

Markborough's Debt Structure

The level of development activity in 1985 led to a substantial increase in the total debt of the company. The total debt outstanding at the end of fiscal 1985 was anticipated to be $984 million. During the year, Markborough obtained permanent financing for five shopping centres. These financings resulted in a reduction of the floating rate debt, and a corresponding increase in the fixed rate debt, of $115 million. For January 31, 1986 which was the end of fiscal 1985, the debt structure was anticipated to be as follows:

Markborough Debt Structure (Est.)
January 31, 1986
(Cdn$ – Millions)

	Amount	% of Total
Fixed Rate Debt	$395	40
Floating Rate Debt	589	60
Total	$984	100

In original currency, the floating rate debt was made up as follows:

Markborough Floating Rate Debt by Currency (Est.)
January 31, 1986
(Millions)

		Amount	Cdn.$ Equivalent	% of Total
Canadian	Cdn.$	18	18	3.1
U.S.	U.S.$	398	538	91.3
U.K.	U.K.£	19	33	5.6
		435	589	100.0

Note: Conversion rates are U.S.$ = 1.35 and U.K.£ = 1.75.

By the end of fiscal 1985, more than 90% of Markborough's floating rate debt would be concentrated in the U.S. This was a direct consequence of the company's expansion in the U.S., and the fact that the U.S. land development projects were necessarily financed with floating rate debt. Land projects could not be financed with fixed rate debt because lenders were wary of the lengthy development period, the cyclical nature of the industry and the lack of guaranteed cash flows. Likewise, income property developments were usually financed with floating rate debt until the project was on-stream and generating sufficient cash flows.

Despite the fact that Markborough continued to create floating rate debt to finance the acquisition and development of new land projects in the U.S., the total floating rate debt in the U.S. was expected to gradually decrease to US$341 million in fiscal 1990 from its projected level at January 31, 1986 of US$398 million. The decline of the floating rate debt was anticipated because various land projects would be maturing over the next five years, and the outstanding principal was to be paid down.

Markborough Floating Rate Debt (Est.)
January 31, 1986 – 1991
(Mixed Currencies – Millions)

	Cdn.	U.S.	U.K.
1985	18	398	19
1986	—	284	42
1987	—	294	18
1988	—	285	18
1989	—	326	18
1990	—	341	18

During the next five to ten years, Markborough was projected to have at least US$250 million of floating rate debt in the form of operating and project loans.

The Problem

The annual rates for Markborough on its floating rate obligations were approximately U.S. Prime plus 50 basis points or LIBOR[1] plus 100 basis points on the US$398 million floating rate debt that the company would have at the end of the 1985 fiscal year. Of this amount, approximately US$250 million would be in LIBOR contracts and US$148 million would be floating with the U.S. Prime Rate. In November 1985, the U.S Prime Rate was $9\frac{1}{2}$ percent and the six-month LIBOR rate was at $8\frac{1}{4}$ percent. Exhibit 5 presents a list of the Eurocurrency deposit rates, which reflected the indicative LIBOR rates.

Though the floating rate debt was reduced from 71.5% to 60% of the total debt with the permanent financing of five shopping centres, Don Prowse and John Brough thought that the company's exposure to interest rate fluctuations was still too high. Although interest rates did not seem likely to fluctuate substantially in the short term, the demise of many real estate developers in the early 1980's served as a constant reminder of the devastating effect of exposure to interest rate fluctuations. As a result of the potential downside risk, Don Prowse and John Brough thought that Markborough should lower the proportion of floating rate debt to between 20% and 40% of the total debt of the company. Over the previous few years Markborough's policy of "going short" on LIBOR contracts had allowed the company to benefit from the declining interest rates. However, a change in strategy seemed in order.

Alternatives

(i) Interest Rate Swap

The possibility of an interest rate swap had been discussed with several banks and investment dealers. In its simplest form, an interest rate swap was the exchange between two counterparties of interest payment obligations — one with a fixed interest rate and the other with an interest rate which floated in accordance with a benchmark such as the Prime rate, LIBOR rate or Bankers' Acceptance rate.

Investment dealers such as Wood Gundy and Burns Fry, and banks such

---

[1] LIBOR is the acronym for London Interbank Offered Rate and represents a series of borrowing rates available in London, England, by major banks from around the world. LIBOR rates may be quoted in various currencies and for different time periods. LIBOR is a base rate for comparison in most financial markets.

as the C.I.B.C., Citibank and Morgan Guaranty were very active in the swap market and were able to locate counterparties rather easily. In order to eliminate the credit risk, and ensure that the parties carried out their payment obligations over the period of the agreement, a bank was usually appointed as guarantor in the swap transaction. Each party made payments to the guaranteeing bank. A guarantee fee of approximately 1/8 percent of the notional principal amount was payable annually to the bank. The swap was for interest obligations only and there was no exchange of principal repayment obligations. Thus, no identification to any particular liability was needed and original credit facilities were not affected. An interest rate swap was not a vehicle to raise new funds. It simply fixed the interest rate on existing debt. Floating rate debt was effectively converted to fixed rate debt without issuing fixed rate debt directly.

Rates for various types of swaps were quoted by dollars. Swap rates formed part of the total network of rates available in the market. In November 1985, fixed swap rates at LIBOR for U.S. dollar obligations were quoted on:

Term	US$ Swaps at Libor
3 Years	10.04%
5 Years	10.50
7 Years	10.62
10 Years	10.84

Any premium a borrower paid over LIBOR was added to the swap rates.

Additionally, a one-time arrangement fee equal to 1/8% of the notional principal amount was required up-front. Amortized over the period of a seven year swap, the arrangement fee amounted to 2.7 basis points per annum[2].

(ii) Interest Rate Cap

A second alternative under consideration was an interest rate cap. A cap was another technique for hedging long-term interest rate risk which established the maximum rate the firm would pay on floating rate debt. Caps were available from commercial and investment bankers. A seven-year cap agreement with a LIBOR rate of 13 percent was available to Markborough in return for an up-front fee of $2\frac{1}{2}$ percent of the notional principal amount. Amortized over seven years, the fee amounted to 50 basis points per annum. As with interest rate swaps, Markborough had not previously used this hedging technique.

---

[2] The formula for calculating the amortization of arrangement fee where n is term in years and where Interest Rate includes the appropriate LIBOR or U.S. prime rates plus the firm's premium plus other fees, is:

$$\text{Annual Arrangement Fee} = \text{Arrangement Fee in \%} \times \frac{\text{Interest Rate}}{1 - (\text{Interest Rate} + 1)^{-n}}$$

(iii) Long-Term LIBOR Contracts

A third alternative available to Markborough was to fix LIBOR contracts for longer periods. Markborough could fix the U.S. floating rate loans in the LIBOR market for periods from 30 days to 5 years. This had to be done on a loan-by-loan basis, subject to the terms of the loans and the availability of long-term LIBOR contracts. Since the excessive interest rates of the early 1980's, Markborough had followed a policy of "going short" (usually 30 to 60 days) on LIBOR contracts. By following this policy, Markborough had been successful in taking advantage of the declining interest rates by lowering its effective interest rate along with the movements in the LIBOR market. Now faced with the possibility that interest rates may have "bottomed out", John Brough thought that a strategy of locking in LIBOR contracts for a longer term may be appropriate. Although long-term contracts were usually difficult to attain, John Brough was confident that Markborough could fix US$150 million in the LIBOR market for at least two years. The current indicative LIBOR rates for U.S. funds for two, three, four and five years were $9\frac{3}{8}$ percent, $9\frac{7}{8}$ percent, $10\frac{1}{8}$ percent and $10\frac{3}{8}$ percent, respectively.

The Decision

As Don Prowse sat back in his chair and gazed over the Toronto skyline on a crisp November morning, he couldn't help but think that interest rate hedging could provide some peace of mind during a period when the future direction of U.S. interest rates was confounding the experts. While some economists believed that there was still room for interest rates to move lower, others predicted that rates had already "bottomed out". If the latter proved true, it would be in Markborough's best interest to fix a portion of the floating rate debt for a longer period of time. This would reduce the company's interest rate risk.

A decision had to be made quickly on a proposal for interest rate hedging for the upcoming Board meeting. Was it an appropriate time for Markborough to hedge its floating rate debt? If so, how much and using what vehicle? In addition, Don Prowse realized that his presentation to the Board needed to be clear and concise because several of the Board members had not had any previous exposure to these interest rate hedging techniques.

EXHIBIT 1

MARKBOROUGH PROPERTIES INC.

Assets by Geographical Location
January 31, 1985
(Cdn $000s)

Assets	*Canada*	*U.S.*	*Total*
Land Operations	$ 195 580	$330 436	$ 526 016
Income Property Operations	649 017	60 537	709 554
Other	197 865	177 873	375 738
Total	$1 042 462	$568 846	$1 611 308

135

Case 12
Markborough
Properties Inc.

EXHIBIT 2
MARKBOROUGH PROPERTIES INC.

Land for Sale and Future Development, October 31, 1985

Location	Year(s) of Acquisition	Original Acreage	Total Remaining Acreage	%	Markborough's Interest Total Remaining Acreage
Canada					
Ontario					
Meadowvale	1972/85	2 905	944	100%	944
Mississauga	1977	284	258	100%	258
Other (including sites)	Various	899	644	100%	644
Alberta					
Woodbine	1976	634	209	100%	209
Other	1984	156	156	100%	156
Other (including sites)	Various	549	416	100%	416
		5 427	2 627		2 627
United States					
Arizona					
Scottsdale Ranch	1978	1 119	112	50%	56
Gainey Ranch	1980	562	394	100%	394
Other	1979	135	28	100%	28
California					
Sunnymead Ranch	1980	1 366	689	100%	689
Other (including sites)	Various	330	221	100%	221
Florida					
Boca Pointe	1979	1 019	225	100%	225
Hunter's Green	1985	1 980	1 980	100%	1 980
Homestead	1974	3 276	3 026	50%	1 513
Texas					
Northview Park	1985	128	128	80%	102
Harvest Bend	1977	599	191	80%	153
Northchase	1980	487	265	82%	217
First Colony	1980	760	272	80%	218
New Territories	1984	3 082	2 982	80%	2 386
Vicksburg	1982	411	139	80%	111
Other	Various	2 832	144	80%	115
Other	Various	658	219	100%	219
		18 744	11 015		8 627
		24 171	13 642		11 254

EXHIBIT 3

MARKBOROUGH PROPERTIES INC.

Ten Year Sumary – Financial Highlights
(Cdn $000s)

	1984	1983	1982	1981	1980	1979	1978	*1977	1976	1975
Operating Results for the Year										
Revenue from Land Operations	$253 936	$120 790	$74 698	$97 964	$39 003	$57 409	$29 648	$23 825	$40 933	$16 925
Revenue from Housing Operations	16 111	21 610	17 665	13 848	15 180	14 819	5 607	—	—	—
Revenue from Income Properties	121 117	22 402	22 697	22 653	16 271	13 789	12 260	13 281	8 720	7 741
Net Income Before Taxes	71 716	20 435	6 121	13 554	12 415	10 245	8 994	8 270	18 109	8 906
Net Income After Taxes	38 500	11 663	4 118	9 979	6 629	5 025	4 524	4 681	9 489	4 283
Per Common Share (weighted average)										
Net Income After Taxes	3.48	2.56	0.90	2.24	1.49	1.13	1.06	1.17	2.37	1.07
Cash Flow	6.49	4.96	1.87	3.58	3.14	2.58	2.15	1.39	3.54	1.70
Financial Position at the Year End										
Undeveloped Land	$272 077	$258 278	$265 438	$227 893	$231 321	$141 574	$112 226	$97 994	$83 719	$63 215
Income Properties	709 554	131 319	156 378	143 000	134 190	97 200	78 007	64 711	57 062	51 292
Total Assets	1 611 308	626 672	624 774	573 435	500 497	345 394	276 046	224 767	186 381	142 105
Bank Debt and Other Short Term Advances	264 788	117 012	143 942	105 058	98 605	72 851	46 323	23 094	9 972	9 609
Long Term Debt	622 871	297 112	298 059	288 913	256 479	147 995	119 587	100 573	90 261	70 808
Share Capital	233 223	26 125	26 125	26 125	25 112	25 112	25 112	20 956	20 956	20 956
Retained Earnings	188 886	69 135	57 472	53 354	43 375	36 746	33 054	29 196	26 076	17 467
Statistical at the Year End										
Common Shares Outstanding	11 054 624	4 555	4 555	4 555	4 440	4 440	4 440	4 002	4 002	4 002
Ratio of Income Properties to Undeveloped Land	2.6:1	0.5:1	0.6:1	0.6:1	0.6:1	0.7:1	0.7:1	0.7:1	0.7:1	0.8:1
Ratio of Debt to Equity	2.1:1	4.3:1	5.3:1	5.0:1	5.2:1	3.6:1	2.9:1	2.5:1	2.1:1	2.1:1

* As a result of a change in year end, operating results for 1977 are for fifteen months.
Note: Fiscal year-end is January 31 of the following year

EXHIBIT 4
MARKBOROUGH PROPERTIES INC.

Public Canadian Real Estate Developers
Financial Highlights – Fiscal 1984
(Cdn $000s)

Company	Total Assets	Shareholders' Equity	Total Long Term Debt	Net Income	Cash Flow
Bramalea	2 204 000	200 900	1 653 700	15 100	64 400
Cadillac Fairview	3 009 159	225 437	1 653 615	76 812	129 472
Cambridge Shopping Centres	648 194	175 006	383 769	5 553	15 813
Campeau	1 164 230	182 506	988 694	27 170	61 651
Costain	418 728	77 689	227 743	6 526	8 909
Daon	1 292 806	159 325	N/A	50 063	35 624
Marathon	1 276 366	175 446	812 569	27 323	51 508
Markborough	1 611 308	422 109	622 871	38 500	71 721
Nu-West	559 768	40 114	N/A	(83 710)	2 647
Trizec	3 453 200	578 400	2 522 000	55 400	124 100

EXHIBIT 5
MARKBOROUGH PROPERTIES INC.

Eurocurrency Deposit Rates
1975 – 1985

	1975 Dec.	1976 Dec.	1977 Dec.	1978 Dec.	1979 Dec.	1980 Dec.	1981 Dec.	1982 Dec.	1983 Dec.	1984 Dec.	1985 Nov.
Euro – US$											
1 Month	$5\frac{3}{8}$	$5\frac{1}{8}$	$6\frac{7}{8}$	11	$14\frac{5}{8}$	$19\frac{1}{8}$	$13\frac{1}{8}$	$9\frac{3}{16}$	$9\frac{11}{16}$	$8\frac{5}{16}$	$8\frac{1}{8}$
3 Months	$5\frac{13}{16}$	5	$7\frac{3}{16}$	$11\frac{11}{16}$	$14\frac{15}{16}$	$17\frac{5}{8}$	$13\frac{3}{4}$	$9\frac{3}{16}$	$9\frac{13}{16}$	$8\frac{9}{16}$	$8\frac{1}{16}$
6 Months	$6\frac{5}{8}$	$5\frac{3}{8}$	$7\frac{1}{2}$	$12\frac{5}{16}$	15	$16\frac{1}{2}$	$14\frac{3}{4}$	$9\frac{3}{8}$	10	$9\frac{1}{8}$	$8\frac{1}{4}$
12 Months	$7\frac{3}{16}$	$5\frac{9}{16}$	$7\frac{11}{16}$	12	$13\frac{1}{4}$	$14\frac{3}{4}$	$14\frac{3}{4}$	$9\frac{5}{8}$	$10\frac{5}{16}$	$9\frac{13}{16}$	$8\frac{3}{16}$
Euro – Can$											
1 Month	8	$7\frac{7}{8}$	$6\frac{1}{2}$	$10\frac{3}{16}$	$13\frac{11}{16}$	$17\frac{1}{2}$	$15\frac{1}{4}$	$9\frac{7}{8}$	$9\frac{1}{4}$	$9\frac{7}{8}$	$9\frac{1}{8}$
3 Months	8	$8\frac{3}{4}$	$6\frac{3}{4}$	$10\frac{3}{4}$	$13\frac{7}{16}$	$15\frac{5}{8}$	$15\frac{5}{8}$	10	$9\frac{9}{16}$	$9\frac{7}{8}$	9
6 Months	$8\frac{1}{8}$	8	$7\frac{1}{8}$	$10\frac{13}{16}$	$12\frac{15}{16}$	$15\frac{5}{8}$	$15\frac{7}{8}$	$9\frac{5}{8}$	$9\frac{11}{16}$	$10\frac{1}{8}$	9
12 Months	$8\frac{3}{8}$	8	$7\frac{1}{4}$	$10\frac{5}{8}$	$12\frac{9}{16}$	$14\frac{5}{8}$	$15\frac{1}{2}$	$10\frac{1}{8}$	10	$10\frac{3}{8}$	$9\frac{1}{8}$
Euro – Sterling											
1 Month	$11\frac{1}{8}$	$16\frac{3}{8}$	$6\frac{1}{2}$	12	$16\frac{13}{16}$	$14\frac{5}{8}$	$14\frac{7}{8}$	$10\frac{1}{2}$	$9\frac{1}{8}$	$9\frac{9}{16}$	$11\frac{5}{8}$
3 Months	11	$16\frac{1}{8}$	$6\frac{5}{8}$	$12\frac{5}{8}$	$16\frac{15}{16}$	$14\frac{5}{8}$	$15\frac{1}{8}$	$10\frac{3}{8}$	$9\frac{5}{16}$	$9\frac{15}{16}$	$11\frac{1}{2}$
6 Months	$11\frac{1}{4}$	$14\frac{3}{4}$	$7\frac{1}{8}$	$13\frac{1}{4}$	$16\frac{7}{8}$	$14\frac{1}{4}$	$15\frac{3}{8}$	$10\frac{1}{4}$	$9\frac{1}{2}$	$10\frac{1}{16}$	$11\frac{5}{16}$
12 Months	$11\frac{7}{8}$	$14\frac{1}{2}$	$7\frac{3}{8}$	13	$15\frac{5}{16}$	$13\frac{3}{4}$	$14\frac{7}{8}$	$10\frac{1}{4}$	$9\frac{7}{8}$	$10\frac{3}{16}$	$11\frac{1}{8}$
Euro – Yen											
1 Month	$6\frac{15}{16}$	7	$\frac{5}{8}$	$-\frac{11}{16}$	$8\frac{5}{8}$	$8\frac{3}{4}$	$6\frac{1}{4}$	$6\frac{11}{16}$	$6\frac{1}{4}$	$6\frac{1}{8}$	$8\frac{1}{16}$
3 Months	$6\frac{1}{8}$	$6\frac{5}{8}$	$1\frac{13}{16}$	$\frac{5}{8}$	$8\frac{7}{8}$	$9\frac{1}{8}$	$6\frac{3}{4}$	$6\frac{3}{4}$	$6\frac{5}{16}$	$6\frac{1}{8}$	$7\frac{5}{8}$
6 Months	$6\frac{3}{16}$	$6\frac{7}{16}$	$2\frac{3}{4}$	$1\frac{7}{8}$	$9\frac{1}{8}$	$9\frac{1}{8}$	$6\frac{15}{16}$	$6\frac{11}{16}$	$6\frac{3}{8}$	$6\frac{1}{8}$	$7\frac{1}{8}$
12 Months	$6\frac{1}{8}$	$6\frac{1}{4}$	$3\frac{1}{4}$	$2\frac{3}{16}$	$7\frac{11}{16}$	$9\frac{1}{4}$	7	$6\frac{3}{4}$	$6\frac{7}{16}$	$6\frac{1}{8}$	$7\frac{1}{8}$
Euro – D.M.											
1 Month	$3\frac{13}{16}$	$4\frac{5}{8}$	$2\frac{3}{16}$	$3\frac{3}{16}$	$9\frac{5}{16}$	$8\frac{7}{8}$	$10\frac{3}{8}$	$5\frac{3}{4}$	$5\frac{3}{4}$	$5\frac{7}{16}$	$4\frac{5}{8}$
3 Months	$3\frac{13}{16}$	$4\frac{11}{16}$	$2\frac{1}{2}$	$3\frac{5}{16}$	$9\frac{1}{8}$	$8\frac{7}{8}$	$10\frac{3}{8}$	$5\frac{3}{4}$	$5\frac{7}{8}$	$5\frac{9}{16}$	$4\frac{5}{8}$
6 Months	4	$4\frac{3}{4}$	$2\frac{13}{16}$	$3\frac{11}{16}$	$8\frac{3}{4}$	$8\frac{7}{8}$	$10\frac{3}{8}$	$5\frac{13}{16}$	$6\frac{1}{8}$	$5\frac{1}{2}$	$4\frac{11}{16}$
12 Months	$5\frac{1}{16}$	$4\frac{13}{16}$	$3\frac{1}{16}$	$3\frac{13}{16}$	$8\frac{1}{4}$	$8\frac{7}{8}$	$10\frac{1}{8}$	$5\frac{1}{8}$	$6\frac{3}{8}$	$5\frac{9}{16}$	$4\frac{7}{8}$
Euro – S.F.											
1 Month	$2\frac{1}{2}$	$\frac{15}{16}$	$1\frac{5}{16}$	$-\frac{1}{16}$	$5\frac{3}{16}$	$4\frac{3}{4}$	$8\frac{3}{4}$	$2\frac{3}{4}$	$3\frac{3}{8}$	$4\frac{1}{2}$	4
3 Months	$2\frac{3}{4}$	$1\frac{7}{16}$	$1\frac{3}{8}$	0	$5\frac{15}{16}$	$5\frac{1}{8}$	9	$3\frac{3}{16}$	$3\frac{3}{4}$	$4\frac{3}{4}$	4
6 Months	$3\frac{1}{4}$	$2\frac{1}{8}$	$1\frac{7}{8}$	$\frac{1}{8}$	6	$5\frac{3}{8}$	$9\frac{1}{8}$	$3\frac{1}{2}$	$3\frac{15}{16}$	$4\frac{15}{16}$	$4\frac{1}{16}$
12 Months	$4\frac{1}{16}$	$2\frac{1}{2}$	$2\frac{1}{4}$	$\frac{5}{8}$	$5\frac{9}{16}$	$5\frac{1}{8}$	$8\frac{3}{8}$	$3\frac{7}{16}$	4	$4\frac{3}{4}$	$4\frac{1}{8}$

EXHIBIT 6
MARKBOROUGH PROPERTIES INC.

Outstanding LIBOR Contracts
as of November 1, 1985

Election Date	Loan	Lender	Value Date	Maturity Date	Term	LIBOR	Spread	All-in	LIBOR Contract	Interest	Daily Interest
20-Nov-85	Alcorn (Texas)	B.O.M.	21-Oct-85	22-Nov-85	32	8.4405%	1.25%	9.6905%	$3 200 000.00	$27 564.09	$861.38
05-Nov-85	Boca Pointe (Florida)	B.O.M.	10-Oct-85	07-Nov-85	28	8.3760%	1.00%	9.3760%	5 110 000.00	37 264.39	1 330.87
19-Nov-85	Boca Pointe (Florida)	B.O.M.	24-Oct-85	21-Nov-85	28	8.4405%	1.00%	9.4405%	2 655 000.00	19 494.63	696.24
26-Nov-85	Boca Pointe (Florida)	B.O.M.	28-Oct-85	29-Nov-85	32	8.5050%	1.00%	9.5050%	2 580 000.00	21 798.13	681.19
04-Dec-85	Boca Pointe (Florida)	B.O.M.	04-Nov-85	06-Dec-85	32	8.3315%	1.00%	9.3315%	3 510 000.00	29 114.28	909.82
28-Jan-86	Boca Pointe (Florida)	B.O.M.	28-Jan-86	30-Jan-86	367	9.7940%	1.00%	10.7940%	2 175 000.00	239 334.46	652.14
20-Nov-85	Clayton Facility #2 (Texas)	B.O.M.	21-Oct-85	22-Nov-85	32	8.4405%	1.00%	9.4405%	24 980 391.63	209 624.34	6 550.76
20-Nov-85	Clayton Tract (Texas)	B.O.M.	21-Oct-85	22-Nov-85	32	8.1250%	1.00%	9.1250%	3 912 140.00	31 731.80	991.62
12-Nov-85	Gainey Ranch (Arizona)	C.I.B.C.	10-Oct-85	14-Nov-85	35	8.1250%	1.75%	9.8750%	6 000 000.00	57 604.17	1 645.83
14-Nov-85	Gainey Ranch (Arizona)	C.I.B.C.	17-Oct-85	18-Nov-85	32	8.1250%	1.75%	9.8750%	9 000 000.00	79 000.00	2 468.75
14-Nov-85	HB Centre (Denver, Colo.)	TD	17-Oct-85	18-Nov-85	32	8.1250%	1.00%	9.1250%	5 000 000.00	40 555.56	1 267.36
20-Nov-85	HB Centre (Denver, Colo.)	TD	21-Oct-85	22-Nov-85	32	8.1250%	1.00%	9.1250%	5 000 000.00	40 555.56	1 267.36
21-Nov-85	HB Centre (Denver, Colo.)	TD	24-Oct-85	25-Nov-85	32	8.1250%	1.00%	9.1250%	5 000 000.00	40 555.56	1 267.36
09-Jan-86	HB Centre (Denver, Colo.)	TD	17-Jul-85	13-Jan-86	180	8.1250%	1.00%	9.1250%	5 000 000.00	228 125.00	1 267.36
15-Jan-86	HB Centre (Denver, Colo.)	TD	17-Jul-85	17-Jan-86	184	8.1250%	1.00%	9.1250%	5 000 000.00	233 194.44	1 267.36
09-Jul-86	HB Centre (Denver, Colo.)	TD	17-Jul-85	11-Jul-86	359	8.5000%	1.00%	9.5000%	11 000 000.00	1 042 097.22	2 902.78
27-Dec-85	Homestead (Florida)	B.O.M.	26-Sep-85	31-Dec-85	96	8.4405%	1.50%	9.9405%	5 250 000.00	139 167.00	1 449.66
29-Jan-86	L.D.C. Acquisition (Texas)	B.O.M.	06-Jun-85	31-Jan-86	239	8.2470%	1.50%	9.7470%	2 500 000.00	161 773.13	676.88
06-Nov-85	M.C.I. Operating (California)	C.I.B.C.	02-Oct-85	06-Nov-85	35	8.0625%	0.75%	8.8125%	3 919 842.30	33 584.07	959.54
19-Nov-85	M.C.I. Operating (California)	C.I.B.C.	17-Oct-85	21-Nov-85	35	8.1250%	0.75%	8.8750%	1 765 687.51	15 235.19	435.29
26-Nov-85	M.C.I. Operating (California)	C.I.B.C.	25-Oct-85	29-Nov-85	35	8.1250%	0.75%	8.8750%	1 959 584.97	16 908.22	483.09
03-Dec-85	M.C.I. Operating (California)	C.I.B.C.	31-Oct-85	05-Dec-85	35	8.1250%	0.75%	8.8750%	3 753 853.80	32 390.02	925.43

EXHIBIT 6 (continued)
MARKBOROUGH PROPERTIES INC.

Outstanding LIBOR Contracts as of November 1, 1985

Election Date	Loan	Lender	Value Date	Maturity Date	Term	LIBOR	Spread	All-in	LIBOR Contract	Interest	Daily Interest
05–Nov–85	M.H.I. Operating (US)	C.I.B.C.	04–Oct–85	07–Nov–85	34	8.0625%	0.75%	8.8125%	3 000 000.00	24 968.75	734.38
06–Nov–85	M.H.I. Operating (US)	C.I.B.C.	04–Oct–85	08–Nov–85	35	8.0625%	0.75%	8.8125%	3 500 000.00	29 986.98	856.77
12–Nov–85	M.H.I. Operating (US)	C.I.B.C.	11–Oct–85	14–Nov–85	34	8.1250%	0.75%	8.8750%	5 000 000.00	41 909.72	1 232.64
13–Nov–85	M.H.I. Operating (US)	C.I.B.C.	15–Oct–85	15–Nov–85	31	8.1250%	0.75%	8.8750%	4 000 000.00	30 569.44	986.11
14–Nov–85	M.H.I. Operating (US)	C.I.B.C.	15–Oct–85	18–Nov–85	34	8.1250%	0.75%	8.8750%	5 000 000.00	41 909.72	1 232.64
19–Nov–85	M.H.I. Operating (US)	C.I.B.C.	17–Oct–85	21–Nov–85	35	8.1250%	0.75%	8.8750%	5 000 000.00	43 142.36	1 232.64
20–Nov–85	M.H.I. Operating (US)	C.I.B.C.	21–Oct–85	22–Nov–85	32	8.1250%	0.75%	8.8750%	3 500 000.00	27 611.11	862.85
20–Nov–85	M.H.I. Operating (US)	C.I.B.C.	23–May–85	25–Nov–85	186	8.2500%	0.75%	9.0000%	6 500 000.00	302 250.00	1 625.00
26–Nov–85	M.H.I. Operating (US)	C.I.B.C.	01–Nov–85	29–Nov–85	28	7.9375%	0.75%	8.6875%	2 000 000.00	13 513.89	482.64
27–Nov–85	M.H.I. Operating (US)	C.I.B.C.	28–Oct–85	02–Dec–85	35	8.1875%	0.75%	8.9375%	5 000 000.00	43 446.18	1 241.32
03–Dec–85	M.H.I. Operating (US)	C.I.B.C.	01–Nov–85	05–Dec–85	34	7.9375%	0.75%	8.6875%	2 000 000.00	16 409.72	482.64
04–Dec–85	M.H.I. Operating (US)	C.I.B.C.	04–Nov–85	06–Dec–85	32	8.0000%	0.75%	8.7500%	2 000 000.00	15 555.56	486.11
13–Mar–86	M.H.I. Operating (US)	C.I.B.C.	20–Jun–85	17–Mar–86	270	7.8750%	0.75%	8.6250%	5 000 000.00	323 437.50	1 197.92
27–Mar–86	M.H.I. Operating (US)	C.I.B.C.	14–Jun–85	31–Mar–86	290	8.1875%	0.75%	8.9375%	3 000 000.00	215 989.58	744.79
20–May–86	M.H.I. Operating (US)	C.I.B.C.	23–May–85	22–May–86	364	8.7500%	0.75%	9.5000%	6 000 000.00	576 333.33	1 583.33
04–Jun–86	M.H.I. Operating (US)	C.I.B.C.	06–Jun–85	06–Jun–86	365	8.3750%	0.75%	9.1250%	5 000 000.00	462 586.81	1 267.36
03–Dec–85	M.N.I. (Nevada)	R.B.C.	31–Oct–85	05–Dec–85	35	8.1250%	0.75%	8.8750%	7 000 000.00	60 399.31	1 725.69
05–Dec–85	M.N.I. (Nevada)	R.B.C.	04–Nov–85	09–Dec–85	35	8.0000%	0.75%	8.7500%	7 000 000.00	59 548.61	1 701.39
06–Nov–85	Markborough Corporate	C.I.B.C.	08–Nov–84	08–Nov–85	365	10.5000%	0.75%	11.2500%	3 000 000.00	342 187.50	937.50
27–Nov–85	Markborough Corporate	C.I.B.C.	29–Nov–84	29–Nov–85	365	10.1250%	0.75%	10.8750%	2 000 000.00	220 520.83	604.17
22–Jan–86	Markborough Corporate	C.I.B.C.	24–Jan–85	24–Jan–86	365	9.5625%	0.75%	10.3125%	3 500 000.00	365 950.52	1 002.60
28–Jan–86	Markborough Corporate	C.I.B.C.	28–Jan–85	30–Jan–86	367	9.4375%	0.75%	10.1875%	4 000 000.00	415 423.61	1 131.94
14–Nov–85	Sunnymead (California)	C.I.B.C.	25–Oct–85	18–Nov–85	24	8.1250%	1.75%	9.8750%	3 000 000.00	19 750.00	822.92
21–Nov–85	Sunnymead (California)	C.I.B.C.	25–Oct–85	25–Nov–85	31	8.1250%	1.75%	9.8750%	3 956 902.69	33 647.41	1 085.40
27–Nov–85	Sunnymead (California)	C.I.B.C.	28–Oct–85	02–Dec–85	35	8.1875%	1.75%	9.9375%	3 734 424.00	36 079.98	1 030.86
03–Dec–85	Sunnymead (California)	C.I.B.C.	31–Oct–85	05–Dec–85	35	8.1250%	1.75%	9.8750%	3 176 599.38	30 497.56	871.36
22–Jan–86	Sunnymead (California)	C.I.B.C.	24–Jan–85	24–Jan–86	365	9.5625%	1.75%	11.3125%	3 000 000.00	344 088.54	942.71
21–Nov–85	Tampa (Florida)	R.B.C.	25–Oct–85	25–Nov–85	31	8.1250%	0.75%	8.8750%	6 000 000.00	45 854.17	1 479.17
26–Nov–85	Tampa (Florida)	R.B.C.	27–Sep–85	28–Nov–85	62	8.0625%	0.75%	8.8125%	6 000 000.00	91 062.50	1 468.75
27–Nov–85	Tampa (Florida)	R.B.C.	31–Oct–85	02–Dec–85	32	8.1250%	0.75%	8.8750%	6 000 000.00	47 333.33	1 479.17
20–Nov–85	Vicksburg (Texas)	B.O.M.	21–Oct–85	22–Nov–85	32	8.4405%	1.25%	9.6905%	6 850 000.00	59 004.38	1 843.89
TOTAL					106	8.3342%	1.00%	9.3339%	$251 989 426.28	$7 157 640.17	$65 334.71

NIAGARA CONSTRUCTION LIMITED

On April 11, 1990, Phil Granger, the Vice-President of Finance for Niagara Construction Limited, was pondering several financing options that had been suggested by Marilyn Foster, a Confederation Bank account manager. Niagara Construction had decided to acquire seven Caterpillar construction machines costing a total of $1 million and they were exploring options to find the most appropriate way to finance the equipment. The company had over $1,000,000 in cash available in its bank account, but they were looking at long term financing alternatives that included leasing the equipment or financing it with a fixed rate or floating rate term loan. Foster had suggested that Niagara Construction consider FedLease, the Confederation Bank's leasing subsidiary, as well as various other long-term lending products that the Confederation Bank had available.

Company Background

History

Niagara Construction was incorporated in 1949 by Thomas Balboni. Initially the company specialized in road construction but had gradually evolved into major excavation projects, water and sewer pipelines, road construction, equipment rentals and land development. After graduating from college, sons Mike (43) and Tony (40) Balboni joined the firm on a full-time basis and eventually assumed day-to-day managerial responsibilities as President and Vice President, respectively. Both Balbonis, together with their sister Maria Miele (39), assumed control of Niagara Construction in 1977 when the company's shares were purchased by 69655 Ontario Limited, a company established for this purpose. The company was well-respected in the Hamilton area with the majority of contracts originating from government agencies and major developers.

Operations

The primary activities of the firm were excavation, road construction, equipment rentals and the development of land. Land development had grown from 0% of revenues in 1987 to 11% in the most recent fiscal year. Gross margins for the company had ranged from 9% to 21% over the past four years. Land development had much greater margins than the other business of the company, averaging about 40%.

Niagara Construction's fixed assets consisted of machinery and mobile equipment used in day-to-day operations, including crawler tractors, hydraulic shovels, compressors, trucks, trailers and automobiles. The company performed their own on-site maintenance of equipment. When Foster had visited the equipment yard and field sites recently, Phil Granger had shown her the equipment and Foster was satisfied that the equipment's book value was a reasonable approximation of its market value.

Financial Management

As seen in the financial statements in Exhibit 1, Niagara had experienced a modest revenue increase in fiscal 1990 which, combined with tight control over direct costs, led to a substantially increased gross profit. On the other hand, net income remained modest because of the company's policy of declaring bonuses in order to reduce taxable income. The company's marginal tax rate was estimated to be 42%.

As of March 31, 1990, Niagara had $15.2 million account/holdback receivables less than 90 days and $6.75 million in account/holdback payables. The company had several accounts receivable from governments and large reputable developers and contractors. The largest account receivable was for $3.6 million due from the City of Hamilton. Bad debt experience had been minimal. Trade payables were maintained on a current basis and the company provided an aged list monthly. Approximately $5.1 million of the fiscal 1990 bonus payable remained payable as of April 1990. The company had agreed to postpone $5.0 million of the bonuses payable in favour of the Confederation Bank.

Niagara Construction had been banking with the Confederation Bank since 1949. Niagara had authorized credit facilities totalling $8.9 million. Use of the operating lines fluctuated with the ebb and flow of business. Currently only modest use was being made of the operating lines. The authorized credit summary is in Exhibit 2 and the collateral security schedule is in Exhibit 3.

Equipment Needs/Caterpillar Purchase

The Caterpillar excavation equipment that Niagara Construction wanted to purchase consisted of two excavators, three bulldozers, and two loaders. The cost of the new equipment was $1 million. The equipment fell into CCA class 38 for income tax purposes, and carried a CCA rate of 30%. In accordance with current tax rules only one half of the CCA could be claimed in the first year. Phil Granger believed that the equipment would last well beyond 5 years.

Financing Alternatives

Leasing

One financing option that Phil Granger was considering was leasing the equipment. Under this alternative the lessor would purchase the equipment and hold title to it, and Niagara Construction, as lessee, would obtain use of the equipment for a fixed period of time in return for rental payments.

Since equipment leasing companies had not been particularly aggressive in attempting to arrange leasing for this new equipment Foster recognized an opportunity for Confederation Bank's leasing subsidiary, FedLease.

In the past, Phil Granger had been approached by representatives from National, Lloyd's and Chase Manhattan Banks to discuss financing arrangements. He knew that each of these banks also offered leasing through subsidiary firms, although he was unsure of the rates available. Lloyd's/ Continental Bank had been particularly aggressive in wanting to do business with Niagara Construction.

Following discussion of Niagara's needs Foster had proposed an arrangement under which FedLease would purchase the equipment and lease it to Niagara over a 60-month period. Monthly lease payments would be $21,984.69 at the beginning of each month and the lessee would have the option to purchase the equipment at the end of the 60th month for $100,000. If the purchase option was not exercised, the lessee would be required to pay an additional four months' rent at the regular monthly rate. No bank fees would be assessed and the very modest legal costs would be covered by the bank. Foster had noted that, assuming the purchase option was exercised, this amounted to an effective cost of 14.25% per annum.

Term Loan Financing

A second method of financing available from Confederation Bank was a fixed rate term loan. Under this alternative the client would make fixed monthly payments sufficient to repay the principal and interest over a five-year period. The interest rate charged was expected to be the Fixed Rate Base Rate (FRBR) plus a premium for the risk. At the time the FRBR had been set by the bank at 14.25% and Foster felt that the risk premium would be 75 basis points. In addition, the bank was expected to ask for an approval fee of $2500 which was payable immediately by the client if the loan was approved and an offer made to the client.

Under this financing alternative the account manager would outline the nature of the arrangement in an offering letter. If the arrangement was acceptable to the client he would have to sign a loan agreement and promissory note detailing the legal obligations of the parties including a number of positive and negative covenants. In addition, the bank would likely require collateral security such as a chattel mortgage on the equipment being purchased. Under some circumstances the bank would require its customer to grant a fixed and floating debenture, the creation of which could cost the customer $1500–$2500.

Floating Rate Term Loan Financing

Confederation Bank also offered a floating rate term loan package. Under this arrangement the loan was paid off in fixed monthly amounts over the five-year term and interest was paid monthly on the outstanding amount of the loan during the preceding month. The interest rate charged the client was based on the prime lending rate of the bank plus a premium for the credit risk of the client. Foster quoted Niagara a rate of Confederation Bank Prime plus 75 basis points. Administration, documentation and collateral security arrangements for this type of loan would be similar to those for a fixed rate term loan.

The Economy and Interest Rate Movements

Phil Granger was aware that the Canadian economy had been growing for an unprecedented period of time and that a number of economists were forecasting either a recession or minimal growth in 1990. Deteriorating levels of leading indicators such as capital spending intentions, factory new orders, housing starts and auto inventories all added weight to the recession scenario. The financial press had reported recent decreases in industrial production largely related to cutbacks in auto sector output. It also pointed out that Canada experienced lower exports due to a high Canadian dollar and gradual slowing of the US economy. Inflation had been picking up recently and Phil knew that the Bank of Canada had been entering markets from time to time in an effort to keep the dollar strong and to prevent inflation from grabbing hold of the economy as it had done in the 1970s and early 1980s. The result had been a steady increase in interest rates. The Minister of Finance had reiterated the government's determination to reduce the budget deficit to $15 billion by 1993/94 but recent high interest rates made it difficult to believe that this goal could be achieved. Granger was also somewhat worried about the effect of the GST introduction on both the economy and interest rates.

Given this environment Granger was very uncertain about the future course of interest rates yet he knew they may have an effect on his choice of leasing versus purchasing the equipment. He also knew that if the equipment was purchased expected future interest rates would affect his choice of fixed or floating rate financing of a term loan. The Confederation Bank prime interest rate stood at 14.25% on April 11, 1990. Data on recent interest rate movements can be found in Exhibit 4, and a forecast of future movements in interest rates published by Confederation Bank is quoted in Exhibit 5.

EXHIBIT 1
NIAGARA CONSTRUCTION LIMITED

**Statement of Income and Retained Earnings
for the four years ending January 31**
(in $000s)

	1990	*1989*	*1988*	*1987*
Revenue (1)	$56 580	$53 911	$46 889	$53 257
Direct costs	44 960	49 102	39 459	44 072
Gross profit	11 620	4 809	7 430	9 185
Expenses				
Operating	3 622	2 919	2 573	2 402
Depreciation and Amortization	1 589	1 171	1 153	909
Executive Salaries and Bonuses	6 317	145	2 031	2 130
Interest on long term debt on equipment	159	131	140	144
Interest on obligations under capital leases	156	190	193	109
Other interest	145	132	70	14
	11 988	4 688	6 160	5 708
Other income (losses)				
Interest and Dividends	391	591	480	254
Sundry Gains and Losses	108	(64)	145	157
	499	527	625	411
Income before taxes	131	648	1 895	3 888
Income taxes				
Current (recovery)	204	(974)	306	60
Deferred (reduction)	(94)	1 344	551	1 830
	110	370	857	1 890
NET INCOME	$ 21	$ 278	$ 1 038	$ 1 998

See accompanying notes.

EXHIBIT 1 (continued)

Balance Sheet as at January 31
(in $000s)

	1990	1989	1988	1987
Assets				
Current Assets				
Cash	$ 8 707	$ 0	$ 6 342	$ 2 401
Marketable securities	251	567	1 151	231
Accounts receivable (2)	18 997	19 781	15 221	17 389
Income taxes recoverable	59	1 986	0	10
Deposits	0	0	441	104
Land under development (3)	1 425	3 229	597	0
Work in progress (4)	400	689	876	603
Prepaid expenses and other	325	219	24	13
	30 164	26 471	24 652	20 751
Other Assets				
Mortgages and loans receivable	312	347	425	463
Land under development	0	0	0	1 188
Investment in affiliated company	2 350	2 329	1 343	1 340
Deferred pension costs	270	293	449	0
Other investments	223	223	34	15
	3 155	3 192	2 251	3 006
Rental Property Under Construction (5)	1 409	0	0	0
Equipment and Leasehold Improvements: (6) (7)				
Machinery & other equipment, Net	3 190	3 283	2 870	3 050
Leasehold improvements, Net	235	51	67	71
Equipment under capital lease, Net	2 407	1 261	1 577	1 024
TOTAL ASSETS	$40 560	$34 258	$31 417	$27 902

See accompanying notes.

EXHIBIT 1 (continued)

Balance Sheet as at January 31
(in $000s)

	1990	1989	1988	1987
Liabilities and Shareholders' Equity				
Current Liabilities				
Bank indebtedness	$ 0	$ 3 207	$ 378	$ 0
Accounts payable and accrued liabilities (8)	12 943	12 040	11 711	10 251
Bonuses payable	6 200	30	1 800	1 500
Mortgage, interest free, secured by land under development	0	0	467	0
10% Notes payable to directors	0	0	510	0
Payable to directors and officers, without interest	0	0	49	190
Income taxes payable	0	0	933	0
Mortgages and notes payable	2 672	3 136	0	0
Current portion of obligations under capital leases (9)	0	0	439	220
Principal due within one year on long term debt	0	0	264	684
	21 815	18 413	16 551	12 845
Other Liabilities				
Obligations under capital lease	1 849	829	1 356	918
Finance contracts secured by equipment	0	0	829	1 261
Note payable to parent company	0	0	189	189
Mortgage secured by land under development	0	0	0	1 090
Long term debt (10)	2 858	904	0	0
Deferred income taxes	5 344	5 516	4 261	4 860
	10 051	7 249	6 635	8 318
Shareholders' Equity				
Capital Stock	1 211	1 133	1 044	591
Retained earnings	7 483	7 463	7 187	6 148
	8 694	8 596	8 231	6 739
TOTAL LIABILITIES AND SHAREHOLDERS' EQUITY	$40 560	$34 258	$31 417	$27 902

See accompanying notes.

EXHIBIT 1 (continued)

Notes to Financial Statements
for the four years ending January 31

Note 1: Revenues
Revenues from construction contracts are recognized on a percentage of completion basis while revenues from the sale of land under development are recognized at closing when title passes to the purchaser.

Note 2: Accounts Receivable

	1990	1989	1988	1987
Accounts and progress claims receivable	$13 284	$15 254	$13 952	$16 441
Receivables from related companies without interest from:				
Directors and officers	970	160	583	910
Affiliated companies	2 401	1 518		
Parent company	209	33		
Note receivable	0	1 789	0	0
Principal due within one year on mortgages and loans receivable	2 133	1 027	686	38
	$18 997	$19 781	$15 221	$17 389

Note 3: Land Development
Land under development is recorded at cost. The costs of holding and developing this land are capitalized and charged to direct costs as individual lots are completed and sold.

Note 4: Work in Progress
Work in progress is recorded net of deferred revenue.

Note 5: Rental Property
Rental property under construction is recorded at cost.

Note 6: Equipment and Leasehold Improvements
Equipment and leasehold improvements are stated at cost. Depreciation and amortization are provided on the declining balance basis using the following annual rates:

Tractors, shovels, compressors, trucks, trailers, misc. and office equipment	20%
Automobiles	30%
Radio equipment	25%
Leasehold improvements	5%
Equipment under capital leases	20%

EXHIBIT 1 (continued)

Notes to Financial Statements
for the four years ending January 31

Note 7: Capital Leases

	1990 Net	1989 Net	1988 Net	1987 Net
Machinery & other equipment, Net	$ 3 190	$ 3 283	$ 2 870	$ 3 050
Leasehold improvements, Net	235	51	67	71
Equipment under capital lease, Net	2 407	1 261	1 577	1 204
Total Net Equipment and Leaseholds	5 832	4 595	4 514	4 145
Plus: Accumulated Depreciation	5 748	5 299	4 310	3 867
Total Cost, Equipment and Leaseholds	11 580	9 894	8 825	8 012

Note 8: Payables

	1990	1989	1988	1987
Trade payables and accrued liabilities	$12 254	$ 9 777	$11 605	$10 002
Payable to affiliated companies	689	2 263	106	249
	12 943	12 040	11 711	10 251

Note 9: Obligations Under Capital Leases

The following is a schedule of future minimum lease payments under capital leases expiring between 1991 and 1995, together with the balance of the obligations under capital leases at January 31, 1990.

Year ending January 31, 1991	$ 998
1992	686
1993	648
1994	498
1995	355
Total minimum lease payments	3 185
Less amount representing interest	562
Balance of obligations, January 31, 1990	2 623
Less current portion included in notes and mortgages payable	774
	$1 849

Note 10: Long-Term Debt

	1990	1989	1988	1987
11.5% Note payable, secured by a bankers' acceptance, due May 1993	2 347	0	0	0
12% Note payable to parent company, due May 1991	189	189	189	189
Finance contracts, secured by equipment, at interest rates ranging from 11% to 13.75% or at prime bank rate plus 1%	1 098	1 152	1 093	1 945
	3 634	1 341	1 282	2 134
Less principal due within one year, included in mortgages and notes payable	776	437	264	684
	2 858	904	1 018	1 450

Principal is due on long-term debt as follows:

1991	$ 776
1992	303
1993	2 492
1994	55
1995	8
	$3 634

Note 11: Contingent Liabilities

(a) The company is guarantor to the bank indebtedness and the liabilities of companies included in other investments to a maximum of $312 000. The company is also guarantor of the liabilities of a company included in other investments to a maximum of $120 000 U.S.

(b) The company is guarantor of the bank indebtedness of an affiliated company to a maximum of $475 000. The bank indebtedness for this company totalled $nil at January 31, 1990.

(c) Letters of credit totalling $3 134 140 have been issued, the majority of which guarantee the fulfillment of agreements with municipalities. The letters of credit are secured by a general assignment of book debts and a fixed and floating charge debenture of $950 000 on all company assets.

EXHIBIT 1 (continued)

Note 12: Lease Commitments
The company rents buildings from an affiliated company under long-term operating leases which expire in 1991 and 1998. The aggregate rental charged in 1990 for these buildings amounted to $213 787 (1989, $179 214).

Future minimum rental payments required under these long-term operating leases are approximately as follows:

1991	$ 195 190
1992	181 440
1993	181 440
1994	181 440
1995 and thereafter	786 240
	$1 525 750

EXHIBIT 2
NIAGARA CONSTRUCTION LIMITED

Credit Facilities

		Credit Applied For	Facility Type & Term	Rates/Fees	Prev. Auth.	Currently Outstanding
(1)	(a)	$3 800 000	Loans, Operating	CBP*	$3 800M	$ 100M
			Tender Loans	@ 2%		
			Bankers' Acceptances	CBPAF**		
	(b)	$3 800 000	LC's/Guarantee	@ 1%	$3 800M	$2 601M
		$6 500 000	*Total Segment (1) Not to Exceed $6 500M*			
(2)		$ 45 000	VISA Expense	Sched. Rates	$ 45M	$ 45M
(3)		$2 347 000	Fixed Rate Term Loan 3 yr. term, 25 yr. am.	11.5%	$2 347M	$2 347M
		$8 892 000	Total Single Name Risk		$8 892M	$5 089M

*CBP   =   Confederation Bank Prime
**CBPAF =   Confederation Bank Prime Acceptance Fee

EXHIBIT 3
NIAGARA CONSTRUCTION LIMITED

Collateral Security Schedule

Realizable
General Corporate Security   *Value ($M)*

Floating debenture, for $950M; no prior charges, PMV $16 500M.

Supported by Full Covering Fire Insurance with loss payable to the Confederation Bank of Canada as their interest may appear.

General Security Agreement covering:

	Book Value on August 31, 1989	Prior Encumbrances
Cash & Equivalent	$ 2 765	$ 592
Accounts Receivable	12 119	NIL
Mortgages Receivable	1 565	NIL
Machinery & Equipment	5 398	3 143
	$21 847	$3 735
Lending value @ 75% less priors		10 428

Guarantees as follows:

$750M signed by Mike Balboni (Net Worth $5 000M – October 1989).

$750M signed by Tony Balboni (Net Worth $6 000M – October 1989).

$750M signed by Maria Miele (Net Worth $4 250M – October 1989).

$950M signed by 69655 Ontario Limited, parent company of Niagara Construction Limited.

Supported by the usual Directors' Resolution. Outside net worth $250M as per statement of file dated February 5, 1989.

TOTAL GENERAL CORPORATE SECURITY $10 428

EXHIBIT 4
NIAGARA CONSTRUCTION LIMITED

Recent Rate Trends
April 11, 1990

	90 Day B.A. Rate	Government of Canada			Swaps			Fixed Rate Base Rate	Prime
		2 Yrs.	5 Yrs.	10 Yrs.	2 Yrs.	5 Yrs.	10 Yrs.	5 Years	
July 31/89	12.30	9.70	9.07	9.21	10.53	10.07	10.18	12.00	13.50
August 31	12.33	10.22	9.54	9.44	11.04	10.53	10.45	12.25	13.50
September 29	12.32	10.36	9.92	9.75	11.21	10.98	10.78	12.25	13.50
October 31	12.28	10.08	9.56	9.39	11.16	10.78	10.50	12.50	13.50
November 30	12.31	10.37	9.99	9.69	11.35	11.11	10.73	12.50	13.50
December 31	12.32	10.52	9.69	9.52	11.44	10.86	10.65	12.50	13.50
January 31/90	12.50	10.85	10.12	10.06	11.70	11.32	11.16	12.50	13.50
February 28	13.40	11.90	11.05	10.64	12.66	12.25	11.72	13.50	13.50
March 30	13.42	12.51	11.56	11.07	12.36	12.71	12.12	13.50	14.25
April 02	13.43	12.57	11.58	11.11	13.32	12.73	12.16	13.75	14.25
April 03	13.52	12.60	11.67	11.18	13.35	12.82	12.23	13.75	14.25
April 04	13.50	12.57	11.69	11.15	13.32	12.84	12.20	13.75	14.25
April 05	13.50	12.69	11.86	11.25	13.44	12.98	12.30	13.75	14.25
April 06	13.55	12.76	11.90	11.27	13.49	13.00	12.30	13.75	14.25
April 09	13.65	12.95	12.15	11.47	13.67	13.25	12.48	13.75	14.25
April 10	13.56	13.01	12.28	11.59	13.73	13.38	12.60	13.75	14.25
April 11	13.52	12.86	12.21	11.57	13.58	13.31	12.58	14.25	14.25

EXHIBIT 5
NIAGARA CONSTRUCTION LIMITED

Interest Rate Commentary and Forecast
Confederation Bank of Canada
March 5, 1990

What Happened to the Canadian Dollar and Why?

During the months of January and February the Canadian dollar fell dramatically from 86.5 cents U.S. to below 83 cents U.S. This significant decline was related to an apparent change in Bank of Canada monetary policy.

In recent years the Bank has monitored inflationary pressures in the economy through such measures as wage increases, growth in demand for credit and total spending. In the Bank's judgement these inflationary pressures have remained strong, leading the Bank to pursue a relatively tight money (high interest rate) strategy. One result of these relatively high interest rates has been steady support for the Canadian dollar relative to its U.S. counterpart.

In January, in spite of suggestions that the economy still had inflationary pressures, the Bank of Canada suddenly added liquidity to the markets, causing a decline in rates. This increase in liquidity persisted and on January 18 the Bank rate fell by 29 basis points. At the same time interest rates in other major economies such as the United States and Japan continued to rise causing the spread between Canadian and U.S. short term rates to narrow considerably.

As a result of these Bank of Canada actions the capital markets interpreted the Bank as discarding its previous hard line against inflation and also felt that the interest rate spread between Canadian and U.S. capital market instruments would not be sustained. Both of these conclusions led currency traders to abandon the Canadian dollar, causing it to fall in value dramatically.

Perceiving these effects, the Bank resumed its high interest rate policy, pushing rates back up and restoring the spreads between Canadian and U.S. short term instruments. In the mean time the Canadian dollar only gradually began to regain its previous levels.

The Interest Rate Outlook

As a result of its recent experience the Bank of Canada is unlikely to ease interest rates in Canada until there are clear and persistent signs of abatement in inflationary pressures. In addition, other major economies are pursuing anti-inflationary policies including high interest rates. These two observations lead us to the conclusion that interest rates will not be falling in the near term and there may even be some additional upward pressure. Our forecast reflects this scenario.

We continue to see signs that the economy is slowing down and performance may be flat over the remainder of 1990. This should result in some easing of inflationary pressures and a modest lowering of rates toward the end of the year and into 1991. The major uncertainty remains the impact of the GST on the rate of inflation.

EXHIBIT 5 (continued)

Canada Interest Rate Forecast Detail
(Quarterly and Annual Averages)

Forecast Period		Bank Rate	30-day Bankers' Acceptances	90-day Commercial Paper	3-5 year Govm't Bonds	Corporate Long-term Bonds (Scotia McLeod)
1989	1	11.82	11.31	11.76	10.69	11.71
	2	12.44	12.40	12.40	10.21	10.76
	3	12.39	12.32	12.29	9.76	10.57
	4	12.46	12.33	12.34	10.10	10.68
	Year	12.28	12.09	12.20	10.19	10,80
1990	1	12.93	12.80	12.81	10.76	11.21
	2	13.29	13.05	13.19	11.19	11.68
	3	12.29	12.08	12.23	11.23	11.85
	4	11.79	11.59	11.75	11.23	11.85
	Year	12.58	12.38	12.50	11.10	11.64
1991	1	11.79	11.59	11.75	11.23	11.85
	2	11.79	11.59	11.75	11.23	11.85
	3	11.62	11.42	11.58	11.10	11.76
	4	11.32	11.17	11.33	10.91	11.63
	Year	11.64	11.44	11.60	11.12	11.77

Cost of Capital

NORTEX, INC.

Bill Quinn, Treasurer of Nortex, Inc. (Nortex), had just returned from a finance committee meeting. The purpose of the meeting had been to set preliminary guidelines for determination of the cost of capital for Nortex. As part of the development of the strategic plan, the finance committee had been asked by the newly appointed President, Paula Thomas, to determine Nortex's cost of capital. This information would be used in the evaluation of potential capital expenditures.

Nortex's Operating History

Nortex was a retailer and manufacturer of clothing. Ten years earlier in 1974, Nortex and Dylex Ltd., a competitor, had been of similar size. However, in the interim, Dylex had grown through acquisitions and aggressive internal expansion, and was now four times the size of Nortex. Although Nortex's sales had grown by 75 percent over the last five years, net operating income and earnings per share had remained stagnant (Exhibits 1 and 2). The former president had persuaded the Board of Directors to increase the dividend payout rate from 20 percent of earnings to 30 percent in an attempt to bolster the market price. Despite these efforts, the trading range of the stock had remained relatively stable. The current share price was $8.50, only $0.78 above the book value per share.

Nortex operated several chains of specialty clothing stores for both men and women. Operations had expanded gradually in both Canada and the United States. A significant portion of revenue came from a license agreement with a national department store. Under the license agreement, Nortex operated the men's and boys' wear departments of all the chain's Canadian stores. Plans to expand the arrangement into the United States were currently being investigated. In addition, Nortex owned several clothing manufacturers in Canada which marketed products not only through Nortex's outlets but also distributed widely throughout specialty and department stores in Canada. Currently, Nortex had no manufacturing facilities in the United States.

158

In the past five years, Nortex had spent significant sums in opening new stores and in developing its computer information systems. These investments had expanded Nortex's sales, but not its profit margins. Because of lagging performance, the Board of Directors decided to hire an executive from outside the organization to replace the retiring President and, in mid-1983, appointed Paula Thomas. Her mandate was to revitalize the company, with the stated expectation that within three years a dynamic improvement in profitability would occur.

After her initial investigation, Thomas concluded that if she was to succeed, Nortex would have to undertake an aggressive campaign of internal growth and acquisitions. In early 1984, as part of her plan to implement this strategy, she asked the finance department to prepare capital budgeting procedures and to recommend a cost of capital for use in evaluating projects. Because the procedures and the cost of capital rate would have to stand up to the challenges of senior managers promoting their pet projects, Quinn knew he would have to organize and prepare the project carefully.

During meetings in late 1983, the Nortex finance committee ranked the tasks to be done. The development of an information system for capital budgeting analysis and the creation of capital budgeting procedures were given the highest priority. Next was the determination of a cost of capital. In March 1984, Quinn believed the finance committee had made significant progress in the improvement of the capital budgeting procedures. Consequently, he had called a meeting to focus on the determination of the cost of capital. Quinn sought the comments of three people: Dave Furnish (a member of the finance department), who had joined Nortex three years previously as a graduate from a well-known business school; Terri Gilmour, Assistant Treasurer, who had taken an extensive financial management program the previous summer; and Steve Lewis, the comptroller.

The Finance Committee Meeting

All members of the finance committee had been briefed on the main topics and had come prepared. Quinn had anticipated that there would be some unanimity regarding concepts. However, he found there were continual arguments about almost every aspect of determining a cost of capital.

The Weights of the "Weighted" Average Cost Capital

One of the first arguments that had developed was whether book weights or market weights should be used in determining cost of capital. In the initial discussion, Lewis had suggested that the book values for the various sources of long-term capital should be used. Specifically, he presented the past weights (Exhibit 3) and suggested including both bank loans and the current portion of long term debt and leases. He argued that bank loans were really used as interim financing until equipment, plant and fixtures were in place and permanent financing was arranged. Moreover, he said, the current portion of long-term debt was only an accounting designation of a long-term liability.

After Lewis had concluded, Furnish put forth his position that market values should be used. He argued that new investments, at least, should preserve market values. He presented figures (Exhibit 4) to show the impact of market value weights. Lewis interjected, wondering how you could possibly use market values when these values fluctuated so much, and pointed out that the market value of Nortex's five million shares had varied between $62.5 million, at a $12.50 price (the high for the previous five years) and $29.4 million, at a $5.8750 price (the low for the previous five years). In addition, he stated that the deferred tax liability had been a real liability in the 1982 fiscal year, and while the amount was small in relation to other sources of capital, there was no guarantee that this account would not expand with Nortex's aggressive approach to asset acquisition.

At this stage of the discussion, Terri Gilmour spoke up. From her discussions with Thomas and Quinn, she believed that once the current excess cash was utilized, there would be board approval for a significant expansion of Nortex's long-term debt and capital leases. Gilmour had undertaken initial discussions with the syndicate of financial institutions that had bought Nortex's previous debt issues. The syndicate stated that if Nortex could improve its operating performance, the syndicate would be prepared to finance up to a 1:1 debt/equity ratio, where debt included bank loans, long-term debt and capital leases. If performance was not improved, the syndicate would institute a covenant of 2:3 debt/equity ratio.

In conclusion, Gilmour stated her belief that the appropriate weights should be either 1:1, 2:3 or somewhere in between and suggested that it might make sense to do a sensitivity analysis on the impact different weights would have on the cost of capital.

In an attempt to focus the discussion, Quinn summarized the points made and stated that the underlying purpose of the meeting was to pull Nortex's performance up to Dylex's level. Dylex, he noted, had a book debt/equity ratio of .3/.7 and its recent share market price was 1.5 times book value with a price/earnings multiple of ten.

Still unable to agree on the weights, the finance committee decided to move on to the next issue, the cost of the sources of capital.

Cost of Debt Capital

The basic disagreement of market value versus book value continued. Steve Lewis argued that debt costs actually "booked" or signed by Nortex adjusted for taxes should be used. Fortunately, there was little difference between Nortex's current actual tax rate (45 percent federal and provincial tax rate) and the effective tax rate (actual tax paid over taxable income from financial statements). Because debt costs averaged ten percent on long-term debt, most of which was issued before 1980, and 15 percent on capital leases, Steve Lewis calculated that after-tax cost of long-term debt was 5.5 percent [.10 × (1 − .45)], and the after-tax cost of capital leases was 8.25 percent [.15 × (1 − .45)]. Furnish countered that he had enquired about the interest rate the syndicate would charge on new debt. The syndicate had indicated that the rate would be 13.5 percent. Consequently, Dave Furnish had used 13.5 percent to value the long-term debt and capital leases. He recommended an after-tax cost of 7.425 percent [13.5 × (1 − .45)] for both sources.

Cost of Equity

Quinn stated that the Board of Directors placed considerable importance on dividends and he believed the appropriate method of determining the cost of equity should probably involve a dividend approach. While the current dividend yield of approximately five percent was not sufficient, Quinn believed that with an additional amount added for growth potential, the cost of equity was properly calculated. Here he was stuck; in the past, the actual earnings per growth of Nortex had been zero, but the compound growth rate of dividends since 1980 had been ten percent per year. Gilmour suggested an alternative approach to determining the growth rate: the earnings retention rate of Nortex, 70 percent, times the average return on equity over the last four years, 20 percent. Gilmour proposed that with the growth rate at 14 percent, the cost of equity capital would be 19 percent after tax. Lewis supported this last figure, noting it was close to Nortex's and Dylex's historical return on equity.

It was at this juncture that Dave Furnish entered the conversation. He pointed out that the dividend model was based on general expectations, but made no adjustment for risk. He suggested that the capital asset pricing model could be used to appraise the risk and set the cost of equity capital. He explained that the capital asset pricing model established return expectations based on risk, defined as the variation of asset returns in relation to the returns for all assets. Unfortunately, Furnish observed, it was impossible to generate the theoretical portfolio of all assets at market prices. The stock market was believed to be representative of the market value for the portfolio of all assets. The capital asset pricing model set a value for beta, which measured the response of a security to a change in stock market returns. Furnish had estimated Nortex's beta at 0.45. The beta had been calculated using 60 months of monthly returns in the following regression:

Monthly Return on Nortex Stock − Risk-free rate (3-month Treasury Bills) = $\alpha + \beta$ (monthly market return − risk-free rate)

Using the regression results, Furnish estimated the cost of equity capital to be 14.55 percent, the risk-free Treasury bill rate, 10.5 percent, plus the beta (.45) times the stock market risk premium, nine percent. The risk premium had been an estimate of the average risk premium, given studies of Canadian and American stock returns. Because Paula Thomas and the board were interested in approaching the performance of Dylex, Furnish obtained the beta estimate for Dylex, .6.

At this point, Gilmour interjected. From her experience, the regression generally explained less than 30 percent of the variation in the monthly returns, and many times the betas were not significantly different from zero. Consequently, Gilmour cautioned the group about using the capital asset pricing model to set a cost of equity capital.

Unable to form any consensus, Bill Quinn ended the meeting. Confused and uncertain as to what he should do next, Quinn asked Gilmour to prepare cost of capital estimates within a week, using the best method available.

EXHIBIT 1
NORTEX INC.

Income Statements for Years Ended January 31
($000 000)

	1984	1983	1982	1981	1980
Sales	$ 168.3	$ 152.9	$ 147.3	$ 126.5	$ 96.3
Cost of sales and general expenses	151.1	140.7	131.2	109.8	82.3
Depreciation and amortization	3.3	3.3	2.9	2.1	1.3
Interest	2.4	3.4	4.6	3.3	1.3
Other income	1.3	1.2	1.5	2.6	1.3
Net income before tax	12.8	6.7	10.1	13.9	12.7
Taxes — deferred	0.1	0.1	(0.2)	0.3	0.1
current	5.4	2.4	4.6	5.6	5.3
Net earnings	$ 7.3	$ 4.2	$ 5.7	$ 8.0	$ 7.3
Common stock dividends	2.2	2.2	2.2	1.8	1.5
Addition to retained earnings	$ 5.1	$ 2.0	$ 3.5	$ 6.2	$ 5.8
D.P.S.	0.44	0.44	0.44	0.36	0.30
E.P.S.	1.46	0.84	1.14	1.60	1.46
Share Price — high	12.50	8.625	10.50	10.875	10.625
— low	8.25	5.875	7.125	8.00	7.50

EXHIBIT 2
NORTEX INC.

Balance Sheets as of January 31
($000 000)

	1984	1983	1982	1981	1980
Current assets					
Cash and marketable securities	$ 18.4	$ 17.5	$ 16.0	$ 18.5	$ 17.1
Accounts receivable	6.9	5.8	5.7	5.3	4.6
Inventories	25.1	26.2	25.9	23.2	18.0
Other current assets	0.8	0.6	1.2	0.6	0.8
Total current assets	51.2	50.1	48.8	47.6	40.5
Investments	5.9	5.3	4.7	5.4	4.2
Property, plant, and equipment	17.2	18.3	17.7	14.4	8.6
Intangible assets	6.1	7.2	7.5[1]	11.5	7.9
TOTAL ASSETS	$ 80.4	$ 80.9	$ 78.7	$ 78.9	$ 61.2
Current liabilities					
Bank loans	$ 0	$ 0.6	$ 0.6	$ 2.6	$ 0
Accounts payable	20.7	22.6	19.9	17.4	12.6
Taxes and accrued liabilities	3.2	2.4	4.2	5.7	6.7
Current portion — long-term debt and leases	1.7	2.7	1.6	2.4	0.1
Total current liabilities	25.6	28.3	26.3	28.1	19.4
Long-term debt	13.0	15.6	17.9	17.4	16.7
Capital leases	2.6	3.0	2.6	2.8	1.0
Deferred income taxes	0.6	0.5	0.4	0.6	0.3
Total liabilities	41.8	47.4	47.2	48.9	37.4
Common stock	5.0	5.0	5.0	5.0	5.0
Retained earnings	33.6	28.5	26.5	25.0	18.8
Total equity	38.6	33.5	31.5	30.0	23.8
TOTAL LIABILITIES AND EQUITY	$ 80.4	$ 80.9	$ 78.7	$ 78.9	$ 61.2

[1] There was an extraordinary writeoff of goodwill, amounting to $2.0 million.

EXHIBIT 3
NORTEX INC.

Steve Lewis' Calculations for Cost of Capital Weights
Using Book Values from Exhibit 2
(in decimals)

	1984	1983	1982	1981	1980
Bank loans	.000	.011	.011	.047	.000
Current portion long-term debt and capital leases	.030	.048	.029	.043	.002
Long-term debt	.230	.279	.328	.312	.399
Capital leases	.046	.054	.048	.050	.024
Deferred income taxes	.011	.009	.007	.011	.007
Equity	.683	.599	.577	.538	.568
TOTAL	1.000	1.000	1.000	1.000	1.000

Note: Because of rounding, detail may not add to totals.

EXHIBIT 4
NORTEX INC.

Dave Furnish's Calculation of Market Weights
Using January 31, 1984 Market Values

Source	Explanation	Amount ($000 000)	Weight
Bank loan	Variable rate: book value = market value	$ 0	.00
Long-term debt including current portion	Annual principal and interest payments discounted at Nortex current market debt rates of 13.5	12.8	.22
Capital leases including current portion	Lease payments discounted at Nortex current market debt rates of 13.5%	2.9	.05
Deferred income taxes	A bookkeeping entry, not a source of cash	0	
Equity	Number of shares outstanding (5.0 million) times current market price ($8.50)	42.5	.73
TOTAL		58.2	1.00

BRITISH COLUMBIA
TELEPHONE CO.

Susan Cox and Bob Chabot, two managers from British Columbia firms, were attending a three-week management training course at a well-known Canadian business school in May 1989. Both had read an article dealing with the cost of capital as preparation for the next day's classroom session. As they vigorously discussed the concept, it became clear that they had several differences of opinion. To clarify their thinking, they decided to calculate the cost of capital for a well-known British Columbia employer, the British Columbia Telephone Co. (B.C. Tel). The data they gathered are presented in Exhibits 1–5.

Sue   What we really want to know is the hurdle rate that B.C. Tel should use for its capital investment projects.

Bob   Yes, and we should decide whether the rate ought to be different for different types of projects, such as the purchase of labour-saving equipment or the building of the fibre optics underground telecommunications corridor from Vancouver to the Alberta border.

Sue   Looking at the balance sheet, I can see that the firm raises funds from quite a few different sources. The best place to start is to look at the cost of the capital raised from each of these sources. The current liabilities are mostly trade credit, so their cost is zero.

Bob   The cost of deferred taxes is also zero. A fellow in the accounting department told me the other day that this is an interest-free loan from the government.

Sue   Well the long-term debt isn't interest free, but at least some of it is quite cheap. For example, the March 1991 bonds were issued with a $6\frac{3}{8}$ percent coupon. The company must be pleased that it has locked in such a low rate.

Bob   But shouldn't we be using current yields which are much higher than the firm paid in the past? I see in the newspaper that the firm's 11.35 percent issue has an asking price of $104.00 to yield 10.82 percent

165

while the 16.375 percent issue has an asking price of $112.25 to yield 11.33 percent[1]. Other outstanding bonds have yield to maturity ranging from 10.11 percent to 11.63 percent.

Sue   B.C. Tel seems to borrow at a pretty good rate. The newspaper says that long-term Government of Canada bond yields are only about 30 basis points lower at 10.50 percent.

Bob   Notice that B.C. Tel borrows money from the banks and through the short-term money market as well. In fact most of its short-term debt is obtained by issuing commercial paper.

Sue   Well, the prime rate from banks is $13\frac{1}{2}$% and I suppose that B.C. Tel would qualify for the prime rate. On the other hand, the commercial paper rate is currently 12.50% which should be much more attractive to the firm. In case we need the information, I also noted that the current rate on 91-day, Government of Canada treasury bills is 12.25%.

Bob   B.C. Tel was able to issue preferred stock at a cost of only 7.00 percent in the past. That's a lot cheaper than the debt, even though about $3.50 for every $100 par value share went to the underwriter.

Sue   *The Globe* has these stocks closing at $20\frac{1}{2}$ on April 28. But that may all be irrelevant. Since the recent tax changes fewer firms are issuing preferred shares.

Bob   Well, if that's true, maybe we can ignore the preferred in our calculations.

Sue   Calculating the cost of common stock is reasonably straight-forward. Since the shareholders are getting regular dividends, we should use the dividend yield.

Bob   No, no! All of the earnings belong to the shareholder, not just the dividends. We should use the earnings-per-share divided by the market price.

Sue   What about issuing costs? Although the current stock price is $31\frac{3}{4}$ per share, B.C. Tel would likely have to pay the underwriter and others about $1.60 per share to issue new stock.

Bob   It's not likely that B.C. Tel will raise more than one-quarter of its new equity by issuing stock. The rest of the new equity will be retained earnings, which have no cost.

Sue   Retained earnings aren't free capital. They belong to the shareholders. Surely they must want some type of return!

Bob   I notice from the firm's financial statements that the return on equity for the company has averaged about 11 per cent over the last five years (9.60, 10.66, 10.96, 11.68 and 12.12 in 1984 through 1988

---

[1] After allowing for a fee to the underwriter, the cost to the company of these two sources of financing would be 11.07% and 12.16% respectively.

respectively). I realize this is an accounting rate of return computed on the book value of the equity but I wonder if it can be used to compute the cost of equity capital?

Sue   I would guess that the funds generated by depreciation are free and they are available in large amounts. For example, last year earnings were over $145 million after deduction of preferred dividends, and depreciation was over $322 million. Capital expenditures for next year are expected to be about $540 million, so perhaps the bulk of the money can come from depreciation.

Bob   The assigned reading mentioned the beta of a stock. As requested by the instructor, I regressed the monthly return for B.C. Tel against the monthly market return on the TSE over the period 1984 to 1988, and got a beta of 0.348 and an R squared of 0.21. The beta seems to be an index of the riskiness of the common stock, but it has to be converted into a required return somehow. What I don't understand is how that return compares with the one we get by simply dividing the earnings-per-share by the stock price.

Sue   What do we do once we have the costs of all sources of financing? Do we just take their average?

Bob   Somehow the average cost doesn't make sense to me. I think we should just use the cost of the next source of financing. For example, B.C. Tel expects to issue $30 million in debt next month. Maybe the interest rate on that issue should be used as the hurdle rate for any new projects which are undertaken with those funds.

Sue   After we get this cost of capital, would you advise B.C. Tel to use the net-present-value method or the internal-rate-of-return method to evaluate projects?

Bob   I don't think it matters. The two methods both give the same answer.

Sue   Well, let's get on with this calculation. We have a long night ahead of us.

EXHIBIT 1
BRITISH COLUMBIA TELEPHONE CO.

Balance Sheet[1] as of December 31, 1988
($millions)

Assets		Liabilities and Equity		
Telecommunications Property		Common Shares[2]		$ 735
(net)	$2 812	Retained Earnings		380
Manufacturing Property	26	Preferred Shares[3]		215
Investments (at cost)	38	Long Term Debt[4]		1 168
Current Assets	311	Current Liabilities		
Deferred Charges	15	Bank Demand Loan[5]	24	
	$3 202	Promissory Note[6]	53	
		Accounts Payable	188	
		Other Accruals		342
		and Payables	77	
		Deferred Taxes		362
				$3 202

[1] This balance sheet has been simplified somewhat for ease of discussion.
[2] At the end of 1988, there were 50 284 000 shares outstanding.
[3] One preferred share issue was outstanding. The issue had a par value of $25 and a coupon rate of 7.00%.
[4] At the end of 1988 there were several debt issues outstanding of which the four major ones were: (1) a $125 million issue due to expire in November, 2005, with a coupon rate of 11.35 percent, (2) a $90.4 million issue due to expire in April, 1992, with a coupon rate of $16\frac{3}{8}$ percent, (3) a $75 million issue due to expire in November, 2003, with a coupon rate of $9\frac{7}{8}$ percent, (4) a $70 million issue due to expire in March, 1991, with a coupon rate of $6\frac{3}{8}$ percent.
[5] Interest payments are equal to the bank prime rate, which floats over time.
[6] These were several notes all of which expired within one year, bearing rates varying from 9.38% to 12.65%.

EXHIBIT 2
BRITISH COLUMBIA TELEPHONE CO.

Income Statement for the year ended December 31, 1988
($millions)

Revenues		$1738
Operating Expenses	$1243	
Selling and Administration Expenses	66	1309
Net Operating Earnings		429
Interest Payments		118
Earnings Before Taxes		311
Taxes		150
Net Earnings		161
Preferred Share Dividends		16
Ordinary Share Earnings		$ 145

EXHIBIT 3
BRITISH COLUMBIA TELEPHONE CO.

Selected Data 1969–1988

Year	Common EPS	Common Div/Share	Dec. 31 Closing[1] Common Stock Price	Total Return[2] For Year (%)
1969	1.03	0.60	14.40	8.70
1970	1.02	0.60	12.80	−6.94
1971	1.08	0.64	13.00	6.56
1972	1.22	0.64	11.30	−8.15
1973	1.16	0.64	9.80	−7.61
1974	1.00	0.79	9.40	3.98
1975	1.38	0.84	11.00	25.96
1976	1.48	0.92	13.13	27.68
1977	1.54	1.00	15.25	23.81
1978	1.55	1.08	17.00	18.56
1979	1.92	1.17	17.00	6.88
1980	2.04	1.20	17.00	7.06
1981	2.23	1.42	15.25	−1.94
1982	2.11	1.60	17.25	23.61
1983	2.36	1.60	22.00	36.81
1984	2.07	1.66	22.00	7.41
1985	2.21	1.72	26.50	28.27
1986	2.46	1.72	27.38	10.26
1987	2.68	1.75	26.25	1.82
1988	2.90	1.82	28.13	14.08

[1] Adjusted for a 5 for 1 stock split in 1975.

[2]
$$r_t = \frac{D_t + P_t - P_t - 1}{P_t - 1}$$

where

r_t = return for year t

D_t = dividend in year t

P_t = price at the end of year t

Case 15
British
Columbia
Telephone Co.

EXHIBIT 4

TSE Composite Index, Selected Data 1969–1988

Year	Index Value Dec. 31	Dividend Paid on Index Stocks	Total Return[1] for Year (%)
1969	1019.77	33.48	−0.91
1970	947.54	33.15	−3.83
1971	990.54	31.36	7.85
1972	1226.58	32.05	27.07
1973	1187.78	37.70	−0.09
1974	835.42	46.40	−25.76
1975	953.54	47.04	19.77
1976	1011.52	47.34	11.05
1977	1059.59	50.11	9.71
1978	1309.99	57.90	29.10
1979	1813.17	72.34	43.93
1980	2268.53	83.03	29.69
1981	1954.24	87.74	−9.99
1982	1958.08	78.91	4.23
1983	2552.35	82.18	34.55
1984	2400.33	88.81	−2.48
1985	2900.60	90.78	24.62
1986	3066.18	91.67	8.87
1987	3160.05	97.32	6.24
1988	3389.99	113.90	10.88

Arithmetic Average Return 1969–1988   11.22

[1]
$$R_t = \frac{DTSE_t + TSE_t - TSE_{t-1}}{TSE_{t-1}}$$

where

R_t = rate of return earned by the TSE Index stocks during period t

$DTSE_t$ = dividend adjusted to Index paid on TSE Index stocks during period t

TSE_t = value of TSE Index at the end of period t

EXHIBIT 5
BRITISH COLUMBIA TELEPHONE CO.

Average Annual Returns in the Canadian Capital Market
Over the Period 1950–1987
as Derived by Hatch and White[1]

Treasury Bills	5.98
Long-Term Government of Canada Bonds	5.65
Long-Term Provincial Bonds	6.23
Long-Term Municipal Bonds	6.72
Long-Term Industrial Bonds	6.62
Inflation Rate	4.72
Common Shares	12.50

[1] James E. Hatch and Robert W. White, *Canadian Stocks, Bonds, Bills and Inflation: 1950–1987*, The Research Foundation of The Institute of Chartered Financial Analysts, Charlottesville, Virginia, 1988.

Capital Expenditures

TOWNSHIP MOTORS

Township Motors is a franchised dealership employing about 60 people in a town of 45,000 in Western Canada. In early 1990, W.B. Craft, the President and General Manager, was considering a proposal for a new body shop facility. An opportunity to buy a suitable piece of land near the dealership had just come to Craft's attention, and he decided it was time to carefully consider making a major investment in a body shop. On the basis of prior negotiations with the vehicle manufacturer, Craft was sure that the manufacturer would not provide financing or active support for the new venture. If construction began in the next few weeks, the shop could open in January 1991.

The current body shop at Township Motors was in a leased building located about one kilometre from the dealership. This building provided room for five metal working stalls. Two preparation stalls and a small paint booth were located in the mechanical repair area of the main dealership. There was very little storage space, at the body shop location, either for parts and supplies or for damaged vehicles. The lease payments were $680 per month, and did not include heat, light, insurance and business tax. Eight men plus a foreman were employed at the body shop.

The old body shop was usually quite busy. Body shop sales in 1990 were running at just under $340,000 annually, with an almost 60% gross and a net earnings after tax of $51,000. The rate of turnover of staff was quite high.

Competition for body shop business in the dealership's trading area came primarily from another franchised dealer with a 20 stall facility. Three other dealers ran small shops but were not particularly aggressive in soliciting business. In addition, there were a variety of small independent shops operating in the area.

The new body shop proposal had been developed by Craft and his body shop foreman with the help of a local building contractor. Craft was toying with the idea of attempting to change the public image of the body shop business, at least with respect to his own dealership. As a result, the new proposal involved some significant innovations to current body shop facility

174

designs. These changes were planned to create a cleaner, more comfortable and more pleasant environment for both the staff and the customers. Specifically, the proposal included a carpeted, well decorated reception area for customers, complete with washroom facilities, a fully-equipped office for use by insurance adjusters, a heated appraisal area, locker and lunch room facilities with modern washroom and showers for employees, hot and cold water together with air lines in every stall and an efficient air control system in the building to reduce dust levels for both the benefit of employees and to ensure top quality paint work. The painting area would be separated from the metal working area by a fire wall, and included a paint booth large enough to accommodate the largest trucks as well as a conventional drying oven for cars. An under-the-floor frame straightening apparatus would be available in six of the metal working stalls. These features were not without their price tag, and Craft was aware that their inclusion in the proposal raised the estimated cost considerably.

Craft and his foreman believed that sufficient business could be attracted to a really good facility to keep 20 stalls busy, seven of which would be in the paint section. A total of almost 1400 square metres would be required to provide this working space with parts storage and the other features described earlier. The land which was currently available was priced at $170,000 for 0.5 hectares, and the contractor estimated that the building would cost about $730 per square metre to construct or a total of $1,022,000. Equipment for the building, including rails in the floor for frame straightening, wiring, fencing, and a road sign would cost about $85,000. The new truck booth and an air compressor for the entire shop would cost an additional $255,000. The capital cost allowance rates were five percent for the building and twenty percent for the equipment expenditures of $340,000. The corporate tax rate was 46 percent. Incremental working capital would be negligible.

The hourly labour charge for the body shop work was $54.00. Wage and benefit costs were $24.60 per hour. Parts and supply sales averaged $0.75 for every dollar of labour charged and earned a contribution of 27 percent. Consequently, the total gross revenue per labour hour charged was estimated at $94.50, ($54 labour plus .75 of $54 or $40.50 parts and supplies). The variable costs per labour hour were $54.17 ($24.60 hourly labour costs plus .73 of $40.50 or $29.57 parts and supply costs). In addition, the following annual cash expenses were anticipated:

Supervision and Clerical	$120 000
Repairs and Maintenance	35 000
Utilities, Business and Property Taxes and Insurance	80 000
Advertising	35 000
Total	$270 000

Capacity operations for the shop were estimated for planning purposes to be 13 stalls for 2000 hours a year, or 26,000 saleable hours. The revenue from the paint stalls was included in the estimate of parts and supply sales. Craft was not sure how long it would take to attract sufficient business to operate the new facility at capacity. He realized that the new shop would have to absorb more overhead than many of his competitors, but he also believed that productivity would be higher in more convenient, pleasant working conditions, and that customers would prefer to do business in the cleaner, quieter and more attractive environment that the new shop would provide.

Craft estimated that the facility would operate at 60 percent capacity in 1991, 70 percent in 1992, 80 percent capacity in 1993, 90 percent capacity in 1994, and 100 percent thereafter. Craft planned to retire ten years hence in 2001, and at that time expected to be able to sell the land for $170,000 and the building for $500,000. Seventy-five percent of any capital gain from the sale of the land would be taxable at the corporate 46 percent rate. The equipment would be worthless. When considering investment decisions concerning the dealership, Craft used a 20 percent after tax hurdle rate.

Craft had two proposals to consider for financing. One was an offer from one of the limited partners of the dealership for a $850,000 loan at 15 percent interest for ten years. Interest would be paid annually at year end with the principle being repaid at the end of the ten year period.

Craft also had an opportunity to lease the building and land for a ten year period at $240,000 per year, with payment at year end. All other occupancy costs to Craft, such as insurance, property tax and utilities would be the same whether the property was leased or purchased. The lease would be an operating lease for tax purposes, allowing Craft to deduct the full lease payment from taxable income.

RANPRO INC.

In early May, 1985, Bob Whitside, President of Ranpro Inc. (Ranpro), was considering automating the manufacturing facilities to increase operational efficiency. A proposal had been submitted by the sales representative of Gerber Garment Technology Inc. (Gerber) of Connecticut, U.S.A. outlining the cost and savings estimated for Ranpro if their systems were used. Whitside had to decide whether these estimates would be realized and whether they would justify the investment. If he decided to go ahead the equipment could be installed for the start of the 1986 fiscal year.

Background

Ranpro was a manufacturer of protective wear such as rain gear, cold wear, and safety wear which was used extensively in industries such as welding, steel, and fishing. The company was located in Simcoe, Ontario but distributed its merchandise nationwide and in the U.S. with sales reaching $7.1 million in 1984. Material purchases such as nylon and polycottons and coated fabrics for the garments amounting to $2.0 million in 1984 were acquired from around the world. The current manufacturing process from raw material to finished product used standard technology and was a manual operation. Ranpro was looking forward to its sales volume growing at the rate of about ten percent per year over the next five years. Selling price increases matched inflation which had been about four percent annually during the past four years.

Whitside had contacted Gerber to inquire about a cost estimate on some of the machines they offered and to learn how Ranpro might benefit from their use. Gerber sales representatives visited Ranpro to observe present operations and review the situation with management. After a detailed analysis of savings and investment outlays that Ranpro might experience by using its machines, Gerber recommended Ranpro purchase the Modular AM–5 Automatic Marking and Grading System and the Gerbercutter System 91.

The AM–5 at U.S.[1] $115,684 was a fast computerized marker and grader system which allowed the various parts of a pattern to be drawn and fitted tightly together on a piece of fabric. A picture of the mark (a piece of fabric 4.9 metres by 1.2 metres) was projected on a screen and a computer programmer drew a miniature scaled picture of the pieces of garment to be cut. The computer calculated and displayed the efficiency of material usage at all times for the particular layout of pieces. This way the programmer could arrange the layout to determine the best usage of the mark. After determining the best placement of the pieces of fabric, the AM–5 automatically drew, checked, labelled, and made specific splice marks. Information was stored in the computer so that processing of subsequent orders could be carried out quickly. The alteration of pieces, additions, or deletions, could be done easily on screen and stored in memory.

The current manual operations required patterns to be cut from cardboard, placed on tracing paper, and traced. The cardboard patterns (markers) were arranged for optimum usage on the mark based on personal judgment. As old markers wore out from repeated use, new ones were made by tracing around old markers on new cardboard. One particular marker had been used so often in the last ten years that repeated remakes of the marker had increased its dimension by one inch.

Gerber estimated several savings would be associated with the purchase of the AM–5. Material cost savings of three percent in the first year and increasing one half percent for the next two years would result from elimination of the cardboard markers. Labour savings would be achieved as the AM–5 would replace one of the employees who made and cut the patterns. The cost of pattern and marking supplies would decrease by $5,500 per year because of greater efficiency and the use of cheaper pattern paper. Savings could also be accomplished through better quality markers, reduction of space needed for marker making, and accurate cost estimations on new styles.

The estimated shipping cost and site preparation costs would be $8,000, in addition to the manufacturer's price for the equipment. The government imposed a duty of five percent on the cost of this type of equipment; however, it also allowed an investment tax credit of seven percent on the total installed cost of the system. Gerber would service the machine for U.S. $12,338 in the year of purchase after giving consideration to a 45 day parts and labour warranty. Ranpro expected the cost of this maintenance service to increase to U.S. $15,807 in the following year with annual increases of 7 percent thereafter.

The Gerbercutter System 91 would complement the effectiveness of the AM–5. The cost of the cutter was US$318,282 plus the five percent Canadian duty. The Gerbercutter System 91 was an accurate and fast machine that could cut fabric without the buffer margin which was needed

_____

[1] $1.00 Canadian = $.74 U.S.

with manual cutting to allow for operator error. This was expected to yield a material cost saving of three percent, though Gerber salesmen believed that was conservative. In addition, they estimated that the number of employees working at this operation would be reduced from eight to four.

Gerber indicated that other operating cost savings were common among Gerbercutter users as well. These savings were due primarily to the consistent accuracy and quality of cutting by the machine. Reduced variances in each piece allowed sewing machine operators to work more quickly and to lower inspection costs. The Gerbercutter also removed the dependence on more highly trained operators who could compensate for variances in each piece. The cost of reworking partially completed garments with associated fabric losses was also lower. Gerber "conservatively" estimated these savings at $30,000 per year; however, Ranpro managers were unsure if these savings would be realized immediately, if at all. The cutter used about $8,000 of electricity and required $15,000 of supplies (cover film, knives, etc.) annually.

Shipping and site preparation would cost another $15,000 but this machine also qualified for the investment tax credit. The system maintenance contract for the cutter, including the 6 month warranty, would cost US$10,200 for the first year. Annualized, the cost would increase at a rate of seven percent per year.

Whitside doubted whether any of the less tangible activities described by Gerber would net any savings. He thought that termination of employees would cost one month's salary for every year of employment at Ranpro. The average annual wages of workers affected was $15,000 in 1985 dollars. The average length of employment was about ten years. Labour rates increased directly with inflation. Labour costs were thought to be fixed over reasonably large changes in volume. If sales volume decreased, all of Gerber's estimates of savings amounts would be reduced, and Ranpro's ability to meet its debt repayment schedule resulting from the purchase of the equipment would also be affected. Ranpro's borrowing rate for a five year term loan was currently about 12 percent. He knew the equipment qualified for a 50 percent straight line Capital Cost Allowance (CCA) rate for tax purposes subject to the rule that only one-half year's CCA can be taken in the year of acquisition. Ranpro's marginal tax rate was 25 percent. He estimated the life of the equipment as five years with zero salvage value.

Ranpro used a discounted cash flow approach to evaluate capital budgeting decisions with an additional requirement that the project must have a payback of not longer than two years. Any investments made by Ranpro had to return 20 percent to cover financing costs and risks.

As an incentive to Ranpro to purchase its machines, the Gerber salesman offered a 20 percent discount on the price of the machines if both the AM–5 and the System 91 were purchased.

FIRST LONDON
CONGREGATIONAL CHURCH

On Sunday December 4, 1983, the Board of Management of the First London Congregational Church (Church), in London, Ontario, announced a special vestry meeting for the following Sunday, to discuss the proposed sale of its property at 173 Queens Avenue to Middlesex Developments Ltd. (Middlesex). Six prominent members of the congregation gathered on Thursday the 8th at Dr. Harry Harris' home to discuss the pros and cons of the land sale. The six members were on various committees within the Church and knew that their comments would have a major influence on the votes of the rest of the congregation.

Background Information

The property, less than two blocks away from the main intersection of downtown London, was purchased by the Church in January, 1964 for $70 000. Four years later, the Church leased the land to Middlesex, which constructed a $10 million, eight-storey office tower on it in 1969. The 50-year lease generated annual income of $15 000. At the end of the lease the ownership of the building would revert to the Church.

Middlesex wanted to sell the building and in May, 1983, approached the Church to renegotiate their arrangement in order to make the sale more attractive. Two proposals were suggested:

1) To extend the length of the lease to 2033, increase the annual lease payments to $16 800 and add a three percent participation in net cash flow from rentals.

2) To buy the land outright.

The Meeting

The informal meeting was attended by the following members of the congregation:

Dr. Harry Harris, a dentist, was unofficial chairperson of the meeting. He was in his early 40s and had been a member of the Church since his late teens.

Simone Short was a prominent businesswoman with a London financial corporation. She was in her mid-50s and had been a member of the Church for about 10 years.

John Johnson, manager of a major hardware retailing franchise, was about 35 years old and had been a member of the Church for 18 years.

Karen Kravitz was married to Kevin Kravitz, a retired business professor from a major eastern business school. She was attending the meeting in place of her husband who was currently out of the city. The Kravitzes had been members of the Church for four years.

Dr. David Dawson, about 45 years old, was an internist at University Hospital. He had been a member of the Church since 1970.

Frank Morphy, a young lawyer about 30 years old, worked for a small London law firm. He had only recently joined the Church, but was considered very bright and an asset to the congregation and its committees.

All of those attending the informal meeting knew each other from previous meetings and other committees.
The meeting proceeded as follows:

Harris   First, I'd like to thank everyone for coming. As you all know, we're here to discuss the possible sale of the land at 173 Queens Street, to Middlesex. Simone has been kind enough to offer to discuss the financial implications, so I'll just turn the floor over to her.
Morphy   Don't we have to declare the meeting open?
Harris   It's just an informal meeting, Frank.
Short   I've prepared copies of what I believe to be the important financial aspects of this problem. Basically we have three choices; sell the land for $503 000, extend the lease for a total income of $2 189 000 over the next 50 years, or do nothing. In the proposed new lease agreement, Middlesex has offered to raise the annual lease payments to $16 800 as well as add a three percent participation in net cash flow. According to Middlesex, starting with an initial net cash flow of $182 630 and increasing rents at 5.5 percent per year, earnings from the new lease would total $2 189 000. Adding this number to our earnings so far gives this option a total value of $2 429 000. At the end of the lease the Church would own the land and the building.
Kravitz   I didn't approach it quite the same way.
Harris   Maybe if we let Simone finish, Karen.
Kravitz   Sorry.
Short   I looked at the problem from the standpoint of comparing the options on equal terms, in which case the option that gives the highest dollar value is clearly the option to select. For example, we know that selling

the land would net us $503 000. If the $503 000 is added to the $240 000 earned so far, it could be invested and earn interest to the year 2033. Even if we used simple interest at nine percent, our total in 2033 would be $3 343 500 or $914 500 more than the extended lease option. Of course, if we used compound interest, this difference would be even greater. Similarly, we could calculate the value of the do-nothing option. This option is the worst because it means we would only net $510 000 from the present lease over the next 34 years for a total of $750 000.

Johnson Shouldn't we be considering what we can get for the land and the building? They must have some value at the end of either lease.

Short That's true, John. The land would undoubtedly have salvage value but trying to project 50 years in the future is too difficult and any figure used is probably meaningless. The building only has a projected 50-year life and will probably have to be torn down by 2033, so it really doesn't have any salvage value at all.

Johnson What about 2018?

Short Possibly a minor amount but I didn't work it out.

Dawson Did we have the land appraised to see if Middlesex's offer is fair?

Harris We retained the services of Mr. Eglington, one of the top appraisers in the city. His appraisal of the property was $502 000.

Morphy When does the decision actually have to be made?

Harris Middlesex has given us until December 15th, if we plan to sell. That's a week from today.

Kravitz These numbers still seem funny to me. Shouldn't we be comparing returns and not actual figures?

Short I don't think there's much of a difference, Karen. For example, I've already shown that selling the land is the best option. If we look at it on a return basis, we are now receiving $15 000 on a piece of land worth $502 000. That's about a three percent return and not an acceptable ROI — another reason for selling it. Basically, all of my quantitative analysis points to selling the land.

Kravitz Well, I still don't think you're comparing apples and apples.

Dawson Are there any other considerations besides the money? Is this a good time to sell the property?

Short Do you mean where are we on the real estate cycle?

Dawson Maybe. What I mean is land values fluctuate and are they high or low right now?

Short That's the real estate cycle and an important consideration. Real estate can be very difficult to sell and land values do not always rise. This may be the only good opportunity we have to sell this land at a fair price.

Dawson I don't think you quite answered my question. It may be a fair price at today's values but are today's prices high or low?

Short In my opinion, we are getting good value.

Morphy Why did the Church buy this land in the first place?

Harris The Church was worried about protecting the Church surroundings but it's now clear that the present grounds are sufficient to satisfy that requirement.

Morphy There may be another reason for selling the land now. At the present time, churches are considered charitable institutions and as such are not taxable, but the Federal Tax Department is currently reviewing its approach to charitable organizations operating commercial ventures and is suggesting that income from these kinds of ventures be taxed. I know we don't want to pay tax if we don't have to.

Johnson Do you think the Church, as a charitable organization, should even be owning such a highly visible investment like real estate?

Harris An interesting point — and if we did continue to lease the land, I don't think the Church has the expertise to manage a rental property when the building reverts to the Church at the end of the lease.

Short I really believe that selling is the only option.

Kravitz I'd like to get back to these numbers for a minute. Where does Middlesex get their $2 189 000?

Short That figure was based on increasing the net cash flow from rents at 5.5 percent per year and adding three percent of the result to the constant lease payment of $16 800. As far as the 5.5 percent increase is concerned, it's not an acceptable return either, when you consider that we could just plop the $503 000 from selling the land right into a savings account and start making nine percent.

Kravitz How secure is the 5.5 percent compared to the nine percent over the 50 year life of the lease?

Short As I explained earlier, Karen, trying to project 50 years in the future is quite useless.

Kravitz Do you think the land will still have value in 50 years?

Short Well of course, barring any unforeseen disasters.

Kravitz So what you're really saying is that you are sure the land will have value in 50 years but you're not sure whether the money we receive from selling the land will have any value in 50 years.

Short I think you're stretching things a little.

Kravitz Why?

Harris I think what you're both trying to get at here concerns whether we convert a tangible asset, land, into a less tangible asset, paper money. I'm sure everyone here knows that the Church has an annual deficit near $75 000 and the income from our investments has to cover this amount. If we sold the land, part of the proceeds could be used to put the Church back in the black.

Short And the remainder could be invested at a reasonable rate of return; certainly at a higher one than the three percent we're getting now.

Johnson There was a time when the Church would attempt to increase the membership to solve such an operating deficit. After all, we are a Christian organization, not an investment corporation.

Short   But that doesn't mean we should make bad business decisions.

Johnson   No, but it might mean that the business facts have to be weighed in comparison with what the Church is supposed to be accomplishing.

Kravitz   Speaking of investment corporations, Simone, who is going to manage the $503 000 should we decide to sell the land? And are these costs considered in your comparison calculations?

Short   We could easily purchase long-term investment certificates at very little cost.

Kravitz   If all you're going to do is transfer from one long-term investment to another, why not just keep the land?

Short   Because we don't have any control over the price of land and we don't know if we could sell it at the time when we most needed the money. With the investment certificates, we could always get our hands on the money even if there was a small fee.

Kravitz   Apples and apples, Simone.

Dawson   As you all know, I'm from Saint John and used to be a member of the Free Congregational Church. That congregation made the decision to sell its land and now the Church has no place to expand. The Church in Fredericton decided against selling its land and still has a steady income from it today. Those members recommend against selling any land, particularly if it is contiguous with the land on which the church stands.

Short   This isn't the Maritimes, Doc, and besides, the building will have to be torn down at the end of the lease and what good is the land without the building?

Harris   There could be other uses for the land even if the building did have to be torn down. The Church could construct a senior citizens' apartment building for some of our parishioners where they, and others, could enjoy living in the city core adjacent to their Church. This would have an added benefit of providing a ready-made nucleus of an on-going congregation right on our property.

Short   Okay, but what about flexibility? If we sell the land we can not only cover the deficit but invest the remainder in interest bearing securities which offer total flexibility. If we need the money at a later date, we know it is available and we can invest it in different assets depending on expected inflation, stock trends and interest rates. We have to remember that the main consideration in this decision is choosing the option that will give us the best return and secondly, choosing the one with the most flexibility.

Kravitz   Fine, let's get back to deciding which option does provide the best return. Simone, did you happen to calculate the break-even interest rate for the two Middlesex options?

Dawson   What's a break-even interest rate?

Kravitz   Simone can probably explain it, but my husband says its an important number to have.

Short   It's the interest rate at which the $503 000 needs to be invested to equal the cash flows received by the lease option, including any terminal values. I don't have that number but I should be able to run some sort of an IRR on the computer at the office. But I think it's a waste of time and will still show that selling the land is the best option.

Morphy   It sounds like a good number to have.

Harris   I have to agree. By the way Karen, where is Kevin? We could use some of his academic expertise on this matter.

Kravitz   He left for Florida yesterday to get the condominium ready for Christmas.

Short   Those Ivory Tower guys really have it made.

Dawson   Right, Simone. Getting back to this break-even number: if we did have such a number, what would we compare it with to see if we were getting a reasonable return on our money?

Morphy   As Simone mentioned earlier, we could always buy perpetual bonds or very long-term government bonds, so it would seem reasonable to compare the break-even rate with these, since they have a guaranteed income similar to keeping the lease.

Kravitz   I don't think that's quite right, but I'll have to check with Kevin.

Harris   Well, I think we have a good start on the issues behind this decision. I also think that everyone should give the problem some thought between now and the next meeting because it's a little more difficult than any of us thought it would be and we really don't have much time to make the decision. Simone, since you've heard all of tonight's discussion and you're the only one with access to a computer and can calculate that break-even number, I think it's appropriate that you work up the presentation for Sunday's meeting. I suggest you try to give equal weight to both the qualitative and quantitative factors and then recommend a decision. That way the congregation will have all the facts. If you need any help with the draft, I can help you on Saturday afternoon.

Kravitz   I can help on. . . .

Short   Thanks anyway, Harry, but I don't think there'll be any problem.

Morphy   Good, then I move the meeting be adjourned.

NORANDA MINES LIMITED

At the June 1980 meeting of the Board of Directors of Noranda Mines Limited (Noranda), four major capital expenditure proposals were scheduled for discussion. Planned capital expenditures had grown to at least $419 million in 1980 from about $320 million in 1979 as a result of sharply improved financial performance. Generally stronger product prices and a weakening Canadian dollar had contributed to what was considered the first good return overall on net assets since 1974. As a result, $40 to $50 million of new funds were available for commitment at the June meeting.

Return on net assets, however, varied among the various product divisions. These differences, and in particular differences in stability of the earnings levels over time, had prompted several members of the Board to question the current development and use of investment hurdle rates throughout the organization. One concern was whether one corporate wide hurdle rate could be used as a guide in capital budgeting, or whether a separate hurdle rate should be developed for each division or business, in response to estimates of the relative risk of that operation.

Background

Noranda was originally formed in May 1922, strictly as a mining company. Since that time, the company has diversified into metal refining, forest products, manufacturing and oil and gas exploration. Total assets had grown from slightly over $1.0 billion in 1971 to almost $3.5 billion by the end of 1979. Exhibit 1 shows selected financial statistics for Noranda for the years ended 1976 to 1979.

Earnings increased in 1979 to $395 million from $135 million in 1978. Metal prices had strengthened toward the end of 1979 with zinc, silver, gold and copper prices rising well above their 1978 averages. As a result the Mining and Metallurgical Group earnings were substantially higher. Exhibit 2 shows price trends for Noranda's precious and base metal products and the Canadian–U.S. dollar exchange rate.

Earnings were also up in 1979 for the manufacturing operations and while earnings for forest products showed an absolute increase, return on net assets for that division fell in 1979 due to recent large investments in the group. Corporate earnings per share advanced from $1.91 in 1978 to $4.70 in 1979, and dividends per share were raised from $.43 to $.85. Exhibit 3 shows group and corporate financial results for 1972 through 1979. Exhibit 4 provides current market interest rates and selected corporate leverage and risk levels.

The outlook for 1980 was mixed. Some forecasters were anticipating a recession in the U.S., which if it occurred, would clearly affect many of Noranda's products. On the other hand, if demand levels, prices and the Canadian–U.S. dollar exchange rate remained reasonably stable, 1980 could be another very good year.

Capital Expenditure Program

Noranda's fundamental corporate objective had always been to provide satisfactory return on shareholder investment. In the past this had been achieved with an aggressive growth strategy through expansion, new development and acquisitions. About 37 percent of the record 1979 capital budget was spent on environment control, asset replacement and maintenance. Total expenditures for 1980 in this area were not expected to decrease. As a result, the demand for funds was high by historical standards and new proposals were being screened more carefully. In a major policy speech in 1979, the Chairman of the Board had emphasized the need to continue to improve productivity and efficiency by focusing capital spending on improving cost effectiveness of existing operations.

Performance during the 1970s had fallen short of the explicit target, set in 1972, of 11 percent real annual growth in EPS. Given target leverage levels, corporate staff had estimated that with 7 percent inflation, the 11 percent target would require a minimum nominal dollar after tax return on gross assets employed in existing operations of 10 percent. The return on gross assets calculation was based cash flow as opposed to accounting profit, and was as follows:

$$\frac{\text{after tax cash flow from operations}}{\text{total assets less current liabilities excluding current debt}}$$

For new investment, the corporate wide hurdle rate was 15 percent after tax on a discounted cash flow basis, with project returns measured in nominal (current) dollars. Because inflation in early 1980 was running at about 12 percent, many Noranda managers expected the required rate on new projects would soon be increased to perhaps 20 percent for project returns measured in nominal dollars. Project reviews included a careful strategic assessment as well as the ROI hurdles suggested above, but managers were aware that approval for their projects would be much more easily achieved if hurdle rates were met and preferably substantially exceeded.

Processing Capital Expenditure Requests

Capital expenditures at Noranda were controlled at three different levels: 1) manager of the profit or cost center; 2) Toronto senior management or the operations Board of Directors; 3) the Noranda Board of Directors. The annual operating plan forecast the magnitude of capital spending but each capital expenditure required an Appropriation Request (AR) and appropriate justification. Projects less than $100,000 required approval at the plant, mine or area manager level; projects costing between $100,000 and $200,000 required approval at the senior management level of the division or wholly owned subsidiary; projects between $200,000 and $1,000,000 required approval by the president, senior VP, Board of Directors of the subsidiary or Noranda operating committee, and projects in excess of $1,000,000 required Noranda Board of Directors approval. Some projects costing less than $1,000,000 would require Noranda Board approval if they involved entering new businesses.

Appropriate justification varied depending on the complexity of the project but was to include at least the following:

(a) (i) purpose of expenditure
  (ii) the present situation
  (iii) expected results
  (iv) projected consequences if the project was not approved
  (v) alternative courses considered and reasons for rejection

(b) (i) details of revenues and costs
  (ii) discounted cash flow rate of return
  (iii) refined (modified) internal rate of return on projects if early cash inflows substantially exceeded later cash inflows
  (iv) payback period

(c) (i) any supporting technical drawings, sketches, specifications or other material that would assist in the understanding and assessment of the proposal

The four projects being reviewed at the current Board meeting had gone through all required channels and were submitted with the required documentation. The projects were:

(1) extension of a current mine shaft to access deeper ore at the Rendell Mine in Schreiber, Ontario;
(2) purchase and installation of a continuous casting mill at Canadian Wire and Cable's Montreal location;

(3) acquisition of the Thorold Division of Abitibi-Price at Thorold, Ontario;
(4) development of the Gray Eagle Gold mine property in Happy Camp, California.

Mine Shaft Extension, Rendell Mine

Rendell Mine began the open pit mining of its Schreiber, Ontario location in 1967. In 1977, reserves from the open pit mine were projected to be fully depleted by 1980. As a result, funding for exploratory drilling was approved and in 1978, preparations began for a sub-pit mine with production expected to commence in 1980. As the sub-pit mine preparation continued, it became clear that although original estimates of quality and ore reserves had been underestimated, costs had risen much faster than expected to a point where the sub-pit mine was barely economic. Rendell management had therefore requested an additional $17,906,000 for development of a deep mine and related facilities which would not only provide access to more ore and exploratory area but would reduce the cost of raising ore from the sub-pit mine by about $1.90 per ton.

Estimation errors, as described above, were not uncommon in the mining industry. The discovery, extraction, processing and marketing of minerals all involved a high degree of risk. Mineral deposits were generally difficult to assess from the surface and further development underground, involving significant expenditures, could show discoveries to be uneconomic. Generally, it was necessary to commit substantial amounts of capital on the basis of very limited information as to the extent and grade of ore available and with the knowledge that the forecasts of total capital costs were frequently unreliable because of unexpectedly adverse water or rock conditions and more recently, high rates of inflation. Estimating revenues only increased the difficulties since revenue projections required the forecast of metal prices, which were almost impossible to calculate given the international forces acting on metal commodities. Historically metal prices had fluctuated over wide ranges.

The deep ore had been found using exploratory drilling and was estimated to extend from 900 to 1500 feet with a strike length of 500 feet and a maximum width of 150 feet. Assuming the exploratory drilling as representative, company geologists estimated the ore body would contain 1.745 million tons of ore grading 9.19 percent zinc (Zn), 0.25 percent copper (Cu), 0.85 percent lead (Pb) and 1.89 ounces per ton (opt) of silver (Ag). (One ton = 2,000 lb.) At historical recovery and dilution rates, a final recovery of 1,727,550 tons with a grading of 7.35 percent Zn, .19 percent Cu., .37 percent Pb, and 1.22 opt of Ag was expected. Net smelter return varied depending on supply and demand of refining capacity but at the present time refining costs, freight costs, etc., totalled about 62 percent of total revenue for Zn, 42 percent for Cu, 81 percent for Pb and 9 percent for

Ag. Based on these smelter costs and on current (June 1980) metal prices, the income per ton (net smelter return) of ore would be $51.15 Canadian. The prices used in this forecast were, in U.S. dollars per pound of metal, Zn $.34, Cu $1.00 and Pb $.42. The silver price was forecast at US $20.00 per oz. and the Canadian–U.S. dollar exchange rate was assumed to be $0.86 U.S. per $Canadian.

Rendell management had hired a consultant to determine the most cost effective way to reach the deep ore and three possible alternatives were considered: 1) a 1900 foot vertical shaft from the surface; 2) an internal shaft tying in with an existing conveyor; and 3) extending one of the present sub-pit declines at a 15 percent gradient, requiring 5800 feet to reach the 1500 foot level. The vertical shaft was calculated to be the most cost effective and the following production rates were forecast:

PRODUCTION
(000 Tons)

	Open Pit	Sub Pit	Deep Ore	Total Via New Shaft
1980	852	—	—	—
1981	296	339	—	—
1982	—	339	—	—
1983	—	339	200	510*
1984	—	339	339	678
1985	—	339	339	678
1986	—	339	339	678
1987	—	339	339	678
1988	—	264	172	436
TOTAL	1148	2637	1728	3658

*Total of 200 deep ore and 310 sub-pit.

Capital expenditures of $.512, $3.47 and $7.21 million were forecast for the years 1980 to 1982, together with preproduction and development costs of $.750, $3.3, $4.689 and $1.850 million annually, also starting in 1980. Ongoing capital expenditures would be required from 1984 through 1987 of $.2 million in addition to a one time expenditure of $.25 million in 1984 for processing equipment. Operating costs were estimated at $20.00 per ton using historical and other data from recently opened mines in the area. Unless more ore was discovered, both mines would close at the end of 1988 with no salvage value. Rendell was in a taxable position and the deep pit mine would qualify as a major expansion meaning that preproduction and development expenditures would be eligible for earned depletion and unde-preciated assets would be eligible for accelerated depreciation (up to income after production commenced).

Based on the assumed prices, costs and production levels, the net cash taxes would be as follows, in $(000). Cash flows for 80–82 are tax credits (inflows).

	80	81	82	83	84	85	86	87	88
Ontario Mining Tax	181	889	1609	(343)	(1461)	(1755)	(1867)	(1864)	(938)
Ontario Income Tax	12	93	239	—	(833)	(959)	(958)	(957)	(474)
Federal Income Tax	78	557	1312	—	(2010)	(2337)	(2334)	(2332)	(1164)
TOTAL TAX	271	1539	3160	(343)	(4304)	(5051)	(5159)	(5153)	(2576)

Continuous Casting Mill

Canada Wire and Cable Company (CWC) was a wholly owned subsidiary of Noranda engaged in the manufacture of a variety of copper based products including copper rod. Its wire bar mill, which converted copper bar to rod, was built in Montreal in 1930 and had been consistently modified and upgraded over the years to improve quality and production. However, new technologies had developed in the last two decades that could further reduce costs by producing rod directly from cathode copper, eliminating the intermediate step of producing copper wire bar.

The new mills, called continuous casting mills, emerged in the early 1960s and required cathode instead of wire bar as an input for rod production. The cathode copper could be supplied directly from the copper refiner. Because these mills produced higher quality, lower cost and longer length wire when compared to wire bar technology, continuous casting mills had already captured over 50 percent of the world's rod market and it was projected that this figure would increase to a point where wire bar mills were obsolete.

The rolling costs of the continuous casting mill were estimated to be $4.00 per ton less than wire bar mills and this difference was expected to increase at the rate of inflation, currently estimated at 8 percent per year. Current cathode costs were $12.50 per ton less than wire bar (wire bar premium was $12.50) but Phelps Dodge, the largest copper rod manufacturer in the world, had been artificially holding down the price of wire bar in order to protect its investment in conventional mills. Since Phelps Dodge had recently announced that it had contracted for a large continuous casting mill to be operational by 1981 and plans for two additional mills operational at later dates, the wire bar premium was expected to rise to as much as $35.00 per ton by 1983. The Europeans had already announced a premium of $28.00/ton beginning in 1981. Canadian Copper Refiners (CCR), the wholly owned subsidiary of Noranda that produced both cathode copper and wire bar, currently estimated the conversion cost of cathode into wire bar at about $20 per ton. CWC's total requirements for wire bar in 1979 were 73,000 tons, of which 936 tons were produced from shaving scrap,

3,325 tons from No. 1 scrap and 18,100 tons from conversion, leaving 50,639 tons required for purchase from CCR. These figures would suggest that $2.1 million could be saved in 1983 alone ($4 on 73,000 tons and $35 on 50,639 tons) if the continuous casting mill was operational at that time, assuming no volume growth from 1979 to 1983. Mill tonnage had been growing at about 4 percent per year.

Not only were the costs lower but the higher quality rod produced from continuous casting mills also translated directly into savings. Rod produced using conventional technology for use as magnetic wire needed to be shaved before enameling. This shaving would not be required with the continuous casting mills. As noted above, shaving scrap from magnetic wire volumes had been running at about 936 tons per year. The shavings were shipped to CCR, for remelting and reprocessing into wire bar, at a total cost to CWC of $173.60 per ton. In addition, two men at $30,000 each were required to handle the shavings, and container costs were estimated at about $20,000 per year on 1979 volumes. All these costs were expected to rise with inflation.

Other savings were also expected. Wire used for communications products was drawn and extruded at 5,000 to 6,000 feet per minute. This high speed caused poor quality rod to break creating equipment downtime and unnecessary scrap. The higher quality rod produced from continuous casting would decrease this downtime and scrap production considerably. These savings were too difficult to quantify but were still considered important. Further, it was projected that as new technologies continued to replace the old, future machines would be capable of even higher speeds. Conventional rod would severely restrict CWC's ability to take advantage of these expected innovations.

All No. 1 scrap from the wire bar mill was returned to CCR for recasting. Scrap of this type could be fed directly into a continuous casting furnace. However, with the new mill and the use of cathode copper the casting operation would be eliminated entirely at CCR, which would produce the savings already suggested on new stock, but also about $20/ton for the No. 1 scrap and $170/ton for conversion of scale scrap from the casting process itself. In 1979 there were about 3300 tons of No. 1 scrap produced and 300 tons of scale scrap. Finally, between CCR and CWC, perhaps $3.9 million of inventory could be eliminated in the year the new mill became operational.

Continuous casting mills produced longer length coils than wire bar mills. The shorter coils required 2 welders at the high speed and heavy drawing machines to weld the shorter coils together. The longer coils would require only one welder for an additional savings of $40,000 per year.

Without the higher quality continuous cast rod, CWC management believed there was little doubt that current annual exports of 12,800 tons would decline. The decline was estimated to begin in 1983 with a loss of 25 percent of export volumes, increasing to a loss of 75 percent of current volume by 1991. If the continuous casting mill was approved, not only would the exports to current customers remain at the current percent of mill production, but as the mill was the first of its type in Canada, it was likely that customers who had not previously purchased from CWC would switch to the higher quality, lower cost rod. Marginal profit (contribution) from export business had been running at about $120/ton. Actual annual export lost sales, for years 1983 through 1992 were forecast, in tons, as 3,000, 4,300, 5,300, 6,300, 7,300, 8,200, 9,000, 9,700, 9,700 and 9,700.

Based on these assumptions and projections, the total increase in before tax cash flows would be as follows:

COST SAVINGS
($000)

Year	Rolling Cost	Raw Materials	Shaving Recovery	#1 Scrap	Scale	Shaving & Welder Salaries	Export Sales Retained	Total Increase Before Tax Cash Flows
1983*	$328	$1139	$183	$74	$57	$100	$360	$2241
1984	342	1185	190	77	60	100	516	2470
1985	355	1232	198	80	62	100	636	2663
1986	369	1281	206	84	65	100	756	2861
1987	384	1333	214	87	67	100	876	3061
1988	400	1386	222	90	70	100	984	3252
1989	416	1442	231	94	73	100	1080	3436
1990	432	1499	241	98	75	100	1164	3609
1991	450	1559	250	102	79	100	1164	3704
1992	468	1621	260	106	82	100	1164	3801

*1983 cash flow estimates are as follows:
– volume increase is assumed to be 4 percent per year, however inflation has not been factored in.
Rolling Cost = Tons produced × $4.00 per ton: tons produced = 73,000 $(1.04)^t$ when t = 1 in 1981 and increases annually.
Raw Materials = Tons purchased × $20.00 per ton: tons purchased = 50,639 $(1.04)^t$
Shaving Recovery = Tons of shavings processed × $173.60 per ton: tons of shavings = 936 $(1.04)^t$
Scrap = Tons of #1 scrap × $20.00: tons of #1 scrap = 3300 $(1.04)^t$
Scale = Tons of scale × $170.00: tons of scale = 300 $(1.04)^t$
Salaries = shaving $60.00 + welder $40.00
Sales Retained = Tons of sales retained × $120.00 per ton.

CWC management considered three possible scenarios for the new mill: 1) build a 150,000 tons per year (TPY) mill with 40 percent equity participation by another major wire rod producer, 2) build a 150,000 TPY mill and contract to sell the excess supply to another producer at $25.00 per ton above cost, or 3) build a 100,000 TPY mill. The 150,000 TPY mill was most desirable if only from an economies of scale standpoint since the capital costs were estimated at $200/ton for a 100,000 TPY mill and $153/ton for the 150,000 TPY mill. If the smaller mill were approved, one of the other three major manufacturers could easily contract to sell excess supply and build the larger mill, undercutting CWC's prices. Option 1 was considered the most desirable.

The mill would cost about $24 million and become operational at the beginning of 1983. Start-up costs, which could be expensed, would be $1 million in 1981 and $0.5 million in 1982. Capital costs for the 150,000 TPY mill were projected as follows:

	1980	1981	1982
Mill, Furnace, Licence	3 617	3 617	4 822
Shaft Furnace, Elevator	—	2 172	—
Building	—	2 500	—
Spare Parts	—	900	—
Installation	—	—	3 000
Installation Supervision	—	—	640
Auxiliary Equipment	—	—	1 688

Capital cost allowance would be 5 percent on the building and 50 percent on remaining capital costs, half rate first year starting in 1981. The 5 percent class was declining balance and the 50 percent class was straight line. CWC's tax rate was 40 percent. For planning purposes, the mill would not have any salvage value at the end of the planning period in 1992.

Paper Mill Acquisition

Fraser Inc., a wholly owned subsidiary of Noranda, had submitted a request for approval of a $32 million ($25 for assets, $7 for working capital) purchase of a paper mill, located on 15 acres of land near Thorold, Ontario. The mill which was currently owned and operated by Abitibi-Price, was well positioned for supply of waste paper which, when available, was a low cost raw material. The mill had a 100 acre dump site nearby to assist in control of undesirable production byproducts.

The Thorold mill produced specialty coated and uncoated papers from four paper machines with a combined capacity of 100,000 tons per year (TPY) of which 25,000 TPY was coated production. The plant provided an excellent opportunity to gain experience in the use of recycled fibres for certain printing and writing papers. Recycled fibres were expected to become an increasingly important fibre source in the future. The mill's products were suitable for use in the business forms and reprographic markets; these markets were expected to increase as tariffs were reduced between Canada and the United States. Reduction of Canadian tariffs would provide increased competition in Canada but reduction of the U.S. rates would provide substantial opportunities given a favourable exchange rate.

Fraser management believed that purchase of the mill was the most cost effective way of entering this type of specialty market. A new mill could not be purchased or constructed because it would include new paper machines that were both wide and fast, and not well suited to specialty paper production. Further, if the Thorold mill were purchased, the product mix could be changed to include more high margin products. This change would be accomplished by transferring products from other Fraser mills more suitable to the Thorold mill's equipment and replacing the transferred products with higher margin products for an overall increase in profits about $15.00 per ton on transferred volume. Fraser management believed that about 5,300 tons could be transferred in 1981, increasing to 14,700 tons in 1982 and to 18,000 tons by 1984.

Purchase of the Thorold plant would include an established customer base and it was expected that the senior operations manager as well as the senior sales manager and at least five other senior sales representatives would be willing to remain with Fraser after the acquisition. The sales people would be moved to Fraser's boxboard sales offices in Toronto and Montreal, with an expectation that fine paper and boxboard sales would be combined at a later date to increase area covered and reduce sales costs.

In 1979, the Thorold mill purchased less than 3,200 tons of hardwood bisulfide from Noranda pulp mills. Although it was of little consequence to Fraser, if the Thorold plant was acquired, Thorold could purchase all of its pulp from Noranda mills, starting with an incremental volume of 1,200 tons in 1980 and increasing to 4,800, 7,200, 20,000 and 22,000 tons from 1981 to 1984 respectively. Noranda management estimated the average profit before tax on a ton of hardwood bisulfide was $50.00.

Since 1977, $17 million in capital expenditures had been spent on the plant with most of the funds being allocated as follows:

(1) rebuilding of the No. 4 paper machine and on-line coater, which was expected to be out of the start-up phase and into full production by the time of purchase. Some start-up problems had been experienced.

(2) purchase of a new 8½″ by 11″ cutsize sheet facility

(3) purchase of a facility for biological treatment of effluent to bring the mill into compliance with environmental standards. The facility was working properly but the mill was still below compliance.

Two other machines were in adequate condition with another currently idle. Additional capital expenditures would be required to increase efficiency of production and were projected at $1.6, $1.6, $3.65, $3.65, $4.7 million starting in 1980 and remaining at the $2 million level after 1984.

Several areas of the mill were labour intensive and although a new contract had recently been negotiated, salaries and wages had been settled as if the plant were part of a non-integrated operation selling to the domestic market. This would not be the case after the Fraser acquisition. Domtar, another major paper producer in the area had settled for lower wage costs more in line with the economics of the paper industry but not without a six month strike. It was therefore possible that Fraser could expect difficult negotiations in the future if labour costs were to be brought into line with Domtar's. However, the labour intense areas of the mill did provide an opportunity for Fraser to reduce operating costs and increase efficiency through mechanization.

Fraser management used a $10\frac{1}{2}$ year planning horizon for its ROI projections beginning with the six months ended December 31, 1980. Even though the customer base was already established, projections were still difficult given the sporadic earnings of the past. A $2.35 million loss in 1975, caused by a lengthy labour dispute was followed by mediocre profits of $865 thousand in 1976. The 1977 operating year produced the very large profit of $5.42 million as paper prices strongly outpaced pulp prices and the mill moved to a seven day work week in the last quarter. Profits then declined in 1978 when a tight pulp market caused increased prices and the necessity of accepting low quality pulp when a major supplier shut down for a portion of the year. The mill was struck again in 1979 and the No. 4 paper mill was shut down for rebuilding creating a $3.6 million loss. The first half of 1980 showed a loss of $130 thousand, mostly because of start up problems with the No. 4 paper mill and continued weak markets. The current owner had projected second half EBIT of $1.5 million, assuming No. 4's problems were cleared up. Given the difficulty of forecasting, Fraser management had only calculated revenue and costs for the first five and one half years of production starting with the six months ended December 1980. Forecasts beyond this point were left at 1984 levels except for capital cost allowance (CCA) and taxes which are shown below. All figures are in $(000).

Year	CCA*	Cash Taxes**	Interest
1980	410	nil	1 800
1981	860	nil	3 600
1982	1 030	nil	3 190
1983	1 260	(1 880)	3 190
1984	1 520	(3 760)	3 190
1985	1 730	3 100	2 340
1986	1 850	3 010	2 340
1987	1 980	3 010	2 340
1988	2 100	680	2 340
1989	2 230	940	2 340
1990	2 350	380	2 340

* CCA based on projected capital expenditures.
** Cash taxes based on combined Fraser-Thorold CCA and investment tax credits (ITCs). If Thorold's earnings were less than expected, the company would not be able to take advantage of some ITCs and cash taxes would increase.

Gross profits (before interest and CCA expense) were forecast to increase from 7 percent of sales in 1980 to 12.5 percent of sales by 1984 and annual sales were projected to remain at the 94,000 TPY level through 1982, increasing slightly to 95,700 TPY in 1983 and to 98,700 TPY in 1984–91. Average selling price for the mill's products had been fluctuating around $1,000 per ton since the beginning of the year, and for planning purposes was assumed to remain at that level. Incremental selling and corporate expenses were also projected to increase gradually to 1984 increasing from .74 percent to .92 percent of sales for selling expense and from .42 percent to .57 percent of sales for corporate expenses. Working capital additions were required by production volume and sales revenue changes and were expected to be $7 million in 1980, constant at $1.85 million per year from 1981 through 1984, and nil following 1984. Salvage value of the plant would be about $25 million in 1991.

The revenue and cost estimates given above can be summarized as follows:

	Year	Sales $(000)	Gross Profit	Selling Expense	Corporate Expense
				(percent of sales)	
July–Dec.	1980	47 000	7.00	.740	.420
	1981	94 000	8.40	.785	.458
	1982	94 000	9.75	.830	.495
	1983	95 700	11.14	.875	.534
	1984–90	98 700	12.50	.920	.570

Gray Eagle Gold Mine

Noranda had purchased the rights to mine the Gray Eagle property from Siskin Ltd. in 1977 for a royalty of 7.5 percent of gross metal revenues. The mine was located eight miles north of Happy Camp in Siskiyou County, California. The area was served by a paved air strip for private aircraft with the nearest commercial air transportation available at Medford, Oregon, approximately 110 miles by road from the site. Rail transportation was available at Yreka, about 70 miles from the mine.

Gray Eagle management had requested $26,077,000, the amount necessary to put the mine into production at a rate of 80,000 tons per year (TPY) in 1982 and 180,000 TPY subsequently until the estimated ore body was exhausted in 1987. Approximately 44 percent of the total open pit waste would be stripped and placed at a dam site in the south fork of Luther Gulch and waste removal was being accelerated during preproduction in order for the tailings dam to be built in accordance with Federal and State specifications. The mine would utilize a carbon-in-pulp process and have smelting facilities on site to produce a combined gold/silver (dore) metal for sale to a refinery. Ancillary facilities at the site would include water supply, waste water treatment and disposal, service shops, warehousing, change facilities and engineering and administrative offices.

Detailed engineering completed over the past two years had proven 973,000 tons of mineable ore with an average (after dilution) grade of .178 ounces per ton (opt) of gold and .542 opt of silver. Based on historical recovery rates in the area, 90 percent of the gold and 80 percent of the silver could be recovered.

Total operating costs would vary with the stripping ratio but would average $22.59 per ton of ore. Total staff at full production would be 12 salaried and 49 hourly employees. Preproduction and development costs had already amounted to $260,000 with projected expenditures of $6.521 million in 1981 and $4.986 million in 1982. Major capital expenditures were forecast at $8.125 million and $4.375 million in 1981 and 1982 respectively. Ongoing capital expenditures were expected to be $125,000 per year 1983–1986 and property acquisition costs would be $800,000 spread evenly over 4 years starting in 1980. Property acquisition costs were neither depreciated nor expensed. Working capital, that could be recovered at mine closure, was projected at $1 million in 1981. All depreciation for tax purposes would be deferred to the first or later years of production with preproduction and development costs being depreciated straight line over the six years of production and major and ongoing capital expenditures depreciated on a declining balance basis changing to straight line in the most advantageous year. Depletion expense would vary with projected net income but was expected to average 36.6 percent of income after depreciation expense but before tax over the life of the project. State and Federal taxes would be 9.5 percent and 41.5 percent of income before tax respectively, with an investment tax credit of $41,000 in 1981 and $792,000 in 1982 available to reduce the Federal tax in those years. Gray Eagle had prepaid $220,000 of the first year's royalties to Siskin in anticipation of 1982 production of 80,000 tons. Gold and silver prices were expected to move with inflation, so the 1980 gold price of $620 per ounce and silver price of $20.00 per ounce were used as price estimates for the entire planning period. All dollars are U.S. dollars.

EXHIBIT 1
NORANDA MINES LIMITED

Selected Financial Statistics
for the years ended December 31
($millions)

	1979	1978	1977	1976
Income Statement				
Net Sales	$2 484.7	$1 691.1	$1 386.5	$1 232.4
Operating Income	770.6	347.2	215.3	184.5
Depr., Depl., & Amort.	96.7	82.1	83.1	70.2
Interest[1]	65.3	64.8	71.9	61.7
Pre Tax Income	694.4	260.2	102.5	81.9
Net Income	410.2	145.0	67.2	46.7
Cash Flow	564.4	203.3	129.3	73.8
Capital Expenditures	284.9	115.1	119.6	115.6
Balance Sheet				
Cash & Equivalent	25.4	17.7	36.3	89.9
Current Assets	1 488.8	882.7	751.9	750.1
Gross Plant & Equipment	2 329.9	1 810.1	1 667.1	1 564.7
Net Plant & Equipment	1 407.4	1 065.9	998.4	954.9
Total Assets	3 320.2	2 374.8	2 152.9	2 092.7
Bank Advances	170.3	133.6	206.1	164.2
Current Portion LTD	45.2	65.1	99.3	103.7
Current Liabilities	801.4	601.1	588.6	559.3
Long Term Debt (LTD)	602.6	604.1	588.9	603.4
Capital Stock	512.3	109.5	85.4	86.3
Retained Earnings	1 113.5	789.4	680.8	636.9
Debt/Common Equity[2]	0.37	0.67	0.79	0.83
Interest Coverage	11.64	5.01	2.43	2.33
Return on Common Equity	30.35	16.42	8.60	6.21
EPS as Reported	4.89	1.89	0.95	0.66
Share Price — High	22.88	13.00	11.46	13.25
— Low	12.13	6.88	6.54	8.79

Case 19
Noranda
Mines Limited

[1] In 1979 bank loan interest rates had averaged about 12 percent, and 1979 bank interest charges were about $20 million. Coupon rates on long term debt outstanding averaged about 7 percent and average maturity was about four years. Current long term debt coupons (new issues) would be about 13 percent.
[2] In June, 1980, the target long term debt to common equity ratio was 0.50. The beta for Noranda was estimated at 1.4, and the tax rate was about 42 percent.

Source: Financial Post Investment Data bank

EXHIBIT 2
NORANDA MINES LIMITED

Past and Forecast Metal Prices and Exchange Rates
(US$)

		Copper ($/lb)	Zinc ($/lb)	Lead ($/lb)	Gold ($/oz)	Silver ($/oz)	$U.S./ $CDN.
1976		0.64	0.32	0.20	125	4.35	1.014
1977		0.60	0.27	0.28	198	4.62	0.940
1978		0.62	0.27	0.30	193	5.40	0.887
1979	1st Q	0.86	0.35	0.49	238	7.04	0.843
	2nd Q	0.89	0.36	0.57	258	8.13	0.864
	3rd Q	0.89	0.32	0.56	318	10.81	0.857
	4th Q	0.96	0.33	0.56	415	18.39	0.851
	Year	0.90	0.34	0.55	308	11.10	0.854
1980	1st Q	1.18	0.36	0.52	632	32.47	0.859
	2nd Q	0.93	0.31	0.38	544	14.26	0.860
Est. Year 1980		1.00	0.34	0.42	620	20.00	0.860
Est.	1981	1.10	0.35	0.40	400	15.00	0.880
Est.	1982	1.10	0.34	0.45	450	11.00	0.850
Est.	1983	1.30	0.40	0.45	500	12.00	0.850

EXHIBIT 3
NORANDA MINES LIMITED

Summary of Financial Performance
($millions except per share data and returns)

	72	73	74	75	76	77	78	79
Mining & Metallurgy								
Earnings[1]	62	91	128	53	58	49	83	292
Net Assets	580	643	774	963	994	1008	941	1420
Return on N.A. %	10.7	14.2	16.5	5.5	5.8	4.9	8.8	20.6
Manufacturing								
Earnings[1]	10	19	38	20	8	35	21	69
Net Assets	270	282	378	510	498	503	595	660
Return on N.A. %	3.7	6.7	10.1	3.9	1.6	7.0	3.5	10.5
Forest Products								
Earnings[1]	11	16	12	11	17	36	61	69
Net Assets	106	112	147	138	196	241	258	380
Returns on N.A. %	10.4	14.3	8.2	8.0	8.7	14.9	23.6	18.2
Noranda Consolidated								
Earnings After Tax	69	122	155	50	47	72	135	395
Earnings Per Share	.98	1.72	2.20	.71	.66	1.01	1.91	4.70
Dividends Per Share	.40	.47	.60	.67	.40	.40	.43	.85
Price Per Share Dec. 31	13⅞	16¾	9½	9¾	9¾	8¼	12¼	22⅜
Selected Market Data[2]								
Equity Returns[2] %	27.0	−2.7	−27.2	22.6	11.5	14.0	29.2	51.5
Treasury Bills, 3 mos., %	3.4	4.8	7.7	7.1	9.1	7.6	7.9	11.1
Inflation, C.P.I., %	5.1	9.3	12.3	9.5	5.9	9.5	8.4	9.8

[1] Earnings before interest charges and income tax.
[2] All returns are on an annual basis. Equity returns are sum of dividend yield and capital gain, and are those of an index of 783 Canadian listed common stocks, value weighted. The longer term average real equity return premium over treasury bills had been 8.4%.

Source: Hatch, J. E. and R. W. White. *Canadian Stocks, Bonds, Bills, and Inflation: 1950–1983*, The Financial Analysis Research Foundation, 1985.

EXHIBIT 4
NORANDA MINES LIMITED

Financial Information as of June 1980

Market Yields

Government of Canada	
Treasury Bills – 90 days	10.38
Bonds 1 – 3 Years	10.48
Bonds 3 – 5 Years	10.48
Bonds 5 – 10 Years	10.74
Bond > 10 Years	11.29

Corporates	
MYW average over 10 years	12.15
Bank Prime	13.25
Yield on Noranda's outstanding bonds	12.35

Stock Prices

Noranda Mines Limited	$25½

Stock Data	Beta	$\dfrac{\text{Debt}}{\text{Debt + Equity}}$
Noranda Mines Limited	1.48	.33
Public companies with business activities as follows:		
(i) *Zinc, Lead, Copper, Silver, Mining*		
Brunswick Mining & Smelting Corp.	1.38	.35
(ii) *Cable*		
Philips Cables Ltd.	.64	.03
(iii) *Paper Products*		
Fraser Inc.	.63	.39
(iv) *Gold Producers*		
LAC Minerals Ltd.	.95	.04

PART SIX

Dividend Policy

FINNING TRACTOR AND EQUIPMENT COMPANY LTD.

In mid July, 1982, Vinod K. Sood, President and Chief Operating Officer of Finning Tractor and Equipment Company Ltd. (Finning), was preparing a presentation on dividend policy for the Board of Directors meeting later that week. Two months earlier, because of the depressed economic conditions and poor company earnings, he had postponed the declaration of the second quarter dividend, usually announced in mid-May and paid in early June, until after he had had a chance to analyze the second quarter results. The restraint measures instigated over the past several months had done little to restore profitability and the second quarter earnings received by Sood the previous day confirmed that the company faced ongoing financial problems. Sood's task was to present a comprehensive financial plan to the Board, one important aspect of which concerned dividend policy. The Board would have to approve any change in dividend.

Background

Finning was North America's largest distributor of Caterpillar equipment, and as such sold, leased, rented and serviced a wide variety of Caterpillar products through its 23 branches, 9 depots and 19 residences as shown in Exhibit 1. The branches provided full service, parts and service facilities, depots provided service and limited parts supplies and residences had one or more field service representatives who serviced equipment at nearby customer locations. Some examples of Caterpillar equipment handled by Finning were track type tractors, pipelayers, motor graders, wheel dozers, wheel tractor-scrapers, hydraulic excavators, lift trucks, off-highway trucks, truck, marine, and industrial engines and electric power generating equipment.

The Caterpillar dealership was not Finning's only source of revenue. Finning also held dealership agreements for several other products with companies including Gardner Denver air equipment, JLG and Smith Tool aerial work platforms, Perkins diesel engines, Grove hydraulic cranes, RayGo-

Wagner log stackers, JCB hydraulic excavators and backhoes, DJB Engineering off-highway trucks and Driltech rotary drills.

Finning extended financing to its customers with leases and conditional sales contracts. Leases were generally operating leases with payments based on a residual value that was Finning's best estimate of the market value of the equipment at the end of the lease term. Financing periods ranged from a few months to seven years, but two to four years was most common. The company could compete successfully with other financing institutions because of its expertise in estimating residual values and its access to Finning Tractor's refurbishing facilities and used equipment market. Finning financed about one-third of its total sales.

205

Case 20
Finning
Tractor and
Equipment
Company Ltd.

Company History

Finning was incorporated under the laws of British Columbia in 1933 and converted to a public company in September, 1969. Considered a growth company by the management, Finning embarked on a series of expansion and acquisition projects beginning with the acquisition of G.M. Philpott Co. Ltd. (air compressors, rock drills, etc.) in 1971. Any acquisitions were meant to complement the Caterpillar line of products and to achieve a degree of market diversification. The Philpott purchase was followed in 1976 by the acquisition of part of the Northern Commercial Company Ltd., through which Finning became the Caterpillar dealer in the Yukon Territories in 1977 by the investment of $2.5 million in Dome Petroleum's Beaufort Sea project for .5 percent participation in net earnings, the purchase of Philpott Close Equipment Co. of Seattle/Spokane in 1979, Portland/Springfield in 1980, Percival Machinery and Supply in 1981 and, as of June, 1982, the agreement in principle to acquire Bowmaker (Plant) Limited, the Caterpillar dealership for southwest England and Wales.

Exhibit 2 shows that sales, profits and stock price had grown at impressive rates through 1980. In mid 1980, analysts considered Finning stock underpriced and were recommending it as a best buy. Dividends had grown from $.025 per share annually (adjusted for splits), paid quarterly starting in May, 1970, to $.30, in March, 1980. The stock had split three times since 1969, first in 1972, then in April of 1980 and 1981. Exhibits 3 and 4 show income statements and balance sheets for the years ended 1977 to 1981.

In January 1981, the Series A preferreds were issued to employees as part of a profit sharing plan. The preferreds were convertible into voting shares after January 27, 1983 and before January 28, 1991, at $18.40 per share. They paid a dividend of one half the prime rate plus one half percent per annum ((Prime Rate/2) + .5%), effectively giving those employees that borrowed to purchase the stock no after tax carrying costs.

In May, the common shares were reclassified into class A voting and class B non-voting shares in preparation for the June issue of $65 000 000,

11 1/2 percent convertible debentures. The debentures were convertible into class B shares so that even after conversion the two majority shareholders would maintain their 70 percent voting control of the company.

In July, Canada's financial press was still publishing articles suggesting that British Columbia's economy was expanding, but Finning was showing signs of an approaching downturn. With the majority of its revenues resource based, 45 percent from forestry, 30 percent from mining and 15 percent from construction, Finning was considered an indicator of B.C.'s economic activity. Sales appeared to continue to climb in 1981 but, adjusted for inflation, they had actually declined. Units sold, total revenue hours and parts sold were all down from 1980. Second and third quarter profits showed a decline that continued into 1982. Exhibits 5 through 8 present the four quarterly reports for 1980 and 1981 and the two quarterly reports for 1982.

In October when Sood, previously executive vice president, replaced the retiring John Frazee as President and Chief Operating Officer, several restraint measures had already been instigated. New equipment inventories had been cut by $50 million and additional cuts were expected. By year end, employment had been cut by 24 percent from its high of 2400 in February, 1981. Sood, an advocate of active management, believed that the major costs for Finning Tractor were wages and interest and both could be managed so that the equity of the company would be protected throughout recession.

By the end of 1981 the recession had settled in. U.S. housing starts had declined from a seasonally adjusted annual rate of 1.66 million in January 1981, to a low of 863 000 in November. U.S. lumber shipments fell from 2813 million board feet to 1637 million board feet over the two year period beginning in January 1979. Copper prices, based on closing prices of May copper futures, dropped 42 percent over the 1981 year. Similar declines could be found in most resource based areas. It was barely a profitable year for Finning. Bad debts had increased from an average of 0.25 percent of sales prior to 1981 to a staggering 1.5 percent of sales. Interest expense had increased 61 percent from 1980, but with all of the bad news, Finning still had a backlog of orders. Even so, when the 1982 forecast of $550 million in sales was presented, Sood knew it was unattainable.

In January of 1982, Sood requested that market inequities in salaries be removed and the majority of the employees received raises. This was a very unusual move considering that most other companies were either freezing or rolling back wages. He did reserve the right to return to the employees should the economy deteriorate to a point where alternate salary proposals would be necessary, but Sood strongly believed that salary cuts were very bad for morale and should be avoided if at all possible. The quarterly dividend of $.075 was declared as usual for March, 1982. Both of these decisions helped dispel false rumours that Finning was on the edge of bankruptcy and would soon begin to close down some of its branches. These rumours had reached many of Finning's branches and newspapers such as the Prince George Citizen had called for verification on the closures. The revaluation downward of the secured and convertible debt to BB and B from BBB and BB respectively along with the bankruptcy of a major competitor did not help matters.

Sood considered the whole situation ironic since the company's balance sheet had never looked better. Because of the staff layoffs and the inventory and capital expenditure reductions, Finning's short term debt had been reduced to its lowest levels in years. The debenture issue of June, 1981 had helped to reduce and stabilize the company's interest costs. The parts and service areas of the company, although affected by the recession, continued to cover all expenses and the company still had substantial lines of untapped bank credit on which to draw. Cash flow had not become a problem. Sood expected that there was considerable pent-up demand for Finning's products, since the forest industry had not had a chance to recover from its strike in 1981 before entering the recession. Several mining and construction projects had been suspended during the economic downturn but would start again as the recession eased.

207

Case 20
Finning
Tractor and
Equipment
Company Ltd.

The Dividend Decision

The March 31, 1982 dividend had been the third consecutive dividend declared by the company that was not covered by quarterly earnings. As the mid-May second quarter dividend declaration date approached, Sood thought it would be prudent to postpone any announcement until after the next Board meeting, especially given the unusual environment — low earnings but satisfactory cash flow, and an improved balance sheet but rumours of impending bankruptcy. Also, by the July 22nd meeting, he would have had a chance to analyze the second quarter results and ascertain if the recession was easing or if additional restraint measures would be necessary.

As the July Board meeting approached, Mr. Sood knew that several issues could be discussed pertaining to dividend policy including: amount of payment, stock or cash payment, desirable long term dividend policy, preferred dividend policy and effect of dividend policy on stock price. Ultimately, the Board would have to decide on continuation of the current policy or a specific change. The two major shareholders, descendants of the founder, were represented on the Board and each was receiving over $1.5 million a year in dividends from Finning. But the stock price had fallen to half its level of a year ago and a dividend cut might force the price even lower. Eliminating the dividend might affect institutional investors holding the stock, because of the requirement for dividends in acts governing various companies and funds such as Pension Benefits Standards Act (Canada), Pension Benefits Act (Ontario), Supplemental Pensions Plans Act (Quebec), Loan Companies Act (Canada), Foreign Insurance Companies Act (Canada) and the Canadian and British Insurance Companies Act, of which excerpts are shown in Appendix A. In general, if a company paid or earned enough to pay a dividend of at least four percent of the average value of the common stock over the year in four of the previous five years, including the last year, it would meet virtually all statutes. Some exceptions include the Trust Companies Act (Canada) which required the four percent rule for every year in the preceding five years, and the Trust Companies Act (Alberta) which required the four percent rule apply to earned profits in each of the preceding five years. The Board had always approved dividend changes in a routine way in the past, but they had always been increases. Exhibit 9 shows the weekly stock prices for Finning for the 42 weeks leading up to the meeting.

EXHIBIT 1

FINNING TRACTOR AND EQUIPMENT COMPANY LTD.

Company Locations as of February 1, 1982

209

Case 20
Finning
Tractor and
Equipment
Company Ltd.

Source: Company Records

EXHIBIT 2
FINNING TRACTOR AND EQUIPMENT COMPANY LTD.

Selected Growth Statistics

(Dollar figures in thousands except per share data)

Year	Revenue	Earnings Before Tax	Net Income	EPS	Stock Low	High	Div
1972	$ 126 622	$ 9 732	$ 5 084	$ .32	$ 1.53	$ 3.69	$ .038
1973	148 157	11 241	5 475	.34	2.19	3.75	.060
1974	162 101	15 424	7 286	.46	1.63	2.88	.070
1975	173 812	15 675	7 942	.50	1.72	2.56	.100
1976	199 795	14 583	8 609	.54	2.19	3.56	.100
1977	246 761	19 625	12 202	.76	2.69	5.13	.125
1978	287 933	24 012	14 769	.93	4.69	7.25	.125
1979	375 417	28 322	19 459	1.23	6.28	9.75	.225
1980	438 327	28 180	18 237	1.15	8.50	17.44	.300
1981	454 377	1 092	3 485	.20	7.50	16.00	.300

Source for Exhibits 2–8: Company Records

EXHIBIT 3
FINNING TRACTOR AND EQUIPMENT COMPANY LTD.

Income Statement
For the years ended December 31

	1981	1980	1979	1978	1977
Revenue	$ 454 377 077	$ 438 327 098	$ 375 417 004	$ 287 933 418	$ 246 760 983
Expenses					
Cost of Sales	370 706 718	356 496 469	307 236 286	236 432 076	202 547 062
General and Admin.	32 381 898	22 544 168	18 519 632	16 683 343	15 830 032
Interest	50 196 061	31 106 229	21 338 814	10 805 908	8 731 936
Total Expenses	453 284 677	410 146 866	347 094 732	263 921 327	227 109 030
Income Before Tax	1 092 400	28 180 232	28 322 272	24 012 091	19 651 953
Provision for Income Taxes	(2 392 587)	9 943 564	8 862 804	9 243 416	7 650 353
Net Income	3 484 987	18 236 668	19 459 468	14 768 675	12 001 600
Beginning Retained	95 637 387	82 166 399	66 281 191	53 498 216	43 482 316
Dividends Paid	4 997 072	4 765 680	3 574 260	1 985 700	1 985 700
Ending Retained	$ 94 125 302	$ 95 637 387	$ 82 166 399	$ 66 281 191	$ 53 498 216

EXHIBIT 4

FINNING TRACTOR AND EQUIPMENT COMPANY LTD.

Balance Sheet
For the years ended December 31

	1981	1980	1979	1978	1977
Assets					
Accounts receivable	$ 61 537 736	72 752 461	55 584 343	42 616 803	30 211 081
Installment Notes	63 361 092	61 968 696	54 089 792	49 315 241	45 930 381
Income Taxes Refundable	—	591 259	—	—	943 997
Inventories					
Equipment	110 953 365	133 598 453	95 114 682	69 075 396	54 471 698
Parts and Supplies	41 945 998	49 641 113	36 153 273	33 655 018	25 183 978
Total Current Assets	277 798 191	318 551 982	240 942 090	194 662 458	156 741 135
Leased Equipment	90 057 226	97 737 107	78 887 287	51 827 491	40 780 316
Net Land, Buildings and Equipment	54 097 262	47 617 776	40 453 850	29 413 773	21 481 628
TOTAL ASSETS	$ 421 952 679	463 906 865	360 283 227	275 903 722	219 003 079
Liabilities					
Bank Debt	$ 165 011 604	246 525 775	179 458 055	35 212 147	107 395 310
Accounts Payable	21 509 239	46 023 641	30 391 020	32 212 147	28 722 876
Income Taxes Payable	1 244 699	—	299 764	1 440 982	—
Long Term Debt[1]	28 200 000	28 800 000	29 400 000	30 000 000	153 094
Convertible Debentures[2]	65 000 000	—	—	—	—
Deferred Taxes	35 509 873	37 823 500	29 471 427	25 706 409	20 137 021
Total Liabilities	316 475 415	359 172 916	269 020 266	200 525 969	156 408 301
Equity					
Share Capital[3]	11 351 962	9 096 562	9 096 562	9 096 562	9 096 562
Retained Earnings	94 125 302	95 637 387	82 166 399	66 281 191	53 498 216
TOTAL LIABILITIES AND EQUITY	$ 421 952 679	463 906 865	360 283 227	275 903 722	219 003 079

[1] The long-term debt carried several covenants, one of which restricts the declaration and payment of dividends and the reduction of share capital. Under the most restrictive of these provisions, the amount available for dividends was $12 976 296 at December 31, 1981.

[2] The 11.5% convertible subordinated debentures were convertible into class B non-voting shares at $18.00 per share prior to June 24, 1986 and at $18.75 from June 25, 1986 to June 24, 1991.

[3] Share capital in 1981 was divided as follows: Series A Preferred — $2 255 400; Class A Common — $4 544 392; Class B Common — $4 544 170

EXHIBIT 5
FINNING TRACTOR AND EQUIPMENT COMPANY LTD.

First Quarter Report For the three months ended March 31

	1982	1981	1980
Revenue	$ 84 232	$ 119 753	$ 92 224
Cost of Sales, etc.	75 884	101 678	78 715
Interest	8 277	12 287	7 265
Total Expenses	84 161	113 965	85 980
Income Before Taxes	71	5 788	6 244
Provision for Taxes	(589)	1 978	2 185
Net Income	$ 660	$ 3 810	$ 4 059
EPS	$ .04	$ .24	$ .26
Outstanding Shares (adjusted)	15 885 600	15 885 600	15 885 600

Statement of Changes in Financial Position

	1982	1981	1980
Cash Generated:			
Net Income	$ 660	$ 3 810	$ 4 059
Depreciation:			
Leased Equipment	6 013	5 551	4 521
Buildings and Equipment	1 316	1 263	1 118
Deferred Income Taxes	(281)	780	1 703
Total Sources From Operations	7 708	11 404	11 401
Cash Used:			
Accounts Receivable	(754)	6 473	(20)
Instalment Note Receivable	(4 209)	1 391	(978)
Inventories:			
Equipment	3 010	42 938	24 195
Parts and Supplies	(2 625)	654	2 226
Net Leased Equipment	(1 228)	1 167	5 152
Accounts Payable and Accruals	(8 888)	(4 802)	8 514
Income Taxes	304	(1 019)	(482)
Total Uses From Operations	(14 390)	46 802	38 607
Net Cash Used in Operations	(22 098)	35 398	27 206
Other Uses (Sources) of Cash:			
Additions to Land, Buildings etc.	755	4 621	2 877
Purchase of Secured Debentures	600	300	300
Issue of Preferred Shares	—	(2 519)	—
Redemption of Preferred Shares	92	—	—
Dividends Paid	1 239	1 233	1 191
Total	2 686	3 635	4 368
NET INCREASE IN BANK INDEBTEDNESS	$ (19 412)	$ 39 033	$ 31 574

EXHIBIT 6
FINNING TRACTOR AND EQUIPMENT COMPANY LTD.

Second Quarter Report For the months ended June 30

	3 Months			6 Months		
	1982	1981	1980	1982	1981	1980
Revenue	$ 91 983	128 289	118 196	176 215	248 042	210 420
Cost of Sales, etc.	83 802	113 327	101 130	159 686	215 005	179 845
Interest	7 934	13 476	8 858	16 211	25 763	16 123
Total Expenses	91 736	126 803	109 988	175 897	240 768	195 968
Income Before Taxes	247	1 486	8 208	318	7 274	14 452
Provision for Taxes	(379)	87	2 873	(968)	2 065	5 058
Net Income	$ 626	1 399	5 335	1 286	5 209	9 394
EPS	$ .04	.09	.34	.08	.33	.59
Outstanding Shares (adjusted)	15 885 600	15 885 600	15 885 600	15 885 600	15 885 600	15 885 600

Statement of Changes in Financial Position

	6 Months		
	1982	1981	1980
Cash Generated:			
Net Income	$ 1 286	$ 5 209	$ 9 394
Depreciation: Leased			
Equipment	10 918	11 507	9 447
Buildings and Equip.	2 568	2 466	2 234
Deferred Income Taxes	(518)	847	3 770
Total Sources From Operations	14 254	20 029	24 845
Cash Used:			
Accounts Receivable	(6 190)	3 997	8 879
Instalment Note Receivable	(5 045)	5 066	3 084
Inventories: Equipment	(3 482)	22 762	27 952
Parts and Supplies	(977)	(402)	1 630
Net Leased Equipment	(2 916)	12 168	15 881
Accounts Payable and Accruals	(4 116)	7 748	7 164
Income Taxes	550	(979)	(448)
Total Uses From Operations	(22 176)	50 360	64 142
Net Cash Used in Operations	(36 430)	30 331	39 297
Other Uses (Sources) of Cash:			
Additions to Land, Buildings etc.	1 212	8 276	5 705
Purchase of Secured Debentures	600	300	300
Proceeds on Issue of Debentures	—	(65 000)	—
Issue of Preferred Shares	—	(2 519)	—
Redemption of Preferred Shares	181	47	—
Dividends Paid	1 282	2 488	2 383
Total	3 275	(56 408)	8 388
NET INCREASE IN BANK INDEBTEDNESS	$(33 155)	$ (26 077)	$ 47 685

EXHIBIT 7

FINNING TRACTOR AND EQUIPMENT COMPANY LTD.

Third Quarter Report For the Months ended September 30

	3 months		9 months	
	1981	1980	1981	1980
Revenue	$ 113 682	$ 106 425	$ 361 724	$ 316 845
Cost of Sales, etc.	102 005	93 343	317 010	273 188
Interest	13 570	6 388	39 333	22 511
Total Expenses	115 575	99 731	356 343	295 699
Income Before Taxes	(1 893)	6 694	5 381	21 146
Provision for Taxes	(260)	2 343	1 805	7 401
Net Income	(1 633)	4 351	3 576	13 745
EPS	$ (.10)	$ .27	$ .23	$ .87
Outstanding Shares (adjusted)	15 855 600	15 885 600	15 885 600	15 885 600

Statement of Changes in Financial Position

	9 months	
	1981	1980
Cash Generated:		
Net Income	$ 3 576	$ 13 745
Depreciation: Leased Equipment	18 263	15 302
Buildings and Equipment	4 007	3 216
Deferred Income Taxes	1 956	5 055
Total Sources From Operations	27 802	37 318
Cash Used:		
Accounts Receivable	4 264	5 457
Instalment Note Receivable	2 460	3 987
Inventories: Equipment	1 080	31 006
Parts and Supplies	(6 748)	3 145
Net Leased Equipment	18 368	23 546
Accounts Payable and Accruals	12 544	5 115
Income Taxes	397	(699)
Total Uses From Operations	32 365	71 557
Net Cash Used in Operations	4 563	34 239
Other Uses (Sources) of Cash:		
Additions to Land, Buildings etc.	9 901	7 490
Purchase of Secured Debentures	600	600
Proceeds on Issue of Convert Deb.	(65 000)	—
Issue of Preferred Shares	(2 519)	—
Redemption of Preferred Shares	99	—
Dividends Paid	3 748	3 574
Total	(53 171)	11 664
NET INCREASE IN BANK INDEBTEDNESS	$ (48 608)	$ 45 903

EXHIBIT 8
FINNING TRACTOR AND EQUIPMENT COMPANY LTD.

Fourth Quarter Report For the months ended December 31

	3 months 1981	1980	12 months 1981	1980
Revenue	$ 92 653	$ 121 482	$ 454 377	$ 438 327
Cost of Sales, etc.	86 079	105 853	403 089	379 041
Interest	10 863	8 595	50 196	31 106
Total Expenses	96 942	114 448	453 285	410 147
Income Before Taxes	(4 289)	7 034	1 092	28 180
Provision for Taxes	(4 198)	2 542	(2 393)	9 943
Net Income	(91)	4 492	3 485	18 237
EPS	$ (.01)	$ .28	$ .22	$ 1.15
Outstanding Shares (adjusted)	15 885 600	15 885 600	15 885 600	15 885 600

Statement of Changes in Financial Position

	12 months 1981	1980
Cash Generated:		
Net Income	$ 3 485	$ 18 237
Depreciation:		
Leased Equipment	24 952	21 234
Buildings and Equipment	5 223	4 657
Deferred Income Taxes	(2 314)	8 352
Total Sources From Operations	31 346	52 480
Cash Used:		
Accounts Receivable	(11 215)	17 168
Instalment Note Receivable	1 392	7 879
Inventories: Equipment	(22 645)	38 484
Parts and Supplies	(7 695)	13 488
Net Leased Equipment	17 272	40 084
Accounts Payable and Accruals	24 515	(15 633)
Income Taxes	(1 836)	891
Total Uses From Operations	(212)	102 361
Net Cash Used in Operations	(31 558)	49 881
Other Uses (Sources) of Cash:		
Additions to Land, Buildings etc.	11 702	11 821
Purchase of Secured Debentures	600	600
Proceeds on Issue of Convert Deb.	(65 000)	—
Net Issue of Preferred Shares	(2 255)	—
Dividends Paid	4 997	4 766
Total	(49 956)	17 187
NET INCREASE IN BANK INDEBTEDNESS	$ (81 514)	$ 67 068

EXHIBIT 9
FINNING TRACTOR AND EQUIPMENT COMPANY LTD.

Weekly Stock Prices

Week ending		Class A			Class B		
		High	Low	Close	High	Low	Close
1981 October	2	$10\frac{1}{2}$	9	$10\frac{1}{2}$	10	9	10
	9	$10\frac{1}{2}$	$10\frac{1}{2}$	10	$10\frac{1}{4}$	$9\frac{1}{2}$	$9\frac{3}{4}$
	16	$9\frac{1}{2}$	9	9	$8\frac{3}{4}$	$8\frac{1}{2}$	$8\frac{1}{2}$
	23	$8\frac{3}{4}$	8	8	$8\frac{1}{2}$	8	$8\frac{1}{4}$
	30	8	$7\frac{1}{2}$	8	$8\frac{1}{2}$	$7\frac{1}{2}$	8
November	6	$10\frac{1}{2}$	$8\frac{1}{4}$	$10\frac{1}{2}$	$8\frac{1}{2}$	8	8
	13	$9\frac{3}{4}$	$8\frac{1}{2}$	$9\frac{3}{4}$	8	8	8
	20	$9\frac{1}{4}$	$8\frac{1}{2}$	$9\frac{1}{4}$	$8\frac{1}{2}$	8	$8\frac{1}{2}$
	27	$9\frac{1}{4}$	$8\frac{3}{4}$	$9\frac{1}{4}$	$9\frac{1}{4}$	$8\frac{1}{2}$	$9\frac{1}{4}$
December	4	$10\frac{1}{4}$	$9\frac{1}{4}$	10	10	$9\frac{1}{4}$	10
	11	10	$9\frac{1}{2}$	10	$9\frac{1}{2}$	$9\frac{1}{2}$	$9\frac{1}{2}$
	18	10	$9\frac{1}{2}$	10	10	$9\frac{1}{2}$	$9\frac{1}{2}$
	24	10	$9\frac{3}{4}$	10	10	$9\frac{1}{2}$	10
	31	$10\frac{1}{4}$	$10\frac{1}{4}$	$10\frac{1}{4}$	$9\frac{3}{4}$	$9\frac{3}{4}$	$9\frac{3}{4}$
1982 January	8	$10\frac{1}{2}$	10	10	$10\frac{3}{8}$	$10\frac{1}{8}$	$10\frac{1}{8}$
	15	$10\frac{1}{4}$	10	10	10	10	10
	22	$10\frac{1}{2}$	$9\frac{3}{4}$	$9\frac{3}{4}$	10	10	10
	29	10	$9\frac{3}{4}$	$9\frac{3}{4}$	9	9	9
February	5	10	$9\frac{3}{4}$	$9\frac{3}{4}$	9	9	9
	12	$9\frac{1}{2}$	$8\frac{1}{2}$	$8\frac{1}{2}$	$7\frac{1}{2}$	$7\frac{1}{2}$	$7\frac{1}{2}$
	19	$8\frac{1}{2}$	$7\frac{3}{4}$	$8\frac{1}{2}$	$7\frac{1}{4}$	7	$7\frac{1}{4}$
	26	$8\frac{1}{2}$	$8\frac{1}{2}$	$8\frac{1}{2}$	$8\frac{1}{2}$	$7\frac{3}{4}$	8
March	5	$8\frac{1}{4}$	8	8	8	$7\frac{3}{4}$	8
	12	8	8	8	8	8	8
	19	9	8	8	8	$7\frac{3}{4}$	$7\frac{3}{4}$
	26	8	8	8	8	$7\frac{3}{4}$	$7\frac{3}{4}$
April	2	8	8	8	8	$7\frac{3}{4}$	$7\frac{3}{4}$
	9	$8\frac{1}{2}$	8	$8\frac{1}{2}$	$7\frac{3}{4}$	$7\frac{3}{4}$	$7\frac{3}{4}$
	16	$8\frac{1}{2}$	8	8	$7\frac{3}{4}$	$7\frac{3}{4}$	$7\frac{3}{4}$
	23	8	8	8	8	$7\frac{3}{4}$	$7\frac{3}{4}$
	30	8	8	8	8	$7\frac{3}{4}$	$7\frac{3}{4}$
May	7	$7\frac{1}{2}$	7	$7\frac{1}{2}$	8	$7\frac{1}{8}$	$7\frac{1}{8}$
	14	$7\frac{1}{2}$	$7\frac{3}{8}$	$7\frac{3}{8}$	$7\frac{1}{2}$	$7\frac{1}{4}$	$7\frac{1}{4}$
	21	$8\frac{1}{4}$	$7\frac{1}{4}$	$7\frac{1}{4}$	$8\frac{1}{4}$	7	7
	28	8	$7\frac{3}{8}$	$7\frac{3}{8}$	$7\frac{1}{4}$	7	$7\frac{1}{4}$
June	4	$7\frac{1}{8}$	7	7	7	$7\frac{3}{4}$	7
	11	7	$6\frac{3}{8}$	$6\frac{3}{8}$	$6\frac{1}{4}$	5	5
	18	$6\frac{3}{8}$	$5\frac{1}{2}$	$5\frac{3}{4}$	$4\frac{1}{2}$	4	$4\frac{1}{2}$
	25	6	5	5	5	5	5
July	2	$5\frac{1}{4}$	$5\frac{1}{4}$	$5\frac{1}{4}$	$4\frac{1}{2}$	$4\frac{1}{2}$	$4\frac{1}{2}$
	9	$5\frac{1}{2}$	5	5	5	$4\frac{1}{2}$	$4\frac{1}{2}$
	16	$5\frac{1}{2}$	5	$5\frac{3}{8}$	5	4	$4\frac{1}{2}$

Source: Public Data

APPENDIX 1

The Canadian and British Insurance Companies Act (Selected paragraphs)

63. (1) A company may invest its funds or any portion thereof in

217

*Case 20
Finning
Tractor and
Equipment
Company Ltd.*

(E) the bonds, debentures or other evidences of indebtedness of a corporation that are fully secured by statutory charge upon real estate or upon the plant or equipment of the corporation used in the transaction of its business, if interest in full has been paid regularly for a period of at least ten years immediately preceding the date of investment in such bonds, debentures or other evidences upon the securities of that class of the corporation then outstanding;

(L) the preferred shares of a corporation if

 (i) the corporation has paid a dividend in each of the five years immediately preceding the date of investments at least equal to the specified annual rate upon all of its preferred shares, or

 (ii) the common shares of the corporation are, at the date of the investment, authorized as investments by paragraph (M);

(M) the fully paid common shares of a corporation where during a period of five years that ended less than one year before the date of investment, the corporation

 (i) paid in each of at least four of the five years, including the last year of that period, a dividend upon its common shares, or

 (ii) earned in each of at least four of the five years, including the last year of that period, an amount available for the payment of a dividend upon its common shares, of at least four percent of the average value at which the issued common shares of the corporation were carried in the capital stock account of the corporation during the year in which the dividend was paid or in which the amount was earned as the case may be, but

 (iii) except as provided in sections 64, 65, 90 and 91, a company shall not purchase more than 30 percent of the common shares of any corporation,

 (iv) except as provided in sections 45.1 and 91, a company shall not purchase its own shares,

 (v) if, at the date of a proposed investment, the corporation owns beneficially, directly or indirectly, more than 50 percent of the common shares of one or more other corporations, and if the accounts of the corporation and those other corporations are normally presented to the shareholders of the corporation in consolidated form, a company shall not make an investment under this paragraph unless the requirement in subparagraph (i) or (ii) is met on the basis of the consolidated accounts of the corporation and those other corporations,

 (vi) where the proposed investment is in the shares of a corporation continuing or formed as a result of the amalgamation or merger of two or more corporations, that corporation is deemed, for the purposes of this paragraph, to have dividend and earnings records for any relevant period prior to the date of the amalgamation or merger identical with the dividend and earnings records of the amalgamated or merged corporations determined on the basis of a consolidation of their accounts and,

(vii) except as provided in sections 65 and 90, a company registered to transact the business of life insurance shall not purchase the shares of a corporation transacting in the business of life insurance.

Source: The Canadian and British Insurance Companies Act, 1983

218

Dividend
Policy

Valuation of a Business Interest

ECLIPSE GOLF LIMITED

"I'm sorry, but I'm only authorized to wait until Monday for your answer."
After hearing this comment, Sean Hall left the lawyer's office. He had just
been offered $10 000 for his 4000 shares in Eclipse Golf Limited (Eclipse),
a company with a unique state-of-the-art process that guaranteed perfect
replication and matching between golf clubs. The offer came from Irene
Sakellis, wife of the founder of the company. The product had been well
accepted by better golfers and sales had increased 350 percent over the past
two years.

Hall had paid $2000 for 1000 of his shares two years earlier and received
the other 3000 for services rendered. He knew that taking the offer would
give him a substantial return on investment but he was not sure if the
$10 000 was the full value of the shares. Since the shares were not traded
on any exchange, their value could not be determined by market forces.
Hall was playing successfully on the PGA tour and he did not need the money
in its own right, but he felt that there was a principle involved since he had
helped get the company on its feet.

Precision Machine

John Sakellis, the principal shareholder in Eclipse, had emigrated from
Yugoslavia with his wife in 1946. Although they found it very difficult at
first, with language problems and a shortage of money, John was persistent
and finally found a job using his knowledge of machining. He was a hard
worker and very skilful and within a few years became the person that
everyone consulted on difficult or complex jobs. He was very proud of his
accomplishments and enjoyed his job, but his main goal had always been
to own his own company. Several years later, in 1964, Sakellis realized this
ambition and started Precision Machine Co. Ltd., (Precision), an aerospace/
aircraft parts machining company, located in Malton, Ontario, five miles from

Lester B. Pearson International Airport. Contracts were not easily found, but after several months Precision won its first contract with De Havilland Aircraft. The quality of Precision's products, along with its competitive prices, ensured that Precision never again had difficulty winning contracts.

The company's reputation grew and by 1978 it was considered one of the top three or four machining companies in North America. Precision developed the reputation of being able to build parts that no other companies could build. This was possible because Sakellis and his vice president, Ray Summers, designed and built many of Precision's machines to their own exacting specifications. Their equipment was always in the forefront of technology and Sakellis and Summers were constantly testing new ideas and designs to increase quality or decrease production times.

In mid-1978, Sakellis decided to step down as president of Precision and leave the business to his son Maurie, who had worked part-time for Precision for several years and was about to complete his degree in chemical engineering. Sakellis felt that Maurie could continue to learn the business under Summers, who was to become president. By the time Summers retired, Maurie would have the knowledge necessary to manage Precision.

With retirement in mind, Sakellis started playing more of his favourite sport, golf. It was a total coincidence that on one of his weekend outings Sakellis met a "master" club builder from a major North American golf club company. After hearing of Sakellis's machining background, the club builder invited him for a tour of the Canadian facilities. Although he never mentioned it during the tour, Sakellis could not believe how inefficient and inaccurate the whole process was, and he was sure he could devise a far better method. Just to be cautious, he decided to check other golf manufacturing facilities and found the same manufacturing problems. He knew it would be difficult to design machines that would accurately reproduce golf club heads because the heads would have to be cut on several planes at the same time. He thought that this complexity might be the reason why no one else had attempted production of this type before, but building the machines would only be the beginning of the problem. Finding proper iron castings, wood turnings, shafts, grips and other supplies to meet the same high standards would not be easy either. The entire golf business seemed to survive on marketing alone and few, if any, of the internationally published claims and advertisements for golf equipment had any basis in physical fact. Sakellis was also worried about suggesting that his product would be superior to the already so-called "perfect" clubs currently on the market, since the perfect matching of golf clubs had been claimed by the golf industry for many years. Sakellis knew these claims to be untrue, but how could a small Canadian company dispute the statements of sporting giants such as Wilson, MacGregor and Ben Hogan? Ping, a small golf club manufacturing company based in Southern California, had managed to overcome the odds, but it had taken ten years to do so and was considered one of the "lucky" ones.

The Golf Club

By June 1979, Sakellis had successfully designed and built several numerically controlled machines capable of accurately machining both iron and wood golf club heads. Even though the prototypes were perfect from an engineering standpoint, Sakellis thought that the clubs were not aesthetically pleasing so he sought out a prominent Canadian tour player to correct the appearance of the clubs and to test several metal alloys in order to find that elusive quality golfers call "feel." Sean Hall was the professional approached and he agreed to help finish the product in exchange for shares in the company.

It took the better part of a year to complete testing and designing, but when the club was finally ready, everyone was confident it would take the market by storm. Hall believed the clubs would give him a two shot advantage over the rest of the tour field, but, more importantly, he felt that the ability to replace broken clubs with exact duplicates, so that no retraining period was required, was virtually priceless. The confidence in the superiority of the clubs exhibited by all those involved in its production led Sakellis to suggest the name *THE GOLF CLUB*, "undoubtedly the finest available on the market."

Eclipse

Sakellis decided to call the new golf club company Eclipse Golf Limited. Sakellis also decided to restructure the management of both his businesses and have Summers take charge of the golf machining sections. He put his son-in-law, Derrick Kouzounas, who had an M.B.A. from a well-known Eastern Business School, in charge of Precision and put Maurie in charge of marketing the golf clubs. Sakellis then was free to oversee both companies in an unofficial capacity, leaving time to continue designing, redesigning and building better equipment.

The clubs were introduced at the Canadian Professional Golfers' Association's fall buying show in October of 1979. Sakellis and Maurie decided to introduce the product at a price near the lower end of what consumers would consider were comparable products, as shown in Exhibit 1. Sales were slow at first mainly because of lack of funds for advertising and the difficulty of overcoming the "Canadian product" stigma.

By the end of 1983, Eclipse had secured a small niche in the Canadian market and had entered several foreign markets such as West Germany, Spain and Australia. But there had been some problems. Everyone involved with the running of Eclipse found golf professionals difficult to understand. They seemed to come to the annual buying shows simply to have a good time with some old friends. It was not unusual to have several pros visit the Eclipse booth partially or even totally inebriated. Senior management could not understand why sales had not increased more rapidly. In the aerospace industry, all a manufacturer had to do was produce a superior product at competitive prices, send out a prototype, and then watch the orders roll in. This method did not seem to work in the golf business. Various reasons for this difficulty were discussed, but the one Eclipse management kept returning to was that golf professionals were more interested in selling something easily, rather than working at selling the best. Everyone thought that if the golf pros were properly educated, it would only be a matter of time until they recognized the quality of the product and started to purchase in larger quantities. In any case, management believed that sales had climbed to a point where entry into the U.S. and Japanese markets seemed possible for the summer of 1984. The American market was huge in comparison to all other markets and even a 0.1 percent market share would double Eclipse's total sales volume. Exhibits 2 and 3 show income and balance sheets for Eclipse for the years 1980 to 1983.

The Share Situation

In Eclipse's early years funds were scarce. Sakellis was totally against public financing, either debt or equity, but was willing in special cases, to issue small numbers of shares to employees as payment beyond their regular earnings. Sakellis himself worked long hours for virtually no pay, since he was drawing a pension from Precision. Eclipse was housed in the same building as Precision and Precision equipment and labour were used when available to keep Eclipse's costs to a minimum.

A total of 16 000 of the 20 000 authorized shares had been issued. Sakellis and his wife, who had worked as a bookkeeper, owned 3000 shares each. Maurie owned 3000, Hall owned 4000 and the remaining 3000 were distributed among other employees, mostly to Summers. Sakellis was interested in repurchasing Hall's shares and those of the employees because of his desire to have the company completely family-owned. Hall was currently on the Board of Directors because of the number of shares he held, but believed his position was really a token gesture since he was rarely consulted on decisions other than product testing.

Hall knew he had little time to make his decision on whether to accept the $10 000 for his 4000 shares. He had dabbled in the stock market for several years and was quite capable of reading financial statements. He thought that other information would be necessary to make his decisions and proceeded to gather the facts shown in Exhibit 4.

Hall had been friends with the Sakellis family for a number of years and did not want to create any animosity. On the other hand, he wanted to be treated fairly for his involvement in Eclipse and his contribution to the company's success. If worse came to worst, he was not against hiring a lawyer to increase his chances of receiving fair value for his shares.

EXHIBIT 1
ECLIPSE GOLF LIMITED

Wholesale Prices for Top Line Golf Sets[1]
(as of 1982)

Walter Hagen	$ 450
Wilson Staff	495
Ben Hogan	508
THE GOLF CLUB	516
Dunlop Maxfli Australian Blade	525
Ram Tour Grind	550
Spalding XL-4	580
Titleist Tour Model	669
MacGregor Nicklaus Muirfield	795[2]
Ping	822
Sounder	853

---

[1] All prices were for 11 piece sets, 3 laminated woods and 8 irons.
[2] Available in solid persimmon woods only.

Source: Manufacturer's wholesale price catalogs.

EXHIBIT 2

ECLIPSE GOLF LIMITED

Income Statement
for the years ended 1981–1983
(Unaudited)

	1983	1982	1981
Sales	$ 522 904	$ 366 036	$ 148 447
Gov't Grants	4 169	8 230	12 714
Gross Revenue	527 073	374 266	161 161
Cost of Sales	326 126	209 961	85 674
Operating Profit	200 947	164 305	75 487
Expenses			
Office Wages	57 304	55 109	42 348
Accounting & Legal	914	1 325	3 760
Travel	3 617	2 992	4 327
Rent	6 998	6 426	6 006
Insurance	7 436	7 436	7 436
Advertising[1]	21 215	19 196	38 111
Repair & Maintenance	6 312	5 604	5 143
R & D	15 900	11 400	8 866
Interest	5 248	13 319	7 745
Office Supplies	964	978	1 004
Telephone	826	711	787
Depreciation	14 411	12 124	11 361
Miscellaneous	319	425	531
Total Expenses	141 464	137 045	137 425
Net Profit Before Tax	59 483	27 260	(61 938)
Tax	9 376	1 192	(12 410)
Net Profit	$ 50 107	$ 26 068	$ (49 528)

[1] Includes cost of CPGA buying shows held annually in 5 cities across Canada.

EXHIBIT 3

ECLIPSE GOLF LIMITED

Balance Sheet
as at December 31, 1981–1983
(Unaudited)

	1983	1982	1981
Assets			
Cash	$ 4 756	$ 5 112	$ 11 406
Accounts Receivable	94 053	64 307	28 939
Inventory	76 158	54 639	40 517
Total Current Assets	174 967	124 058	80 862
Equipment, Cost less accumulated Depreciation	202 169	248 568	242 875
TOTAL ASSETS	$ 377 136	$ 372 626	$ 323 737
Liabilities			
Bank Loan	$ 42 244	$ 88 196	$ 67 193
Accounts Payable	17 245	16 890	15 072
Total Current Liabilities	59 489	105 086	82 265
Loans From Shareholders	275 000	275 000	275 000
Capital Stock (16 000 issued, 20 000 authorized)	16 000	16 000	16 000
Retained Earnings	26 647	(23 460)	(49 528)
TOTAL LIABILITIES & EQUITY	$ 377 136	$ 372 626	$ 323 737

EXHIBIT 4
ECLIPSE GOLF LIMITED

Selected Statistics

Long-Term Government Bond Yield	12.73%[1]
T-Bill Rate	9.24%[1]
TSE Composite P/E	22.41 times[1]
Consumer Products P/E	11.48 times[1]

Company		Sales	EPS	Div	Price[2]	High[3]	Low
Cooper	82	$ 66 883 000	$1.08	—	$ 3.38	$ 4.00	$ 2.25
	81	66 988 000	(.24)	—		4.13	2.50
Irwin	82	88 639 000	.88	$ .15	11.00	15.25	6.38
	81	60 787 000	.41	.10		8.88	2.00

[1] Statistics as of December 31, 1983.
[2] Share Price as of December 31, 1982.
[3] High and low share price for year specified.

Case 21
Eclipse Golf
Limited

TREMBLAY LTEE.

In June 1987, Susan Spencer, a Montreal based Royal Bank of Canada account manager for the Tremblay Ltee. (Tremblay) account, was assessing her client's financial position and needs. The company had $18 million in term loans outstanding with the Royal Bank and required additional financing to buyout a minority equity interest in Tremblay held by Le Groupe Marechal (Marechal). Term debt was clearly an option, however, Spencer had some concern about the impact of additional term debt on Tremblay's leverage position. Spencer had suggested to Tremblay's president and majority owner, Andre LeBlanc, that additional equity be considered, and she now wondered if a referral to Royal Bank Capital Corporation (RBCC) was appropriate.

Spencer knew that LeBlanc had received overtures from Societe d'Investissement Independent Ltee. (SDIL), a major Quebec based securities firm, about taking Tremblay public by way of an initial public offering. LeBlanc had obtained a $2.5 million loan from SDIL in February 1986 to assist in his purchase of the controlling interest in Tremblay, and SDIL was eager to play a larger role in the company's financing activities. In addition, the Confederation Bank, which had been the company's banker before the Royal, had recently made several calls on Tremblay.

Company Background

Tremblay, headquartered in Montreal, was the holding company for two operating subsidiaries as shown in Exhibit 1. The original subsidiary, Transport Tremblay Ltee., had been incorporated in Quebec by Marc Beaubien and a partner in 1966. Beaubien had bought out his partner in 1971 and watched the company grow to become one of Canada's major trucking firms.

Andre LeBlanc, who worked as a vice president with SDIL up until 1978, was a longtime friend of Marc Beaubien. In 1978, LeBlanc left SDIL to pursue several real estate investments and, within a year, LeBlanc made

$400,000 in two land development transactions. He parlayed this gain into an investment in a Montreal packaging company with several partners. LeBlanc managed this company for one and a half years and then sold it to a major competitor at ten times the original investment value, leaving LeBlanc with a gain of over $4.0 million. In 1980, LeBlanc joined Transport Tremblay Ltee. as the company's Chief Financial Officer (CFO).

In 1986, the elderly Beaubien decided to sell off a controlling share of his ownership in Transport Tremblay Ltee. He had been highly impressed with the performance of LeBlanc as CFO, and approached him with an offer for an 80% interest in Transport Tremblay Ltee., which LeBlanc accepted and paid for with the personal capital he had accumulated from his earlier ventures and the $2.5 million loan from SDIL. LeBlanc was a very private individual and he had not disclosed to Spencer the terms of the loan with SDIL. However, Spencer speculated that SDIL wanted to take the company public and would likely have structured repayment of the loan to a public stock issue.

Subsequent to this transaction, LeBlanc became chief executive officer and Beaubien retired, agreeing to serve as a consultant for the next three years and to retain his seat on the board. Beaubien's salary and bonuses had previously amounted to roughly $1 million per annum; however, LeBlanc set his own compensation at $300,000 per year.

As seen in the financial highlights presented in Exhibit 2, Beaubien and LeBlanc managed the company profitably through the recession of the early 1980s, and revenues increased on average 12% yearly during this period. In fiscal 1985, Transport Tremblay Ltee. acquired several routes from a competitor, which caused revenues to increase by 42%. LeBlanc felt that the scheduled deregulation of the transport industry would result in increased competition and only the large players would be able to survive. As a consequence, he began to actively pursue acquisition opportunities. LeBlanc learned that Marechal was interested in divesting Transport Larochelle Ltee. from their group. Negotiations followed and Beaubien and LeBlanc reviewed the Transport Larochelle Ltee. operation in detail. They developed specific plans to combine Larochelle into Transport Tremblay Ltee. and to improve operating efficiency by eliminating Larochelle's excessive middle management, demarketing marginal accounts, closing down several unprofitable terminals, and introducing Tremblay's state-of-the-art computer costing and logistics system.

On August 23, 1985, an agreement was reached and the deal was set to close on March 12, 1986. Transport Tremblay Ltee. acquired Transport Larochelle Ltee. from Marechal for $21,204,000, paid for with $10,704,000 in cash (drawn from cash on hand and Royal Bank loans) and $10,500,000 in convertible preferred shares. The preferred shares carried an 8% annual dividend, a term of 5 years, and were convertible at any time at Marechal's option into an equivalent number of common shares of Tremblay Ltee., which was incorporated as the holding company. As part of the agreement, Marechal retained two seats on Tremblay's board until the preferred shares were redeemed. Assuming conversion of Marechal's preferred shares, shareholdings in Tremblay (as shown in Exhibit 1) would consist of 64% held by LeBlanc, 16% by Beaubien, and 20% by Marechal.

Transport Larochelle Ltee.'s longtime banker had been the Royal Bank, and when the acquisition occurred, the Royal made a concerted effort to gain as much of the connection's business as possible. Tremblay split its banking connection, with Transport Tremblay Ltee. maintaining its outstanding loans with the Confederation. The acquisition needs and Transport Larochelle Ltee.'s facilities were financed by the Royal. In October 1986, Spencer successfully persuaded LeBlanc to move all banking to the Royal Bank.

Industry Overview

Freight could be transported over land by truck or by rail. Poolcar and piggyback operators were trucking firms that combined these two modes of transportation by using trucks to transport freight to or from rail terminals and using rail to transport freight between terminals. Poolcar operators sorted freight at terminals and loaded it on empty cars, while piggyback operators drove loaded trailers onto rail flatcars. Tremblay was engaged in all of these operations.

There were two main types of carriers in the trucking industry. The first group consisted of public carriers, like Tremblay, whose main activity was for-hire-carriage and accounted for 45% of truck freight movements. The second group entailed private carriers (captive carriers of companies such as Sears or Canada Post) that owned their own fleets and generated the other 55% of industry shipments. The division of revenues between public and private had remained stable for much of the past decade. Most public carriers utilized a mixture of employee-operated and owner-operated equipment to move freight over a long distance. A single trailer could often be hauled by several different tractors over the course of its movements.

There were two basic services offered by the industry: full truckloads (TLs) and less than truckloads (LTLs). The larger trucking firms, which had sufficient infrastructure to pick up, group and deliver loads according to their destination, were able to service both the LTL and TL clients. The smaller trucking firms competed exclusively in the TL market which experienced significantly more price competition and lower profit margins than the LTL market.

Large trucking companies enjoyed economies of scale. A large volume of traffic enabled firms to achieve a more efficient pickup and delivery network and have fewer empty trips. However, heavy traffic required complex and sophisticated logistical systems. The larger trucking companies tended to be unionized and any independent truckers were contracted on union terms. Smaller carriers were generally not unionized which gave them the advantage of lower labour costs and increased operational flexibility.

Deregulation

All trucking operations in the US were deregulated as a result of legislation introduced in June 1980, and this had facilitated entry into the US market for Canadian firms. In Canada, deregulation of trucking operations was to be introduced in January 1988 and was expected to follow the US model. Under current regulation, operators were required to hold licenses in order to transport on the roads and across provincial borders, and these licenses were awarded once the transporter could demonstrate to the regulatory authority that the public required the service. License applicants had to demonstrate sufficient market demand and a lack of adequate service by companies presently servicing the market. With deregulation, licenses were to be awarded provided an operator could meet certain financial and safety criteria.

The impact of deregulation was not expected to be as severe[1] on the Canadian industry as the American deregulation had been for U.S. transporters. Deregulation in the US had coincided with the deep economic recession of the early eighties and caused numerous bankruptcies to occur. Economists expected most new entrants into the industry would compete in the TL segment of the market which did not require terminal facilities to sort and pool partial freight loads into full truckloads. In the long run, deregulation was expected to translate into efficiency gains for the industry as the larger, LTL/TL carriers acquired smaller and less efficient TL carriers. However, many were opposed with feelings summed up by the owner of Reimer Transport who was critical of deregulation:

> "I'm a firm believer in the maxim: If it ain't broke, don't fix it. We have a system with good rates and a great deal of competition. Why ruin it? The new legislation will spawn over-competition and in the long run, higher prices, poorer service, and more concentration of ownership. There is more competition today then I've seen in 35 years in the business, and a lot of companies are in financial trouble. If shippers are expecting lower rates when the bill takes effect, they're going to be surprised. Rates are as low as they're going to go."

Economic Outlook

Exhibit 3 presents Canadian trucking industry data over the 1981 to 1984 period. Revenues were estimated to have exceeded $8.5 billion in 1986. The Canadian trucking industry had benefitted in recent years from strong economic growth. Over the 1983 to 1986 period, the annual average growth

---

[1] The initial impact of deregulation in the US was an upsurge in new entrants into the industry, with a 39% increase in certificates issued in 1982, a recession year. Despite the increase in the number of firms, the business failure rate was below that of American industry and was more influenced by the recession than by deregulation. From 1978–1983, the rate of failure rose from 0.10% to 0.50%, while the comparative failure rate for American industry rose from 0.24% to 0.61% during the same period.

in operating revenues had been roughly 10% and reflected an increased volume of traffic as well as the industry's success in enlarging its share of total freight traffic, primarily to the detriment of the railways. Trucking carriers had steadily increased their share of the total freight market, handling 25% of tonnage shipped in 1986 as compared to 19.1% in 1983 and 13.7% in 1965. The top ten trucking competitors accounted for only 25% of the total industry revenues and a financial profile of the companies can be found in Exhibit 4. Detailed stock market information on publicly traded companies are provided in Exhibit 5.

A 1987 sectoral analysis from the Royal Bank's Economics Department predicted that growth would moderate and price increases would be minimal due to heightened competition resulting from deregulation. The Department forecasted volume growth to average 4% over the 1987–1990 period and to increase slightly to 6% thereafter.

Included in the forecast was a marginal increase in revenue growth as a result of an anticipated "free trade" deal that would emerge from discussions between the Canadian and U.S. governments. However, some industry analysts worried that free trade might eventually mean the end of Canadian east-west transport as trade became more regionally oriented in the North American market.

Company Overview

Tremblay Ltee. was one of Canada's major trucking haulage firms and was able to offer its customers a broad range of services: LTL or TL freight, poolcar, rail piggyback, local pickup/delivery, freight brokerage across borders, and cargo express. The majority of Tremblay's revenues were from the LTL products which accounted for roughly 65% of its revenues, and the company's 16,000 active client accounts were spread across all major industry sectors. No client accounted for more than 2% of revenues. Client freight movements were tracked by way of a sophisticated computer system, and this had led to almost perfect delivery reliability (98% on-time) and claim-free (99% without claims) performance. Tremblay's operations were nationally balanced with Transport Tremblay Ltee. specializing in Canada east-west freight while Transport Larochelle Ltee. was concentrated in the east, serving Quebec, Ontario and the northeastern U.S. In June 1987, Tremblay owned 275 tractors, 1,000 trailers, 75 trucks, and 2 cranes. The company followed a conventional replacement policy and its fleet was considered to be reasonably well-maintained.

Management

LeBlanc, at 41, was a large, heavyset man, and a tough, open-door manager. While experienced in dealing with senior level managers, he could be at ease talking to truckers down in the terminals. He knew he had not been in the industry very long, but made up for this by soaking up information on the industry at every opportunity. He was also a pragmatist, often telling Spencer: "I'm not married to this business [trucking]. If the right offer came along tomorrow, I'd grab it." LeBlanc personally dabbled in the stock market, always investing in very safe, blue-chip stocks. His lifestyle was modest and unassuming.

Tremblay's senior management team had experience in the freight forwarding/trucking business dating back to the 1960s. After acquiring his controlling interest in the company, LeBlanc became the driving force behind the company, while Beaubien adopted a more laidback management stance. Operationally, the company was managed by Raymond Brousseau, 38, the vice president of operations and Martin Coutlee, 50, personnel manager. Jean Tardiff, 48, was promoted to replace LeBlanc as chief financial officer, and Rene Rousseau, 42, remained as vice president of sales. All of the key officers had been with the company for a number of years and LeBlanc was confident that his management team would continue to be successful in the highly competitive trucking industry.

Employee Relations

Tremblay employed 2,000[2] people in the various facets of its operations. This total included 350 tractor owner-operators working under contract to the company. Approximately one-half of the company was unionized, and these workers were represented by nine separate collective bargaining units. Contracts with various provincially based unions were for varying terms and expired on an ongoing basis. Employee relations were stable, and Tremblay, like many of its competitors in the industry, had been able to obtain favourable contracts in recent negotiations with various unions due to an oversupply of truckers. Transport Tremblay Ltee. and Transport Larochelle Ltee. had not suffered a strike or other significant labour disruption since the early 1970s. Tremblay negotiated separately with its owner-operators usually under exclusive one year contracts that set prices on a negotiable basis and complied with union safety and benefit stipulations.

If Tremblay decided to go public at some future date, LeBlanc was considering establishing an employee share option plan which would enable certain employees to subscribe in the aggregate for up to 5% of the common shares of the company.

Buyout of Marechal's Minority Interest

Marechal's preference shares carried an annual dividend of 8% and were to be fully redeemed by Tremblay five years after the date of the Transport

---

[2] By occupation, drivers 772; clerical 500; dockhands 348; marketing/sales 141; management and supervisory 172; and maintenance 67.

Larochelle acquisition. LeBlanc realized that a refinancing of the preferred shares with interest-bearing, tax deductible long-term debt could generate substantial savings. In addition, he was dissatisfied with the presence of the two Marechal members on the Tremblay board who were continually questioning and trying to obstruct the company's plans to streamline operations by closing down inefficient terminals and laying off redundant employees. In LeBlanc's opinion, Marechal contributed little to the management of Tremblay. Marechal was opposed to LeBlanc's expansionary plans and had made it clear that it did not want to increase its investment in Tremblay and would retire its preferred shares at maturity. LeBlanc stated that even if he had to pay the full $10.5 million now, "it would be worth it just to get rid of Marechal's influence".

LeBlanc knew that Marechal had alternative uses for the money it had invested in Tremblay so he approached Marechal's president with an offer to retire the preferred shares prior to the March 1991 maturity date. The negotiations were tough and protracted, but finally Marechal agreed to a $8 million payment. Marechal's willingness to accept a $2.5 million discount reflected their cash needs for other investments and their concern about the future of the trucking industry.

Financial History

Tremblay's consolidated financial statements for the year ending March 31, 1987, can be found in Exhibit 6. Revenues and expenses had increased as a result of the Larochelle acquisition.

As of March 31, 1987, the company had long term debt outstanding of $18,000,000 as part of a total Royal Bank facility of $26,000,000 in revolving[3] term loans. The revolving term loan had initially been set at $21 million to assist in financing the Transport Larochelle Ltee. buyout, but had been increased by $5 million in October 1986 to payout the Confederation Bank loans and to allow the Royal Bank to become exclusive banker to the connection. At this time, the debt was moved to the holding company level. The loan rate on the first $16 million was set at the Royal Bank Prime (RBP) or the Royal Bank Prime Acceptance Fee (RBPAF) for bankers' acceptances; and the remaining $10 million was set at RBP[4] plus $\frac{1}{4}$% or RBPAF plus $\frac{1}{4}$%. The credit facility was secured by accounts receivable and inventory as well as a fixed and floating charge over all of the company's assets.

---

[3] The revolving term loan was for general operating purposes and for realignment of acquisition financing for Transport Larochelle Ltee. It was revolving until April 1, 1988, with the balance outstanding after that date to be split as follows:
(a) demand, operating loans to a maximum of 75% of good accounts receivable;
(b) amount in excess of (a) to be termed out over a period not exceeding 5 years, repayable in 20 equal quarterly installments.
[4] RBP was 9.5% in June 1987.

The revolving term facility was seen by both Spencer and LeBlanc as a bridge financing arrangement until a more permanent capital structure evolved. LeBlanc had discussed the possibility of arranging mortgage financing to pay down some of the term facility. He felt that a fixed rate might help in stabilizing financing costs and place Tremblay in a stronger financial position to deal with industry restructuring and future expansion.

Company Prepared Forecasts

Income and expense forecasts can be found in Exhibit 7. These forecasts assumed a 15% drop in volume in fiscal 1988 caused by three factors: an anticipated economic recession, the pruning of unprofitable Larochelle accounts and price reductions expected to result from deregulation.

Despite the anticipated sales drop, LeBlanc was optimistic about the upcoming year. The bottom line would be improved by several actions: a saving in financing costs due to the replacement of the preferred shares with debt; a reduction in CEO salaries; and an annual $1.1 million year pre-tax saving from closing down unprofitable terminals and reducing layers of redundant middle management, although these moves would necessitate a one-time expense of $1.6 million in separation and restructuring costs.

LeBlanc envisaged making further acquisitions over the next five years. He believed that deregulation and free trade would create numerous opportunities to pick off weaker competitors and this would give Tremblay growth well above the industry averages. LeBlanc saw the three main goals of Tremblay as: (1) expansion through acquisition, (2) an eventual public issue to strengthen the company's capital base, and (3) an emphasis on providing reliable on-time delivery to maintain its competitive edge and preserve its market share.

Financing Alternatives

Spencer knew that LeBlanc was considering financing the Marechal buyout with $8 million in term debt, the unused portion of the revolving term loan facility. Spencer had come to understand LeBlanc quite well. She observed a classic dealmaker, with a highly analytical mind that was challenged by complexity. LeBlanc enjoyed taking "well calculated risks." He knew the trucking industry well, and at their meetings he would often relate interesting developments that were ongoing at competitors.

LeBlanc estimated Tremblay's real estate assets (land and buildings) had a market value between $16 and $18 million, and he thought that mortgage financing on these properties might result in lower and more stable interest costs over the long term. He had had preliminary discussions with several trust and insurance companies about fixed rate mortgage financing.

Royal Bank Capital Corporation (RBCC)

During their meeting, Spencer told LeBlanc that she would gather some background information on RBCC (see Exhibit 8). Spencer called Daniel Mathews, a vice president at RBCC and discussed some of the guidelines that RBCC sought in new investment decisions. Mathews told her that RBCC invested by way of a convertible subordinated loan or a common stock purchase. RBCC had a target return on investment of 20%. However, Mathews pointed out that since a portion of RBCC's portfolio earned little, if any, returns, the successful investments would have to generate a return in excess of 20% for RBCC to achieve its overall target.

SDIL's Financing Proposal

Spencer knew that SDIL wanted very badly to underwrite an initial public offering (IPO) of Tremblay stock. That motive was evident in their extending to LeBlanc a $2.5 million personal loan to assist in consolidating his ownership. SDIL were attracted to Tremblay because of their strong track record and solid industry reputation and believed Tremblay was an exciting story they could successfully market in selling shares. SDIL were in the process of determining an offering price. LeBlanc told Spencer that SDIL were attempting to price the issue at a price/earnings (P/E) ratio comparable to other trucking companies in the market, but that he thought they would propose an offering of 750,000 common shares at a price of about $7 per common share. Underwriting fees and the legal and audit costs associated with the examination and prospectus would amount to roughly 10% of the gross proceeds from a stock issue. SDIL had just about completed their due diligence examination of Tremblay. If an underwriting agreement was reached, SDIL planned to market the issue in September 1987.

EXHIBIT 1
TREMBLAY LTEE.

Corporate Structure
June 1987

Shareholdings By	LeBlanc	Beaubien	Marechal
Common Shares	80%	20%	0%
After Conversion of Preferred Stock	64%	16%	20%

TREMBLAY LTEE.
(Quebec)
Holding Company

100%	100%
Transport Tremblay Ltee.	Transport Larochelle Ltee.
Canada wide service	Ontario, Quebec, Atlantic, US
LTL, TL, & poolcar	LTL, TL & piggyback freight

Revenues	35%	65%
Employees	625	1375

EXHIBIT 2
TREMBLAY LTEE.

Selected Consolidated Financial Information
for the years ended March 31, 1987
(in $000s)

	1987	1986**	1985*	1984*	1983*	1982*
Operating Data						
Revenues	$156 289	$92 831	$40 258	$28 250	$24 641	$21 960
Operating Profit Before Interest and Tax	8 580	4 505	2 692	2 369	1 402	2 084
Net Income	3 967	1 673	563	8	79	132
Balance Sheet Data						
Total Assets	$ 55 111	$57 023	$10 995	$ 8 958	na	na
Long Term Debt	18 365	16 649	418	687	na	na
Equity	16 620	13 493	3 169	2 733	na	na

*Transport Tremblay Ltee. figures only.
**1986 results include Larochelle from August 1985, the effective date of acquisition.

EXHIBIT 3
TREMBLAY LTEE.

Canadian Trucking Industry Data[6]
($000 000s)

	1981	1982	1983	1984
Total Revenues	6 047	5 929	6 088	7 115
Net Income	130	70	156	231
Cash Flow	465	411	473	594
Balance Sheet Data				
Working Capital	−94	−215	−117	−78
Total Liabilities	2 473	2 384	2 502	2 727
Long-Term Liabilities	1 096	1 024	1 079	1 252
Shareholders' Equity	974	941	1 010	1 052
Financial Ratios				
Current Ratio	0.93:1	0.84:1	0.92:1	0.95:1
Liabilities/Equity	2.54:1	2.53:1	2.48:1	2.59:1
Long-Term Liab./Equity	1.12:1	1.09:1	1.07:1	1.19:1
Interest Coverage	2.04X	1.60X	2.45X	2.82X
Other Data				
Employees	90 782	83 989	80 546	83 689
Total Equipment	135 002	133 523	133 178	138 819

[6] *Source: The Canadian Year Book*, Statistics Canada

EXHIBIT 4
TREMBLAY LTEE.

The Top 10 Canadian Trucking Companies
(ranked by revenues)
($millions)

Name Fiscal Yr.	Where	Revenue	Income	Assets	Fixed Assets	Total Liab./ Equity	ROE
1. CP Trucks (1986)	Canada/US	$410	subs.[7]				
2. TNT Canada (1986)	Canada/US	410	subs.[7]				
3. Kingsway (1986)	Canada/US	300	pvt.[8]				
4. Trimac (1986) —Trucking Division	Canada/US	202					
—Total Company		294	3.5	357.5	245.4	1.59	1.3%
5. Canadian Motorways (1986)	Canada/US	175	pvt.[8]				
6. Reimer (1986)	Canada	171	.7	94.1	43.6	6.41	5.5%
7. GTL (1986)	Ont/Queb	169	4.7	128.4	90.8	5.90	25.2%
8. Tremblay (1987)	Canada/US	156	4.0	55.1	24.1	2.22	23.9%
9. Cabano (1987)	Queb/Marit	93	1.3	64.8	33.3	2.72	7.5%
10. Laidlaw (1986) —Trucking Division	Ont/Queb/US	77					
—Total Company		717	66.2	901.7	454.7	.38	18.3%

[7] Subsidiary does not report results separately.
[8] Privately held company — no public data available.

EXHIBIT 5
TREMBLAY LTEE.

Stock Market Information
on Selected Canadian Trucking Firms[9]

	Laidlaw Transportation		Trimac		Transport Dorval	
	Aug 31 85	Aug 31 86	Dec 31 85	Dec 31 86	Dec 31 85	Dec 31 86
EPS	$ .31	$ .42	$ .06	$ .04	$ .74	$ .65
EPS % growth	34%	34%	−122%	−33%	12%	−12%
Revenue % growth	23%	31%	3%	−18%	5%	−16%
Dividends/share	$ .06	$ .07	$ .09	$ .09	—	—
Average P/E ratio	21.4	34.1	54.1	69.4	not	10.8
Average market/book value of stock	4.2	5.3	1.1	.9	listed	1.8
Book value per share	$ 1.61	$ 2.69	$ 3.06	$ 3.05		$ 3.90
Return on common equity	21.8%	18.3%	1.9%	1.3%	13.2%	13.0%
Debt/equity ratio	.47	.38	1.69	1.59	1.35	1.41

Historical P/E Ratio

Transportation		TSE 300	TSE Sector*
1980		8.8	5.9
1981		7.9	5.2
1982		19.3	10.6
1983		22.4	26.1
1984		15.2	13.0
1985		14.5	14.9
1986		17.4	28.9
1987	January	18.9	28.6
	February	19.3	33.1
	March	21.4	30.2
	April	20.9	28.1
	May	20.3	31.5

*Includes Algoma Central, Greyhound Lines, Laidlaw Transportation, Pacific Western Airlines, and Trimac

[9] *Source:*   Royal Bank Information Resources

EXHIBIT 6

TREMBLAY LTEE.

Consolidated Statement of Income
(in $000s)

	March 31	
	1987	1986
	(note 1)	
Revenue	156 289	92 831
Operating Expenses	144 214	86 136
Depreciation and Amortization	3 495	2 190
Earnings Before Interest and Taxes	8 580	4 505
Interest Expense	1 424	1 017
Income from Operations Before Income Taxes	7 156	3 488
Provision for Income Taxes	3 549	1 814
Income Before Extraordinary Items	3 607	1 674
Extraordinary Items (note 5)	360	
Net Income for the Period	3 967	1 674
Preferred Dividends	840	28
Net Income Available for Common Shareholders	3 127	1 646
Income Per Common Share:		
Income Before Extraordinary Items	$0.69	$0.41
Net Income	$0.78	$0.41

Consolidated Statement of Retained Earnings
(in $000s)

Retained Earnings, Beginning of Period	2 677	1 031
Add Net Income for the Period	3 967	1 674
Less Preferred Dividends	840	28
Retained Earnings, End of Period	5 804	2 677

See accompanying notes.

EXHIBIT 6 (continued)

Consolidated Balance Sheet
(in $000s)

	March 31	
	1987	1986
Assets		
Current Assets		
Cash	1 714	
Accounts receivable	22 554	22 092
Inventories	553	649
Prepaid expenses	1 845	2 210
	26 666	24 951
Other Assets (net of depreciation)		
Fixed Assets (note 2)	24 075	27 640
Licenses	833	833
Goodwill	3 537	3 599
TOTAL ASSETS	$55 111	$57 023
Liabilities and Shareholders' Equity		
Current		
Bank Indebtedness	0	4 084
Accounts Payable and Accrued Liabilities	16 468	19 605
Income Taxes Payable	2 025	1 155
Current Portion of Long Term Debt (note 3)	105	809
	18 598	25 653
Long Term Debt (note 3)	18 260	15 840
Deferred Income Taxes	1 633	2 037
Shareholders' Equity		
Capital Stock (note 4)		
Preferred Shares	10 500	10 500
Common Shares	316	316
Retained Earnings	5 804	2 677
	16 620	13 493
TOTAL LIABILITIES AND SHAREHOLDERS' EQUITY	55 111	57 023

See accompanying notes.

EXHIBIT 6 (continued)

Consolidated Statement of Changes in Financial Position
(in $000s)

	1987	1986
Cash Provided By (used in)		
Operating Activities		
Income Before Extraordinary Items	3 607	1 673
Items Not Involving Cash		
Depreciation and Amortization	3 495	2 190
Deferred Income Taxes	− 404	995
Gains on Disposals of Fixed Assets	− 400	− 329
Net Change in Non-Cash Working Capital	−2 699	−1 607
Cash Provided By (used in)		
Operating Activities	3 599	2 922
Financing Activities		
Increase in Long-Term Debt	1 716	14 312
Issue of Preferred Shares	0	10 500
Preferred Dividends	− 840	− 28
Cash Provided By Financing Activities	876	24 784
Investing Activities		
Purchase of Transport Larochelle Ltee. (note 1)	0	− 21 204
Addition to Fixed Assets	− 861	− 6 050
Proceeds from Disposals of Fixed Assets	517	665
Proceeds from Sale of Extraordinary Items (net of tax)	1 667	0
Cash Provided By (used in)		
Investing Activities	1 323	− 26 589
Net Change in Cash During the Period	6 638	1 117
Bank Indebtedness Acquired on Acquisitions	0	− 3 393
Bank Indebtedness, Beginning of Period	−4 084	−1 836
Bank Cash Balance (indebtedness), End of Period	+ 1 714	− 4 084

See accompanying notes.

243

Case 22
Tremblay Ltee.

EXHIBIT 6 (continued)

Excerpts from
Notes to Consolidated Financial Statements
(in $000s)

March 31, 1987

1. *Purchase of Transport Larochelle Ltee.*

Effective August 23, 1985, the company acquired 100% of the issued shares of Transport Larochelle Ltee. from Le Groupe Marechal. Transport Larochelle Ltee.'s business consists of over-the-road freight transportation. The acquisition was accounted for using the purchase method and the results of operations are included in the consolidated financial statements from the effective date of acquisition. Details of the net assets acquired at assigned values and the consideration paid on the acquisition are as follows:

Working Capital (including bank indebtedness of $3 393)	648
Fixed Assets	20 418
Licences	762
Goodwill	1 016
	22 844
Long-Term Debt	608
Deferred Income Taxes	1 032
Purchase Price of Net Assets Acquired	$21 204
Consideration	
Cash, including cash on acquisition	$10 704
Preferred shares (note 5)	10 500
	$21 204

The closing date for this acquisition was March 12, 1986.

2. *Fixed Assets*

		March 31, 1987		March 31, 1986
	Cost	Accum. Depr.	Net B.V.	*Net Book Value*
Land	5 459	0	5 459	5 666
Buildings	8 776	3 514	5 262	5 540
Trucks, Tractors and Trailers	36 291	24 504	11 787	13 992
Other Equipment	5 234	3 790	1 444	2 296
Leasehold Improvements	161	38	123	146
	$55 921	$31 846	$24 075	$27 640

EXHIBIT 6 (continued)

3. Long-Term Debt	March 31, 1987	March 31, 1986
Revolving Loans	$18 000	$15 028
Lease Obligations	365	512
Term Loans, at Varying Interest Rates from Prime Plus ½% to Prime Plus 1%	0	1 109
	18 365	16 649
Less Current Portion	105	809
	$18 260	$15 840

The terms of the revolving loans extend to April 1, 1988 at which time the company has the option to convert the amount not designated as an operating loan to term loans which are repayable in equal quarterly installments over five years. Interest during the revolving period is at prime when loans outstanding are under $16 million and prime plus ¼% when loans exceed $16 million. Interest on the term loans will be at the fixed money market rate (as defined) plus ¾%.

Under the loan agreement, the company is required to maintain the following financial ratios: a minimum equity of $13 000 000; a working capital ratio greater than 1 to 1; a debt/equity ratio not exceeding 3.5 to 1 until April 1, 1988 and reducing to 2 to 1 thereafter. As at March 31, 1987, the company complied with all restrictive covenants and financial tests.

4. *Capital Stock*
Issued
As at March 31, 1987 and March 31, 1986, issued share capital consisted of:

	Number	Amount
Preferred	1 000 000	$10 500
Class A common	4 000 000	316

5. *Extraordinary Items*
During the year, the business, goodwill, and all tangible assets of certain Transport Larochelle Ltee. properties and terminals were sold. Total proceeds of $1 841 were received resulting in a gain of $360 (net of taxes of $174).

6. *Segmented Information*
Geographic segmented information is as follows:

	USA	Canada	Total
1987			
Revenue	23 786	132 503	156 289
Net Income for the Period	749	3 218	3 967
Identifiable Assets	548	36 832	37 380
1986			
Revenue	12 841	79 990	92 831
Net Income for the Period	233	1 441	1 674
Identifiable Assets	609	32 384	32 993

EXHIBIT 7

TREMBLAY LTEE.

Income Forecasts
for the five years ending March 31, 1988–1992

	1988	1989	1990	1991	1992
Revenues	$138 835	$130 505	$168 352	$191 921	$211 113
Operating Expenses	129 117	121 370	153 200	174 648	192 113
Depreciation and Amort.	3 691	3 810	3 871	4 104	4 413
	132 808	125 180	157 071	178 752	196 526
Operating Income (EBIT)	6 027	5 325	11 281	13 169	14 587
Interest on Existing Revolving Term Debt[10]	2 160	2 160	2 160	2 160	2 160
Net Income Before Taxes, Dividends or Any Other Incremental Financing Costs	3 867	3 165	9 121	11 009	12 427
Taxes @ 50%	1 933	1 582	4 560	5 504	6 213
Net Income After Taxes	$ 1 934	1 583	4 561	5 505	6 214

[10] Assumed to be 12%.

EXHIBIT 7 (continued)
Pro Forma Balance Sheets
for the five years ending March 31, 1988–1992

	1988	1989	1990	1991	1992
Assets					
Current Assets					
Accounts Receivable	$22 822	$21 594	$27 674	$31 549	$34 704
Inventory	554	577	599	623	648
Prepaids	1 845	1 845	1 845	1 845	1 845
	25 221	24 016	30 118	34 017	37 197
Fixed Assets	24 810	25 221	26 770	28 832	31 192
Licences	833	833	833	833	833
Goodwill	2 811	2 722	2 634	2 545	2 457
	28 454	28 776	30 237	32 210	34 482
TOTAL ASSETS	$53 675	52 792	60 355	66 227	71 679
Liabilities & Equity					
Current Liabilities					
Accounts Payable	17 687	16 626	20 986	23 924	26 317
Income Taxes Payable	1 258	1 258	1 258	1 258	1 258
	18 945	17 884	22 244	25 182	27 575
Revolving Term Loan	18 000	18 000	18 000	18 000	18 000
Deferred Taxes	2 874	2 874	2 874	2 874	2 874
Total Liabilities	39 819	38 758	43 118	46 056	48 449
Common	316	316	316	316	316
Contributed Surplus	2 500	2 500	2 500	2 500	2 500
Core Retained Earnings[11]	5 804	5 804	5 804	5 804	5 804
New Retained Earnings	1 934	3 517	8 078	13 583	19 797
Total Equity	10 544	12 137	16 698	22 203	28 417
TOTAL LIAB. & EQUITY	50 373	50 895	59 816	68 259	76 866
FINANCING NEED	3 302	1 897	− 539	− 2 032	− 5 187
TOTAL LIAB. & EQUITY	$53 675	52 792	60 355	66 227	71 679

Assumptions:

Contributed surplus represents the difference between the $10.5 million face value of the preferred shares and the $8 million redemption value.

    Retained earnings were $5 084 at March 31, 1987. Year over year additions to retained earnings do not reflect any new financing.

[11] These numbers exclude the costs of any new financing.

EXHIBIT 8
TREMBLAY LTEE.

Royal Bank Capital Corporation (RBCC) Profile

Background

Royal Bank Capital Corporation (RBCC) provides capital to well managed and established companies, through equity and subordinated debt. RBCC's experience, expertise, financial resources, and track record of innovative deal structures are fully committed to help businesses succeed.

RBCC is a wholly owned subsidiary of The Royal Bank of Canada. Chartered in 1869, the Royal Bank is Canada's largest bank with assets in excess of one hundred billion dollars, a network of 1500 branches and 5300 correspondent banking relationships in nearly every country in the world. With its 75% ownership of RBC Dominion Securities, the Bank has consolidated its position as Canada's leading financial institution.

Originally established as a financial services company in 1974, RBCC today represents one of Canada's most active merchant banking/private investment pools, with corporate offices located in Montreal, Toronto, and western Canada.

Financial Flexibility

RBCC invests its own funds and can therefore be highly flexible in structuring financial packages that best suit individual needs. The scope of operations encompasses a wide range of minority equity and mezzanine capital investments beyond the limitations of conventional bank debt.

RBCC's investment professionals are skilled in analyzing, structuring, financing, and monitoring a diverse investment portfolio.

Investment Opportunities

RBCC will provide risk capital to dynamic, privately owned and emerging public companies with potential for significant capital appreciation and cash flow generation. Preferred areas of investment are Canadian manufacturing or service oriented firms beyond the startup stage. RBCC will also assist in the structuring of management and leveraged buyouts and advise clients concerning the optimum use of senior and secured debt.

Products and Services

RBCC investments normally take the form of common shares and/or participating debentures with a typical horizon of three to five years (maximum eight years). Funds are directed primarily toward working capital support, capital expenditures, and corporate acquisitions.

RBCC works best with companies as a value added participant at the board of directors level. RBCC expertise relates to all phases of financing, ranging from planning and conceptualization, legal review, operational and financial due diligence, to implementation and closing. RBCC contributes financial skills, networking, and a variety of connections to private or public funding as the company matures.

Investment Size

Individual investments typically range from $1 million to $10 million. Larger financings can be handled through syndication supported by RBCC's extensive network of investment partners.

Investment Criteria

RBCC investments are characterized by the following:

(1) *Management.* The businesses sought should have highly skilled and financially committed management teams with entrepreneurial flair.

(2) *Market Advantage.* The company's products or services should be distinctive and demonstrate a strong market potential.

(3) *Strategic Planning.* The company should have a clearly defined and an achievable long-term strategic plan.

(4) *Profitability.* Growth in revenue and cash flow should be sufficient to enable the company to provide a return to RBCC commensurate with the risks assumed.

(5) *Divestiture Opportunity.* Exit opportunities should be available to repurchase RBCC's interest through: cash flow from operations; puts to (calls by) management and/or the company; private or public placement to third parties; or sale to corporate partners.

Investment Process

Typically, an investment is established as follows:

(1) *Initial Evaluation.* Management, product or service, market growth rate, competition, margins and cash flow are assessed quickly and professionally to determine the investment potential. All enquiries are treated in strictest confidence.

(2) *Outline.* A facility outline is issued by RBCC establishing general parameters for the proposed investment.

(3) *Due Diligence.* RBCC completes due diligence and provides a firm financing offer.

(4) *Disbursement.* Legal and other disbursement conditions are completed and funds disbursed.

Managing the Investment

Through regular meetings with management and by having representatives on the board of directors, RBCC contributes to the growth and development of its portfolio companies.

RBCC can often assist in major operating decisions, strategic planning, mergers and acquisitions, executive recruiting and introductions to investment bankers, lawyers, accountants and other professionals, as well as access to the financial services of The Royal Bank of Canada and RBC Dominion Securities. RBCC is a resource for information, practical experience, and contacts.

RBCC — FLEXIBILITY, CREDIBILITY, INNOVATION: A STRONG FINANCIAL PARTNER!

PART EIGHT

Pricing Securities Issues

AIR CANADA

Claude Taylor, now Chairman of the Board of Air Canada, and previously the Chief Executive Officer (CEO) for the airline from 1976 to 1984, nervously paced across his hotel suite on Toronto's airport strip on a late September 1988 Friday afternoon. The meeting to establish the price for Air Canada's initial public offering of common shares was set to start at about 4:00 p.m. after the market closed. From the federal government's decision to privatize Air Canada through to the road-show in downtown Toronto, Taylor with Pierre Jeanniot, President and CEO, and other key Air Canada executives had dedicated themselves to achieve a successful transition from a government-owned to a privately-owned global airline. Taylor had pressed the government for years to turn Air Canada over to the private sector and the decision was a personal victory for him. Now just as his goal was at hand, a serious question arose as to an acceptable price for shares the company intended to issue. While the price of the shares was always a concern for the government officials from the Department of Transport and Finance, the perception among the Air Canada officers was that the government would be flexible on price in order to get the issue accomplished. Now as the pricing decision was imminent, Taylor realized that the government officials had a minimum acceptable price in mind and it was rigid. As one senior bureaucrat told him, "if we don't get it, we'll pull the issue."

History of Air Canada

Trans-Canada Airlines (TCA), the forerunner of Air Canada, came into being through an act of parliament, the Trans-Canada Air Lines Act, on April 10, 1937. TCA was organized as a subsidiary of the Canadian National Railway Company, a crown corporation, although there were several businessmen who wanted to set up an independent airline at the time.

At TCA's inception, the Canadian airways system was virtually non-existent. However in the United States several commercial airlines such as

Pan-Am were already well established. In 1937, the Canadian airline industry consisted of a few operators whose main source of revenue was in mail transport. TCA's task was to build the infrastructure for a national airline and it did that by instructing pilots, constructing runways, setting up navigational beacons across the country and developing a meteorological service. TCA made its maiden commercial voyage on September 1, 1937, a mail run from Vancouver to Seattle with two passengers.

TCA was an innovative airline, initiating many firsts for the North American airline industry, including the first airline to have turbine-powered aircraft, and the first North American airline to serve Moscow.

In 1965, the crown corporation changed its name to Air Canada and, in 1977, the Government of Canada acquired direct control of the corporation from Canadian National.

By 1988, Air Canada was one of the world's largest airlines and one of the most recognizable names in the global airline industry (Exhibit 1). The company had expanded operations to include not only a collection of regional airlines, but also industry-related companies such as airline maintenance services, tour operations, reservation systems, a credit card company and an interest in an aircraft leasing company.

Airline Industry

The airline industry was a very competitive and cyclical industry. The factors of fuel prices, fare wars, landing rights, market share battles, number of business people flying, and labour disputes made an airline tough to manage.

Globally the airline industry was undergoing drastic changes. Traditionally the airways were tightly controlled and regulated by the domestic governments. Deregulation in the United States brought on many changes in the competitive nature of the industry. No longer could airlines rely on profitable regulated routes with restricted competition. Start-up carriers fought for market share with established airlines. These new carriers often leased available aircraft and subcontracted the maintenance. As a result, they required a small initial investment. Major airlines expanded their scope of operations to global markets as their home market profit levels became squeezed.

Internationally, an airline's operations were an inter-governmental issue. Bilateral agreements between governments determined landing rights, flight frequencies, airline capacities, number of air carriers and tariffs to be charged. It was a give and take process with reciprocal rights usually being given to another country's air carriers.

The Minister of Transport negotiated landing rights for a Canadian carrier in another country, and then decided which Canadian airline would service that route. The selection process often brought charges of favouritism towards Air Canada by the other Canadian carriers.

Canadian Airline Industry

Before 1984, domestic flights were regulated by the federal government. The government regulations permitted two national airlines, Air Canada and Canadian Pacific (CP) Air, and four regional airlines in Canada. Then in 1984, as an introduction to deregulation, the distinction between regional and national carriers was removed. Further deregulation occurred allowing free entry into the market place and permitting the airlines to establish fares and routes for southern Canada based on economic conditions. Routes in northern Canada were still tightly regulated by the federal government.

Dramatic changes took place in the Canadian airline industry as a result of deregulation. In 1986, Wardair, until then a charter-only airline, applied for and received permission to become a regularly scheduled airline with national routes. In 1987 Pacific Western Airlines (PWA) bought CP Air and merged it with Eastern Provincial Airways, Nordair and Pacific Western Airlines to form Canadian Airlines. Air Canada took over control of Air BC, Northwest Territorial Airways, Air Ontario, Air Alliance and Air Nova. Now there were three national airlines, a number of strong regional carriers linked to the national carriers, and more competition for the Canadian air traveller.

The major Canadian airlines began to concentrate on the longer, more profitable flights with larger more fuel-efficient aircraft. The regional airlines with smaller airplanes could more economically serve the shorter routes.

Demand in Canada for airline passenger service was highly seasonal. A major challenge for the airlines was to stimulate demand during the slow seasons through selective price discounting practices. Airline profits were very sensitive to successfully managing these swings in demand.

Growth in Canadian passenger service was lagging behind worldwide growth (Exhibit 2). While competition increased, Air Canada had to expand its network of international flights and achieve market share in the global market if it intended to grow.

Air Canada

The corporation included a number of businesses all related to airline, travel and related business. A corporate organization showing the various companies and operations that make up Air Canada is shown in Exhibit 3. Each major segment is described in the next few paragraphs.

Financial statements for the consolidated company are set out in Exhibit 4, including a forecast for the last six months of 1988.

Air Canada's Airline Business

Air Canada operated an average of 430 scheduled flights each day involving 28 Canadian cities and 33 cities in Europe, the U.S., the Caribbean and Asia. Connector airlines linked another 81 North American communities to the Air Canada network. Passenger traffic accounted for 76 percent of total revenues and cargo revenues 13 percent.

Air Canada's fleet included 103 passenger aircraft and 8 cargo aircraft. The operating statistics and average age of the aircraft are shown in Exhibit 5. The company had 34 Airbus 320 planes on order. The company estimated the life of a plane at thirty years. A recent evaluation of the fleet established its value at $200–300 million over book value. The Airbus 320 was scheduled to begin replacing the Boeing 727 in 1990.

Other Business

The other components of Air Canada's business were less visible than the passenger airline, but valuable components. The enRoute card was the world's largest airline-operated credit card system with over 280,000 cardholders. Revenues amounted to $36 million in 1987 with a compound annual growth rate of 21 percent. Touram Inc. (100 percent owned) was a major tour operator which provided travel packages. In 1987, Touram generated $139 million in revenues. As well, Air Canada sold aircraft maintenance and servicing to other airlines. In 1987, the company generated revenues of $134 million from this activity. Other airline related activities generated revenues in 1987 of $102 million.

Air Canada and another airline formed a limited partnership called the Gemini Group in 1987 to operate an airline passenger reservation system. The Gemini Group had assets and revenues in 1988 of over $100 million and employed over 600 computer professionals.

Many analysts considered Air Canada's 22.4 percent holding (879,925 shares) in GPA Group Limited (GPA) a significant component of its total value. GPA was a privately held financial service company with headquarters in Shannon, Ireland. The company was engaged in aircraft leasing, sales and service with airlines and financial institutions. In April 1988, GPA completed a private placement of 331,650 common shares at a price of US $250 per share. The GPA shares were carried on Air Canada's balance sheet as an investment of $118.5 million.

The GPA Group reported earnings after tax of $101 million for the fiscal year ended March 31, 1988 on revenues of $650 million. Air Canada included $24 million in its earnings for 1988 reflecting the contribution of GPA and received $6 million in dividends from GPA.

Privatization Drive

Company officials believed that it was essential for Air Canada to achieve private ownership. With three large and established Canadian carriers, the role of a national airline to aid in the development of the country was no longer necessary. Waiting for government approval on key business decisions put Air Canada at a disadvantage. Air Canada wanted to upgrade its air fleet with newer, more cost efficient planes. Requests to the government for funds were subject to delay and review which took longer than capital market funding.

Air Canada officials were not the only ones who thought that the airline would be better off in private hands. In a Financial Times / Decima Poll, taken in June 1987, over 60 percent of survey respondents said that they would support the privatization of Air Canada.

Political Situation

The Progressive Conservative government of the day, led by Prime Minister Brian Mulroney, was committed to privatization of crown corporations. Companies that the government had already privatized included: Teleglobe Canada, Canadair, de Havilland, Canada Development Corporation, Northern Transportation Company, Canadian Arsenals, Nanismith Mines, Pecheries Canada and Fishery Products International. The privatization of Fishery Products International and Canada Development Corporation were accomplished by stock offerings. The other companies were sold intact to corporate buyers.

During the 1984 election campaign, the question of selling Air Canada arose and Mulroney stated emphatically that "Air Canada is not for sale". After the Conservatives were elected this statement was thought by many to be the reason that Air Canada was not included in the set of companies sold by the government. Taylor and other Air Canada officials did not give up hope and continued with their efforts towards privatization.

In February 1987, British Airways, the British government-owned airline, was successfully sold by the Thatcher government as part of an extensive privatization program. In the British Airways sale, the shares were sold mainly to institutional money managers. British Airways stock was listed on foreign stock exchanges including the Toronto and New York Stock Exchanges. However the British government kept a "Golden Share" which could be used to control the company in exceptional circumstances. Demand for shares of British Airways was strong. Although there were allegations that the British government "gave the company away", the sell-off of British Airways was considered to be a textbook case of how a government should privatize a company.

The Government's Decision

On April 12, 1988, the Honourable Donald Mazankowski, the Deputy Prime Minister, made the surprise announcement that Air Canada was to be privatized. Speculation on the reasons for the announcement included the fact that Air Canada was requesting additional capital to buy new planes at a time when the government was strapped for funds. The success of the British Airways sale was considered to be another factor in the decision.

The announcement set in rapid motion the plan that Air Canada officials had prepared for such a situation. Airline officials had ideas that assisted in drafting legislation that the government could use in getting the needed Commons and Senate approval.

At this stage there were two tricky political issues to be managed. One was getting the proper legislation passed allowing the sale. Another issue was price. The price had to be set high enough that criticism of "giving the company away" would be negligible. As well, the government wanted to avoid having the stock price set so low that it was below the carrying value on its books (just under $8.00). To have sold at less than the carry value would have created an accounting loss which would increase the budget deficit.

On August 18, legislation allowing the issue passed the Senate and received final government approval. By August 20, the underwriting syndicate was formed, on August 25 the red-herring prospectus was filed with the various provincial securities commissions, and by September 26 the prospectus for the issue was cleared.

The Privatization Plan

The plan was for Air Canada to issue new shares to the public. These shares would constitute approximately 45 percent of the total shares outstanding. The issuing of new treasury shares by the company rather than a secondary offering of the shares held by the government provided several advantages. First, the proceeds went to the company which required funds to acquire aircraft. Second, it deflected attention away from the government as the seller of the shares. Third, it enabled the company to manage the investment banking process without very much government involvement.

The government imposed various restrictions on the sale. The government would retain 55 percent of the shares; it declared that it would not vote its shares although it retained the right to do so. The government indicated its intention to sell its holdings when market conditions were favourable. Foreign ownership was to be restricted to 25 percent. Any single shareholder could not control more than 10 percent of the shares. These restrictions were not unique in the airline industry as KLM Royal Dutch Airways and British Airways had similar ownership restrictions, as did airlines in the US at least with respect to foreign ownership.

The shares were to be listed on the Toronto, Montreal, Vancouver, Alberta, and Winnipeg stock exchanges, but not on any foreign exchanges. In addition there was not to be any initial organized foreign offering of the shares, although the Canadian investment banking syndicate members were not prohibited from offering shares through their foreign distribution networks as permitted by local securities laws.

Marketing

The government wanted the shares to be as widely distributed among Canadians as possible. Mazankowski said in the House of Commons that every Canadian would have an opportunity to buy Air Canada shares. To accommodate this objective the government encouraged Air Canada and its investment banking advisors to set up an innovative approach to marketing the shares which would make this one of the most extensively promoted initial public offerings ever in Canada.

A large number of shares was reserved for the traditional customers of the investment dealers, namely institutional and retail investors. However retail customers of investment dealers were also offered a subscription-type plan to buy shares similar to that designed for the public-at-large.

The offering to the public-at-large took place in stages. First Air Canada sent a bulletin to enRoute credit card holders (Exhibit 6). When the red-herring prospectus was prepared and filed, advertisements were run in various Canadian newspapers announcing the issue with coupons to clip and mail for information. Subsequent advertising included a toll free number that potential investors could use to request information about the issue. The information they received included the red-herring prospectus, an application form, and a process for submitting orders. Air Canada officials expected a strong response to this promotion based on Decima research and had 600,000 prospectuses printed.

In addition the traditional "road shows" were conducted for institutional investors and retail securities sales representatives. In keeping with the plan of a wide distribution of shares, Air Canada officials staged road shows in sixteen different Canadian cities in every Canadian province using three different road show "teams". The road shows were very successful. Over 1000 sales representatives from securities firms attended the road show in Toronto the day before.

Even the actual share certificates were a marketing tool as they were printed on attractive blue paper with a special design showing off the Air Canada logo when viewed at a particular angle.

Finally, the government asked Air Canada, as part of its objective to encourage the small investor, to permit purchase by subscription in a block of 25 shares instead of what is considered the usual minimum of 100 share lots. The opportunity to subscribe for 100 share lots also existed.

While Air Canada shares were being marketed to the general public, officers of the company were busy educating employees about the share issue. A block of shares was reserved for company employees. To encourage employee participation, Air Canada offered several attractive features including interest-free loans to finance the purchase of shares, discounts off the offer price, instalment purchases and payroll deductions. The response from employees was expected to be strong, although some union leaders were advising their members to boycott the issue. The pilots union had publicly supported the offering.

The Financial Data

At this stage the major items not decided were the price of the shares and the size of the issue. The number of shares to be issued from the company's treasury was not yet determined. During discussion, the number of shares to be issued was estimated at 30.8 million with the government retaining 41.1 million for a total of 71.9 million shares outstanding. An offering price of $10 per share was regarded as most likely by the company officials although the investment bankers set a range of $8 to 10.

Airline stock prices tended to be volatile. Financial statistics for Air Canada, PWA, Wardair and various American and international airlines are presented in Exhibit 7. Just a week earlier, financial analysts had presented lower earnings estimates for PWA for the quarter ended August 31st. The actual results for PWA were due at any moment.

Consolidated balance sheets and income statements for Air Canada are presented in Exhibit 4. Air Canada's performance in the fourth quarter of 1987 was significantly below expectations. The company's ground maintenance workers went on a costly strike during that busy last quarter. The first quarter of 1988 reflected the costly efforts to regain market shares. As well, Wardair was aggressively cutting fares in order to attract customers and this meant Air Canada had to follow suit.

As a private company, Air Canada was expected to become even more cost competitive. An Economic Council of Canada report concluded that between 1964 and 1981, the company had spent 18 percent more on administrative costs because it was under government control.

Having the government as a major shareholder was thought to be of some comfort to the small investor. However Canadian institutional investment managers were known to be unhappy about investing in a company where the government was involved in any way as an owner. If the Conservatives lost power in the upcoming election, then it was conceivable that a new government would rescind the legislation to sell the remaining shares or delay the process inordinately. The possibility that this new government would use its ownership position to influence the company to act in pursuit of its public policy objectives frightened many investors. Many analysts argued that the shares would have to be discounted because of the government involvement.

Speculating on the share price provided a bonanza for the business press. Almost every day there was another analyst's assessment of the firm quoted in the press. Exhibit 8 presents one such newspaper article.

The Investment Bankers

The choice of lead underwriter for the Air Canada issue was carefully considered because of its unique characteristics. The issue was large by Canadian standards and required an investment banking firm with substantial resources. In order to satisfy the government's promise to have the shares as widely distributed as possible, the underwriters had to be able to organize an effective distribution system. As well, the unique marketing techniques the Air Canada officials introduced like newspaper coupons and direct telephone lines, required patience and flexibility. The members of the underwriting syndicate were chosen with these criteria in mind.

The underwriting process involves three steps. At each step, a single investment banking firm or a syndicate of firms may carry out the functions involved. The first step involves the preparation of the prospectus, the marketing of the issue through the road shows and the presentation of an offer to the issuer. This is referred to as the underwriting function. In the second step the investment bankers involved in the first step sell the deal which has been agreed upon with the issuers to a large group of securities firms. This larger group, known as the banking group, includes the underwriting firms. Each member of the banking group takes financial responsibility for a specified percentage of the issue. The function of the banking group is to share the risk of the issue. Finally, the selling activity involves members of the banking group and others selling the issue to investors. Major institutional investors are assigned to specific members of the banking group for the sales effort.

The scarcity of initial public offerings since the stock market crash of October 1987 and the size and high profile of the Air Canada issue, created a great competition among the Canadian investment banks to act as the lead underwriter. Air Canada invited securities firms to submit proposals for this position. The "bake-offs" or "beauty contests" to select the lead underwriter began shortly after the privatization plan was announced. Eleven different investment banking firms made presentations to Air Canada officers, its advisors and the government. RBC Dominion Securities Inc. (RBC Dominion) was chosen to act as lead underwriter with Wood Gundy Inc. chosen as co-lead. Seven additional firms formed the underwriting syndicate including Scotia McLeod Inc., Nesbitt Thomson Deacon Inc., Richardson Greenshields of Canada Inc., Burns Fry Ltd., Merrill Lynch Canada Inc., Levesque Beaubien Inc. and Pemberton Securities Inc.

The underwriting spread is shared among the various investment banking participants generally in the following proportions:

Underwriters' Fee	20 percent
Banking Syndicate	40 percent
Selling Concession	40 percent

For an issue of $250 to $300 million, the spread of $12 to $15 million (5 to 6 percent) of the total proceeds represented a significant pool of revenues for the investment banking firms.

Derek Brown and his team at RBC Dominion were well aware of the pressures involved in setting the price for a new issue. Brown was the RBC Dominion executive managing the Air Canada issue and he had been through it many times before. However, the Air Canada issue was the largest, and certainly the most visible initial common stock offering of his career. As he prepared for the meeting that afternoon with the Air Canada officers and the government officials, he kept referring to the order book that the various securities firms had compiled. While the orders were in hand to sell the 30.8 million shares, the price to clear the market was well below the $10 per share price which he knew the government and company officials had initially counted upon. The investment bankers referred to a price of $8 to $10 per share in the road show presentations and in the marketing material. He wondered if a renewed sales campaign with the institutional investors might lift the orders and the price; but he knew that there was resistance among institutional portfolio managers to the issue. More importantly, there was very little confidence among the investment bankers in orders obtained through the application scheme for the general public.

Brown, a vice-president of RBC Dominion, the largest securities firm in Canada, and his colleagues had to consider the other members of the underwriting and banking syndicates as well. He knew that setting a price too high for an issue of this size would result in a huge block of unsold shares for the investment banking group to manage, ultimately a failed issue, and financial losses in the millions to the underwriting group.

The investment bankers (underwriters) for a securities issue, like Air Canada's proposed offering of 30.8 million shares, undertook the key role of buying the securities from the company and selling them to investors. The spread between the purchase price to the company and the selling price to investors, usually expressed as a percentage of the selling price, compensated them for the risk and work involved in the process. In the Air Canada issue, five percent was negotiated as the underwriting spread.

But the underwriters had a much greater role in the initial public offering of stock than just buying and selling the shares. They advised the company on all aspects of the offer including type of securities to issue, the reorganization of the existing capital structure, preparation of the prospectus, and the marketing of the company, including establishing expectations about the price and size of the issue. After the issue the underwriter was expected to maintain an orderly market in the shares up to the time of completing the distribution.

The lead underwriters, in this case RBC Dominion and Wood Gundy, managed the new share issue process. This involved co-ordinating with the company on the preparation and submission of the prospectus, working with the other managing underwriters to form a banking syndicate, and organizing the marketing program for the sale of the shares. The plan for the road shows was a key component of the total marketing effort.

RBC Dominion was prominent in conducting the road shows and managing the marketing activity with institutional investors. The intense marketing program for the shares with retail investors required extra work to insure that no securities commissions guidelines were broken in any province. The newspaper promotion to sell stock to the public required special permission from the various securities commissions.

A major activity for the underwriter was negotiating the price for the shares and the size of the issue. The lead underwriter took the initiative to conduct financial analysis leading to a price, but the others conducted some research as well and pricing parameters were established on a collaborative basis. Setting the price too low meant that the issuing company would not receive full value. Also a rapid run-up in the share price would attract speculators or "riders" with the result that legitimate long term investors would be put-off and the after market would be in disarray. Setting the price too high meant that the underwriters would be left holding inventory while the price in the secondary market dropped below issue price. If this happened the underwriters would suffer a financial loss. In either event the underwriters' reputations would be damaged and both the government and Air Canada officials would be unhappy.

In developing the price proposal, the underwriters reviewed the share prices of similar publicly-traded companies, as well as the company's own particular situation and potential. These data are presented in Exhibit 2. During the road shows, and in meetings with institutional investors, the underwriters attempted to determine what investors would pay. In Air Canada's case it appeared that the majority of the institutional investors were wary of the issue and were unwilling to put a high value on the shares. The enthusiasm of the retail investor for the shares was difficult to gauge because of the large number of dealers promoting the shares and the unpredictable nature of orders in the priority subscription system. However, it was believed that there was a strong demand at the retail level and among employees for the shares. As well, several articles appeared in the financial press suggesting that the Air Canada issue would rapidly sell out.

Orders for the issue were compiled by the lead underwriters in an order book. Institutional sales representatives for the managing underwriters communicated the number of shares and the price information for all institutions contacted. Retail allocations were reviewed but were not considered as price sensitive as institutional orders.

At the meeting to set the price and size of the issue, the lead underwriter in conjunction with the others presents the offer to the company, the number of shares and the price per share. The underwriter bases the proposals on the state of the market, the order book, and the outlook for the industry and the company. The underwriter attempted to condition the issuer to the price during the road shows and in meetings. The intention was that the pricing meeting would not result in "surprises" for the issuer.

The Price

Over the course of the past three years, Air Canada officials produced several studies to determine the value of the company and the shares. Obviously the value of a share was a function of two variables, the value of the company and the number of shares outstanding. The various studies had different assumptions about shares issued therefore making comparisons of per share values meaningless; nevertheless, the per share price arrived at in a study often stayed in people's minds. Since some valuation studies took place prior to the market crash of October 1987, the comparable market values of airline stocks were higher then. Prices as high as $20 per share had been presented by consultants to Air Canada and the government.

In the spring of 1988 Morgan Stanley and S.G. Warburg, both prominent global investment banking firms, provided studies to Air Canada which concluded about stock price. These studies indicated that the market value of the equity in Air Canada was approximately $800-900 million. The market price per share was then estimated by dividing by the estimated number of shares outstanding after the initial share offering. Now in discussions with Brown and his colleagues from RBC Dominion, $10 per share based on the share capitalization established just prior to filing the preliminary prospectus was set as the upper bound of possible prices.

The various per share prices presented in the different studies obviously affected the expectations of the Ministers of Transport and Finance, their deputy ministers and advisors. The generally held opinion was that they were expecting at least $10 per share and anything less than that would cause the government to seriously reconsider the sale of Air Canada shares.

During the past month many articles appeared in the financial press concerning the Air Canada issue (Exhibit 8). All seemed to agree on one thing – it was not a great time for an initial public offering for an airline stock.

At 4:00 p.m., just as Taylor was leaving his hotel suite for the meeting, the phone rang. "Did you know that PWA announced its quarterly earnings today and they were significantly below the analysts' expectations? The stock dropped $1.00. I thought you'd want to know."

EXHIBIT 1
AIR CANADA

The Top World Airlines
1987 Revenue Passenger Kilometres

Rank	Airline	(million)
1	Texas Air Corp.	121 034
	Continental Airlines	
	Eastern Airlines	
2	United Airlines	106 685
3	American Airlines	91 329
4	Delta Airlines	74 667
5	Northwest Airlines	63 650
6	TransWorld Airlines	53 452
7	U.S. Air/Piedmont	46 320
8	British Airways	46 299
9	Japan Air Lines	44 002
10	Pan American World Airways	41 992
11	Lufthansa	31 771
12	Air France	31 440
13	Qantas Airways	22 709
14	KLM Royal Dutch Airlines	21 801
15	Air Canada	21 165
16	Iberia	19 404
17	Alitalia	18 094
18	Saudi Arabian Airlines	15 640
19	Canadian Airlines International	15 479
20	Swissair	13 724

EXHIBIT 2
AIR CANADA

Airline Passenger Growth
Revenue Passenger Miles (RPM)
(billions)

	International	Canadian
1987	981.8	25.0
1986	901.6	24.1
1985	848.8	22.1
1984	793.5	21.1
1983	739.4	19.3
1982	709.6	19.8
1981	695.3	21.9
1980	676.7	22.3
1979	658.7	21.2
1978	581.6	18.1
Ten Year Annual Compound Growth Rate	5.8%	2.8%

EXHIBIT 3
AIR CANADA

Corporate Organization

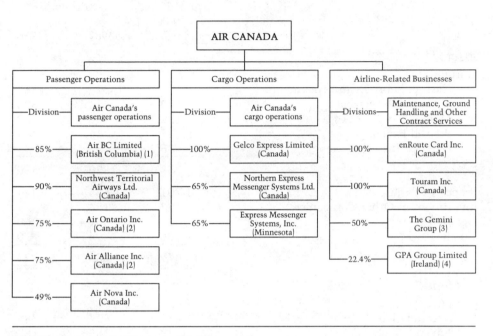

Passenger Operations			Cargo Operations			Airline-Related Businesses		
—Division—	Air Canada's passenger operations		—Division—	Air Canada's cargo operations		—Divisions—	Maintenance, Ground Handling and Other Contract Services	
—85%—	Air BC Limited (British Columbia) (1)		—100%—	Gelco Express Limited (Canada)		—100%—	enRoute Card Inc. (Canada)	
—90%—	Northwest Territorial Airways Ltd. (Canada)		—65%—	Northern Express Messenger Systems Ltd. (Canada)		—100%—	Touram Inc. (Canada)	
—75%—	Air Ontario Inc. (Canada) (2)		—65%—	Express Messenger Systems, Inc. (Minnesota)		—50%—	The Gemini Group (3)	
—75%—	Air Alliance Inc. (Canada) (2)					—22.4%—	GPA Group Limited (Ireland) (4)	
—49%—	Air Nova Inc. (Canada)							

(1) On a fully diluted basis. Air Canada's interest would be 80%.

(2) Indirectly held through 152160 Canada Inc., a 75% owned subsidiary of Air Canada, which holds 100% of the common shares of Air Ontario Inc. and of Air Alliance Inc.

(3) Air Canada holds a 50% interest in The Gemini Group Limited Partnership, as well as a 50% equity interest in the general partner. The Gemini Group Automated Distribution Systems, Inc.

(4) On a fully diluted basis at the date hereof, Air Canada's interest would be 16.1%.

EXHIBIT 4
AIR CANADA

Consolidated Balance Sheet
($000,000s)

	June 30 1988 (unaudited)	December 31 1987	1986
Assets			
Current			
Cash & Short Term Investments	$ 7	$ 223	$ 382
Accounts Receivable	583	414	326
Materials & Supplies	122	131	99
Prepaid Expenses	17	16	14
Deferred Income Taxes	35	36	39
	764	820	860
Property & Equipment	1 701	1 665	1 744
Investment in Other Companies	183	154	59
Deferred Charges	325	351	260
Goodwill	106	94	0
	$3 079	$3 084	$2 923
Liabilities			
Current			
Accounts Payables & Accruals	$ 437	$ 427	$ 385
Advance Ticket Sales	239	186	187
Current Portion Long Term Debt & Capital Lease Obligations	66	67	74
	742	680	646
Long Term Debt & Capital Lease Obligations	1 033	1 097	1 064
Other Long Term Liabilities	30	28	22
Deferred Credits	322	335	302
	2 127	2 140	2 034
Minority Interest	9	9	0
Subordinated Perpetual Bonds	336	336	336
	2 472	2 485	2 370
Equity			
Share Capital	329	329	329
Retained Earnings	278	270	224
	607	599	553
	$3 079	$3 084	$2 923

EXHIBIT 4 (continued)

Consolidated Statement of Income
($000,000s)

	Six Months Ended June 30				Year Ended December 31		
	1988	1987	1987	1986	1985	1984	1983
Operating Revenues							
Passenger	$1 225	$1 187	$2 383	$2 218	$2 110	$1 989	$1 844
Cargo	254	182	412	354	319	280	255
Other	180	188	336	313	293	230	199
	1 659	1 557	3 131	2 885	2 722	2 499	2 298
Operating Expenses							
Wages & Benefits	539	459	954	873	910	873	831
Aircraft Fuel	243	225	467	481	565	542	538
Depreciation	85	97	192	189	193	165	144
Other	783	673	1 414	1 216	1 053	876	757
	1 650	1 454	3 027	2 759	2 721	2 456	2 270
Operating Income	9	103	104	126	1	43	28
Interest Expense	56	60	129	125	114	102	80
Gain on Disposal of Assets	(32)	(25)	(30)	(24)	(14)	(31)	(19)
Other Expenses	(16)	(19)	(51)	(30)	(43)	(34)	(34)
	8	16	48	71	57	37	27
Income Before Taxes & Extraordinary Items	1	87	56	55	(56)	6	1
Provision for Taxes	(7)	34	10	19	(34)	(16)	(5)
Net Income Before Extraordinary Items	8	53	46	36	(22)	22	6
Extraordinary Items	–	–	–	4	7	6	(3)
Net Income	$ 8	$ 53	$ 46	$ 40	$ (15)	$ 28	$ 3

EXHIBIT 4 (continued)

Consolidated Statement of Changes in Financial Position
($000 000s)

| | Six Months Ended June 30 | | | | Year Ended December 31 | | |
	1988	1987	1987	1986	1985	1984	1983
Cash by Operations							
Net Income Before Extraordinary Items	$ 8	$ 53	$ 46	$ 36	$ (22)	$ 22	$ 6
Extraordinary Items	—	—	—	7	(5)	(26)	(5)
Non-cash Items Included in Income	8	51	97	148	129	114	105
	16	104	143	191	102	110	106
Change in Net Trade Balances	(155)	(135)	(35)	12	(33)	18	(21)
Increase in Advance Ticket Sales	53	38	(3)	16	18	7	(4)
Change in Supplies	7	(7)	(31)	(13)	(19)	(16)	5
Other	(27)	(3)	(4)	(16)	(4)	(18)	(3)
	(106)	(3)	70	190	64	101	83
Financing							
Long Term Debt	40	35	76	9	137	308	282
Repayment of Debt & Lease Obligations	(37)	(47)	(139)	(129)	(137)	(87)	(72)
Debt Deference	—	—	(6)	(269)	—	—	—
Subordinated Perpetual Bonds	—	—	—	336	—	—	—
Other	(9)	(11)	(29)	(9)	16	18	(4)
	(6)	(23)	(98)	(62)	16	239	206
Investments							
Additions to Fixed Assets	(170)	(78)	(199)	(87)	(104)	(430)	(343)
Disposal of Assets	83	88	294	294	37	58	20
Investment in Other Companies & Subs.	(20)	(115)	(232)	(19)	(4)	33	(2)
Dividends Received	3	2	6	4	2	4	4
	(104)	(103)	(131)	192	(69)	(335)	(321)
NET CHANGE IN CASH POSITION	(216)	(129)	(159)	320	11	5	(32)

EXHIBIT 4 (continued)

Forecast Consolidated Statement of Income
($000 000s)

	Forecast Year Ending Dec. 31, 1988	Forecast Six Months Ending Dec. 31, 1988	Actual Six Months Ending June 30, 1988
Operating Revenues	3 512	1 853	1 659
Operating Expenses	3 367	1 717	1 650
Operating Income	145	136	9
Non-operating Income	2	(6)	8
Income Before Taxes & Extraordinary Items	143	142	1
Provision for Taxes	40	47	(7)
Extraordinary Items	(3)	(3)	0
Net Income	100	92	8
Net Cash Flow	172	156	16

	Operating Assumptions		
	Forecast Six Months Ending Dec. 31, 1988	Actual Six Months Ended Dec. 31, 1987	Actual Six Months Ended Dec. 31, 1986
Revenue Passenger Miles (RPM) millions	8 099	7 076	7 368
Available Seat Miles (ASM) millions	11 300	9 871	10 558
Passenger Load Factor (%)	71.7	71.7	69.8
Yield per RPM (cents)	16.1	16.1	15.9
Available Ton Miles (ATM) millions	2 002	1 732	1 879
Operating Expense/ATM (cents)	73.5	81.1	70.4

EXHIBIT 5
AIR CANADA

Aircraft Fleet

	Number of Seats	Average Age	Owned	Leased	Ordered
Passenger					
Boeing 747	264–496	13.5	3	3	—
Lockhead L1011	214–306	10.9	8	4	—
Boeing 767	179	3.7	10	6	5
Airbus A320	137	—	—	—	34
Douglas DC-9	100	18.3	11	25	—
Boeing 727	136	9.5	25	8	—
Total Passenger			57	46	39
Cargo					
Douglas DC-8		18.8	8	—	—

EXHIBIT 6
AIR CANADA

Privatization Bulletin to enRoute Cardholders
August 18, 1988

Today the Government of Canada proclaimed into law "Bill C-129 – An Act to provide for the continuance of Air Canada under the Canada Business Corporations Act and for issuance and sale of shares thereof to the public".

The genesis of the legislative process occurred April 12, 1988 when the Deputy Prime Minister and President of the Queen's Privy Council for Canada, the Hon. Donald Frank Mazankowski, rose in the House of Commons to announce: "The Government has decided to allow Air Canada the freedom and financial options it needs to grow and continue to serve Canadians while remaining Canadian-owned and controlled".

At the same time, Mr. Mazankowski indicated that "The Government will instruct the Chairman of Air Canada's Board of Directors to vote its (the Government's) shares in accordance with the majority of the public shareholders. It will be a clear arms-length relationship".

On May 19, 1988, Mr. Mazankowski tabled in the House of Commons "Bill C-129 – The Air Canada Public Participation Act". Following are some of the highlights of the Bill:

- The corporation will be continued as a Canadian business corporation under the Canada Business Corporations Act, which means that Air Canada will operate under the same corporate rules as other Canadian businesses and when shares are sold will cease to be a crown corporation.
- Individuals will be allowed to own up to 10 per cent of the publicly-available shares.
- Non-residents of Canada will be restricted from collectively holding more than 25 per cent of the publicly-available shares.
- The Government's shares in Air Canada will be held by the President of the Queen's Privy Council instead of the Minister of Transport.
- Both the Government and the corporation are authorized to sell or issue shares as the case may be.
- Members of the Board of Directors will be elected by the public shareholders at the first shareholders' meeting following the initial sale of shares.
- The corporation will be required to maintain operational and overhaul centres in Winnipeg, Mississauga and Montreal.
- Air Canada will continue to follow the requirements of the Official Languages Act.
- Air Canada's head office will remain in Montreal.

On June 7, 1988 the Bill passed second reading in the House and was referred to a Legislative Committee of the House for clause-by-clause study. That Committee convened on June 20, 21 and 22 and heard testimony from 10 interested parties including leaders of the major unions representing workers at Air Canada, members of the Air Canada Employee Ownership Committee, the senior executives of the airline and the Deputy Prime Minister.

On June 23, 1988 the Bill was referred back to the House and was passed by the House of Commons on July 18, 1988.

EXHIBIT 6 (continued)

First reading of the Bill in the Senate took place on July 19, 1988 followed by second reading on July 21, 1988 and referred to the Standing Senate Committee on Banking, Trade and Commerce. After inviting communities and labour groups across Canada to submit written briefs, the Committee met on August 2, 3, and 4 to give consideration and study to these briefs and to the legislation itself. On August 16th, the Senate Committee presented its report on Bill C-129 to the Senate. That report observed that the government's decision to give the Chairman the proxy to vote its shares in accordance with the desires of the majority of the private shareholders is "a skillful way of managing the issue of government majority ownership in the corporation. . . ."

Finally, the legislation received Royal Assent today and became law. In the coming weeks and months, newspapers across Canada will be informing the public as to how the share offering will take place.

Your interest in this process and your confirmed support of Air Canada is appreciated.

EXHIBIT 7
AIR CANADA

Selected Financial Statistics for Airline Companies
Fiscal 1987

	Air Canada ($C)	Allegis ($US)	Delta ($US)	Pan Am ($US)	TWA ($US)
Revenues	3 131	8 538	6 607	3 734	4 153
Operating Expenses	3 027	8 242	6 152	3 839	3 896
EBIT	104	348	475	(145)	385
Net Income	48	78	262	(255)	48
Cash Flow from Operations	70	888	600	(89)	295
5 Year Compound Growth in Operating Revenues	7.8	10.5	8.5	14.5	2.4
Labour Cost as % of Revenues	30.5	33.5	48.0	36.3	31.2
Number of Employees	22 000	63 000	51 054	21 907	29 919
Number of Aircraft	109	382	374	126	213
Return on Assets %	0.0	1.2	4.9	− 12.2	1.3
Return on Equity %	0.1	11.6	13.2	N.M.	31.9
Passenger Load Factor %	71.1	65.4	55.7	63.3	63.4
5 yr. Compound Growth %	1.7	1.3	1.4	− 1.6	− 1.3
Yield Per Passenger Mile $	13.16	10.3	12.81	9.77	10.39
Revenue Mix					
Passenger Domestic	41.7	82.7	92.5	14.9	53.3
Passenger International	33.6	N.A.	0.0	71.7	30.9
Cargo	13.2	5.9	5.3	N.A.	5.6
Other	11.5	11.4	2.2	13.4	10.2
Stock Price					
52 week high		105.88	60.25	5.50	36.25
52 week low		57.00	32.00	2.38	14.00
Beta		N.A.	1.00	1.05	N.A.
Debt as percent of capital employed			17%	218	

EXHIBIT 7 (continued)

Selected Financial Statistics for Airline Companies
Fiscal 1987

Unit of Currency Unless Otherwise Noted	PWA ($C)	Wardair ($C)	British Airways (£)	KLM (DG)	Swissair (SFr)
Revenues	2 060	538	3 756	5 377	3 905
Operating Expenses	1 879	533	3 520	5 077	3 831
Rental Expenses	30	8	151	29	83
EBIT	205	10	259	491	199
Net Income	67	(2)	151	301	72
Cash Flow from Operations	175	29	369	719	463
5 Year Compound Growth in Operating Revenues	42.4	6.6	9.5	4.0	1.7
Labour Cost as % of Revenues	28.4	19.3	N.A.	31.6	36.6
Number of Employees	13 097	3 890	36 096	21 235	3 890
Number of Aircraft	78	N.A.	151	83	52
Return on Assets %	3.3	−0.3	5.8	3.2	1.6
Return on Equity %	17.1	−1.2	24.4	11.1	6.1
Passenger Load Factor %	68.0	N.A.	70.2	65.4	63.7
5 yr. Compound Growth %	5.9	N.A.	1.6	1.1	−0.1
Yield Per Passenger Mile $US	12.50	N.A.	15.82	206.08	N.A.
Revenue Mix					
Passenger Domestic	44.4	N.A.	93.8	61.3	65.2
Passenger International	28.4	N.A.	0.0	0.0	0.0
Cargo	8.5	N.A.	0.0	19.9	11.5
Other	18.7	N.A.	6.2	17.8	23.3
Stock Price					
52 week high	26.58	16.94	$37.50	$27.75	1440
52 week low	14.97	7.99	22.12	13.25	830
Beta	N.A.	N.A.	1.00	.80	N.A.
Debt as percent of capital employed				51%	57%

EXHIBIT 8

AIR CANADA

Bumpy ride for Air Canada issue
Election talk, shaky market pose threats

August 15, 1988
By James Bagnall
and Richard Blackwell
Financial Post

STOCK MARKET turmoil, combined with rising election fever, are causing headaches for the executives and financial advisers planning **Air Canada's** privatization.

The airline is determined to move ahead this fall with a public issue of common shares, representing 45% of its ownership. It has been a cherished goal of Air Canada management for years.

"It would take a significant market downturn to change plans," an Air Canada spokesman says. "We want to get the ball rolling before an election call."

A fall federal election, which is increasingly forecast, could scuttle the deal. And this past week a sudden rise in U.S. interest rates sent stock markets tumbling, making new equity issues (already in disrepute among investors) even riskier.

Aside from timing the issue, the offering price is the critical decision to be made by Air Canada and its advisers — including **Dominion Securities Inc.** of Toronto, **Morgan Stanley & Co.** of New York and **S.G. Warburg Securities Ltd.** of London.

The price must be high enough to give the airline the money it needs for fleet expansion, yet low enough to attract retail investors leery of new issues in the post-crash climate.

Share split

(A British study has estimated that **British Airways**, privatized before the crash, could have received 30% more for its stock if it had not underpriced it to encourage investor acceptance.)

Frederick Larkin, analyst at Alfred Bunting and Co., Toronto, suggests that Air Canada stock will likely be priced at about $11 a share. He speculates that the 329,000 Air Canada shares now owned by the government will be split 100-for-one, giving Ottawa a total of 32.9 million shares. To dilute this holding to 55%, another 27 million new shares could be issued to the public.

Air Canada's book value, as of Dec. 31, 1987, was about $1,821 per share, equivalent to $18.21 after a split. The shares would likely be discounted by about 40%, suggests Larkin, giving a price of about $11 per share.

At this price, 27 million shares would generate about $300 million. At recent Senate hearings into the privatization bill, Michael Reilly, a principal of Morgan Stanley, confirmed the market "target point" would be a $300 million issue. The net cost of the underwriting is estimated to be 4%-6% of total proceeds, or $15 million.

The price/earnings ratio generated by a stock price of $11 depends, of course, on the airline's profits this year. The other two major Canadian airlines are trading at p/e ratios of about 6.3 (**PWA Corp.,** parent of Canadian Airlines International) and 3.8 (**Wardair Inc.**) In the U.S. major airlines trade at between six and 18 times earnings, averaging about eight or nine.

Assuming that 60 million shares will be outstanding after privatization, Air Canada's 1987 profit of $45.7 million would yield earnings per share of about 76¢. At a share price of $11, the p/e would be 14.

In its most recently reported four quarters, Air Canada had slim earnings of $800,000, largely the result of a $29.1-million loss in the first quarter of 1988, ended March 31.

EXHIBIT 8 (continued)

The ideal time for Air Canada to privatize — at least in terms of presenting an attractive p/e to investors — would be in late 1988 after the release of third quarter earnings, usually the strongest of the year.

But other factors may intervene, chief among them being the growing possibility of an early autumn election. That would not give the airline much time to get the issue launched.

No stopping

The Senate is still preparing a report on the Air Canada privatization bill. Even if the upper house proposes no amendments, it may be late this month before the airline has the legal authority to proceed with the issue.

Air Canada executives would like to issue a prospectus very soon after the Senate approves the bill. Their thinking is that once the share sale is set in motion, there could be no stopping it.

If the Liberals or New Democrats — both opposed to the privatization — wound up in power, they would find it far more difficult to reverse the process if Air Canada shares were already in the hands of investors.

In spite of the political uncertainty, international airline analysts believe the 45% share issue will be well received. Many larger U.S. airlines have reported an earnings surge in the second quarter of this year.

"U.S. airlines generally are reporting a record level of earn-ings this year," says Louis Marckesano, vice-president of Philadelphia-based Janney, Montgomery & Scott Inc. "That kind of background won't hurt Air Canada at all."

However, Air Canada is the first major airline to test privatization waters since the October crash. "It's not the best time to come to market, but what can you do?" notes Anthony Hatch, an airline analyst with New York-based Argus Research Corp.

Hatch points out that "airline stocks are still trading at a pretty big discount in the U.S. The general feeling is that the market hasn't caught up to the fact the airline industry has already gone through its rough phase."

Analyst Steve Garmaise of First Marathon Securities Ltd. in Toronto says Air Canada has a spotty track record of earnings to present to investors. In the past five years, the company's bottom line has ranged from a net loss of $14.8 million in 1985 to a last year's profit of $45.7 million on sales of $3.1 billion.

'Quite accustomed'

Garmaise says investors tend to be wary of the cyclical nature of the airline business at the best of times, and many won't like the government's majority interest in the airline.

John Stancliffe, director of Warburg Securities, told the Senate committee that continuing government control of Air Canada is not likely to put off foreign investors. They are "quite accustomed" to this sort of arrangement in the airline industry, he says.

Foreign ownership in the airline will be limited to 25%, and individual purchasers will be prevented from buying more than 10%.

One positive indicator is the fact post-crash privatizations in other industries have been well received. **Matra,** the French defence and electronics group, was five times oversubscribed when the government sold its majority share early this year.

British Airways, whose initial privatization in early 1987 attracted 1.2 million investors, has recently been making the rounds in Switzerland and the U.S. with a view to making private placements.

However, analysts have been leery of BA stock since its 1987 acquisition of **British Caledonian.** Its former rival has been taking larger-than-expected losses, which contributed to a first-quarter drop in BA profit to £53 million from £58 million the previous year.

Potentially volatile

Air Canada is expected to try to emulate BA's initial approach to privatization. Prior to the launch in February, 1987, BA officials conducted marketing campaigns to prepare employees and the investment community for a potentially volatile stock. Already Air Canada has sent a letter to all members of its Aeroplan frequent flyer program

EXHIBIT 8 (continued)

explaining its approach to privatization.

Priority will be given to Air Canada employees who want to buy stock, and it appears that most workers will welcome the opportunity. This should strongly boost the airline's attempt to sell out the issue.

One factor influencing the share price could be the hint from Deputy Prime Minister Donald Mazankowski that if the issue is vastly oversubscribed, the government might consider diluting further its 55% stake in the airline.

Even if that does not happen, Air Canada executives want to show there is widespread investor interest in the stock, because this might encourage a future government to expedite plans to sell off its majority stake.

[1] This article was reprinted with the permission of the *Financial Post*.

EXHIBIT 9[1]

AIR CANADA

Comparable Trading Statistics

The following table compares the indicated pricing range for Air Canada with the major Canadian and U.S. airlines on a multiple of net income, net cash flow and book value basis.

Company	Price August 29, 1988	Price/Earnings (1) (2)	Price/ Cash Flow (1) (3)	Price/ Book Value (4)
PWA Corporation (Canadian Airlines International)	$20.25	8.7X	2.9X	0.94X
AMR Corporation (American Airlines)	43.00	8.4	2.8	0.94
Delta Airlines, Inc.	47.88	7.4	3.3	1.20
NWA Inc. (Northwest Airlines)	44.00	14.7	2.8	0.84
USAir Group, Inc.	36.00	9.0	3.4	0.82
AVERAGE		9.6X	3.0X	0.95X
Air Canada (5) (6)	$ 8.00	5.1X	2.2X	0.73X
(1988 Forecast)	9.00	6.0	2.6	0.79
	10.00	6.8	2.9	0.84
Air Canada (5) (7)	$ 8.00	3.4X	1.4X	0.73X
(Strike Adjusted)	9.00	4.0	1.7	0.79
	10.00	4.5	1.9	0.87

(1) Based on 1988 estimates. Canadian estimates provided by RBC Dominion Securities. US estimates provided by Value Line. Air Canada multiples based on prospectus forecast, proforma the sale of 45% of Air Canada Common Shares from treasury (resulting in approximately 74.8 million Common Shares outstanding after this offering).
(2) Fully diluted net income before extraordinary items.
(3) Fully diluted net income before extraordinary items plus non-cash items included in net income.
(4) Based on last completed fiscal year end.
(5) Assigns a value of $190 million ($2.50 per Common Share) to Air Canada's holding in GPA Group Limited as discussed under "Valuation Approach".
(6) Based on forecast 1988 results, proforma the sale of 45% of Air Canada Common Shares from treasury in this offering.
(7) Based on trailing 12 months to September 30, 1987, proforma the sale of 45% of Air Canada Common Shares from treasury in this offering

The indicated pricing range for Air Canada represents multiples below most other major North American airlines based on 1988 forecasted earnings and cash flow and significantly below these airlines based on the earnings and cash flow achieved in the 12 months prior to the fourth quarter 1987 labour disruption.

---

[1] This exhibit was taken from material prepared and distributed by the underwriters.

Corporate Acquisitions

MARSHALL STEEL LTD.

Early in September 1981, Jeffrey Marshall, President and Chief Executive of Marshall Steel Ltd. (Marshall), knew he had to make a final decision about an offer to acquire control of Drummond McCall Inc. (DMC), a firm about four times the size of Marshall. The acquisition strategy had been a closely kept secret within the Marshall firm for several months. Jeff Marshall had headed a team of three whose members had devoted themselves almost exclusively to studying the DMC acquisition. The team had concluded that the fit was a good one, offering considerable potential for growth and profits. Only these three knew of the on-going effort to acquire DMC and they knew that surprise was of strategic importance to their success.

The target date for the public announcement and offer was set for September 15. The offer price had not yet been determined. Although the Toronto-Dominion Bank had agreed to lend the funds to Marshall on relatively favourable terms of prime plus 3/4 percent with repayment spread over 12 years, Marshall knew that with the prime interest rates at 21 percent, the additional financial cost and risk from such a large loan were significant. He had to make his mind up on whether to go forward with an offer and if so, at what price?

Background
The Industry

The secondary metal products industry consists of four major sectors: distributing, processing, fabricating and erecting. Steel and other metals are supplied to this industry by Canadian and foreign primary metal producers. Examples of Canadian primary metal producers are as follows:

Steel	— Algoma Steel Corp., Dofasco, and Stelco
Aluminum	— Alcan Products Can. Ltd. and Reynolds

Stainless Steel	— Atlas Steels Co. Ltd.
Copper and Brass	— Noranda Metal Ind. Ltd., Arrowhead Metals Ltd.
Cold Finished Steel	— Union Drawn Steel Co. Ltd.

Metals are supplied to the secondary metal products industry in three basic forms:

Flat Products which are referred to in the trade as either sheet or plate, the difference being determined by thickness. Sheet metal, which is thinner, is supplied by the primary industry in coils (rolls) which the secondary industry resells as is or flattened and cut to size. Plate metal products, which are thicker, are supplied in either coil form or in flattened rectangles.

Bar Products common shapes are round, square and rectangular solid bars of various lengths.

Structural Products are supplied in many shapes and sizes. Common shapes include lengths of square, rectangular or circular hollow sections, H-beams, I-beams, and angles.

The secondary steel industry performs the following functions:

Distributing Metal service centres act as distributors of primary metal. A service centre buys large volumes of metal products in mill forms and sizes and sells smaller volumes. The key success factors for this business are strong purchasing skills and careful inventory management.

Processing The distribution function often evolves into the processing business to serve customers who require some processing of the metal but do not carry specialized equipment. Processing includes operations such as cutting to length, slitting to width, shearing, painting, sawing and flame cutting according to customer specifications.

Fabricating Fabricating involves preparing specially processed steel pieces such as beams and girders with the related fittings so that they can be used directly in the construction of a particular structure.

Erecting The erecting activity involves the on-site assembly and putting in place of fabricated metal into products such as buildings, bridges, and cranes.

Marshall Steel Ltd.

Marshall had its head office in Montreal and operated out of facilities in Montreal and Toronto. Marshall operated as a distributor of structural steel as well as a fabricator and erector of steel products. Sales of $62 million for the fiscal year ended April 1, 1981 were up ten percent over 1980. Profit from the two operating divisions was up 45 percent; however, overall profits before tax remained level at about $5 million because revenue from joint venture construction projects declined, as shown in Exhibits 1 and 2. Marshall was 60 percent owned by the Marshall family and 40 percent owned by management in 1981. Management was a tight-knit group described by Jeff Marshall as "bottom-line-oriented entrepreneurs."

Marshall management believed that flexibility was the key to success. The Marshall group had concluded that very large service centres offered economies of scale for inventory control and opportunities to use new technologies to move products most effectively, but required strong management with the capability to make significant changes quickly. Marshall's inventory, its largest single asset, was reduced during the 1981 fiscal year as interest rates increased. The Canadian primary steel industry was considered "soft" and sources of supply were monitored continually within Canada and abroad for attractive deals. Marshall engaged in joint ventures to reduce risk on very large construction jobs.

Marshall's management followed a strategy of growth through acquisition followed by periods of consolidation. Expansion into new product lines or new territories had never taken place until both the financial and the structural integrity of the base was established. Marshall had just been through a period of consolidation. The systems, procedures and business philosophies of its two plant locations were compatible. Long-term debt had been eliminated and bank loans and other short-term debt had been reduced to $6 million. The stated company target of 20 percent return on average shareholder's equity had been exceeded for five consecutive years.

The short-term outlook for the steel fabrication and distribution markets was unpredictable due to the volatility of steel supply, fluctuations in short-term interest rates, the attitude of confrontation among government leaders and the inability of politicians to settle oil price regulations. However, current demand for Marshall's products was strong. The balanced inventory put Marshall in a position to take advantage of distribution opportunities as they occurred and the fabricating plants were fully contracted through to the fall of 1982. Further development of the existing facilities in Toronto and Montreal was planned for the 1982 fiscal year at an estimated cost of $3 million.

The Marshall management team was young and aggressive. Jeff Marshall, in his late 30s, was the grandson of the founder of Marshall Steel and the heir of a family which had been involved in the business for 50 years. His educational background included an engineering degree and an M.B.A. He attracted and kept his management team by paying fair salaries, offering substantial equity participation in Marshall and paying annual bonuses based on the company's return on average shareholder's equity in excess of five percent.

Drummond McCall Incorporated

DMC, also headquartered in Montreal, began operations as a wholesaler of iron in 1881. One hundred years later DMC processed and distributed a wide range of ferrous and non-ferrous metal products from 25 locations across Canada and three U.S. locations in Maine and Connecticut. DMC stocked steel products such as sheet, plate, bar and structural forms and other products such as aluminum, brass, copper, alloy steel, stainless steel, carbon steel, chain and nickel in most mill forms and sizes.

DMC had expanded the geographic scope of its operations substantially over the past decade. In 1972 DMC had combined plants and sales offices in Halifax, Montreal, Toronto, Hamilton, Winnipeg and Calgary and sales offices in Quebec City and Vancouver. DMC began its rapid territorial expansion in 1977 with the acquisition of Quadra Steel Limited (Quadra). Quadra, with its headquarters in British Columbia, was a steel service centre. The Quadra acquisition added six warehouses in B.C. and one in the Yukon to DMC operations. Two new Canadian sales offices were opened in 1978, additions were added to two existing plants and operations at Quadra locations were expanded to include metals other than steel. Inclusion of Quadra results for 1978 resulted in substantial increases in sales and net income. The devaluation of the Canadian dollar not only made Canadian suppliers more competitive with imported metal in the domestic market but also in the U.S. market. During 1978 DMC opened its first sales office in the U.S. at Portland, Maine. In 1979 DMC amalgamated Quadra under the DMC name and established four new plants across Canada. The expansion strategy was to establish a sales office in a promising market and to follow with the warehousing and processing facilities as they were required. By the end of 1979 DMC had 16 combined sales offices and plants in six provinces and the Yukon and one plant under construction at the Portland, Maine sales office. A list of 1979 locations with sales office and plant roofed floor areas and land area statistics is presented in Exhibit 3. Sales offices were also located in Quebec City, Saint John and Thunder Bay. The book value of land, buildings, and equipment net of depreciation on September 20, 1979 was $17.9 million.

In 1980, despite a weak economy with high interest rate and declining sales in several key industries, DMC established two additional Canadian sales offices in Newfoundland and New Brunswick and established plants in Kitimat and Quebec City. Production began from the new plant in Portland, but demand was weak and performance was not up to expectations. Both the Winnipeg and Calgary plants were expanded. Sinking fund debentures totalling $10 million at a floating rate of prime less 1/4 of one percent were placed privately to finance the expansion.

DMC sales in 1980 totalled $223 million, up six percent over 1979. However, net income declined 52 percent as tonnage shipped declined seven percent, as shown in Exhibits 4 and 5. Return on stockholders' equity was

8.2 percent. In 1981 DMC serviced 13 000 customers in Canadian primary and secondary industries such as construction, agriculture, petrochemical, automotive, electrical, shipbuilding and mining.

Despite discouraging results in its U.S. operation, DMC acquired Hunter & Havens Inc., with two plants in Connecticut, paying over $4 million in cash for the acquisition.

DMC first issued 442 000 shares of class A stock to the public in 1971 at $10.00 per share. During 1979 all common shares were split on a two-for-one basis and a second public offering of 500 000 common shares at $12.50 per share was made. The capital structure of the company was also altered. Class A and B common shares were changed to Series A and B Common stock. Series B shares would henceforth be paid stock dividends in Series B shares at a rate equal to Series A cash dividends. These series were interconvertible.

The Employee's Pension Plan and the Drummond and McCall families collectively held 42 percent of DMC stock. Management owned less than three percent of the shares. DMC stock traded on both the Toronto and Montreal Stock Exchanges. Trading statistics for DMC since 1976 are shown in Exhibit 6. Comparative data for several firms in the steel and metal industries are compiled in Exhibit 7.

DMC had maintained its family orientation since 1881. Although the current senior management team did not include a member of either the Drummond or McCall families, both were represented on the Board. Douglas T. Bourke, President and Chief Executive Officer, had joined DMC in 1951 as a salesman and had risen through the ranks to become President in 1972. Management was centralized and emphasis was placed on sales volume. When asked by *Metal Center News* in September 1981 why expansion had been so rapid recently, Bourke replied, "This was a family-run company, and as such it probably didn't expand as fast as it might have under different circumstances."

In 1981 a DMC policy document stated that its business was in the service industry and that it would continue to emphasize service through expand and more numerous outlets, an increased number of products and increased specialization in processing.

Marshall Investment Opportunities

The Marshall group had looked at various options for investment and they concluded from studying the industry that growth and profit potential were higher, relative to the risk, in the service-centre sectors than in the fabricating and erecting sectors of the market. Economies achieved by volume buying of metals for processing and distributing gave the service-centre business a relatively high return with a high ratio of sales to assets. The relationship of the fabricating and erecting sectors with the construction industry made any venture in these sectors relatively more risky for the potential returns.

The aim of Marshall management was to broaden the product line and achieve larger regional coverage. If Marshall had distribution channels in place in Western Canada, it could add fabricating and erecting as the next phase in Marshall's expansion.

Members of the Marshall management team examined many companies, both public and private, as take-over targets.

The DMC Prospect

The Marshall group's review of potential acquisitions focused on DMC for three reasons:

(1) Marshall believed that the addition of smaller warehouses was making DMC less and less flexible at a time when the opposite strategy was required to maintain earnings. The five-year DMC expansion program had not included any time for consolidation and it was obvious to Marshall that such a period was not planned in the near future.

(2) DMC was exceptionally well represented in all major geographical locations in Canada and minimal product overlap existed between the two entities. The only overlap involved processing and distributing structural steel in Eastern Canada.

(3) DMC shares continually sold below book value.

The Marshall team realized the fundamental difference between the two firms lay in contrasting strategies. The relative size of the two corporations was a major factor for Marshall to consider in any bid to take over DMC. DMC sales for the year ended December 31, 1980, were 3.5 times Marshall's sales for the year ended April 1, 1981 (Exhibits 1 and 4). DMC total assets were almost four times Marshall's total assets for the same periods (Exhibits 2 and 5).

Previous Merger Attempts

In December of 1979 DMC management had approached Marshall to discuss a possible merger. However, Marshall had made it clear it was interested in a share exchange, not cash, and the discussions had ended.

In December of 1980, Marshall had extended to the Drummond and McCall families and the DMC pension plan a private offer to purchase all of their shares. Marshall stated that acceptance by a portion of this group would trigger an offer for all remaining shares outstanding. Marshall had arranged to take on a new partner if the offer were acceptable, in order to finance the 100 percent acquisition. However, the shareholders allowed the offer to lapse.

Takeover Bid

Over the past nine months, top management at Marshall had decided that an appeal to the public shareholders of DMC was the best route to follow if the acquisition was to be pursued. A strategy was developed, a team was formed to concentrate on the project and the financing was arranged. The team consisted of Marshall, the Secretary of the Corporation, who was a lawyer, and a financier who was also a member of the Board.

The team consulted with economic advisors and set out to project financial statements that would help determine DMC's value and future profitability.

They advised the team that the floating rate on prime bank loans would average 14 percent between 1981 and 1985. Interest on Marshall's and DMC's short-term debt was at the bank's prime rate. Marshall knew that earnings would be highly sensitive to interest rates. The inflation rate was also projected to 1985. The Portland operaton had opened in 1980 and its marginal sales contribution for five years had been estimated. Marshall decided to begin with a conservative zero real growth. He projected the historical cyclical patterns in the ratio of operating margin before depreciation, interest and taxes to sales forward to 1985. These assumptions are summarized in Table 1.

TABLE 1

Bases for Projecting DMC Performance

	Inflation Rate	Sales Portland (millions)	Gross Margin/Sales
1981	9%	$ 4	8%
1982	11%	5	13%
1983	11%	6	10%
1984	8%	7	6%
1985	8%	8	9%

Depreciation rates were straight line and ranged from 2.5 percent to 20 percent, as described in the notes to Exhibit 6, but the average annual amount would be 7.6 percent of fixed assets at cost. New investment was assumed to be for replacement purposes only and equal to depreciation charges. Interest rates on long-term debt and repayment requirements are outlined in the notes to Exhibit 4. Special income tax provisions were available to firms in the industry. Taxes after these provisions would average 42 percent of earnings. Dividends were forecasted at five percent of opening equity. DMC's inventory to sales ratio was expected to be level at .25 and the accounts receivable to sales ratio was estimated at .16. The ratio of accounts payable to sales was estimated at .11.

The Post-Acquisition Strategy

A post-takeover business plan for DMC had not been incorporated into the projections. The team thought that once they gained control of DMC, an in-depth consideration could be given to the following strategy in order to decrease pressure on operating lines of credit and provide the funds needed for future expansion.

1. *Centralized Inventories* The team believed a substantial reduction in the number of operating units in DMC would result in reduced operating costs (economies of scale), lower "base" stocks of inventory and lower financing charges. With fewer square feet in service, a reduction in sales was expected, but the relationship between the sales reduction and the space reduction would not be linear. The decrease in operating costs and inventories should be direct. An analysis of profitability by location would be an immediate priority on assuming control.

2. A more sophisticated *distribution system* would be developed in order to replace the apparent decline in distribution capacity from the customer's perspective. Fast delivery would have to be maintained through effective communications and trucking operations.

3. The revised operations strategy and policy of *centralization* and *direct accountability* would require fewer personnel.

4. *No product duplication* within regions would be allowed.

5. A *steel fabrication plant* with a capacity of approximately 7500 tons per annum would be a medium-term objective for the western region. This expansion was expected to be financed by savings resulting from cutbacks in present locations. This plant would become the structurally oriented facility for the region.

6. All products would be prices on the basis of *NIFO* (next-in-first-out).

7. *Equity participation* Marshall management intended to continue its policy of management motivation through equity participation and to extend it to include key personnel in the DMC division over a period of time.

The Marshall group concluded that direct cost reductions amounting to $4 million per year were possible from implementing this business strategy in DMC.

The Regulatory Requirements

The team investigated the various securities laws and regulations pertaining to takeovers. They found that any offer that would give a purchaser in excess of 20 percent of all voting securities outstanding was deemed a takeover bid by the Ontario Securities Commission (OSC). To protect minority share-holders in a takeover bid, all holders of the same class of securities had to be offered the same consideration. The OSC had jurisdiction over all stocks trading on the Toronto Stock Exchange (TSE). In a bid to acquire control of DMC any buyer would have to comply with both the OSC and the Quebec Securities Commission (QSC) regulations. The procedure outlined by OSC stated that a bid had to be sent to all Ontario holders of the class of securities sought and a deposit period of no less than 21 days and no more than 35 days was required. Deposited securities could not be taken up during the first 10 days of the deposit period to allow depositors to withdraw their securities if they chose to do so. If less than 100 percent of the shares were sought, the shares could not be taken up until the deposit period expired and then had to be taken up on a pro-rata basis. In this way all shareholders were treated equally. The Canada Business Corporations Act, to which DMC was subject, also contains takeover bid conditions which are similar to those of Ontario, except that the percentage is 10 percent instead of 20 percent.

A private agreement exemption was possible if the private agreement was made with less than 15 shareholders to achieve a takeover. However, if the price paid was greater than the market price plus reasonable fees, the pur-chaser was required to make a followup offer to remaining Ontario share-holders within 180 days of the first private agreement. The market price was determined by averaging the closing price over the preceding ten busi-ness days and adding 15 percent. The consideration per share in the follow-up offer had to be at least equal in value to the greatest consideration paid in a private agreement. Th QSC had similar regulations to protect Quebec minority shareholders. This followup offer requirement would have applied if the Drummond and McCall families had accepted the private offer made to them in December 1980.

Financing

Marshall made an agreement with the Toronto-Dominion Bank to provide for a 12 year term loan at prime plus 3/4 percent to finance the acquisition. The loan would enable Marshall to buy 51 percent of DMC common stock outstanding. The loan would be repayable in equal consecutive monthly instalments beginning on the third anniversary of the loan acceptance. A commitment fee would be payable to the bank monthly at 1/8 percent per year beginning on the date of acceptance. This commitment fee would in-crease from the date of the first principal repayment to 3/8 percent per year on the unused portion. On or before December 31, 1983, Marshall would be allowed to convert any portion of the loan up to $15 million into a fixed rate Euro-Canadian facility at the bank's Euro-Canadian rate plus 1 1/4 percent.

The basis for the loan was Marshall's known earning capacity and its long relationship with the bank. The loan would be secured by a registered general assignment of Marshall's book debts, an assignment of Marshall's inventory, a fixed and floating charge under a Trust Deed to a trustee covering all of Marshall's other assets and a pledge of the common stock acquired through the offer. Covenants were placed on Marshall regarding additional borrowing, certain capital expenditures, dividends and working capital.

Marshall realized that a loan large enough to acquire DMC would be considerably more than Marshall's net worth. Interest payments, which were deductible from pre-tax income, would be less than Marshall's projected pre-tax earnings.

With 51 percent of the shares, the Marshall group intended to operate DMC in the best interests of all the shareholders. The loan and the interest expense would be on Marshall's books, with only dividends from DMC as a means to offset the costs.

Brokerage fees to Marshall's consultants on the project would be $75 000 plus another $75 000 if the takeover succeeded. Legal and other fees were estimated at $400 000. Marshall would also pay each soliciting dealer $0.20 per share deposited, taken up and paid for by Marshall to a minimum of $25 and a maximum of $2000 for any one owner.

Marshall Steel had experienced high points in its business cycles two or three times in each decade. When reviewing the large debt requirements, Marshall thought the three year reprieve from principal repayment would enable Marshall Steel to accumulate funds for repayment of the loan during a high in the business cycle. He believed the loan could be repaid within the decade if the two to three cycle pattern held and he predicted that dividends from DMC at its historical rate of payment would generate sufficient cash flow to Marshall for principal and interest payments.

The takeover team also considered the option of financing the takeover by an offer of Marshall stock. The time involved in preparing a prospectus for Marshall would significantly delay the offer to DMC shareholders and there was considerable doubt that Marshall's directors would be willing to give up the flexibility a private company enjoyed.

As each day passed more and more people at Marshall were either becoming aware of the project or that something important was going on. The Marshall team knew that surprise was a necessity for maximum impact for pricing of the offer.

With a well thought-out strategy in place for the takeover, Marshall knew that his firm had the initial advantage over an unprepared DMC management if an unfriendly takeover battle developed. Based on the approaches made by both sides over the past two years, there was every reason to believe the takeover would not be easy. His legal advisors had indicated the types of retaliatory practices he could expect. Surprise would reduce DMC's preparation time and decrease the likelihood of DMC finding a more attractive buyer.

The price of the offer would be critical. The price of DMC stock was about $10 in light trading throughout August, but had reached a high of 15 3/8 during April 1981. Trading volume had increased significantly in that month due to rumours of the December 1980 takeover attempt. The lack of a follow-up offer had apparently convinced the market that no takeover would be attempted. The April high was the only time DMC shares had traded above book value in recent years. The team considered the value of DMC's fixed assets to be an important issue in determining an appropriate price. An informal appraisal of DMC real estate indicated that the market value was considerably more than the book value. Equipment was considered to be well valued at book value.

The pressures from the secrecy of the operation, the size of the acquisition and the financing were beginning to tell on everyone. Marshall knew that a leak at this point could undo the months of preparation. He also knew that the emotional momentum to acquire DMC could lead to a decision to go ahead that was not in Marshall's best interests. He concluded that everything was done that could be done by the team — now he had to make his decision.

EXHIBIT 1

MARSHALL STEEL LTD.

Consolidated Statement of Income and Retained Earnings
Year Ended April 1
($000)

	1981	*1980*
Sales	$ 61 921	$ 56 038
Costs and Expenses		
Cost of sales and operating expenses	55 401	51 256
Depreciation	488	471
Interest on long-term debt		106
Other interest	1 799	1 321
	57 689	53 154
	4 232	2 884
Income from joint ventures	770	2 082
Income before income taxes	5 002	4 966
Income taxes		
Current (recovery)	2 614	(103)
Deferred (reduction)	(527)	1 927
	2 087	1 824
Net Income	2 915	3 142
Retained Earnings at Beginning of Year	10 927	8 358
	13 842	11 500
Dividends	610	573
Retained Earnings at End of Year	$ 13 232	$ 10 927
Earnings per Share	$ 23.92	$ 26.03
Fully Diluted Earnings Per Share	$ 23.08	$ 24.46

Note: Figures are rounded and therefore may not add to totals.

Source: Marshall Steel Ltd. annual report

EXHIBIT 2

MARSHALL STEEL LTD.

Consolidated Balance Sheet as at April 1
($000)

	1981	1980
Assets		
Current		
Cash	$ 707	$ 135
Accounts receivable	10 145	10 302
Due from joint ventures	1 072	2 859
Accounts and notes receivable from shareholders and director	440	196
Income taxes recoverable		442
Inventories	14 594	20 024
Prepaid expenses	89	58
	27 047	34 015
Fixed		
Land, buildings and equipment	7 021	6 485
Less accumulated depreciation	3 676	3 246
	3 346	3 238
	$ 30 392	$ 37 253
Liabilities		
Current		
Bank and short-term borrowings	$ 5 707	$ 15 147
Accounts payable and accrued liabilities	5 585	7 206
Income taxes payable	2 322	108
Deferred income taxes	2 696	3 241
	16 311	25 703
Deferred Income Taxes	266	248
Shareholders' Equity		
Capital Stock		
123 000 Common shares		
(1980 — 120 700)	584	375
Retained Earnings	13 232	10 927
	13 816	11 302
	$ 30 392	$ 37 253

Exhibit 2 (continued)

Notes to Consolidated Financial Statements
Year Ended April 1

1. *Inventories (000)*

	1981	1980
Work in process	$ 6 153	$ 8 276
Less progress billings	3 951	5 147
	2 201	3 130
Steel and supplies	12 392	16 894
	$ 14 594	$ 20 024

2. *Fixed Assets (000)*

		Accumu- lated Depre- ciation	1981	1980
	Cost		Net	Net
Land	$ 445	$ —	$ 445	$ 445
Buildings	2 436	923	1 514	1 273
Machinery and Equipment	4 140	2 753	1 387	1 520
	$ 7 021	$ 3 676	$ 3 346	$ 3 238

3. *Bank and Short-Term Borrowing*

	1981	1980
Bank indebtedness	$ 894	$ 5 421
Bankers' acceptances	2 500	7 000
Loans from shareholders	1 948	1 217
Advances from joint ventures	365	1 510
	$ 5 707	$ 15 147

Figures are rounded and therefore may not add to totals.

Source: Marshall Steel Ltd.

EXHIBIT 3

MARSHALL STEEL LTD.

Drummond McCall Inc.
Floor Area and Land Area of
Plant/Sales-Office Sites

	Roofed Floor Area (Sq. Feet)	Land Area (Acres*)
Canada		
Nova Scotia		
Halifax	40 000	5.37
Quebec		
Montreal	256 000	28.74
Jonquiere	13 000	2.82
	269 000	31.56
Ontario		
Toronto	235 000	15.34
Hamilton	193 000	22.80
Sudbury[1]	38 000	2.98
	466 000	41.12
Manitoba		
Winnipeg	87 000	6.98
Alberta		
Calgary	32 000	7.05
Edmonton	31 000	7.69
	63 000	14.74
British Columbia		
Vancouver	120 000	14.99
Victoria[1]	42 000	.96
Prince George[2]	19 000	2.43
Nanaimo[1]	11 000	1.49
Kelowna	10 000	2.00
Campbell River[2]	9 000	2.00
	211 000	23.87
Yukon Territory		
Whitehorse[1]	21 000	.48
United States		
Portland, Maine[3]	45 000	12.47
TOTAL	1 202 000	136.59

Notes: [1] Leased land and buildings
    [2] Leased land
    [3] Under construction
* 1 acre = 43 560 square feet

Source: Drummond McCall Inc. Prospectus 1979

EXHIBIT 4
MARSHALL STEEL LTD.
DRUMMOND McCALL INC.

Consolidated Statement of Earnings
for the year ended December 31
($000)

	1980	1979
Sales	$ 223 477	$ 210 827
Cost and Expenses		
Cost of sales and expenses before the undernoted depreciation	209 652	191 515
Depreciation	1 877	1 494
Interest on long-term debt	2 414	1 633
Other interest	3 341	2 016
	217 284	196 658
Earnings Before Income Taxes	6 194	14 169
Income Taxes		
Current	1 747	5 705
Deferred	523	291
	2 270	5 996
Net Earnings	$ 3 924	$ 8 173
Earnings per common share	$1.15	$2.82

Consolidated Statement of Retained Earnings
for the year ended December 31
($000)

Retained Earnings at beginning of year	$ 39 957	$ 34 066
Net Earnings	3 924	8 173
	43 881	42 238
Dividends on Common Shares $0.80 per share (1979 — $0.80)	2 727	2 281
Retained Earnings at end of year	$ 41 154	$ 39 957

Note: Figures are rounded and therefore may not add to totals.

Source: Drummond McCall Inc. annual report

EXHIBIT 5
MARSHALL STEEL LTD.
DRUMMOND McCALL INC.

Consolidated Balance Sheet
for the year ended December 31
($000)

	1980	1979
Assets		
Current		
Cash	$ 42	$ 30
Accounts receivable	33 405	33 745
Inventories	52 254	65 496
Prepaid expenses	298	130
	85 999	99 402
Fixed Assets, at cost less accumulated depreciation	26 002	21 194
Share Purchase Plan Loans	259	—
Unamortized Long-Term Debt Issue Expense	276	239
	$ 112 536	$ 120 835
Liabilities and Shareholders' Equity		
Current		
Bank indebtedness	$ 16 977	$ 30 803
Accounts payable and accrued liabilities	15 843	21 338
Income and other taxes	2 186	4 009
Long-term debt maturing within one year	975	525
	35 981	56 675
Long-Term Debt	25 138	15 231
Deferred Income Taxes	2 632	2 110
Shareholders' Equity		
Stated capital		
Common shares	7 631	6 863
Retained earnings	41 154	39 957
	48 785	46 820
	$ 112 536	$ 120 835

Figures are rounded and therefore may not add to totals.

Exhibit 5 (continued)

Notes to Consolidated Financial Statements
for the year ended December 31

1. *Fixed Assets (000)*	*1980*	*1979*
Land	$ 2 271	$ 2 218
Buildings and leasehold improvements	20 942	18 171
Equipment	17 926	14 141
	41 138	34 530
Less: Accumulated depreciation	15 136	13 336
	$26 002	$ 21 194

2. *Long-Term Debt (000)*

	1980	1979
11 1/8% Sinking Fund Debentures Series A due July 31, 1990	$ 5 400	$ 5 925
10 1/4% Sinking Fund Debentures Series C due October 15, 1993	9 000	9 000
Floating Rate Sinking Fund Debentures Series D due June 10, 1995	10 000	—
Industrial Building Revenue Installment Note due to September 26, 1994 (u.s. $1 467)	1 713	831
	26 113	15 756
Less: Amounts due within one year	975	525
	$ 25 138	$ 15 231

The series A, C and D Debentures are secured by a floating charge on assets.

The Series D Debentures bear interest at a floating rate of 1/4 of 1% less than the prime rate of a Canadian chartered bank.

The Industrial Building Revenue Installment Note, in the maximum principal amount of u.s. $1 650 000, is guaranteed by the Corporation and repayable by the subsidiary commencing in 1982. The Note bears interest at 7% to 1984, then at 7 1/4% to 1989 and thereafter at 75% of the lending bank's base rate and is secured by specific property, plant and equipment. Up to December 31, 1980 the subsidiary had drawn down u.s. $1 466 561 of the available funds.

Sinking fund and other repayment requirements in the next five years are (in dollars) 1981 — $975 000; 1982 — $1 015 140; 1983 $1 135 559; 1984 — $1 135 559; 1985 — $1 135 559.

3. *Shareholders' Equity*
   (a) Stated Capital

	Authorized	*Shares outstanding December 31*	
		1980	*1979*
Preferred shares	Unlimited	—	—
Common Shares	Unlimited		
Series A		2 931 393	2 516 443
Series B		523 720	867 398
		3 455 113	3 383 841

Exhibit 5 (continued)

Under a Certificate of Amendment dated April 30, 1980, the Corporation's Articles of Continuance were amended to authorize it to issue an unlimited number of Preferred Shares.

The Series A and Series B Common Shares are interconvertible at any time at the option of the holders on a one-for-one-basis and rank equally in all respects. Payment of dividends on the Series B Common Shares may be in the form of stock dividends.

During 1980 the Corporation adopted an employee share purchase plan. Under the plan, 90 000 series A Common Shares have been reserved for allotment during the period ending December 31, 1982. Employees designated by the Board may purchase their shares in the year of allotment at a price, also established by the Board, of not less than 90% of the market price on the date of acquisition.

Following is a summary of the changes in Common Shares for the years ended December 31, 1980 and 1979:

	1980		*1979*	
	Number	*$*	*Number*	*$*
Total outstanding at beginning of year	3 383 841	$ 6 862 657	1 418 650	$386 500
Increase due to two-for-one subdivision of shares	—	—	1 418 650	—
Shares issured				
Public offering	—	—	500 000	5 887 500
Payment of dividends	44 322	502 731	46 541	588 657
Share purchase plan	26 950	265 258	—	—
	71 272	767 989	546 541	6 476 157
Total outstanding at end of year	3 455 113	$ 7 630 646	3 383 841	$ 6 862 657

(b) Dividend Restrictions

The trust indentures securing the Series A, C and D Sinking Fund Debentures, and the covenants in connection with the Industrial Building Revenue Installment Note, place certain restrictions on the payment of dividends. The most restrictive of these requires that total dividend payments subsequent to December 31, 1977 be limited to the aggregate of $5 000 000 and the consolidated net earnings and the consideration received by the Corporation for shares of its capital stock subsequent to December 31, 1977. In addition, as long as the Industrial Building Revenue Installment Note is outstanding, the Corporation is required to maintain its consolidated net worth at at least $28 000 000 plus 40% of the consolidated net earnings exclusive of any losses subsequent to December 31, 1978.

Source: Drummond McCall Inc. annual report

EXHIBIT 6
MARSHALL STEEL LTD.
DRUMMOND McCALL INC.

Stock Trading Statistics for A and B Series
Common Stock on the Toronto and Montreal Exchanges

	High	Low	Volume	Year End Book Value
1981				
January	$12\frac{2}{8}$	$10\frac{7}{8}$	26 631	
February	$12\frac{1}{8}$	$11\frac{4}{8}$	29 360	
March	$12\frac{4}{8}$	$11\frac{2}{8}$	13 773	
April	$15\frac{3}{8}$	$11\frac{6}{8}$	37 390	
May	$13\frac{3}{8}$	$10\frac{4}{8}$	10 535	
June	13	$11\frac{2}{8}$	18 740	
July	$11\frac{5}{8}$	$11\frac{2}{8}$	36 930	
August	$11\frac{2}{8}$	10	14 900	
Aggregate	$15\frac{3}{8}$	10	188 259	
1980				
January — August	$12\frac{2}{8}$	10	139 386	
January — December	$12\frac{2}{8}$	10	255 610	14.12
1979				
January — August	$14\frac{6}{8}$	$9\frac{4}{8}$	116 000	
January — December	$14\frac{6}{8}$	$9\frac{4}{8}$	209 605	13.84
1978[1]				
January — August	$10\frac{4}{8}$	$6\frac{4}{8}$	48 000	
January — December	$10\frac{4}{8}$	$6\frac{4}{8}$	81 630	12.15
1977[1]				
January — August	$7\frac{5}{8}$	$5\frac{3}{8}$	12 780	
January — December	$7\frac{5}{8}$	$5\frac{3}{8}$	19 480	11.35
1976[1]				
January — August	$7\frac{7}{8}$	$5\frac{7}{8}$	93 350	
January — December	$7\frac{7}{8}$	5	120 265	10.83

[1] Prices adjusted for 1978 2 for 1 stock split

Source: TSE Review and Montreal Stock Exchange

EXHIBIT 7
MARSHALL STEEL LTD.

Comparative Data
($000 000)

	DMC	Russel[2]	Slater[3]	Harris	Niagara[4]
Fiscal Year End	Dec. 31/80	Dec. 31/80	Mar. 28/81	Dec. 31/80	
Sales ($000 000)	223	524	114	142	67
Net Income ($000 000)	4	7	7	5	.8
Net Income/Sales	2%	1%	6%	4%	1%
Net Income/Total Assets	4%	2%	5%	8%	3%
Long-Term Debt/Shareholders' Equity	51%	34%	57%	35%	67%
Earnings per Share					
1980	1.15	1.73	2.60	.97	1.61
1979	2.82	4.84	3.60	.65	1.67
1978	1.66	3.15	4.16	.03	(2.49)
1977	1.08	1.25	1.31	.50	1.14
1976	.79	.88	.63	.41	1.44
Market Price (Average 1980)		11.13	—	17.32	4.20
Price Range[1]					
1980	12.25 –10.00	—	19.63–15.00	4.50–3.90	—
1979	14.75 –9.50	16.00–11.75	20.00–14.75	4.60–3.95	—
1978	10.50 –6.50	13.25– 8.50	20.00–12.75	—	—
1977	7.625–5.375	9.88– 7.50	13.38– 7.00	—	—
1976	7.875–5.00	13.00 – 8.25	8.88– 6.75	—	—
Price/Earnings Average					
1980	9.7	—	6.7	4.2	—
1979	4.3	2.9	4.8	6.6	—
1978	5.1	3.5	3.9	—	—
1977	6.0	7.0	7.8	—	—
1976	8.1	12.1	12.4	—	—
BETA	.59	.60	.69		
Sales Growth					
1980	6%	(2%)	9%	19%	8%
1979	42%	25%	9%	86%	44%
1978	46%	26%	48%	16%	54%
1977	10%	17%	16%	(7%)	17%
Net Income Growth					
1980	(50%)	(50%)	(30%)	67%	—
1979	60%	56%	(9%)	1848%	214%
1978	67%	125%	175%	(92%)	(217%)
1977	50%	100%	100%	—	(14%)

Exhibit 7 (continued)

Net Income Return on Average Shareholders' Equity

1980	8%	6%	10%	23%	15%
1979	21%	19%	16%	16%	18%
1978	14%	16%	20%	1%	(14%)
1977	10%	8%	8%	11%	11%

Dividend/Share

1980	.80	.63	.80	.22	(see note 5)
1979	.80	.73	.95	.04	
1978	.875	.64	.70	—	
1977	.50	.64	.32	—	
1976	.50	.58	.68	—	

[1] Calendar year.
[2] Extraordinary loss 1980 of $1 million. Net Income before extraordinary loss $8 million; EPS $2.16 before extraordinary loss. Delisted Nov. 25/80, H-L to June 30/80 20.75–12.00 with average P/E 4.6.
[3] Fiscal year end March 28, therefore, 1980 figures are for 1981 fiscal year, etc.
[4] Fiscal year end August 31; therefore, 1980 figures are for 1981 fiscal year, etc. Only Preferred trades on stock exchange.
[5] Data unavailable.

York Russell Ltd.

York Russel is an industrial distributor of steel products, replacement bearings and power transmission components, plumbing and heating supplies, hardware and other home products. York Russel also designs and manufactures specialized machinery for the wire and cable industry. The metals group distributes and processes carbon and alloy steel through 17 steel service centres in Canada and the U.S. Hugh Russel was taken over by York Steel Consturction Ltd. in 1980 and became a privately owned corporation under the name York Russel Ltd.

Slater Steel Industries Limited

Slater has three operating divisions with headquarters in Hamilton. Slater produces a variety of rolled steel products for industry and pole line hardware for power utilities. It produces stampings, forgings and aluminum castings for industry and manufactured various bars and shapes for application in the automotive, agricultural, construction and utility markets and for the warehousing industry. The Joslyn Stainless Steel division in the U.S. produces a range of stainless and high temperature alloy grades in bar and billet form for service centre markets in the U.S.

Harris Steel Group Inc.

Harris is a fabricator and erector of reinforced steel rods and a manufacturer of steel bar supports. Its Montreal division is a full service outlet involved in steel grating for industrial construction. Through its subsidiaries, Harris fabricates and erects structural steel, designs and installs post-tensioning systems, and manufactures and distributes industrial wire products, heavy industrial steel and aluminum gratings. Subsidiaries are also warehouse distributors of industrial structural steel and bar products.

Niagara Structural Steel Co. Ltd.

Niagara fabricates and erects structural steel out of its head office in St. Catharines. Niagara operates steel service centres in St. Catharines, Sept-Îles and New York State. Although Niagara preferred shares traded on the Toronto Stock Exchange, the company was in the process of buying back and cancelling the outstanding preferred shares.

EXHIBIT 8
MARSHALL STEEL LTD.

Drummond McCall Inc.
Ratio of Margin[1] to Sales and Sales Growth Rates
1972–1980

	Margin/Sales	*Nominal Sales Growth Rate*
1980	6.2	5.8
1979	9.2	40.9
1978	7.2	46.1
1977	6.9	10.2
1976	6.5	1.8
1975	11.7	(11.8)
1974	16.9	36.4
1973	12.8	37.5
1972	7.8	

The eight year compound annual growth rate in sales from 1972 to 1980 is 19%.

[1] Margin is defined as the difference between Sales and Cost of Sales and Expenses.

Source: Drummond McCall annual report

EXHIBIT 9
MARSHALL STEEL LTD.

Selected Financial Statistics
August 31, 1981

Government of Canada Bond Yields	
1–3 years	18.93%
3–5 years	18.68%
5–10 years	17.94%
over 10 years	17.66%
Corporates	
Long term bonds	19.08%
Bank Prime Rate	21.00%
Toronto Stock Exchange	
Composite 300 Index	2176
Price Earnings – Composite	9.2
Dividend Yields	4.8

LAWSON & JONES LIMITED

In January 1985, a group of officers and senior managers at Lawson & Jones Limited (Lawson & Jones) of Mississauga Ontario was preparing a management leveraged buyout (LBO)[1] proposal. The group, led by Lawrence (Larry) Tapp, President and CEO, Donald (Don) Thain, Chairman of the Board and Ralph Steedman, Vice President and CFO, was evaluating a plan to acquire Lawson & Jones from its parent, Mardon Packaging International Limited, a wholly owned subsidiary of BAT Industries plc (BAT) of the United Kingdom. This opportunity arose because of the difference between the Lawson & Jones management group, who believed the company had the potential to grow under their leadership, and the senior executives of BAT, who considered the printing and packaging industries unattractive for further investment.

Tapp faced a major problem; the strategy for the company favoured by management and the Board differed significantly from the plan for Lawson & Jones adopted by the BAT Board of Directors. BAT wanted Lawson & Jones operated as a source of cash, i.e., a "harvest" strategy. Lawson & Jones wanted the cash being paid out for dividends spent on additional investments that would promote growth internally and by acquisition. When Tapp proposed capital projects which he said were needed to meet the RONA[2] objective of 25% set by BAT, the reply from BAT was that no money would be allocated to divisions that couldn't meet corporate RONA objectives. BAT's core businesses of tobacco, retailing and paper provided better returns than Lawson & Jones' printing and packaging sector. BAT set corporate-wide objectives. Although Lawson & Jones outperformed other

---

[1] A leveraged buyout occurs when a company is purchased using debt as the principal financing means. Subsequent divestitures and profitable operations are expected to bring interest coverage to acceptable levels. A management LBO occurs when a company's management executes the LBO.

[2] Return on Net Assets (RONA)

$$= \frac{\text{EBIT or Trading Profit}}{(\text{A/Rec} + \text{Inv} - \text{Trade Cred} + \text{Net Fixed Assets})}$$

printers within the BAT organization and the printing industry, it could not match the earnings performance of BAT's core sectors.

The management group had to answer many questions before it could approach BAT regarding the buyout. It had to establish a reasonable price for Lawson & Jones within the limits of what the group could pay. It had to find a source of financing and determine acceptable terms. The group had to evaluate the risk related to the buyout and to define all areas of potential improvement. It was clear that there would be costs incurred to answer these questions; a plan was drawn up to define how the LBO proposal would be prepared, who would work on it and who would pay for it.

Lawson & Jones Limited[3]

Lawson & Jones was one of Canada's oldest and premier companies in the printing and packaging industries. From 17 operating plants in Canada and two in the United States, the company produced a wide range of products and services, from magazines, labels, catalogues and newspaper advertising inserts to folding cartons, flexible packaging and business forms. Lawson & Jones's sales and pre-tax income for the 12 months ended December 31, 1984 were C$294.8 million and C$15.1 million, respectively. Financial statements for 1979 to 1984 are presented in Exhibit 1.

The company's operations were organized into three main divisions: Commercial Printing (60% of EBIT), Packaging (30% of EBIT) and Business Forms (10% of EBIT). Divisional units operated as separate entities, each managing its own production, marketing, accounting and sales staff, permitting quicker response, higher quality and better service at the customer level. The 19 companies that made up the corporate structure are set out in Exhibit 2.

Lawson & Jones began in 1882 as a partnership between F.E. Lawson and H.J. Jones in London, Ontario. The partnership's first products were labels and calendars. By the 1950's, the company covered the Canadian market for labels and printing, with operations in seven cities. The company entered the business forms market in 1958 and, three years later, acquired its first packaging facility, as well as a printing company in the United States. In 1984, sales reached almost $300 million. Growth was achieved in part by completing 35 acquisitions and expanding to nine new locations, and by maintaining the company's product innovativeness, state-of-the-art equipment and careful attention to the needs of its customers. A representative sample of major customers is set out in Exhibit 3.

---

[3] Major portions of Lawson & Jones company background are reprinted from company documents.

Printing

The printing product line generated C$123 million of sales and C$7.4 million of trading profit in 1984.

In commercial print (brochures, catalogues, newspaper inserts) the company was strongly positioned in Eastern Canada. Management estimated that it held a 30% share of the commercial market and a leading position in specialist in-line finishing of print. Trading profit margins were consistently close to 8% of sales. Major competitors were Southam, Ronalds, Maclean Hunter and Metro Graphics.

In Western Canada and West Coast United States, Lawson & Jones was estimated to have a market share of about 9%. Trading profit margins were 3% of sales. Major competitors included Ronalds and Canadian Publishers in Western Canada, and R.R. Donnelly and Jeffries in the United States.

Lawson & Jones expected the web printing market to grow at about 5% per annum in all regions, reflecting increased demand for direct mail and newspaper insert advertising.

Labels

Label production accounted for revenue of C$56 million, with margins close to 7% of sales.

In Canada, where the total market is about C$90 million, Lawson & Jones was the market leader in Ontario and Quebec, with a share of about 30% and in British Columbia, with about 75%. A plant in Michigan served the United States Midwest. Lawson & Jones was particularly strong in cosmetics, liquor, fish and wine labels. Competitors included MMT and Jonergin in Eastern Canada and Fleming Potter and St. Louis Litho in the United States.

The company estimated that the North American labels market would grow at 3% per annum in real terms.

Cartons

The Packaging Division produced folding cartons for the tobacco, distillery, cosmetics, detergents and beer markets. The total Canadian carton market was valued at about C$600 million and was believed to be growing at about 3% annually. Lawson & Jones held a share of about 12%. Its position was strongest in high quality gravure cartons, which were growing at the expense of litho. The trading profit margin in 1984 was 6% of sales.

Major competitors were Somerville Belkin, Rolph Clark Stone and Reid Dominion.

Flexible Packaging

The Packaging Division also produced flexible packaging for the Canadian food, tobacco and confectionery markets. Lawson & Jones sales of C$20 million represented an 11% share of a C$190 million market which was growing at about 5% per annum. The trading profit margin was 5.5% of sales. The company's main strength was in printed barrier laminates. DRG was the market leader and major competitor.

Business Forms

The company produced a range of continuous forms and multi-part sets for small to medium-sized customers across Canada. Sales attained C$24 million in 1984, with trading profit margins of 5%. Moore Corporation was the market leader and major competitor.

Lawson & Jones was estimated to hold a 5% share of the C$500 million market. The company had strong shares in Alberta and Manitoba and a smaller presence in Eastern Canada. The nature of the packaging and print industries was such that most of the customer relationships were handled on an individual quotation basis. However, a few "agreements to supply" existed for major customers.

Manufacturing Operations

The Lawson & Jones factories ranged from modern single-storey plants such as Lawson Packaging Toronto, Lawson Graphics Toronto and Montreal Lithographing, to older multi-storey factories such as Lawson Packaging Montreal and Michigan Litho. Most of the plants were owned by Lawson & Jones.

Web printing plants were located in Toronto, Montreal and Los Angeles. They were conventionally equipped. Recent investments included a new 48-page press (unique to Canada) in Toronto and a halfweb press with finishing line at the Montreal plant. A plant in Winnipeg had both web and sheet feed litho capabilities, and there were smaller litho printing plants at Calgary and Montreal.

Label plants were in Montreal and Michigan. They were conventionally equipped. All the label plants produced combination label sheets.

Folding carton plants were situated in Toronto and Montreal. They were conventionally equipped, with recent major investment involving rotary gravure equipment.

The flexible plant was in Toronto and had gravure and flexo-printing machinery and laminating equipment.

There were four forms plants, the major ones being in Winnipeg and Calgary.

Additionally, small mixed plants in London (Ontario), Vancouver and Halifax produced cartons, labels and general print.

The company had about 2,300 employees. Of the 1,480 unionized employees, approximately 1,376, or 93% were represented by the Graphics Communications International Union (GCIU). Contract renewals usually proceeded smoothly as labour relations had generally been very good.

In fiscal 1984, salaries, wages and fringe benefits accounted for approximately 31% of total costs and expenses. To strengthen operations and improve productivity, the company had a program in which approximately 100 operating and corporate managers participated in an annual bonus plan based on achieving targeted results. The annual bonus was a substantial portion of the total remuneration.

Management

Tapp had been President and CEO since 1982. He joined Lawson & Jones in 1978 and worked his way up through operations at various locations. Prior to joining Lawson & Jones, Tapp had been VP Operations and Director of Hallmark Canada. He held an MBA from the University of Kansas.

Steedman joined Lawson & Jones as CFO in 1982. He had been VP Finance of Control Data Canada and Controller of Baxter Travenol Ltd. He was a Chartered Accountant with an MBA from York University.

Thain joined Lawson & Jones as a member of the Board in 1980 and was appointed non-executive Chairman in 1983. In addition to being a Professor of Business Administration at the University of Western Ontario, he was a director of several Canadian companies. Thain obtained a doctorate from the Harvard Business School and joined Western's faculty after his graduation.

Share Ownership

Lawson & Jones first sold common shares to the public in 1948. In 1953, BAT Industries plc of London, England, through a subsidiary, purchased 50% of Lawson & Jones and in 1976 increased its ownership to 75%. The Class B shares were listed on the Toronto Stock Exchange but trading was sporadic. In 1984, only about 1000 shares were traded and the price spread was between $305 and $315.

BAT Industries plc

BAT Industries (formerly the British American Tobacco Company) was a U.K.-based multinational with sales of £11,846 million and before-tax profits of £979 million in 1984. The company was organized into operating groups and associated companies. The subsidiaries and divisions comprising tobacco, paper, retailing and printing are described in Exhibit 4. The newly acquired financial services business, Eagle Star Holdings, was the result of a very deliberate plan to be a major player in this industry. Mardon Packaging International Limited (Mardon) was the name of the printing and packaging division which held the 75% interest in Lawson & Jones. A three-year financial summary for BAT is presented in Exhibit 5.

Mardon Packaging International Limited

In 1984 the Mardon Group's business was concentrated in the United Kingdom and in North America. In 1984, Mardon had rationalized its operations, particularly in the United Kingdom and made significant investments in the growth areas of plastics packaging. Mardon had five trading divisions. Although the overseas division was treated separately, its activities also included operations similar to those of the major divisions.

		Sales (£ million)
(1) Carton & Print Division		97.9
(2) Corrugated Division		38.0
(3) Flexible Packaging Division		106.8
(4) Rigid Plastics & Metals Division		87.9
(5) Overseas Division		277.0
— Lawson & Jones	198.6	
— Mardon Packaging Corp	70.0	
— Mardon Printers	8.4	
		607.6

Mardon's headquarters were in Bristol, England. The company operated over 80 manufacturing facilities, including 46 in the United Kingdom, 16 in Canada, and eight in the United States with the remainder in Europe and Central Africa. The Mardon group employed over 11,500 worldwide.

The Chairman of the Board of Mardon was E. John Worlidge, an executive director of BAT Industries. Thain reported to Worlidge in regard to strategic issues relevant to the Lawson & Jones Board, and in other matters of concern at the Board level. The reporting format was formal but the overall relationship was friendly.

Three-year profit and loss statements for Mardon are shown in Exhibit 6 and balance sheets are in Exhibit 7.

The Problem

The relationship between Lawson & Jones management and BAT/Mardon management had changed and became less comfortable over the last two years for several reasons. First, printing and packaging was not a core business for BAT. Second, BAT had many investment options which were more financially attractive than Lawson & Jones' capital expenditure program. Finally, the geographic distance and decentralization of Canadian operations allowed few synergies with BAT's core businesses.

The annual BAT Industries guidelines set specific objectives for Return on Net Assets (RONA). Overseas operations objectives were 25% RONA, while UK operations aimed for at least 20%. BAT considered Lawson & Jones' performance unsatisfactory at 14.7%, despite the fact that it performed relatively well within its industry. Mardon Packaging Int'l. had an average RONA of 10% in the same year (1983).

BAT required each division to pay dividends. What was left over after the dividend payout was available to invest either in the business itself through capital spending programs or in another group activity. The dividend objectives for the printing and packaging business did not leave anything for discretionary capital projects. Lawson & Jones capital spending proposals were submitted to BAT each year with the intention of improving RONA, but were always reduced because past RONA performance did not justify the requested amount. The gearing ratio (debt/equity) was to remain below 60%, although specific constraints on Lawson & Jones made its effective gearing maximum closer to 40%. Profit, in real dollar terms, was expected to double over 10 years. Lawson & Jones' RONA had varied between 12% and 16% from 1979 to 1983, and trading profit fluctuated between C$5 million and C$9 million. Results for 1984 were 16.2% RONA and C$9.6 million net earnings.

BAT wanted its portion of Lawson & Jones' dividends to be C$9.5 million for 1985 and to increase by C$1.2 million every year. This left a planned discretionary cash flow of C$15.8 million for 1985, but Lawson & Jones had capital spending plans for C$23 million. BAT would not authorize the additional C$7.2 million.

Executive compensation and bonuses were another topic of disagreement. BAT wanted Lawson & Jones to keep total executive compensation the same but to increase salaries and reduce bonuses. Lawson & Jones' Board preferred to maintain the status quo because of the motivation bonuses gave to its managers and the positive effect they had on results.

BAT requests for information about the capital spending program were a further source of aggravation. During April 1983, Tapp had informed BAT that the equivalent of one person full time was needed to answer queries on a multitude of financial, marketing and operations issues not necessarily needed by the BAT bureaucracy. Canadian management suspected that many requests were made by staff members guessing that their bosses might ask for the information at a later date.

Further differences of opinion existed on restructuring the company. BAT expected an integrated program of divestiture and growth which would reshape Lawson & Jones from 19 companies (Exhibit 2) with total sales of C$294.8 million in 1984 to 13 companies with total sales of C$320 million in 1988. BAT wanted to use the proceeds of divestitures to invest in other divisions. Lawson & Jones, on the other hand, wanted to use the proceeds of divestitures within Lawson & Jones, and had proposed a growth strategy using a comprehensive investment program.

An excerpt in a letter from a BAT Board executive to the President of Lawson & Jones describes the situation:

> In summary, meeting your trading profit budget for 1984 when a number of key financial figures are unlikely to be achieved, will not support your case for a substantial increase in capital spending for 1985. On the other hand, if we see a progression on trading profit well up on budget for 1984 and 1985, you will have the credibility to support capital spending for 1986.

In reply, Tapp wrote:

> I thought Lawson & Jones was genuinely earning adequate credibility but you and I seem to differ on this . . .

> The capital spending that we are asking for will permit us to meet your objectives — I don't know how to get another $1 mm of trading profit this year if our capital spending is delayed.

Tapp was often annoyed about the worsening aspects of the relationship. BAT's harvest strategy could have been implemented by senior executives satisfied with the status quo. Instead two aggressive people who were relatively new to the organization assumed the top positions of President and non-executive Chairman of the Board after their predecessors retired almost simultaneously. The new leaders, Tapp and Thain, hired Steedman who was also aggressive.

The Proposal

The management group expected that if BAT agreed to the LBO, BAT would want to sell all of its stake in the company for cash. Although none of the managers had ever spearheaded a project of this magnitude or type, they were advised that the best way to structure the LBO would be to create a holding company that would buy all of the outstanding common and preferred shares of Lawson & Jones. All the essential elements and potential pitfalls of an LBO had to be researched and documented so the group would be prepared for the proposal and subsequent transaction. Personal concerns of each group member regarding the project had to be brought to the surface.

The proper strategy for Lawson & Jones had to be analyzed. The management group wanted to be sure that a growth strategy was appropriate before proceeding with a buyout. BAT's reasons for a harvest strategy had to be reviewed and debated in the overall analysis.

Financing the project was a formidable task. Tapp expected Colonel Thomas Lawson, who held at least 20% of the equity in Lawson & Jones and still had strong ties to the business that his grandfather had started, would participate in the buyout. Management participation in the form of investment in common shares was expected to be necessary to secure financing. Tapp, Thain and Steedman committed in aggregate approximately C$1 million to equity purchases.

Merrill Lynch Canada Inc. (Merrill Lynch), Lawson & Jones' investment bank, actively pursued candidates who would invest in the buyout with a combination of equity and subordinated debt. It contacted corporate investors, pension funds, venture capitalists and insurance companies to determine whether sufficient financing could be put in place for the proposal. A formula of $2.50 of subordinated debt for every $1.00 of equity was suggested to interested parties. The Tom Lawson family holding company, Woodholme Holdings, had agreed in principle to invest in subordinated debt and equity in this ratio.

A major new investor, Roman Corporation, controlled by Steven Roman, had also agreed to invest in the LBO in the debt and equity proportions proposed. The tentative agreement with Roman indicated that he might invest up to $27 million in the deal.

Senior debt holders were solicited among banks and trust companies. The objective was to obtain about 75 to 80% of the purchase price through senior secured loans from banks, 12 to 15 percent from subordinated loans, and a further 5 to 10 percent from equity.

Key indicators had to be predicted and potential improvements planned. Sensitivities to revenues, costs and interest rates had to be forecasted. Current and potential market niches had to be identified. The strengths and weaknesses of human resources had to be established. Investors had to be convinced that they could trust management and that the price that was paid for the company would allow Lawson & Jones to meet the terms of the financing. Steedman drafted the financing plan shown in Exhibit 8. A total of $120 million was needed for the transaction under this scenario.

Valuation of the firm was one of the tasks at hand. From 1979 to 1984 Lawson & Jones's sales grew at a compound annual rate of 8.6%, while pretax income grew at a rate of 9.9% (Exhibit 1). In fiscal 1981 and 1982, revenues grew, while income before taxes fell, reflecting the generally high interest rates in both Canada and the United States and the ongoing effects of inflation. During the fiscal year ended December 31, 1984, revenues and pre-tax income increased by 14% and 20% respectively.

The company's financial condition and liquidity in early 1985 were the strongest in its history. As of December 31, 1984, the company had working capital of $28.5 million and shareholders' equity of $61.7 million, 77.8% of total capitalization.

The company owned the land and buildings for 12 of its locations in Canada and the United States. These owned premises comprised over 75% of the total building square footage used by the company, with a net book value of $8.8 million, an estimated market value of $21.6 million and debt of $1.9 million. The remaining locations and the corporate office were leased. The company was reviewing its properties to: (i) potentially divest unutilized properties; (ii) determine any benefits resulting from sales and leasebacks; and (iii) move from less productive or unattractive locations.

A projected earnings statement and capital spending program were prepared (Exhibits 9 and 10) to provide a basis for estimating possible outcomes. Financial statements of comparable companies with their respective beta's are presented in Exhibit 11. Since Lawson & Jones operated in three industries, management felt that a weighted average P/E multiple based on the EBIT of each division would assist them in valuing the firm. Exhibit 12 was prepared for that purpose. Interest rates and exchange rates are documented in Exhibit 13.

The management group was eager to prepare a proposal and plan of action that could be implemented before the end of February 1985.

EXHIBIT 1
LAWSON & JONES LIMITED

Income Statements for Lawson & Jones Limited
(C$ millions)

				Fiscal Years Ended December 31		
	1984	1983	1982	1981	1980	1979
Net Sales	$294.8	$258.5	$242.1	$234.2	$215.2	$194.8
Cost of Goods Sold	238.1	206.1	196.5	185.4	169.8	158.0
Depreciation	7.5	7.5	7.3	6.8	6.0	5.1
Gross Profit	49.2	44.9	38.3	42.0	39.3	31.7
Sales, General & Admin.	31.5	30.9	26.4	25.9	23.4	21.6
EBIT (Trading profit)	17.6	14.0	11.9	16.1	15.9	10.1
Interest Expense	2.9	2.1	3.6	3.9	3.0	2.3
Interest Income	0.0	0.0	0.0	0.0	0.0	0.0
Other Income	0.4	0.4	0.7	0.7	2.3	2.0
Earnings Before Income Taxes	15.1	12.5	8.9	12.9	15.2	9.5
Provision for Income Taxes (note 6)	5.5	5.5	3.6	6.1	6.3	3.7
Net Earnings	$ 9.6	$ 7.0	$ 5.3	$ 6.8	$ 8.9	5.8
Common Dividends	5.6	4.4	2.4	3.6	3.5	3.0
Preferred Dividends	0.1	0.1	0.1	0.1	0.1	0.1
Addition to Retained Earnings	$ 3.9	$ 2.5	$ 2.8	$ 3.1	$ 5.3	$ 3.1

EXHIBIT 1 (continued)

Balance Sheets for Lawson & Jones Limited (A)
(C$ millions)

			Fiscal Years Ended December 31			
	1984	1983	1982	1981	1980	1979
Assets						
Current Assets						
Cash and Short Term Investments	$ 1.9	$ 0.0	$ 0.0	$ 0.4	$ 3.2	$ 1.5
Net Receivables	42.7	39.6	38.5	42.1	39.0	36.4
Inventories (note 1)	35.4	31.2	24.4	24.2	23.1	24.1
Other Current Assets	2.2	1.8	2.7	1.3	1.2	1.9
Total Current Assets	82.2	72.6	65.5	68.0	66.4	63.9
Property, Plant & Equipment	104.6	99.7	94.7	90.8	85.8	71.1
Less Accumulated Depreciation (note 2)	61.0	56.4	50.1	43.5	39.9	36.0
Net PP&E	43.6	43.4	44.6	47.4	45.9	35.1
Other Assets	0.5	1.8	1.6	4.0	4.1	3.1
Intangible — Goodwill	0.0	0.0	0.0	0.2	0.2	0.3
TOTAL ASSETS	$126.4	$117.8	$111.8	$119.6	$116.6	$102.3
Liabilities and Stockholders' Equity						
Current Liabilities						
Accounts Payable	$ 36.1	$ 31.3	$ 24.0	$ 27.0	$ 24.8	$ 21.3
Accrued Liabilities	1.3	3.3	1.1	2.6	5.3	2.1
Short Term Debt & Current Ltd.	16.4	14.4	18.1	23.8	23.5	23.2
Total Current Liabilities	53.8	48.9	43.2	53.5	53.6	46.6
Deferred Taxes	9.8	9.6	11.5	10.8	9.6	7.7
Other	0.0	0.0	0.0	0.0	0.0	0.0
Long Term Debt (note 3)	1.1	1.8	2.4	3.4	4.2	1.7
Acquisition Financing						
Bank Revolving Credit	—	—	—	—	—	—
Subordinated Notes	—	—	—	—	—	—
Additional Debt	—	—	—	—	—	—
Total Liabilities	64.7	60.3	57.0	67.7	67.3	56.0
Capital Stock (Classes A and B) (note 4)	0.1	0.1	0.1	0.1	0.1	0.1
Retained Earnings	61.6	57.3	54.7	51.7	49.1	46.2
Total Equity	61.7	57.4	54.8	51.9	49.3	46.4
TOTAL LIABILITIES AND EQUITY	$126.4	$117.8	$111.8	$119.6	$116.6	$102.3

EXHIBIT 1 (continued)

Consolidated Statement of Changes in Financial Position
year ended December 31, 1984
(C$000's)

	1984	1983
Sources of Working Capital		
Operations		
Income before extraordinary item	$ 8 891	$ 6 950
Items not affecting working capital		
Depreciation and amortization	7 510	7 519
Income taxes eliminated by		
application of losses of prior years	1 082	590
Deferred income taxes	240	(1 900)
Equity in net income of associated		
company	(144)	(356)
Gain on disposal of fixed assets	(203)	(239)
Dividends received from associated		
company	–	158
	17 376	12 722
Proceeds from sale of fixed assets	627	1 519
Net proceeds from sale of associated		
company	1 640	–
	19 643	14 241
Uses of Working Capital		
Increase (decrease) in loans and		
mortgages receivable	246	(20)
Additions to fixed assets	7 791	7 530
Dividends	5 720	4 520
Decrease in non-current portion of		
long-term debt	855	507
Foreign currency translation	271	371
	14 883	12 908
Increase in Working Capital	4 760	1 333
Working Capital, Beginning of Year	23 695	22 362
Working Capital, End of Year	$28 455	$23 695

EXHIBIT 1 (continued)

Selected Notes to the Consolidated Financial Statements
December 31, 1984

1. Inventories

(C$000s)

	1984	1983
Raw Materials	$13 706	$12 453
Work in Process	10 663	9 311
Finished Goods	11 071	9 478
	$35 440	$31 242

2. Fixed Assets

(C$000s)

	Cost	1984 Accumulated Depreciation	Net Book Value	1983 Net Book Value	Depreciation Rates
Land	$ 1 263	—	$ 1 263	$ 1 258	—
Buildings	15 147	7 090	8 057	7 666	5–10%
Equipment	84 874	53 138	31 736	33 406	10–30%
Deposits on Purchase of Equipment	2 381	—	2 381	649	—
Equipment Under Capital Leases	932	734	198	371	10–30%
	$104 597	$60 962	$43 635	$43 350	

EXHIBIT 1 (continued)

Selected Notes to the Consolidated Financial Statements
December 31, 1984

3. Long-Term Debt

	(C$000s)	
	1984	*1983*
Note payable without interest, maturing March 1985, unsecured	$ 150	$ 300
Note payable without interest, maturing March 1988, payable U.S. $158 000, unsecured	209	193
8.4% note payable, maturing December 1985, payable U.S. $432 000	571	1 002
11.75% mortgage, maturing January 1987	910	925
Obligations under capital leases	111	257
	$1 951	$2 677
Less amounts due within one year	868	831
	$1 083	$1 846

Principal payments required are

1985	$ 868
1986	119
1987	949
1988	15
	$1 951

The long term debt, other than the non-interest bearing notes payable, is secured by certain fixed assets.

EXHIBIT 1 (continued)

Selected Notes to the Consolidated Financial Statements
December 31, 1984

4. Share Capital

Shares authorized

The company is restricted by its articles as to the maximum number of shares that can be issued, as follows:

(i) 300 000 Class A non-voting shares with a cumulative preferential dividend of $1 per share participating to a maximum of an additional $0.20 per share
(ii) 300 000 Class B shares

Shares issued

	1984	1983
Class A	100 000	100 000
Class B	200 000	200 000
	300 000	300 000

Earnings per Class B share are calculated using the average number of shares outstanding and are calculated after providing for the maximum dividend requirements of $120 000 on the Class A Shares.

5. Lease Commitments

The company has commitments under operating leases which call for future minimum rentals as follows:

	(C$000s)
1985	$1 055
1986	813
1987	813
1988	753
1989	726
After 1990	1 140
	$5 300

Rent expense amounts to $1 097 000 in 1984 and $928 000 in 1983.

EXHIBIT 1 (continued)

Selected Notes to the Consolidated Financial Statements
December 31, 1984

6. *Income Taxes*

The company's basic income tax rate approximates 42%. The consolidated statement of income does not reflect this rate primarily as a result of the 3% allowance on opening inventories and investment tax credits relating to fixed asset replacements and additions, which have been deducted from the current income tax provision.

The subsidiary has accumulated business losses of approximately $5 680 000 available to reduce future income for tax purposes, which expire after 1995. The potential effect on future income taxes of these losses has not been recorded in the accounts.

In addition the subsidiary has tax credits of $1 074 000 available to reduce future years' income taxes. These expire after 1989.

7. *Information by Geographic Areas*

The company operates in one industry, producing printed products.

(C$000s)

	1984		
	Canada	*United States*	*Consolidated*
Sales	$240 935	$53 827	$294 762
Operating Profit	14 083	3 532	17 615
TOTAL ASSETS	$103 607	$22 807	$126 414

	1983		
	Canada	*United States*	*Consolidated*
Sales	$213 482	$45 033	$258 515
Operating Profit	11 389	2 635	14 024
TOTAL ASSETS	$ 97 971	$19 793	$117 764

8. *Capital Commitment*

The company has entered into agreements to purchase four major pieces of equipment for approximately $10 824 000. To December 31, 1984, advances of $1 726 000 have been made with payments of $5 266 000 due in 1985 and the remaining $3 832 000 due in semi-annual installments from 1986 to 1989.

EXHIBIT 2
LAWSON & JONES LIMITED

Coporate Structure

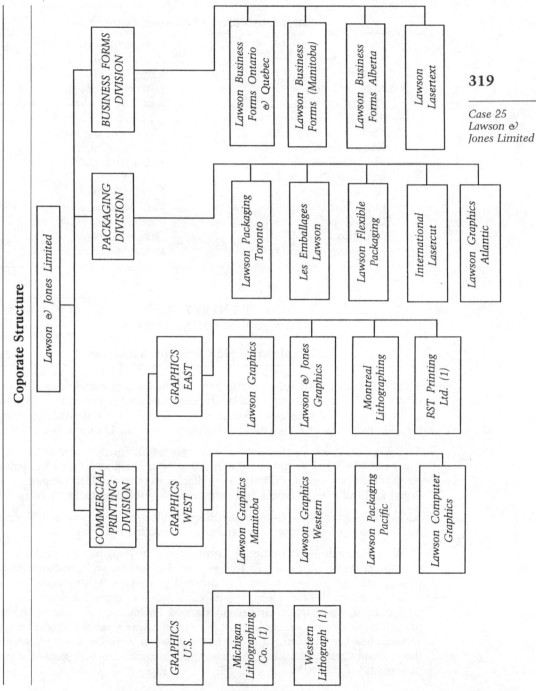

EXHIBIT 3
LAWSON & JONES LIMITED

Major Customers of Lawson & Jones

Kraft	Cheeseborough-Ponds
J.E. Seagram's & Sons	Avon Canada
Labatts	Imperial Tobacco
General Foods	Lowney's Nabisco
Playtex	Smith & Nephew
Brooke Bond	Johnson & Johnson
Shulton Canada	Charles of the Ritz
Canada Starch	Warner Lambert
RJR MacDonald	Rothmans
Brown & Williamson	Eaton's
Woolco	Hudson's Bay
Robert Simpson	Paul Masson
Coca-Cola	Nestle
Carnation	Quaker Oats
Consumers Distributing	Procter & Gamble

EXHIBIT 4[1]
LAWSON & JONES LIMITED

BAT Industries plc Company Background

---

1. The British-American Tobacco Company Limited was responsible for the Group's tobacco interests in 47 countries, with principal subsidiaries in the UK, Europe, Latin America, the Caribbean, Asia and Africa. It also co-ordinated key strategies for all Group tobacco companies, including those in the USA and West Germany.

2. The Wiggins Teape Group Limited was responsible for the Group's interests in paper outside the USA and for co-ordinating on a world-wide basis key strategies for this industry sector. Principal subsidiaries were in the UK, Belgium, France, Brazil and India, with offices and warehouses established in 30 countries.

3. BAT Stores Holdings Limited was responsible for the Group's UK retailing interests, comprising International Stores and Argos Distributors.

4. Mardon Packaging International Limited was responsible for packaging and printing operations in the UK, Europe, North America and Southern Africa. A wide variety of packaging and promotional material was produced, including folding cartons, flexible packaging, fibreboard cases, specialist print and labels, rigid plastics and metal containers. Mardon Packaging was one of the major manufacturers of packaging in the UK, where it was a market leader in folding cartons, flexible packaging and calendars. Lawson & Jones was 75% owned by the Mardon Group and was a major supplier of packaging and printed materials in Canada.

---

[1] Major portions of this exhibit reprinted from the BAT annual report 1983.

EXHIBIT 4 (continued)

BAT Industries plc Company Background

5. British-American Cosmetics Limited, the largest British-owned cosmetics business, was responsible for the Group's worldwide interests in cosmetics manufacturing and marketing.

6. BATUS Inc. was responsible for the Group's US subsidiaries in tobacco, retailing and paper.

7. BATIG GmbH was responsible for the Group's interests in tobacco, home improvements and retailing in West Germany.

8. On January 18, 1984, Eagle Star Holdings PLC became a subsidiary of BAT. On joining the Group, Eagle Star, which was one of the UK's largest composite insurance groups, became a separate operating group within BAT Industries.

Numerous other associated companies such as Imasco Ltd., a major diversified Canadian company with over half the domestic tobacco market, and AMATIL Ltd., a major diversified Australian company with one-third of the domestic tobacco market, completed BAT's portfolio.

Financial reporting at BAT was done by product sector. The four major sectors had the following results:

	Turnover (£millions)	Profit (% of turnover)
Tobacco	£6 138	8.8%
Retailing	3 528	4.7%
Paper	1 051	9.5%
Printing and Packaging	537	4.5%
	£11 254	

EXHIBIT 5
LAWSON & JONES LIMITED

BAT Industries Three-Year Financial Summary
(£millions)

	12 Months to December 31,		
	1984	*1983*	*1982*
Turnover and Profits			
Turnover	11 846	11 507	9 165
Trading Profit	851	783	634
Share of Profit of Associated			
Companies	125	102	87
Profit Before Taxation	979	856	684
Profit After Taxation	606	510	403
Attributable to BAT Industries			
Net Profit Before Extraordinary			
Items	547	454	363
Dividends − ordinary	120	100	84
	(pence)		
Earnings Per Ordinary Share	37.569	31.225	24.975
Dividends Per Ordinary Share			
Net of ACT Credit	8.250	6.875	5.750
Adjusted by the Retail Price Index	8.250	7.240	6.383
	(£millions)		
Balance Sheet			
Tangible Fixed Assets	1 969	1 871	1 388
Other Fixed Assets	617	470	424
Stocks	2 144	2 147	1 731
Other Current Assets	2 174	1 879	1 378
TOTAL ASSETS	6 904	6 367	4 921
Interest of Ordinary Shareholders	3 168	2 721	2 218
Interest of Minority Shareholders	250	270	210
Shareholders' Funds	3 418	2 991	2 428
Provisions for Liabilities and Charges	348	314	280
Borrowings − due beyond one year	844	867	589
Borrowings − due within one year	418	462	322
Other Creditors	1 876	1 733	1 302
TOTAL FUNDS EMPLOYED	6 904	6 367	4 921

EXHIBIT 6
LAWSON & JONES LIMITED

Mardon Packaging International Limited
Consolidated Profit and Loss Accounts
(£millions)

	1984	1983	1982
Net Turnover	607.6	496.7	495.7
Net Operating Charges	573.1	472.1	478.2
Trading Profit	34.5	24.6	17.5
Attributable Profit of Associates	0.3	0.7	0.8
Operating Profit	34.8	25.3	18.3
Interest Payable	11.1	9.6	11.7
Profit Before Tax	23.7	15.7	6.6
Tax	4.8	4.1	1.0
Profit After Tax	18.9	11.6	5.6
Outside Shareholders' Interest	2.1	1.1	1.0
Attributable Profit After Tax	16.8	10.5	4.6
Extraordinary Charges	5.6	3.9	13.1
Attributable Profit/(Loss) After Extraordinary Charges	11.2	6.6	(8.5)
Dividends	8.0	7.0	2.0
Retained Profit/(Withdrawn from Reserves)	3.2	(0.4)	(10.5)

EXHIBIT 7

Mardon Packaging International Limited
Consolidated Balance Sheets at December 31, 1983 and 1984
(£millions)

	1984	1983
Fixed Assets	153.6	143.0
Working Capital		
Stocks	72.2	58.9
Debtors	99.7	87.8
Creditors	(97.1)	(79.8)
	74.8	66.9
Net Trading Assets	228.4	209.9
Investments in Associates	14.2	16.7
Cash and Other Investments	4.7	1.7
	247.3	228.3
Capital and Reserves		
Share Capital	96.0	96.0
Revaluation Reserve	11.3	11.7
Profit and Loss Account	16.7	10.4
Ordinary Shareholders' Interest	124.0	118.1
Outside Shareholders' Interest	16.6	14.0
Deferred Tax	1.0	0.4
Borrowings		
External — including finance leases	67.5	61.0
Inter-group	32.1	29.8
	99.6	90.8
Dividend (2nd interim)	4.5	3.5
Taxation Payable	1.6	1.5
	247.3	228.3

EXHIBIT 8
LAWSON & JONES LIMITED

Potential Lenders and Investors for Proposed New Company

Type of Financing	Max. Amount Available (C$)	Cost	Investor
Senior Debt	$80 million (plus $20 million for seasonal working capital fluctuation excluded from total)	14%	Banks Trust Companies
Subordinated Debt Common Equity	$20 million 7.6 million	12%[1]	Roman Corporation
Subordinated Debt Common Equity	$ 5.0 million 3.7 million	12%	Woodholme Holdings (Colonel Tom Lawson)
Common Equity	$ 1.0 million		Management
Common Equity	Bridge financing and equity if required		Merrill Lynch
Approximately	$120 million		

[1] Subordinated debt was negotiated to cost less than the senior debt because these investors received a package of debt and equity.

EXHIBIT 9
LAWSON & JONES LIMITED

Projected Earnings Statement
(C$ millions)

	1985	1986	1987	1988	1989	1990	1991	Projected Fiscal Years 1992	1993	1994
Net Sales	$ 321.0	$349.6	$381.0	$416.1	$454.2	$494.5	$536.4	$578.3	$618.6	$661.9
Cost of Goods Sold	260.8	282.5	308.5	337.2	368.6	401.4	435.5	469.6	502.2	536.3
Depreciation	8.9	8.9	8.9	9.0	9.2	9.5	10.8	11.6	12.5	14.5
Gross Profit	51.3	58.2	63.7	69.9	76.4	83.6	90.1	97.1	103.9	111.1
Sales General & Admin	31.7	36.0	38.7	41.8	45.4	49.2	53.3	57.2	61.2	65.5
Goodwill Writeoff	0.3	0.6	0.6	0.6	0.6	0.6	0.6	0.6	0.6	0.6
EBIT	19.3	21.6	24.4	27.5	30.3	33.8	36.2	39.3	42.1	45.0

EXHIBIT 9 (continued)

Projected Income Statements
(C$ millions)

Timing

The purchase of the company for accounting and calculation purposes is assumed to take place on June 30, 1985, which coincides with the end of the company's second fiscal quarter.

Economic Outlook and Inflation

With the company's demonstrated record of revenue growth, even during periods of cyclical economic downturn, the projections have been based on the outlook for the company's products and services and not on aggregate levels of economic activity. The projections are based, however, on a long-term average inflation rate of 4%. The inflation rate is assumed to consistently affect revenues, expenses, capital equipment, costs, etc.

Revenue Growth

For each of the company's three divisions, revenues are projected based on inflation rates, the proposed capital expenditure program and real growth rates in the major Lawson & Jones markets, assuming no acquisitions or divestitures.

Division	Business Area	Market Growth Rates 1985–94
Printing	Web Printing	7–9%
	Sheet Fed Printing	1–3
	Labels	1–3
Packaging	Folding Cartons	5–6
	Flexible Packaging	5–7
Business Forms	Business Forms	4–5

Cost of Sales

The cost of sales of the Commercial Printing Division as a percentage of sales is projected to decline from its historical levels of 81.3% to 79.0% in 1994. Similarly, the cost of sales for the Packaging and Forms Division are projected to decline from historical levels of 82.8% and 68.2%, respectively, to 78.8% and 66.4% respectively by 1994. Improved gross margins are forecast as a result of the ongoing installation of new, more cost-efficient equipment and further cost reduction programs.

Depreciation

Depreciation expense is projected as a function of the company's gross fixed assets. With reduced levels of future capital spending (as a percentage of sales) after 1985, depreciation as a percentage of sales is calculated to decrease from a historical average of 2.8% to 2.1% during 1986 to 1995.

EXHIBIT 9 (continued)

Projected Income Statements
(C$ millions)

Capital Expenditures

Capital expenditure requirements are allocated by division primarily for purchases of new equipment and upgrading of existing machinery. For the company to take advantage of new markets and technology, consolidated capital expenditures as a percentage of sales are projected to increase initially from the 1984 level of 2.6% to 5.0% in 1985 and then range between 1.8% and 3.4% during the period of 1986 to 1995. For details of capital spending plans by division, see attached Exhibit 10.

Income Taxes

On a consolidated basis, the company's basic income tax rate is projected to remain at approximately 44% (Canadian income tax rate – 42%, U.S. income tax rate – 46%).

Interest Rates

Interest rates on the senior bank debt (including the operating line of credit) are estimated to annually average 14% over the 10-year period, based on amounts given in Exhibit 8.

The subordinated debt, which will be on a fixed rate basis, is estimated to be 12.0%. The lower coupon is due to the equity participation through the purchase of strips of the common equity (i.e. units of debt and equity).

EXHIBIT 10
LAWSON & JONES LIMITED

Projected Capital Expenditures By Division
(C$ millions)

Division	1985	1986	1987	1988	1989	1990	1991	1992	1993	1994
								Projected Fiscal Years		
Packaging-Maintenance	$0.545	$0.900	$0.750	$1.180	$1.180	$1.180	$1.180	$1.180	$1.180	$1.180
Packaging-Replacement & New	6.045	1.800	5.850	1.100	2.442	2.442	6.063	3.649	3.649	7.673
Packaging-Sub Total	6.590	2.700	6.600	2.280	3.622	3.622	7.243	4.829	4.829	8.853
Printing-Maintenance	1.080	1.000	1.000	1.000	1.000	1.000	1.000	1.000	1.000	1.000
Printing-Replacement & New	7.775	4.130	2.500	5.500	3.781	3.781	8.561	5.374	5.374	10.686
Printing-Sub Total	8.855	5.130	3.500	6.500	4.781	4.781	9.561	6.374	6.374	11.686
Forms-Maintenance	0.175	0.150	0.290	0.460	0.460	0.460	0.460	0.460	0.460	0.460
Forms-Replacement & New	0.400	0.425	0.550	0.550	0.138	0.138	0.736	0.337	0.337	1.002
Forms-Sub Total	0.575	0.575	0.840	1.010	0.598	0.598	1.196	0.797	0.797	1.462
Sub Total-Maintenance	1.800	2.050	2.040	2.640	2.640	2.640	2.640	2.640	2.640	2.640
Sub Total-Replacement & New	14.220	6.355	8.900	7.150	6.360	6.360	15.360	9.360	9.360	19.360
Total Consolidated Capital Expenditures	16.020	8.405	10.940	9.790	9.000	9.000	18.000	12.000	12.000	22.000

EXHIBIT 11
LAWSON & JONES LIMITED

	Packaging Company Comparison (January 1985)				
Company	Lawson & Jones (C$mm)	Ball Corpn (US$mm)	Dorsey Corpn (US$mm)	Triangle Industries (US$mm)	Jefferson Smurfit (IR£mm)
Balance Sheet					
Assets					
Total Current Assets	82.2	264.9	97.4	876.8	265.2
Investments		0.0	0.0	92.6	23.4
Other	0.5	39.5	0.6	39.7	15.1
Intangibles	0.0	0.0	10.6	12.1	0.0
Fixed Assets	43.6	337.3	87.8	456.7	271.3
TOTAL ASSETS	126.4	641.7	196.4	1 477.9	575.0
Liabilities & Shareholders' Equity					
Total Current Liabilities	53.8	135.5	58.1	457.1	171.2
Long Term Debt	1.1	89.9	40.4	790.4	124.6
Deferred Charges	9.8	85.5	15.3	0.0	25.6
Other	0.0	0.0	0.0	90.0	3.6
Minorities	0.0	0.0	0.0	0.0	50.2
Redeemable Stock	0.0		17.8	30.0	
Total Shareholders' Equity	61.7	330.8	82.6	131.6	199.7
TOTAL LIABILITIES & SHAREHOLDERS' EQUITY	126.4	641.7	196.4	1 477.9	575.0
Sales	321.0	1 106.0	532.0	1 645.0	630.0
Profit for 1984	9.6	46.3	7.9	3.2	24.5
Beta	—	0.9	1.0	0.9	0.75
P/E (January 1985)	—	8.4	15.0	11.9	8.0

EXHIBIT 11 (continued)

Packaging Company Comparison (January 1985)

Ball Corporation makes glass containers and metal cans. Food packaging, beer, soft drink and home food preservation are the major markets served. Bell also makes plastic products for electronics, computers and appliances. Technical products made include space systems, components and antennas for NASA and the military. Ball has 21 plants and 9 000 employees.

Dorsey Corporation makes and sells products for the packaging and transportation markets. Plastic containers for use by dairies, food packagers and the soft drink industry are produced by 22 plants in 14 states. Interests are held in a cargo trailer facility and a chain of 28 restaurants. There are 6 100 employees.

Triangle Industries is a major international packaging company. Two of its subsidiaries, National Can and American Can, manufacture metal, glass and plastic containers and closures. Another subsidiary, Triangle PWC, makes electrical wire and cable, steel conduit and related products for the construction industry. Triangle has 14 000 employees.

Jefferson Smurfit Corporation is an integrated manufacturer of paperboard and packaging products. Seven paperboard mills and 60 converting plants are operated in the U.S. and one in Canada. Jefferson has approximately 6 300 employees.

Source: Value Line April 1987

EXHIBIT 12
LAWSON & JONES LIMITED

Price Earnings Multiple
(at January 1985)

Current P/E multiples at January 1985 which include, for most of the companies, earnings for 12 months ended December 31, 1984, are as follows:

Printing

Donnelley	15.3x	Web	11.3
Krueger	14.3	Banta	10.4
Lehigh	13.9	Sorg	8.3
Cadmus	12.4	Average* = 12.5x	

Packaging

Engraph	16.3x	Dixico	10.9
DRG	14.7	Bonar	8.0
Bemis	11.1	Average* = 12.2x	

Business Forms

Wallace	18.1x	Ennis	13.8
R.L. Crain	15.9	Moore	12.3
Standard Reg	15.2	Duplex	9.9
Amer. Bus. Prod.	14.8	Average* = 14.4x	

Summary of Select Acquisitions in
Printing, Packaging and Forms Industries

Acquired Company	Announcement Date	Purchase Price	P/E Multiple	Premium to Book
BA Bank Note	Sept. 22/84	$ 70.7	12.6x	1.9x
Williamhouse — Regency	Aug. 13/82	116.0	11.2x	1.7x
Arcata Corp.	Mar. 15/82	334.0	14.2x	1.2x
Ronalds Federated	July 30/80	50.0	10.0x	1.7x
Stafford-Lowdon	June 19/79	28.0	13.8x	1.8x

* excluding high and low values

EXHIBIT 12 (continued)
(US$ millions)

Comparison of Selected Printing Companies

Market Value (a)

Donnelley	$1 947.6
Krueger	211.8
Banta	164.0
Webb	85.0
Lehigh	41.0
Cadmus	32.9
Sorg	18.2

Current Price to Earnings Multiple (a)

Company	Multiple
Donnelley	13.3x
Krueger	14.3
Lehigh	13.9
Cadmus	12.4
Webb	11.3
Banta	10.4
Sorg	8.3

Current Price to Book Multiple (a)

Company	Multiple
Krueger	3.3x
Donnelley	2.5
Banta	2.0
Cadmus	1.9
Webb	1.8
Sorg	1.6
Lehigh	1.4

Current Capitalization to EBIT (a)(b)

Lehigh	19.1%
Cadmus	9.0
Donnelley	8.5
Krueger	7.5
Webb	7.2
Banta	5.4
Sorg	3.1

Current Dividend Yield (a)(c)

Company	Yield
Webb	2.8%
Krueger	2.2
Banta	2.1
Donnelley	2.0
Cadmus	2.0
Lehigh	0
Sorg	0

Latest 12 Months Net Revenues

Donnelley	$1 715.8
Banta	268.8
Krueger	257.4
Webb	169.6
Lehigh	119.3
Cadmus	74.8
Sorg	57.8
L & J	221.2
Printing	141.8

Latest 12 Months Pre-Tax Income

Donnelley	$221.0
Banta	31.6
Krueger	27.9
Webb	13.5
Sorg	6.2
Lehigh	4.6
Cadmus	4.4
L & J	11.3

Latest 12 Months Net Income

Donnelley	$127.0
Banta	15.8
Krueger	14.8
Webb	7.5
Lehigh	3.0
Cadmus	2.8
Sorg	2.2
L & J	7.2

Latest 12 Months Pre-Tax Margin

Company	Margin
Donnelley	12.9%
Banta	11.8
Krueger	10.8
Sorg	10.7
Webb	8.0
Cadmus	5.9
Lehigh	3.9
L & J	5.1

Latest 12 Months Net Margin

Company	Margin
Donnelley	7.4%
Banta	5.9
Krueger	5.7
Webb	4.4
Sorg	3.8
Cadmus	3.7
Lehigh	2.5
L & J	3.3

5-Year Compound Revenue Growth

Company	Growth
Sorg	14.9%
Krueger	14.3
Banta	13.8
Donnelley	12.4
Lehigh	9.2
Webb	8.8
Cadmus(f)	16.4
L & J	9.4
Printing	5.6

5-Year Compound Pre-Tax Income Growth

Company	Growth
Sorg	78.2%
Banta	24.2
Krueger	16.0
Donnelley	13.8
Webb	11.0
Cadmus(f)	16.5
Lehigh	(3.9)
L & J	8.1

5-Year Compound Income Growth

Company	Growth
Sorg	75.4%
Banta	22.6
Krueger	16.5
Donnelley	15.1
Webb	10.8
Cadmus(f)	20.9
Lehigh	(1.2)
L & J	10.7

5-Year Average Pre-Tax Margin

Company	Margin
Donnelley	12.2%
Banta	9.2
Krueger	8.3
Webb	6.8
Cadmus(f)	5.4
Lehigh	3.8
Sorg	2.5
L & J	5.2

5-Year Average Net Margin

Company	Margin
Donnelley	6.8%
Banta	5.1
Krueger	4.4
Webb	3.9
Cadmus(f)	3.3
Lehigh	2.5
Sorg	1.5
L & J	3.0

EXHIBIT 12 (continued)

Comparison of Selected Printing Companies

Latest 12 Months Return on Assets (d)		Latest 12 Months Return on Equity (e)		Latest 12 Month EBIT Margin		Latest 12 Months Debt/Capitalization	
Krueger	11.9%	Krueger	24.8%	Donnelley	13.1%	Donnelley	1.8%
Banta	11.7	Banta	20.8	Banta	12.8	Sorg	14.1
Sorg	11.8	Sorg	19.7	Krueger	12.1	Lehigh	20.2
Donnelley	9.9	Donnelley	17.2	Sorg	11.1	Banta	20.7
Webb	7.6	Webb	16.7	Webb	8.9	Krueger	26.5
Cadmus	7.2	Cadmus	16.2	Cadmus	7.2	Webb	32.5
Lehigh	4.3	Lehigh	11.0	Lehigh	6.2	Cadmus	43.2
L & J	7.8	L & J	16.1	L & J	6.0	L & J	22.1
				Printing	5.6		

5-Year Average Return on Assets		5-Year Average Return on Equity		5-Year Average EBIT Margin	
Donnelley	10.0%	Krueger	20.8%	Donnelley	12.4%
Krueger	9.7	Banta	17.9	Banta	10.5
Banta	9.4	Donnelley	15.7	Krueger	10.0
Cadmus(g)	6.8	Webb	15.3	Webb	8.5
Webb	6.6	Cadmus(g)	14.7	Cadmus(g)	6.7
Lehigh	5.2	Lehigh	13.0	Lehigh	5.8
Sorg	3.8	Sorg	7.8	Sorg	4.0
L & J	6.5	L & J	14.1	L & J	6.1
				Printing	6.0

(a) As of January 1985
(b) Common equity market value plus book value of debt and preferred stock divided by earnings before interest and taxes.
(c) Indicated dividend divided by market price per share.
(d) Net income divided by average assets.
(e) Net income divided by average equity.
(f) Year compounded rates for Cadmus.
(g) Four-year average rates for Cadmus.

EXHIBIT 13
LAWSON & JONES LIMITED

Table of Interest Rates and Exchange Rates

Interest Rates (%)	Jan. 1985	Jan. 1984	Jan. 1983	Jan. 1982	Jan. 1981
Canadian T Bills — 3 Mos.	9.5	9.7	9.6	14.3	16.9
Government of Canada Long Bond Rate	11.4	11.9	12.2	15.9	13.4
Bank Prime Rate	11.0	11.0	12.0	16.5	18.3

Exchange Rates – January 1985

Canadian $ per US $	= 1.367
Canadian $ per £ Sterling	= 1.699
US $ per £ Sterling	= 1.243
US $ per IR£	= 1.014
Canadian $ per IR£	= 1.386

Source: International Monetary Fund Financial Statistics

Comprehensive Cases

DICKENSON MINES LIMITED

In October 1981, Peter Munro, the new President of Dickenson Mines (Dickenson), sat in the Toronto offices of the gold mining company and wondered what actions he could take to save Dickenson from bankruptcy. In 1979, Dickenson's former management had undertaken a major expansion of the company's mining and milling operations. Subsequently, interest rates on the debt financing of the project had climbed and gold prices had dropped. These problems were compounded by cost overruns on the expansion program and higher operating costs at the mine. These factors combined to produce a cash drain on the company and Dickenson was no longer able to service its growing debt. The company had defaulted repayment of $1.5 million U.S. on a term loan from a Canadian bank. Accordingly, the bank could demand the entire principal of $10 million U.S.; however, the bank at that point had not acted to either waive the default or demand repayment. Several major suppliers were threatening to cut off essential raw materials if accounts payable of over 70 days were not paid. Munro's first priority was to take the necessary steps to ward off bankruptcy, and then to restore profitability.

Company History

In 1981, Dickenson Mines conducted gold mining operations in Ontario and silver mining operations in British Columbia. Dickenson also held a number of investments in oil and gas ventures throughout Canada and the United States. Most of the company's revenues were generated at the Red Lake Gold Mine in northwestern Ontario.

The Dickenson property was first staked during the Red Lake gold rush of 1926. In 1945, Dickenson Red Lake Mines was incorporated and by 1947 a first shaft was sunk, to a depth of 550 feet. The following year, enough reserves had been discovered to justify the construction of a 150 ton per day mill to treat ore. By 1959, the mill was expanded to 450 tons per day, again

336

in response to the discovery of new reserves. In 1961, the first shaft was deepened to 3300 feet and in 1968 a second internal shaft was sunk from the 3300 foot level to 4400 feet. By 1968, Dickenson was conducting mining operations on thirty different levels off the main shafts.

The period 1945–1971 was difficult for the Canadian gold industry. The selling price of gold was fixed at $35.00 U.S./oz. and production costs were rising. Other metal producers were enjoying increasing prices for their products and were therefore able to lure away skilled miners with the promise of higher wages. These problems led to the introduction of the Emergency Gold Mining Act (EGMA) in 1947 to aid the faltering industry. This act made new gold mines tax exempt for the first three years of operation and allowed them to accumulate the depletion and depreciation allowances earned during those years for write-offs in the following years. Over this period government subsidies of this sort worked out to roughly five dollars an ounce produced and allowed many companies to stay in operation. In 1971, when gold prices were allowed to float on the open market, profitability returned to the Canadian industry and the EGMA was no longer needed.

After the deregulation of the price of gold, Dickenson's fortunes improved considerably. By 1974, revenues had risen to $11 million and profits were $3 million as compared to 1971, when revenues were $3 million and profits were $264 000. The company's major activity was still gold mining, but a process of diversification had begun. Dickenson owned a 36 percent share in Kam Kotia Mines which had investments in several mining and oil and gas companies, and which was developing a silver-lead-zinc mine in British Columbia.

In 1975, Dickenson management made the strategic decision to diversify into oil and gas exploration and development. Dickenson entered into a joint venture agreement with Conventures Ltd. of Calgary to develop a gas field in Alberta. Conventures acted as the operating partner and Dickenson supplied a portion of the capital. From June 1975 to December 1978, Dickenson purchased 700 000 Conventures shares for a total of $2.1 million. In 1979 Dickenson invested an additional $1 million and supplied Conventures with some oil and gas leases in Alberta in exchange for 225 000 shares at a share purchase price valued at eight dollars per share by the two companies. Also in 1979, Dickenson loaned the company money on the basis of a $4.7 million note from Conventures that was convertible into another 681 000 common shares at $6.90 per share until December 31, 1981. If Dickenson decided to exercise the conversion option, they would own roughly 25 percent of the oil and gas company.

By early 1980, the Dickenson group of companies operated the Red Lake Gold Mine in Ontario and the Silvana silver mine in British Columbia. Besides Conventures, Dickenson held non-operating interests in several oil and gas plays throughout Alberta, other parts of Canada, and the U.S. In addition, Kam Kotia Mines Ltd. held similar oil and gas interests. Dickenson also held a portfolio of investments in Canadian junior mining companies.

The Mine and Mill Expansion

By 1979, after 31 years of production at the Red Lake Gold Mine, new high-grade ore reserves were no longer being discovered in sufficient quantities to maintain gold production at previous levels. However, Dickenson management believed that large quantities of low-grade ore reserves still existed and that these could best be mined by changing Dickenson from a medium tonnage, high-grade ore producer to a high tonnage, low-grade ore producer. Management believed that this shift in mining strategy could best be accomplished by changing the mining method from labour intensive cut and fill mining to mechanized blast hole mining. Consultants were hired to quantify these low-grade ore reserves and to give an opinion on the application of blast hole mining.

After several months of study, a four part capital expenditure program was approved. This program would increase mill capacity, deepen the #2 internal shaft of the mine, increase ore hoisting capacity and utilize newer, more mechanized methods of mining. It was estimated that the two-year program would cost between $10 and $11 million and would increase the mine's capacity to 1000 tons per day.

Deepening the #2 internal shaft from a depth of 4400 feet to 5700 feet would open up eight more levels for mining (levels 31–38) and allow access to new ore that was believed to be promising. The cost of the project was estimated at $2.5 million.

In order to remove 1000 tons per day from the mine, additional hoisting capacity had to be build. After considerable study, it was decided to modify the #1 shaft to permit utilization of the two hoisting compartments solely for hoisting ore and waste instead of combining this use with the lifting of men and materials. These services were then placed in a third compartment, which required the installation of considerable auxiliary equipment. This was expected to cost $4 million.

Finally, milling capacity had to be increased to accommodate the increased ore volumes from the mine. To accomplish this, the consultants proposed that the ore crushing process be speeded up by reducing the crushing time for a batch of ore and therefore increasing the crusher product size. The size of the crusher would be doubled, which would increase crusher capacity to 1400 tons per day. In addition, the fine ore storage bin would be increased in size from 600 to 2000 tons. The cost of the mill expansion was estimated to be $4 million.

The consultants and Dickenson management believed that these operating changes would allow the company to mine lower ore grades at lower costs per ton. Combined with higher gold prices, these changes would ensure the profitability of the mine in the years to come. Dickenson therefore negotiated a $10 million project term loan at a rate of bank prime plus one percent and an additional $5 million line of credit to finance the expansion program.

By the end of 1980, approximately $8 million had been spent on the expansion program, yet none of the four components was complete. Dickenson had run the term loan up to $6.6 million and the operating line of credit was up to $3.7 million. Gold production for the year had dropped from 44 000 oz. in 1979 to 29 000 oz. in 1980, primarily due to the mining of lower grade ore. The recovery rate at the mill also fell, as an enhanced recovery process involving the roasting of gold sulphide wastes produced by cyanide leaching had to be suspended for environmental and employee health reasons. This had lowered gold recovery from 93.7 percent to 83.3 percent. Lower grade ores and lower mill recovery rates meant that Dickenson had to treat 4.4 tons of ore in 1980 to produce one oz. of gold, as compared to 2.7 tons in 1979. Fortunately the average price received per oz. of gold had risen from $356 to $675. Because of severe cost overruns in 1980, the company had revised its estimates of the cost to complete the four part expansion to an additional $9 million in 1981.

Problems in 1981

As the expansion program moved into 1981, several new developments occurred which all started to work against Dickenson. For 1981, anticipating the beginning of the new mechanized mining operations, the company had set out a production budget to mine 210 000 tons of ore at a grade of .19 oz. of gold per ton, resulting in the production of 34 700 ounces of gold, assuming a mill recovery rate of about 87 percent. Costs of production were expected to be $63.10 per ton or $381.90 per ounce.

However, as the year progressed it became clear that Dickenson could not meet this budget. The expansion work in the mine hindered the efficiency of the mining process, and the control of ore grade quality declined as the new mechanized mining methods were put into use. This resulted in lower tonnages mined at reduced ore grades. The operating and financial statements for the first three quarters indicated clearly the severity of the operating problems at the mine. For the nine months ending September 30, 1981, 133 000 tons of ore had been mined at an average grade of .15 oz. of gold per ton, resulting in production of only 16 471 ounces of gold. Once again, the expansion program was experiencing major cost overruns, as total estimated expenditures for 1981 alone were now expected to be roughly $14 million.

Increased financing costs and lower gold prices added to these operating problems. The prime rate hit a high of 22 percent in 1981 and by October 1981, the price of gold had fallen to $400 U.S. per ounce. At that point, Dickenson's operating costs were estimated to be $631 Cdn/oz. and interest expense was estimated at $91 Cdn/oz. for a total cost of $722 an ounce. These problems were compounded by a complete lack of capital budgetary controls to the extent that the company relied solely on external auditors to develop capital cost and cash flow projections. At this time, the company's major banker was exerting considerable pressure to reduce bank debt and infuse new management.

Dickenson's problems were not limited to the gold mining operations — the silver division was also operating at a loss. This division, Silvana Mines of British Columbia, had been adversely affected by sharply reduced silver prices. For the nine months ending September 30, 1981, Silvana had lost almost $1 million, as opposed to a profit of $493 000 for the same period in 1980.

Dickenson was also involved in a $21 million lawsuit with Willroy Mines Ltd. concerning the results of an exploration program conducted by New Cinch Uranium Mines of New Mexico, a company in which Dickenson held a 12 percent interest. Willroy was accusing Dickenson and 15 other firms of misrepresentation regarding the presentation of the New Cinch assay results. The original assays of New Cinch's reserves were found to be inaccurate, but not before Willroy had purchased a large portion of New Cinch shares. When the drilling cores were re-assayed and found to be worthless, New Cinch stock dropped dramatically and Willroy Mines incurred a substantial loss. Dickenson contended that it had no knowledge of the inaccuracies in the original assays and that it had also suffered a loss on its holdings of New Cinch as a result of the new information.

The Sale of Conventures Ltd.

By September of 1981, Dickenson owed $4.5 million in accounts payable and $33.4 million in bank debt, all of which was technically due and payable because the company was in default on servicing this debt. In light of these obligations, Dickenson management decided to sell the company's interest in Conventures Ltd. of Calgary, which now consisted of 1.4 million common shares and the $4.7 million convertible debenture.

On September 29, Dickenson was able to arrange to sell its interest in Conventures to Oakwood Petroleums of Calgary for $26.5 million. Dickenson received a note from Oakwood for $13.5 million bearing interest equal to the prime rate within a range of 17.5 to 23.5 percent. Dickenson also received $13 million in cash, which was used to reduce the bank debt. In return, Dickenson gave up 1 453 686 shares of Conventures and the five percent - $4.7 million note from Conventures that could be converted into another 680 000 shares by December 31, 1981. On September 24, 1981, Conventures common stock had closed at $9.00.

The Situation in October 1981

When Peter Munro came to Dickenson from Falconbridge in October 1981, he called in his new Vice-President of Finance, John Kachmar (also from

Falconbridge), to review the situation. The cash proceeds of the Conventures sales had reduced the floating rate bank debt to roughly $20.4 million. Interest payments amounted to $325 000 a month. Two creditors in particular had become adamant about receiving payment. One bank wanted $1 million by January, and the company's cyanide supplier was threatening to cut off deliveries, which would shut down the mill, if outstanding bills were not settled.

With regards to the expansion program, which originally had been expected to cost between $9 and $10 million, the deepening of the #2 shaft was now complete and enough equipment had been purchased to begin the mechanized mining processes. However, mill capacity had only reached 700 tons per day and the ore haulage system was not finished. It was estimated that the cost to complete the program, in addition to the $22 million already spent in 1980 and 1981, was $3.2 million in 1982.

Munro and Kachmar knew that they had to raise cash immediately to pay off the company's debts or face bankruptcy. They had drawn up a list of possible options:

(1) A public financing issue to institutional investors,
(2) A rights offering to existing shareholders and corporate management,
(3) Sale of assets,
(4) Increase gold production with possible use of forward sales to ensure stable gold prices,
(5) Reduce costs and cut capital expenditures.

Munro and Kachmar had had some discussions with the company's underwriters regarding the first two financing options. They had come up with a plan to issue a type of "debt unit". This unit would consist of seven $1000 U.S. bonds and 40 gold purchase warrants. Each warrant would allow the holder to purchase one ounce of gold. The warrants would be exercisable in groups of ten in the years 1986, 1987, 1988, and 1989. Dickenson wanted to sell each unit for $14 000 U.S., the purchase price representing seven $1000 U.S. bonds and a prepayment of $175 U.S. towards the exercise price of each warrant. The coupon rate on the bonds, the exercise price of the warrants and the overall size of the issue had yet to be decided.

A rights offering to existing shareholders and management would allow the present shareholders to maintain their proportionate share of ownership, and would give the new management an opportunity to participate in the ownership of the company at a low cost, given the current price level of Dickenson stock. It was, however, a risky proposition, because Dickenson's future was by no means certain.

Selling more company assets was not a pleasant proposition, but had to be considered. First, there was the note from Oakwood Petroleum, with a par value of $13 535 000 and interest rates that varied with the prime rate between a range of 17.5 to 23.5 percent. Munro and Kachmar also had to consider the possibility of selling a portion of Dickenson's oldest asset, the

Red Lake Gold Mine. Munro wondered how much cash he might be able to raise by selling a 50 percent interest in the mine.

Both men clearly recognized the need to cut operating costs and increase gold production. Munro prepared a five year forecast for the Red Lake Mine beginning in 1982 (Exhibit 11). He estimated the additional cost of increasing the capacity of the concentrator to 1000 tons per day at $1.4 million and planned to complete this expansion by the end of 1982. No other capital expenditures were planned. He planned ore mining operations at 95 percent of milling capacity in each year. Munro set his operating budget at $13.5 million for 1982 after cutting $2.3 million in wages, contract diamond drilling, and consulting costs from the previous budget. He established a mining plan that involved returning to traditional mining methods, working the higher grade stopes and pillars that remained, at least in the short term, while gradually adopting the high volume/low grade proposals.

Munro estimated his variable costs of production at about $40 per ton, mined and milled, and his fixed costs at $4 million for 1982. At the higher volumes and with the capital program completed, he estimated that his real variable costs would decline by about five percent each year starting in 1983, just enough to offset the expected inflation increases.

Munro and Kachmar were investigating the use of the gold futures or options markets in order to gain security against further price drops. In addition, Munro was considering delaying the rest of the capital expenditure program.

Both Munro and Kachmar realized that the initial goal of the mine and mill expansion was a good one, in principle. However, it was also clear to them that bankruptcy was imminent if they could not develop a short-run survival plan to raise cash and retire the company's debt.

EXHIBIT 1
DICKENSON MINES LTD.

Mill Operations
Flow Sheet of Concentrator

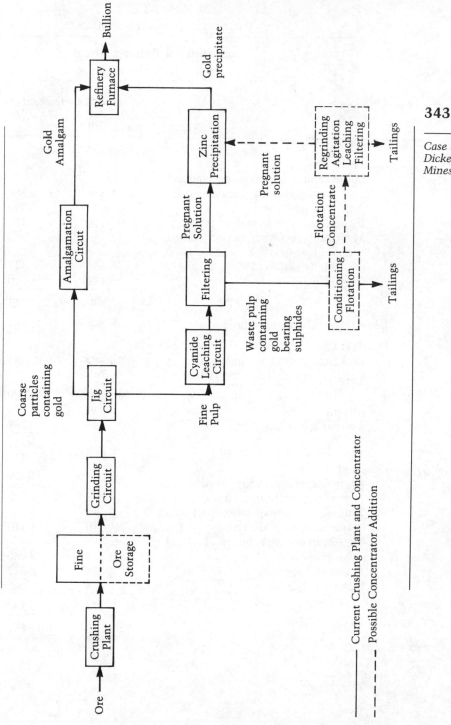

EXHIBIT 2
DICKENSON MINES LIMITED

Consolidated Balance Sheet
($000)

	September 30, 1981 (Unaudited)	December 31, 1980	December 31, 1979
Assets			
Current			
Bullion and concentrates on hand and in transit, at net realizable value	$ 1 646	$ 1 561	$ 2 943
Accounts receivable	422	580	343
Income taxes recoverable	314	314	—
Marketable securities, at cost (quoted market value 1981 — $213; 1980 — $383; 1979 — $965)	365	347	731
Prepaid expenses	133	110	53
	2 880	2 912	4 070
Long-Term Investments (note 4)	18 245	22 881	15 826
Fixed, at Cost			
Buildings, machinery and equipment	24 349	16 383	12 041
Less: Accumulated depreciation	9 749	9 293	8 404
	14 600	7 090	3 637
Mining claims	929	1 089	1 179
Townsite lots	287	282	142
	15 816	8 461	4 958
Other, at Cost			
Shaft deepening and renovation expenditure unamortized	11 838	6 722	2 922
Interest in and expenditure on outside mining properties	530	1 110	1 129
Interest in and expenditure on oil and gas properties	3 961	3 086	1 905
Stores and supplies	2 712	2 317	1 709
Deferred charges	136	348	186
	19 177	13 583	7 851
	$ 56 118	$ 47 837	$ 32 705

Exhibit 2 (continued)

	September 30, 1981 (Unaudited)	December 31, 1980	December 31, 1979
Liabilities			
Current			
Bank indebtedness (note 3)	$ 7 436	$ 4 043	$ 315
Accounts payable	4 378	4 604	2 239
Income and mining taxes payable	142	142	981
Current portion of long-term debt (notes 2 and 3)	6 250	1 043	1 200
	18 206	9 832	4 735
Long-Term Debt (notes 2 and 3)	6 669	7 746	3 500
Deferred Income Taxes	5 435	4 916	3 223
	30 310	22 494	11 458
Shareholders' Equity			
Capital Stock (note 1)			
Authorized			
30 000 000 Class A common shares without par value			
6 000 000 Class B special shares without par value			
Issued			
Class A shares	4 901	4 879	4 489
Class B shares	4 898	4 879	4 489
Contributed Surplus	1 466	1 466	1 466
Retained Earnings	17 002	16 688	12 108
	28 267	27 912	22 552
Deduct Company's share of Kam Kotia Mines Limited's holdings of shares of Dickenson Mines Limited	2 459	2 569	1 305
	25 808	25 343	21 247
	$ 56 118	$ 47 837	$ 32 705

Dickenson Mines Limited
Notes to Financial Statements

1. *Amalgamation*

The consolidated financial statements give effect to the statutory amalgamation (under the Business Corporations Act of Ontario) of Dickenson Mines Limited (Dickenson) and Silvana Mines Inc. (Silvana), both under common control, into the continuing corporation, Dickenson Mines Limited, pursuant to an amalgamation agreement dated October 7, 1980, and the issue of a certificate of amalgamation on October 31, 1980.

Exhibit 2 (continued)

The amalgamation was accounted for on the basis of combining the assets and liabilities of the amalgamating corporations at their carrying value in each corporation's records. The income of the combined corporation includes income of the combining corporations for the year ended December 31, 1980. Income figures for the years 1979, 1978, 1977 and 1976 have been restated on the same basis.

The amalgamation agreement provided that the authorized capital of the amalgamated corporation shall consist of 30 000 000 Class A common shares without par value and 6 000 000 Class B special shares without par value; each Class A share is entitled to one vote and each Class B share is entitled to ten votes at meetings of shareholders. The Class B shares rank equally with the Class A shares in all other respects.

2. *Long-Term Debt*

	September 30, 1981 (Unaudited)	December 31, 1980	December 31, 1979
($000)			
Term bank loan — $10 000 000 U.S., interest at prime plus $1\frac{1}{4}$%	$ 11 919	$ —	$ —
Term bank loan — interest at prime rate plus 1%	—	6 600	4 700
Notes payable — Carl O. Nickle — 7% repayable $1 000 000 in September 1981 and $1 000 000 in September 1982	1 000	2 000	—
Finance contract payable — 14% repayable $3036 U.S. monthly up to and including May 1, 1985. Fixed assets have been pledged as security	—	189	—
	12 919	8 789	4 700
Less: Amounts due within one year	6 250	1 043	1 200
	$ 6 669	$ 7 746	$ 3 500

3. *Bank Loan Security*

The Company has pledged as security for the bank indebtedness and the term bank loan the following:

(a) A $25 000 000 demand debenture creating a fixed charge over the Red Lake Mine, a fixed charge over the major machinery and equipment of the Company and a floating charge over all other assets of the Company.

(b) Security under Section 177 of the Bank Act (Canada) on mineral reserves, inventory and equipment located at the Red Lake Mine site.

(c) Security under Section 178 of the Bank Act (Canada) with respect to the Red Lake and Silvana Mines.

(d) An hypothecation of the Company's portfolio of junior stocks, including oil and gas stocks and Kam-Kotia stock.

(e) An assignment of the promissory note from Oakwood Petroleum Limited.

Exhibit 2 (continued)

			($000)		
			September 30, 1981 (Unaudited)	December 31, 1980	December 31, 1979

4. Investments in companies accounted for by the equity method:
   Shares and convertible notes
   Kam Kotia Mines Limited

	Shares	Quoted Market Value			
at September 30, 1981	2 119 108	$ 4 026 000			
at December 31, 1980	2 119 108	$19 602 000			
at December 31, 1979	2 112 108	$13 465 000	$ 1 041	$ 2 346	$ 2 992

Conventures Limited
   1 453 686 shares and $4 700 000 - 5% convertible
   notes (quoted market value at December 31, 1980
   $31 128 000) — 16 826 —

Other quoted market value
   at September 30, 1981 $ 2 592 000
   at December 31, 1980 $10 365 000
   at December 31, 1979 $ 7 228 000 $ 2 855 $ 2 701 $ 2 826

			3 896	21 873	5 818
Loans and advances, at cost			112	72	315
Sub-total			4 008	21 945	6 133

Investment in Conventures Limited
   At December 31, 1979, 1 084 396 shares and
   $4 700 000 - 5% convertible notes (quoted market
   value at December 31, 1979, $23 406 000) — — 9 938

Portfolio investments, at cost
   Listed shares
      Shares and warrants of New Cinch Uranium Ltd.
         quoted market value
         at September 30, 1981 $ 274 000
         at December 31, 1980 $12 216 000
         at December 31, 1979 $ 1 388 000   275   345   198

Other listed shares quoted market value
   at September 30, 1981 $117 000
   at December 31, 1980 $385 000
   at December 31, 1979 $365 000   278   262   320

			553	607	518
Other shares, bonds, advances and participations			1 878	2 188	1 256
Sub-total			2 431	2 795	1 774

Note receivable from Oakwood Petroleums Limited, due September 5, 1983, bearing interest at the prime rate, not to exceed 23.5% and not less than 17.5%   13 535   —   —

TOTAL			19 974	24 740	17 845
Less: Allowance for decline in value			1 729	1 859	2 019
			$ 18 245	$ 22 881	$ 15 826

Exhibit 2 (continued)

The quoted market values referred to above do not necessarily represent the realizable value of these holdings which may be more or less than that indicated by market quotations.

The investment in Conventures Limited comprising 1 453 686 shares and $4 700 000 convertible notes was sold to Oakwood Petroleums Limited on September 29, 1981 (with effect from September 4, 1981) for the following consideration:

Cash	$ 13 000 000
Note receivable, due September 5, 1983	13 535 000
	$ 26 535 000

The cash portion of the proceeds were applied to reduce the Company's bank indebtedness.

EXHIBIT 3
DICKENSON MINES LTD.

Forecast of Expenditures to Complete
Mine and Mill Expansion
($000)

Expenditure Category	Actual 1980	Actual Jan. 1–Sept. 30 1981	Estimate 1982
(1) Working Capital and New Machinery for Mechanized Cut and Fill Mining	$ 1 042	$ 2 411	$ 35
(2) Mill Expansion	1 163	5 202	2 882
(3) Deepening of #2 Shaft	3 152	531	—
(4) New Hauling System	2 591	5 776	310
TOTALS	$ 7 948	$ 13 920	$ 3 227

EXHIBIT 4
DICKENSON MINES LTD.

Operating Results for the Red Lake Mine
1976 – October 1981

	1981			Years ended December 31				
	Third quarter	Second quarter	First quarter	1980	1979	1978	1977	1976
Ore milled (tons)	49 360	46 467	36 549	128 000	118 000	110 000	129 000	117 000
Average grade of ore milled (ounces of gold per ton)	0.17	0.13	0.15	0.270	0.405	0.576	0.499	0.509
Production of gold (ounces)	7 142	5 047	4 282	29 281	44 367	59 957	60 019	55 488
Operating expenses								
per ton milled	$ 85.21	$ 83.22	$ 97.21	$ 91.79	$ 86.27	$ 80.94	$ 60.89	$ 58.36
per troy ounce recovered	$ 588.33	$ 765.44	$ 798.77	$ 401.25	$ 229.45	$ 149.48	$ 130.89	$ 123.03
Average price of gold per ounce received during the period	$ 501.19	$ 554.04	$ 687.43	$ 675.49	$ 356.33	$ 226.00	$ 160.34	$ 123.30
Revenue received during the period (thousands of dollars)	—	—	—	$ 19 779	$ 15 807	$ 13 560	—	—

EXHIBIT 5
DICKENSON MINES LTD.

Proven Ore Reserves

Year	Tons of Ore	Ounce/ton	Ounces of Gold
1981[1]	653 700	.289	189 300
1980	425 000	.450	191 250
1979	389 000	.529	205 781
1978	350 909	.571	200 369
1977	335 622	.539	180 900
1976	357 382	.536	191 556
1975	393 057	.538	211 464

[1] As estimated by consultants

EXHIBIT 6
DICKENSON MINES LIMITED

Consolidated Statement of Income
(in thousands of dollars except earnings per share)

	Nine months ended September 30		Years ended December 31				
	1981	1980	1980	1979	1978	1977	1976
	(unaudited)						
Revenue							
Gold bullion production	$ 9 439	16 018	19 857	15 973	13 594	9 650	6 857
Lead and zinc concentrates production	4 584	5 560	7 394	5 207	2 793	1 216	164
Expense							
Mining	8 972	6 548	9 299	6 979	6 256	5 227	4 212
Milling	2 484	2 014	3 073	2 257	1 757	1 343	1 057
Mine management, office and general	2 768	2 326	3 511	2 485	1 930	1 357	1 160
Transportation and treatment costs	1 314	1 251	1 666	1 627	597	498	407
Head office administration, general and short-term interest expense	2 703	629	1 015	796	897	340	22
Marketing	37	62	73	66	65	53	45
	18 278	12 830	18 637	14 210	11 502	8 818	6 903
Operating Income (Loss) Before Undernoted Items	(4 255)	8 748	8 614	6 970	4 885	2 048	118
Amortization of shaft deepening and renovations	866	960	1 388	393	121	—	—
Depreciation and depletion	671	676	1 206	826	731	583	329
Outside exploration written off	695	516	757	436	9	28	87
Amortization of oil and gas properties	349	257	343	—	—	—	—
	2 581	2 409	3 694	1 655	861	611	416
Income (Loss) From Mining Operations	$ (6 836)	6 339	4 920	5 315	4 024	1 437	(298)

Exhibit 6 (continued)

Investment and Other Income and Expense							
Share of net income (loss) of companies accounted for by the equity method	$ (106)	104	742	(94)	38	75	(62)
Dividends, interest and net results of security transactions	736	910	1 093	844	267	258	221
Oil and gas revenue	52	53	70	16	—	—	—
Interest expense, long-term	(985)	(465)	(762)	(674)	—	—	—
Fire loss recovery (net)	32	—	464	—	—	—	—
Amalgamation expense	—	(50)	(332)	—	—	—	—
	(271)	552	1 275	92	305	333	159
Income (Loss) Before Income Taxes and Extraordinary Items	(7 107)	6 891	6 195	5 407	4 329	1 770	(139)
Income and Mining Taxes	—	2 200	1 750	2 691	1 648	541	(346)
Income (Loss) Before Extraordinary Items	(7 107)	4 691	4 445	2 716	2 681	1 229	207
Increase in the carrying value of the Company's interest in Kam Kotia Mines Limited arising from share issues by Kam Kotia	—	503	503	1 200	—	—	—
Provision for decline in investment in New Cinch Uranium Ltd.	(477)	—	—	—	—	—	—
Share of extraordinary gains (loss) of companies accounted for by the equity method	(1 285)	93	93	367	(124)	(75)	(40)
Gain on sale of investment in Conventures Limited (net of deferred tax of $520)	9 183	—	—	—	—	—	—
Net Income for the Period	$ 314	$ 5 287	$ 5 041	$ 4 283	$ 2 557	$ 1 154	$ 167
Earnings per Share:							
Before extraordinary items							
Class A	(.76)	.49	.48	.31	.32	.16	.03
Class B	(.76)	.49	.48	.31	.32	.16	.03
After extraordinary items							
Class A	.03	.55	.55	.48	.31	.15	.02
Class B	.03	.55	.55	.48	.31	.15	.02

EXHIBIT 7
DICKENSON MINES LIMITED

Consolidated Statement of Changes in Financial Position
($000)

	Nine months ended September 30		Years ended December 31				
	1981	1980	1980	1979	1978	1977	1976
	(Unaudited)						
Source of Funds							
Income (loss) before extraordinary items	$ (7 107)	$ 4 691	$ 4 445	$ 2 716	$ 2 681	$ 1 229	$ 207
Charges (credits) not affecting funds							
Amortization of shaft deepening and renovations	866	960	1 388	393	121	—	—
Depreciation and depletion	671	676	1 206	826	731	583	329
Outside exploration written off	695	516	757	436	9	28	87
Amortization of oil and gas properties	349	257	343	—	—	—	—
Share of loss (net income) of companies accounted for by the equity method	106	(104)	(742)	94	(38)	(75)	62
Deferred income taxes	—	2 200	1 692	1 705	710	123	2
Gain on sale of investment in Jameland Mines Ltd.	(118)	—	—	—	—	—	—
Funds provided from (applied to) operations	(4 538)	9 196	9 089	6 170	4 214	1 888	687
Long-term debt, non-current portion	(1 077)	4 100	4 246	3 500	—	—	—
Issue of capital stock	39	984	986	2 535	852	1 186	264
Decrease in stores and supplies	—	—	—	—	—	93	—
Decrease in deferred charges	219	—	—	14	147	—	—
Proceeds from sale of long-term investments	26 650	—	—	—	—	—	—
Increase in contributed surplus	—	—	—	—	6	—	—
	$ 21 293	14 280	14 321	12 219	5 219	3 167	951

Exhibit 7 (continued)

Application of Funds							
Purchase of fixed assets	8 196	3 130	4 482	874	869	1 519	1 686
Shaft deepening and reno-vation expenditure	5 982	3 332	5 100	2 185	650	35	—
Increase in stores and supplies	395	706	608	275	349	41	141
Investment in and ad-vances to other companies	13 788	7 631	7 501	8 076	1 600	770	342
Exploration expenditure on outside mining, oil and gas properties	1 338	1 388	2 262	2 238	796	591	115
Increase in deferred charges	—	9	162	—	—	8	173
Dividends paid	—	—	461	190	353	163	259
	29 699	16 196	20 576	13 838	4 617	3 127	2 716
Increase (Decrease) in Funds During the Period	(8 406)	(1 916)	(6 255)	(1 619)	602	40	(1 765)
Funds (Deficiency) at Begin-ning of Period	(6 920)	(665)	(665)	954	352	311	2 076
Funds (Deficiency) at End of Period	$(15 326)	$ (2 581)	$ (6 920)	$ (665)	$ 954	$ 351	$ 311

EXHIBIT 8

DICKENSON MINES LTD.

Common Stock Performance for 1980 and 1981

1981	Dickenson A Shares	Dickenson B Shares	TSE Gold Index	Gold Price $US/oz.
September	$ 4.15	$ 3.60	3423	$ 431.75
August	5.00	5.00	4101	414.00
July	4.85	4.70	3819	401.50
June	5.37	5.12	3573	428.75
May	7.00	5.87	4449	479.25
April	8.50	7.50	4311	477.25
March	10.50	9.25	4288	539.50
February	8.25	8.00	3796	489.00
January	10.50	9.25	4056	506.50
1980 Range	$11.25–16.75	$9.75–$17.00		

EXHIBIT 9
DICKENSON MINES LTD.

Results of Silvana Division[1]

	Nine months ended September 30		Years ended December 31		
	1981	1980	1980	1979	1978
Revenue	$ 3 288 164	$ 4 214 497	$ 5 545 193	$ 3 580 000	$ 1 896 000
Operating income (Loss) (2)	(352 687)	560 190	413 140	1 255 000	246 000
Income (Loss) before income taxes (3)	(954 898)	493 126	369 488	1 006 000	123 000
Average price received:					
Silver (per ounce)	12.49	23.56	22.56	14.82	6.25
Lead (per pound)	0.44	0.48	0.48	0.63	0.37
Zinc (per pound)	0.50	0.42	0.42	0.41	0.33

Notes:
(1) In 1976 and 1977 to August 1, Silvana Mines Inc. leased its property to Kam Kotia. Financial information for years prior to 1978 is not comparable to subsequent years.
(2) Before depreciation and depletion, deferred development expenses, oil and gas interests written off and head office, administration and general expenses and interest income.
(3) Results were adversely affected in 1981 by a change in the method of accounting for depreciation from the straight line method to the unit of production method.

	Years ended December 31			
	1980	1979	1978	1977
Ore milled (tons)	31 110	21 632	17 600	17 499
Average tons per month	2 593	1 803	1 467	1 459
Average grade				
Silver (ounces per ton)	8.63	13.96	14.84	19.34
Lead (%)	3.21	4.87	5.81	7.41
Zinc (%)	3.03	4.51	4.34	6.13
Lead concentrate produced (tons)	1 556	1 654	1 609	2 086
Metal content				
Silver (ounces)	183 684	185 744	174 799	224 311
Lead (pounds)	1 805 561	2 011 863	1 948 464	2 449 345
Zinc (pounds)	258 200	301 586	299 608	427 384
Zinc concentrate produced (tons)	1 359	1 458	1 071	1 582
Metal content				
Silver (ounces)	71 698	104 301	68 876	101 515
Zinc (pounds)	372 240	491 599	1 108 890	1 578 866
Cadmium (pounds)	9 542	10 937	8 209	12 055

EXHIBIT 10
DICKENSON MINES LTD.

Prime Lending Rate of a Major Canadian Bank
January 1980 – September 1981
(at month end)

		Average Monthly Prime Rate (%)
1980	January	15
	February	15
	March	16.12
	April	17.16
	May	15.18
	June	13.25
	July	12.63
	August	12.25
	September	12.25
	October	12.87
	November	13.83
	December	16.91
1981	January	17
	February	17.11
	March	17.75
	April	18
	May	19.25
	June	20
	July	21
	August	22.50
	September	22.00

EXHIBIT 11
DICKENSON MINES LTD.

Pro Forma Production Budget

	Years ending December 31				
	1982	*1983*	*1984*	*1985*	*1986*
Ore milled (tons)	240 000	350 000	350 000	350 000	350 000
Average grade of ore milled (ounces of gold per ton)	0.181	0.176	0.176	0.176	0.176
Recovery	83%	85%	85%	85%	85%
Production of gold (ounces)	36 000	52 500	52 500	52 500	52 500
Operating expenses (1982 dollars)					
Per ton milled	$ 56.25	$ 51.65	$ 51.65	$ 51.65	$ 51.65
Per troy ounce recovered	$ 375.05	$ 344.38	$ 344.38	$ 344.38	$ 344.38
Capital cost (thousands of 1982 dollars)					
Concentrator	$ 1 443	—	—	—	—
Other	$ 1 265	$ 2 853	$ 1 372	$ 1 244	$ 1 244

NATIONAL SEA PRODUCTS LIMITED

Introduction

In early November 1987 Mr. R.A. McCulloch, Executive Vice President Finance and Administration of National Sea Products reflected as he looked out of his Halifax head office window at the ships and pleasure craft which moved about the harbour below. National Sea, one of the largest vertically integrated private enterprise seafood-based companies in the world, had been through some difficult times in the recent past but the industry had been restructured and the company looked forward to the future with confidence. The company had developed a number of marketing, operations and human resources strategies with which to guide its development and over $110 million in pent-up capital expenditure proposals applying to the 1988 fiscal year had recently been submitted to the Management Committee for their consideration. To assist with the financing of these projects the firm, on the advice of its underwriters, was in the process of preparing a preliminary prospectus for a public issue of additional common shares. The market crash of October 1987 had struck like a lightning bolt and suddenly it was very difficult for any public company to issue shares. McCulloch knew that the crash would force a reassessment of a number of the company's priorities and financial policies. With a sigh he settled into the task.

Recent History of the Atlantic Fisheries

Offshore Fishing

The Atlantic fisheries business may be divided into the "inshore fishery" and the "offshore fishery". The inshore fishery business was a highly seasonal industry conducted by self-employed fishermen utilizing about 30,000 vessels of less than 100 feet in length and making trips from one to a few days duration at a time. The offshore fishery business was made up of about 15 companies using vessels of over 100 feet for extended fishing trips of about ten days.

At one time the standard method of fishing on the Grand Banks was to use dories launched from schooners with long lines of hooked and baited trawl which were set by hand. With the development of engine powered trawlers fishing crews were able to catch many times more fish per man using large nets. The only limiting factor was the 12 day duration of each trip, the longest period that iced fish could be held on board before being brought ashore for processing. By the mid-1960's factory freezer trawlers were developed. These vessels were able to quick freeze and pack their catches at sea. There was no limit to the distance that these factory trawlers could travel to fill their holds. The factory trawlers placed great pressure on local fishermen and even greater pressure on the available stocks of fish.

Seafood Processing

Trawlers caught a variety of species of fish, gutting them and storing them in ice until they were brought into port. Fish which were gutted but not filleted were called "dressed". When the trawler returned to shore the fish were placed in boxes in the wharf area. At this stage they could be sold in their dressed form.

Most National Sea fish were processed in what were called "wetfish plants". In these plants the fish were skinned, filleted and trimmed. Fillets were then usually placed in packages and frozen. Many packages were then packed in large corrugated boxes for storage. Sometimes the packages were unmarked so that purchasers could utilize their own brand names and packaging. Unmarked products were often called "semifinished". In most wetfish plants there was little added to the filleted product except perhaps to smoke or salt the fish. Small fish and fish pieces left over from the filleting operation were frozen into large blocks.

Another process was called "secondary processing". The major difference between secondary processing and a wetfish operation was that something was added to the fish. An example of a simple addition was batter or breading. The input into these plants often took the form of frozen blocks of fish. The blocks were cut into shapes (such as for fish sticks) and fish batter, sauces, noodles, vegetables and other ingredients were added. The product was then packed for sale.

National Sea's plants largely combined the wetfish and secondary processing operations.

International Agreements

For years fleets of many nations competed with Canadians to within three miles of the Canadian coast. This heavy uncontrolled competition created a real danger to the viability of the Canadian industry and available fish stocks. In 1964 Canada unilaterally declared a twelve mile limit and in 1977 the Third United Nations Law of the Sea Conference made it possible for

Canada to declare a 200 mile limit. As a result Canada was able to establish and enforce quotas for Canadian and foreign fishermen within the
200 mile zone.

Fish Stock Management

The Federal Government set an annual Total Allowable Catch by foreigners
and Canadians for each species and fishing area. The major fishing areas
may be seen in Exhibit 1. Under the 1987 allocations and those proposed
for 1988 the Canadian Total Allowable Catch was roughly equally divided
between inshore and offshore fisheries. At one time this quota was not
assigned to individual companies so the companies fished as quickly as
possible to obtain as large a portion of the quota as possible. Beginning in
1984 the Enterprise Allocation (EA) system of fish stock management,
control and apportionment was created to manage the offshore fishery for
a trial period of five years. This system advised offshore operators at the
beginning of each year how many tons of each species they were allowed to
catch in each fishing zone. For example, in 1987 National Sea Products was
permitted to catch 548 tons of haddock in zone 4X. This new allocation
system revolutionized offshore fishing by making it easier for corporations
to effectively exploit fish stocks in a systematic way. Inshore fishermen were
still under the old system which did not provide for individual fisherman
quotas but an allocation system was being discussed for this area as well.

Individual company quotas were specified as a percentage of the Total
Allowable Catch for each species in each area. The total allowable catch
varied from year to year in response to Federal Government studies of the
amount of fish that were available. Exhibit 2 contains the 1987 Total
Allowable Catch and Enterprise Allocations for Fishery Products International, National Sea and other offshore fishing fleets. The Department of
Fisheries and Oceans monitored fishing by requiring that each vessel report
its position and catch on a daily basis to its company which forwarded the
daily report to the Government. At the time corporate budgets were being
prepared the Total Allowable Catch had typically not been announced but
some of the studies on which the Total Allowable Catch was determined
were made available.

The Industry Restructuring of the 1980s

In 1977 five major companies accounted for over 80% of the offshore fishing
industry in Atlantic Canada. Three of the corporations were Newfoundland-
based and two were headquartered in Nova Scotia. One Nova Scotia based
company, H.B Nickerson and Sons, owned 57% of the other Nova Scotia
company, National Sea Products. All of these family owned companies

expected a great boom because of the availability of larger quotas for Canadian fishermen resulting from the newly created 200 mile limit.

These expectations led the companies to make a number of strategic moves. First, they dramatically expanded their asset bases through an increase in both fishing fleets and processing plants. Second, they caught more fish than the market required in order to maintain or increase quotas. Third, they financed this massive growth in activity primarily through debt. The large increase in debt occurred largely because the family-owned companies were reluctant to inject new equity that would threaten majority control. Borrowing was also relatively easy due to the competition among the chartered banks to provide funds.

For three years the companies were quite profitable. This euphoric period was followed by a series of unforeseen events that turned the entire Atlantic fishery into a disaster area. First, the demand turned out to be less than expected; fish prices flattened then fell as corporations sold off fish inventory at depressed and then panic prices. Second, there was a serious strike in the Newfoundland sector of the industry. Third, interest rates shot up to unprecedented levels increasing the burden on the highly leveraged industry. Finally, the Canadian dollar rose against other currencies raising the relative cost of Canadian fish in international markets and leading to a large diversion of fish from Europe into North American markets.

Faced with a crisis affecting an entire industry the Government of Canada stepped forward and established a Task Force followed by a Restructuring Team. One result of this initiative, beginning in 1982, was massive infusions of federal and provincial funds into the three Newfoundland companies to form Fisheries Products International (FPI). While this firm was initially government owned, it undertook a public issue of stock in 1987 to buy back all of the government shares and became a widely held public company. By 1987 this Newfoundland based company had assets of $280 million including 66 deep sea vessels and 19 processing plants while employing over 8,600 staff.

At the same time that FPI was being created, National Sea was approached by Scotia Investments Limited, a company jointly owned by the Jodrey family. Scotia Investments, which already had a small equity interest in National Sea, offered to put up $20 million of new equity capital. In addition the Government of Canada put up $10 million, the Government of Nova Scotia supplied $5 million and the Toronto-Dominion Bank took on term preferred shares valued at $75 million. The Royal Bank provided an operating line of credit of $100 million. National Sea then acquired the Canso plant and three trawlers of the now-defunct H.B. Nickerson and Sons, to leave National Sea as the major surviving Nova Scotia based company. This acquisition was financed by an issue of preferred shares to the Federal and Provincial governments.

National Sea's Mission

The company's Mission Statement as of 1985, read as follows:

> The objective of National Sea Products Limited is to increase shareholders' value through planned growth, profit performance and dominance in the marketing of food, particularly seafood. The company will be recognized as the best in the industry by offering its customers the highest quality for value sought by being a good employer and a good corporate citizen.[1]

National Sea carried out this mission with a vertically-integrated structure. The company had the capability to harvest, process and market its product. Of these three activities marketing tended to be dominant and the firm sold more products than it harvested or processed. The shortfall was made up through active purchases from Canadian inshore fishermen and an expanding international trading organization which both sold and acquired products. The company had recently reiterated that its overall strategy was to grow internationally in the seafood business.

Marketing Management

Market Potential

National Sea was enthusiastic about the potential growth in the market for seafood primarily due to increases in per capita consumption of seafood products compared to other sources of protein. For example, the per capita consumption of seafood in the United States grew from 12.8 pounds in 1980 to an estimated 15.4 pounds in 1987. In spite of this growth in per capita consumption in North America it remained only one quarter of the level in such countries as Japan suggesting ample opportunity for further growth. Non-traditional markets such as China were seen as offering tremendous potential. The growth in popularity of seafood was attributed to a number of factors. One was that the product itself had been made much more attractive due to modernized harvesting, processing and shipping methods. Fish was more available in its fresh form or as ready-to-cook dinners. Second, there had been a general upsurge in health awareness in North America and seafood was considered to be very nutritious. It was low in fat, low in undesirable cholesterols and high in proteins and minerals. It had also been associated with a lower incidence of heart disease. Seafood was more commonly being served in restaurants and the fishing industry was attempting to make seafood a more important staple of home cooking through education programs and a greater sensitivity to consumer needs.

[1] Preface to National Sea Products Limited, *Annual Report, 1985*.

As seen in Exhibit 13, the price of fish relative to its major protein competitors had risen recently, placing a dampening effect on the competitive advantage of the product. Moreover, there were a number of substitute seafood species in the market. For example, Alaska pollock from the North Pacific and whiting off the coast of Argentina had some characteristics which were similar to cod from the North Atlantic. Since National Sea currently only had access to cod through its North Atlantic fishery it was somewhat vulnerable to the prices of these other two species. This clearly raised the issue of whether or not the firm should have a presence (as an active buyer or owner of a fleet) in these other two fisheries for strategic reasons.

Marketing Strategy

The company had set a target of becoming a billion dollar company by 1991. This meant that it had to achieve a real sales growth rate of roughly 15% per year.

The products sold included fresh, frozen and processed products. Examples of some of the products included fresh and frozen fillets, breaded and battered portions, fish and chips, canned chowders and heat-and-eat packaged fish meals. Exhibit 14 outlines the major products produced and the customers served by National Sea Products.

National Sea sold its products in North America directly and through distributors to retail stores, hotels, restaurants, institutions and fresh fish and live lobster markets. Products were also sold outside of North America particularly in Portugal, Japan, Australia and France. The company's Highliner brand was the dominant brand in the Canadian market having a 65% share of the retail frozen seafood market. Only 24% of National Sea's output was consumed in Canada; 59% was sold in the United States and 17% in other countries. The Japanese market, serviced largely through purchases from Portugal, was considered to be increasingly important to National Sea. A large proportion of U.S. sales were either unbranded packs for the food service industry or private label products bearing such brands as Topco, Safeway or Kroger. The company had recently acquired two important U.S. brands, Booth and Fisher Boy. The company found that there was a high level of brand-loyalty for their products even when non-fish products such as chicken were marketed under the brand name.

The United States market was a major importer of seafood products. In 1987 consumption of edible fish products was forecasted to exceed 2,700 million pounds. Of this total Canada was expected to be the largest foreign supplier with 675 million pounds followed by Iceland with 165 million and Norway with 74 million.

National Sea was continually involved in new product development to meet evolving consumer tastes and to find markets for previously under-utilized species.

The company saw itself as a market driven versus a supply driven company. This meant that they "read the market, responded to trends, found customers, caught the fish that the customers wanted, processed it the way they liked it and shipped it to them when, as and where they wanted it."[2] This was in contrast to the supply driven company which would catch fish to keep the plants busy then turn to the sales force and ask them to sell whatever was produced.

Each year the marketing department estimated the anticipated sales by species and degree of processing. The company knew its catch capacity and its processing capacity. The difference between sales and available production was met by the international trading business unit which handled worldwide procurement and sales.

The strategy of the company had been to shift from the low margin commodity types of products to the higher margin fresh fish and the rapidly growing value-added products such as single servings and products for the calorie conscious. As a result, in recent years the firm had been willing to allow sales of some products to decline while expanding sales of higher margin products. This emphasis was expected to accelerate.

One of the risks faced by the company was the possibility that other nations would impose tariffs or countervailing duties on the fish products. Another risk was that sales and margins could be affected by exchange rates. When National Sea sold into the United States the sales were made in U.S. dollars and some of the costs were also incurred in U.S. dollars. On balance the result was a net cash inflow of about $11 million per month in U.S. dollars. Assuming a 46% marginal tax rate an increase in the value of the Canadian dollar of 1 cent (for example from $1.32 to $1.31 per U.S. dollar) caused a decline of Canadian after tax profits of roughly $800,000. The company was also concerned about the strength of Canadian and U.S. currencies relative to competitor currencies. If for example the U.S. dollar strengthened relative to the Norwegian Kroner or the Icelandic Kronur it would give Norway or Iceland a competitive advantage in selling their products into the United States rather than their more traditional European markets. In Portugal the company purchased redfish from the Portuguese fleet in Escudos (about $40 million Canadian per year) and purchased cod from National Sea's Canadian operation in Canadian dollars (about $10 million per year). The redfish were then sold to Japan priced in U.S. dollars and the cod were sold to Portuguese dryers and salters priced in Escudos. National Sea's Japanese operation annually purchased squid and other products priced in Yen from National Sea's Canadian operation for resale in the Japanese market.

[2] Notes for an address by Gordon E.M. Cummings, President and Chief Executive Officer, National Sea Products Limited to the Rotary Club of St. John's Newfoundland, July 3, 1986.

Competing Firms

The company competed with a number of firms such as Gortons, Swansons, and Campbells which sold brands such as Gorton's, Mrs. Paul's, and Van deCamp. However, National Sea felt that it had two advantages over these firms. First, National Sea concentrated on seafood. Second, the firm's vertical integration gave them a much better opportunity to respond to market forces and exhibit quality control. Other firms relied on the purchase of fish from around the world in the open market.

The other major integrated fish processor in Canada was FPI. The firm was not very significant in the branded retail market but was strong in the food service area (large institutions and national food chains such as Long John Silvers) particularly in the United States where it had a greater presence in the food service market than National Sea. Over 50% of National Sea's sales were of products past the fillet stage while FPI had less than 20% of sales from this source. National Sea's priorities tended to be focused on the retail market followed by fresh fish, food service and then other products. FPI's priorities tended to place food service first.

Production and Production Strategy

Physical Facilities

National Sea had 59 company owned and operated vessels (42 wetfish stern trawlers, 9 offshore scallop draggers, 2 herring seiners, 1 shrimp vessel, 4 inshore vessels and a factory freezer trawler). The fleet had the capacity to catch 200,000 tonnes of fish annually operating primarily in the North Atlantic Ocean. All of the stern trawlers were ice strengthened enabling them to fish at any time during the year. Enterprise allocations and these reinforced ships allowed the company to operate the fleet and processing plants year round. The company also acquired seafood from independent fishermen and processors. In 1987 purchases of frozen product from other processors around the world were expected to amount to 44 million pounds or 12% of the firm's total supply. In 1986 the company made a $9.3 million investment in Canada's first factory freezer trawler, the Cape North which could stay at sea for six or seven weeks at a time working in around-the-clock shifts.

The company harvested or purchased from inshore fishermen ground fish such as cod, haddock, redfish, flounder, and turbot; pelagic species such as herring, mackerel, and squid; plus shellfish such as crab, lobster and scallops. Less than 20% of all ground fish but virtually all crab and lobster were purchased from others. None of these purchases were based on firm supply contracts so prices were simply determined by supply and demand on a spot basis.

The company also operated 14 processing plants in Atlantic Canada. These plants had the capacity to process 400 million pounds of landed weight annually using a one-shift operation. In 1987 the company expected to process over 350 million pounds or almost 88% of capacity. The company had subsidiaries in the United States including a shrimp plant in Tampa, Florida, and secondary processing plants in Rockland, Maine and Portsmouth, New Hampshire. National Sea was also a partner in a seafood processing plant in Australia and had an investment in a large seafood operation in Uruguay.

The company had a policy of acquiring and developing processing equipment and fishing gear which placed it at the technological forefront of its industry. For example, the company installed a containerization system (plastic containers to hold and store fish on board ship) in 23 of its trawlers. This decreased handling, increased the quality of the final product including the proportion of the catch available as fillets rather than "block," but called for major trawler and processing plant modifications.

The company made fleet and processing plant assignments on the basis of day-to-day market analysis by the corporate planning group. Trawler crews were advised daily of the species and quantity desired, the area to be harvested, the destination of the cargo, and the optimum schedule for arrival at processing facilities.

Importance of Enterprise Allocation

The company's fleet was configured, capital expenditures planned and marketing ventures undertaken based on the assumption of a reasonably predictable EA system. Since 80% of the firm's sales were derived from this EA the firm was clearly vulnerable to any changes in the EA system and had to protect its position vigilantly. It was particularly noteworthy that the five year experiment with EA was to expire in 1988. Although management of National Sea expected the system to be renewed basically as it had been in the past, negotiations were still in process. There was active competition between National Sea and other offshore producers for the share of total offshore allocation and with the inshore fishermen for the split of offshore and inshore allocations. The inshore fishermen had been increasing the capacity of their boats which prompted them to demand a greater share of the allocation and because of their numbers they tended to have a significant lobbying capability. For example, in May 1986 the Minister of Fisheries had succumbed to the lobbying efforts of dragger operators and transferred 8,000 tonnes of the EA of National Sea to one mobile dragger fleet. Surprise moves such as this could jeopardize National Sea's long term planning.

In 1987 the company expected to utilize about 78% of its quota. The firm felt that with more effective utilization there could be a positive effect on future income. It was very difficult to achieve 100% of the quota since there was not always a market for all species and the fish were not always available in the specified localities. The location of fish depended on such factors as food supplies and water temperatures. While the company had sophisticated equipment to assist with their search the task remained very much of an art and depended on the skills of individual captains.

Employees

National Sea was one of the largest private sector employers in Atlantic Canada with a direct work force of over 7,000 who worked in plants, vessels and offices. About 10% of these people worked in the U.S. in one of the three plants or as marketing representatives. Of these employees, approximately 4,000 were full time hourly employees and 900 were salaried. The remainder were seasonal or in the case of trawler crews paid on a co-venture basis. In addition, many independent fishermen relied on the company to purchase their catch. The company had agreements with 15 collective bargaining units of six different unions. A large number of employees were subject to agreements which were to expire in 1988.

Potential Impact of the Free Trade Agreement

Canada and the United States were at the advanced stages of negotiating a bilateral free trade agreement. At the moment there was an 11% ad valorem tariff on secondary processed products (but not fillets) going either way across the border. There was also a lot of debate concerning dumping and countervail duties in the United States. A company was considered to have dumped its product in a market if the selling price in the foreign market was lower than the selling price in the domestic market or if the product was sold below cost. A countervail duty was imposed on an industry if it could be demonstrated that the industry was being subsidized in its home country. National Sea had been charged with dumping dried salt fish in Puerto Rico and as a result a modest duty had been imposed on the product. All Canadian companies lost a countervail case dealing with fresh fish in the United States. As a result the U.S. had imposed a 5% duty on whole round (gutted but not filleted) fish but fillets continued to be imported duty free. Since National Sea did not export much whole round fish management felt that it was not unduly harmed by the duty but the possibility always existed that they would not be so fortunate in the future. Judgements regarding dumping and countervail were made by a U.S. tribunal that was very difficult for Canada to influence and against which the Canadians had no right of appeal. This added uncertainty in marketing in the U.S. As a result of these and other factors there was a tendency to locate processing facilities for the U.S. market in the United States and for the Canadian market in Canada.

With the introduction of the free trade agreement the tariff was expected to be reduced by roughly 1% per year so that it would disappear completely after 10 years. Also, the anti-dumping and countervail tribunal would be replaced by a joint American/Canadian tribunal which was likely to be somewhat more predictable and willing to listen to the Canadian position.

Free trade was expected to make the U.S. market somewhat more open to sales of Canadian product. On the other hand it would also be easier for U.S. competitors to enter the Canadian market. This threat was not considered very great because no U.S. companies were any larger than National Sea. Also, the U.S. companies tended to concentrate only on very large metropolitan areas of 20 million plus people and they were not geared up to distribute to Canada's more dispersed population. Moreover the United States didn't have adequate fish stocks to meet their own current needs let alone engage in major exports.

Financial Management Considerations

Capital Spending Plans

The company recognized four broad types of expenditures depending on their purpose: profit maintenance, profit improvement, unavoidable non-profit and strategic acquisitions. Profit maintenance projects were those where the company would stand to incur greater costs if the projects were not adopted. Thus their benefits were typically measured in terms of cost savings. They tended to be initiated by the operating divisions and included such projects as a new roof or the levelling of a plant floor. Profit improvement projects were expected to lead to enhanced profits or lower costs and there was a choice of whether or not to proceed. Examples of these projects were automated fish filleting equipment or the introduction of containerization into the wetfish fleet. Unavoidable non-profit projects were essential regardless of the cost or had benefits that were difficult to measure. Examples included the introduction of a new computer for accounting purposes, safety devices for vessels or pollution abatement equipment. The final category of expenditures was acquisitions of other companies made necessary by strategic considerations. Examples of these were the purchase of the Booth and Fisher Boy brands in the United States.

Because of National Sea's heavy losses and conditions in the industry the name of the game in 1983 and 1984 was survival. As a result capital expenditures were constrained to the maintenance of existing assets. While the company was beginning to turn around in 1985 there was still a severe capital constraint and the company refused any projects that did not promise at least a 2 year payback. By 1986 and 1987, as conditions improved, the company began to consider projects which were longer term and more strategic in nature. As a result there was beginning to be a large pent up demand for funding for excellent projects. Moreover, the company had initiated an 18 month strategic planning process. This process involved extensive market research and a careful analysis of company goals and alternative strategies. The result was eleven (after rejecting many other) new strategic initiatives, all of which had associated plans and monetary implications.

Each of the National Sea business units had put together its initial capital investment proposals by the end of September. These were then reviewed within the business units during the month of October and by November 1 the formal proposals were submitted to the Management Group for their final assessment. At this time the Committee was faced with over $110 million of potential projects of which about $49 million came from existing operations and the remainder were the result of proposed new strategic initiatives. Of the $110 million, $4 million (3.6%) were carryforwards of commitments from 1987, $17 million (15.5%) were profit maintenance projects, $4 million (3.6%) were non-profit, $54 million (49.1%) were for profit improvement and $31 million (28.2%) were for proposed acquisitions. Most of these profit improvement projects promised a rate of return after tax of at least 20%. McCulloch felt that this was an adequate hurdle rate but thought that the whole question of hurdle rates warranted further discussion. The bulk of the funds would be spent in 1988 but modest amounts would carry over until 1989. Exhibit 15 provides additional detail on these proposed capital expenditures.

Two examples of strategic initiatives were the globalization strategy and the Alaska strategy. It was clear to the company that they had to generate the ability to source and sell products in other countries around the world rather than simply relying on the Canadian fish stock and the Canadian and American markets. Thus they had to set up offices in such cities as Lisbon, Tokyo, Seattle and Hong Kong. Moreover they were contemplating the acquisition of two companies located in Lorient, France for a price in excess of $7 million. The first company had roughly $70 million of seafood sales to France and Germany. The second company was a small company that bought fresh fish at auction and sold fillets and secondary processed products. The acquisition was proceeding satisfactorily although it required the formal permission of the French Government.

Turning to Alaska, the company had no involvement in the North Pacific fishery and wanted access to that source of such species as Alaska Pollock. A number of alternatives were being considered including the purchase of a factory freezer trawler and the acquisition of an Alaskan fishing company.

Income Statements

Exhibit 3 contains the comparative income statements for National Sea for 1985 and 1986. Additional data for previous years are provided in Exhibit 5. The company paid a dividend of 10 cents for each voting common share for 1984 and 1985 and 20 cents per non-voting common share in 1986. The firm expected to pay equivalent dividends in the 1987 fiscal year. McCulloch's staff provided an estimate of 1987 income as seen in Exhibit 6. He noted that 1987 income after tax and before extraordinary items would be improved over 1986 results. Basic earnings per share before extraordinary items was expected to rise to about $1.70 compared to $1.36 in 1986.

Balance Sheets

Exhibit 4 contains the comparative balance sheets for National Sea for the 1985 and 1986 fiscal years. Exhibit 6 contains a projected balance sheet for fiscal 1987 prepared by McCulloch's staff as of October 1987.

The normal terms of the trade were net 30; however it was common to offer $1\frac{1}{2}$%, 15 net 30 terms in Canada. The ratio of accounts receivable to sales had remained reasonably stable in recent years. Inventory levels were carefully managed. At any point in time inventory consisted of round fish, frozen fish, and processed products. Fixed assets were considered by the firm to be undervalued in the books for a number of reasons. First, the company's accounting practice was to deduct investment tax credits from the value of the assets thus lowering their book value immediately upon acquisition. Also, the assets were depreciated at a rate which was somewhat faster than their true value would indicate. Finally, the replacement costs of some assets had risen due to inflation and demand for vessels and other equipment.

The firm's assets were converted for financial statement purposes into Canadian dollars. The U.S. operations were integrated for accounting purposes with the Canadian operations and at the present time these integrated operations represented a net U.S. dollar book asset position of $20 million. Any gains or losses on currency translation were reflected in the company's income statement each year. Losses on foreign exchange for 1987 were expected to exceed $2 million. The only major self sustaining operation was in Australia where the company currently had a net investment of $3.5 million Australian dollars. By accounting convention any annual gains or losses on currency translation for self sustaining operations were recorded as Deferred Foreign Currency Translation Losses in the firm's balance sheet. The Australian dollar had strengthened modestly relative to the Canadian dollar in 1987.

Exhibit 7 contains a graph of the relationship between the selected currencies over the period January 1985 to October 1987. Exhibit 8 contains a series of foreign exchange forecasts and forward rates as supplied by the company's various financial advisors.

Capital Structure

The company had two different types of common shares: voting and non-voting. The two shares were identical in all respects except that the non-voting shares had no vote and were entitled to a 10 cent dividend before any dividend was paid to the voting shares. After the initial 10 cent dividend the two classes of shares were entitled to identical amounts of dividends. A "coattail provision" protected the non-voting shareholders in the event of a takeover offer. As of November 1, 1987 the distribution of holdings of the voting stock was approximately 27% Jodrey family, 13% Halifax Developments Ltd (which was in turn owned $1/3$ Jodrey, $1/3$ Sobey and $1/3$ general public), 20% Government of Canada, 14% Bank of Nova Scotia and the remainder were widely held by the public. The non-voting common shares were similarly distributed.

The company had $20 million of second preferred shares outstanding as a result of its reorganization; $5 million to the Province of Nova Scotia, $10 million to the Government of Canada, and $5 million to Scotia Investments.

As a result of its restructuring National Sea had issued $75 million of term preferred shares to the Toronto Dominion Bank. Those shares were to be repaid at a rate of $25 million per year beginning in 1987. Because of their high cost the company decided to totally pay the shares off in late 1986 and 1987 using $45 million of cash flow from operations, incurring a debt of $30 million in the process.

With regard to leverage McCulloch felt that National Sea's capital structure target should be roughly similar to other food companies such as Campbell Soup and Quaker Oats. He had this opinion because whenever financial analysts did a report on the company these were the companies to which National Sea was compared. He also noted that Campbell Soup was somewhat vertically integrated and into the retail business although its operations were exclusively Canadian while National Sea had a large U.S. component. The company also kept an eye on the ratios of its major Canadian competitor FPI Limited although they felt that FPI's leverage was too low. Selected capital structure and other data for these companies may be seen in Exhibit 9.

National Sea's bankers had recently raised the topic of interest rate swaps. McCulloch wondered whether it would make sense to swap any of National Sea's fixed interest rate debt for floating rate debt or some of the floating rate debt for fixed rate debt. He did not expect long term interest rates to change appreciably over the next couple of years and did not feel that the firm's earnings before interest and taxes was particularly sensitive to the level of interest rates.

Additional Public Financing

In 1987 the firm had considered raising additional financing from the public. The firm first considered a preferred share issue. One rating agency indicated the rating would be a low P2 if the new issue was given priority over other preferred share issues while the other suggested a rating of P4. Preferred shares with this rating would have cost between 9 and $9\frac{1}{2}$ per cent. The firm also considered a public issue of debt. The interest rate on such long term debt, if it could be issued was expected to exceed $10\frac{1}{2}$ per cent. The underwriter had suggested the possibility of a convertible issue but McCulloch wondered if it was appropriate since it would add to the debt burden and might not sell very easily in such uncertain equity markets. While a common share issue had seemed very appropriate the share price had fallen dramatically in the last month and the stock market did not seem very receptive to new issues.

Banking Relationships

National Sea relied primarily on two banks for its operating and term financing: the Royal Bank of Canada and the Toronto-Dominion Bank. The Royal had been the firm's lead bank for many years and, in addition to providing good service, was particularly understanding during the firm's difficult times in the early 1980's. In addition the Royal had a treasury unit in Halifax which was particularly useful for such items as bankers' acceptances, letters of credit and foreign exchange. The Toronto-Dominion Bank had been a major player in the 1984 restructuring through its acquisition of the company's term preferred shares and now shared in the company's operating loans and other banking activities.

National Sea's operating loans were set at the prime rate. The bank term loan which had recently been arranged to repay the remainder of the term preferred shares had a maximum rate of prime plus $\frac{1}{4}$. The company had the opportunity to finance this term debt at lower rates by choosing between the prime-based rate or issuing a series of bankers' acceptances or LIBOR based instruments so the company watched the interest rates on bankers' acceptances and LIBOR rates carefully. The stamping fee on a bankers' acceptance was usually about 50 basis points. The company also had a $30 million revolving loan to repay preferred shares and for other special projects. Typically the Canadian parent company handled most borrowing and supplied funds to its subsidiaries as required although it was considering having the foreign subsidiaries borrow in their own countries.

As a result of its relationships with the chartered banks the company was subject to a number of balance sheets and income statement constraints. Some of the major constraints were as follows:

(1) A minimum of $85 million of equity.
(2) All debt could not exceed equity by more than 2.5 times.
(3) Minimum working capital ratio of 1.4 to 1
(4) For purposes of bank operating loans the margin could not exceed 75% of eligible accounts receivable and 50% of inventories of marketable products.[3]

---

[3] As of the end of 1986 about $3 million of regular accounts receivable and the entire amount identified in the footnote to the statements as "other accounts receivable" did not qualify for margin.

(5) Interest coverage (EBIT/both short and long term interest for a rolling 4 quarters) was not to fall below three times.

If the company borrowed for an asset such as a trawler it could obtain long term fixed rate financing in the neighborhood of fifteen years which was approximately its useful life. The province used to lend such long term fixed rate money to build trawlers in support of ship yards. On the other hand, it was now possible to get long term commitments of funds at rates floating over such short periods as 90 days.

Stock Price Behavior

The stock price behavior of National Sea, and the TSE Index for recent years may be seen in Exhibit 10. National Sea's shares were traded on the Montreal and Toronto Stock exchanges but there was very little public float (about 2 million shares). As a result it made it difficult to interest institutional investors even though recent research reports had been quite favourable. The government appeared willing to sell its holdings but it was less clear whether the Bank of Nova Scotia wanted to do so. The bank was required to lower its holdings to a maximum of ten percent within 2–3 years.

Mr. McCulloch was interested in the behavior of National Sea shares relative to the market at large so he had an assistant regress the return on National Sea against the TSE 300 over the period October 1982 to September 1987. This resulted in a beta of 0.50 and an R squared of 0.038. He also had the assistant regress the Consumer Products Sub Index of the TSE against the TSE 300 which resulted in a beta of 0.91 and an R squared of 0.781.

Funding Needs for 1988

Mr. McCulloch's staff had prepared an estimated income statement and balance sheet for the 1987 fiscal year. These statements are seen in Exhibit 6. Using these as a base he began to focus on the firm's projected income statement and balance sheet for the 1988 fiscal year. He noted that if there were no major acquisitions, sales would increase by about 15% but if he included expected acquisitions, sales in the coming year would increase by at least 20%. Gross margins had been about 25.5% in 1987 but because the acquired firms would have lower gross margins the gross margin overall was expected to fall to 23.5% in 1988. Although Selling and Administrative costs were supposed to have some fixed elements they tended to vary directly with sales. In 1987 they were about 10.4% of sales. Expected interest charges were difficult to estimate since it depended on his financing strategy. Nonetheless he decided to assume interest costs at 1987 levels of 1.9% of sales. Based on anticipated new fixed asset acquisitions the depreciation for the coming year was expected to increase to $16 million. Earnings of affiliates were expected to remain at a level of $800,000. Taxes were expected to be about 46% of earnings. One third of these taxes were payable to the

Government immediately and the remaining two thirds represented deferred taxes. He assumed that there would be a dividend on the preferred shares of $106,000 again in 1988 and that there would be 7,765,000 voting common and 7,960,000 non-voting common shares outstanding. Indications were that the past dividend policy of $0.10 per voting and $0.20 per non-voting share would be paid.

Turning to the projected balance sheet Mr. McCulloch noted that normal sales increases would increase inventories by about $10 million and accounts receivable by another $10 million. In addition, anticipated acquisitions would increase inventories and accounts receivable by $4 million each. The largest increase in assets, over $103 million, would represent an increase in fixed assets.

As the total funding required for the coming year became apparent McCulloch began the task of choosing among alternative means of meeting the need.

EXHIBIT 1
NATIONAL SEA PRODUCTS LIMITED
BOUNDARIES OF THE NORTH ATLANTIC FISHING AREAS

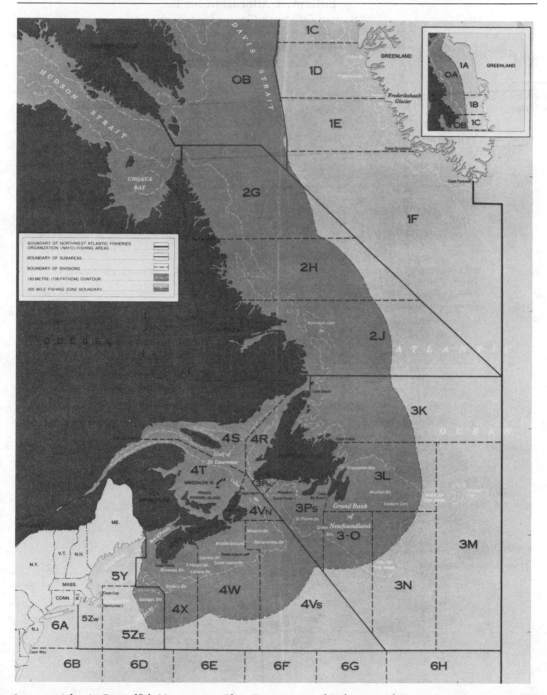

Source: Atlantic Groundfish Management Plan, Department of Fisheries and Oceans, Government of Canada

EXHIBIT 2
NATIONAL SEA PRODUCTS LIMITED

**Enterprise Allocation for the
Atlantic Offshore Groundfish Fisheries**
(in metric tons)

Species	FPI	National	IOC[4]
Cod	82.2	73.5	30.4
Haddock	1.6	6.8	2.4
Redfish	27.0	50.3	39.0
American Plaice	47.3	4.8	1.4
Yellowtail	13.2	1.0	0.5
Witch	7.7	1.5	0.6
Flounder	0.6	6.0	1.8
Greenland Halibut	17.1	9.7	2.7
Pollock	0.3	18.7	2.5
Total	197.0	172.3	81.3
% of Total	43.7	38.3	18.0

[4] This category refers to the group of Independent Offshore Companies which are 17 smaller companies that meet as a group.

Source: Enterprise Allocations For the Atlantic Offshore Groundfish Fisheries, 1987, Atlantic Fisheries Service, Government of Canada Department of Fisheries and Oceans.

EXHIBIT 3
NATIONAL SEA PRODUCTS LIMITED

Comparative Income Statements for the Years Ended
December 31, 1985 and January 3, 1987
($000s)

For the fifty-three weeks ended January 3, 1987
(with comparative figures for the fifty-two weeks ended
December 28, 1985)

	1986	1985
Net sales	$516 415	$454 708
Cost of sales	393 639	375 170
	122 776	79 538
Selling, general and administrative expenses	49 746	43 012
Interest expense (revenue)		
— short term	(1 716)	918
— long term	7 598	7 485
Depreciation and amortization	13 098	14 013
	68 726	65 428
Income from operations before the following	54 050	14 110
Share of affiliated companies' net earnings	347	204
Dividends on preference shares of subsidiary companies	(4 977)	(5 932)
	49 420	8 382
Profit sharing contribution (note 12b)	(4 942)	(838)
Income from operations before income taxes and extraordinary items	44 478	7 544
Income taxes (note 7b)		
Current	848	305
Deferred	21 866	—
	22 714	305
Income before extraordinary items	21 764	7 239
Extraordinary items (note 8)	14 360	2 883
Net income	$ 36 124	$ 10 122

Earnings per share (note 9)

EXHIBIT 4

NATIONAL SEA PRODUCTS LIMITED

Comparative Balance Sheets as of
December 28, 1985 and January 3, 1987
($000s)

	January 3 1987	December 28 1985
Assets		
Current		
Cash and marketable securities	$ 13 644	$ 11 550
Accounts receivable – trade	36 559	33 026
Accounts receivable – fishermen and other	5 382	5 152
Inventories of marketable products and supplies	94 794	83 192
Prepaid expenses	4 736	1 673
TOTAL CURRENT ASSETS	155 115	134 593
Fixed (note 3)	117 403	109 505
Other		
Investments in affiliates	2 995	2 457
Goodwill	4 937	–
Sundry investments and other	7 961	5 543
	15 893	8 000
	$288 411	$252 098
Liabilities and Shareholders' Equity		
Current		
Bank indebtedness (note 4)	$ 4 609	$ 3 880
Accounts payable and accrued charges	45 680	35 085
Income taxes payable	845	–
Current instalments on long-term debt	7 189	3 990
TOTAL CURRENT LIABILITIES	58 323	42 955
Long term debt (note 4)	87 637	65 261
Deferred income taxes	9 806	29
Preference shares of subsidiary companies (note 5)	50 000	95 334
Shareholders' equity		
Share capital (note 6)	44 369	43 869
Retained earnings	39 042	5 326
Deferred foreign currency translation losses	(766)	(676)
	82 645	48 519
	$288 411	$252 098

See accompanying notes

EXHIBIT 4 (continued)

NATIONAL SEA PRODUCTS LIMITED

Notes to Consolidated Financial Statements
January 3, 1987

1. Significant accounting policies

The accompanying financial statements have been prepared on the historical cost basis in accordance with accounting principles generally accepted in Canada and conform in all material respects with International Accounting Standards.

(a) *Basis of consolidation*

The accompanying financial statements consolidate the accounts of the Company and all its subsidiary companies.

(b) *Inventory valuation*

Inventories are valued at the lower of cost and net realizable value with cost determined principally on a FIFO (first-in, first-out) basis.

(c) *Foreign currency*

Assets and liabilities of self-sustaining foreign investments are translated at exchange rates prevailing at the balance sheet date. The revenues and expenses are translated at average exchange rates prevailing during the year. The gains and losses on translation are deferred and included as a separate component of shareholders' equity titled "deferred foreign currency translation gains (losses)".

Assets and liabilities of integrated foreign subsidiary operations and foreign currency denominated assets and liabilities of Canadian operations are translated into Canadian dollars at exchange rates prevailing at the balance sheet date for monetary items and at exchange rates prevailing at the transaction date for non-monetary items. The revenues and expenses, except depreciation and amortization, are converted at average exchange rates for the year. Depreciation and amortization are converted at the same rate as the related assets. Gains or losses on translation are expensed except for the exchange gains or losses on long-term monetary items which are deferred and amortized over the remaining terms of the related items.

Foreign exchange contracts are valued at rates prevailing at the balance sheet date. The resulting gains and losses on contracts acquired to hedge foreign currency denominated monetary assets are offset by the gains and losses on the translation of those monetary assets. The resulting gains and losses on contracts acquired to hedge future foreign currency cash flows are deferred until the hedged cash flows are realized.

(d) *Fixed assets*

Fixed assets are carried at cost with depreciation being provided on the straight-line basis at the following rate per annum:

Brick buildings	2½%
Other buildings and wharves	2½% to 5%
Machinery and equipment	5% and 10%
Trawlers	6% for 5 years, 5% for the next 10 years, and 4% for the last 5 years

The above rates represent a change from previous years based on a review of the estimated useful lives of the Company's fixed assets during 1985. The Company changed the depreciation rates on buildings and trawlers effective December 29, 1985, with the major change being on trawlers where the useful life was increased

EXHIBIT 4 (continued)

from fifteen years to twenty years. If depreciation had remained unchanged in 1986, depreciation expense for the year would have been higher by approximately $2 000 000.

(e) *Investments in shares of affiliates*

These investments represent companies over which National Sea Products Limited has significant influence and are carried at the Company's equity in their net assets; current income is recognized on the basis of the Company's share of their net earnings as reported.

(f) *Sundry investments*

Sundry investments are carried at cost. Income from these investments is included in income for the period only to the extent of dividends received.

(g) *Goodwill*

Goodwill has been recorded on the acquisition of product brands and is being amortized on a straight-line basis over 10 years.

2. *Business Acquisitions*

Effective June 16, 1986, the Company purchased the United States retail seafood marketing business of Booth Seafood Sales Corporation. The principal assets acquired were the trade names "Booth" and "Fisher Boy" (subject to certain license agreements) and the related inventories of seafood products.

This transaction has been accounted for by the purchase method, with the operating results from the date of acquisition included in these financial statements. The net assets acquired with consideration given is as follows:

($000s)

Net assets acquired	
Inventories	$4 279
Goodwill	5 196
Fixed assets	37
	$9 512
Consideration	
Cash	$5 362
Long-term debt	4 150
	$9 512

3. Fixed assets

	($000s)	
	January 3, 1987	December 28, 1985
Land	$ 1 086	$ 986
Buildings, wharves and equipment	122 261	115 639
Trawlers	104 460	88 632
	227 807	205 257
Less accumulated depreciation		
Buildings, wharves and equipment	61 844	53 561
Trawlers	48 560	42 191
	110 404	95 752
	$117 403	$109 505

4. Debt

	($000s)	
	January 3, 1987	December 28, 1985
Current		
Bank indebtedness	$4 609	$3 880
Long term		
Bank indebtedness at bank prime plus ½%	–	366
Bank indebtedness – trawler mortgage loans, interest rates averaging 8.0%, due to 1994 (U.S. $11 430)	15 754	14 966
Trawler mortgage loans, interest rates averaging 8.2%, due to 2004	26 366	21 923
Mortgage loans on land, buildings, wharves and equipment, interest rates averaging 10.1% (10.8% after April 1987), due to 2004	18 287	19 629
Special Purpose Revenue Bonds, interest rate at one-half of a United States bank's prime plus ½%, due to 2005 (U.S. $2 881)	3 971	4 247
Industrial Development Revenue Bonds with a property mortgage as collateral, interest rates averaging 10.2% (6.6% after 1988), due to 1998 (U.S. $5 777)	7 962	8 120
Other indebtedness related to acquisition of Booth/Fisher Boy, without interest, repayable to 1989 (U.S. $2 593)	3 574	–
Unsecured note payable bearing interest at 6% (8.5% after April 1989) due to 2009	18 912	–
	94 826	69 251
Less current instalments	7 189	3 990
	$87 637	$65 261

EXHIBIT 4 (continued)

The Company has pledged as collateral for its bank indebtedness a general assignment of accounts receivable, inventories and a $250 000 000 demand debenture providing a fixed charge over certain assets and a floating charge over all other assets of the Company (note 5).

Principal payments required on long term debt in each of the next five fiscal periods are as follows:

	($000s)
1987	$7 189
1988	7 080
1989	7 095
1990	6 814
1991	6 870

5. *Preference shares of subsidiary companies*

The preference shares of subsidiary companies consist of the following:

	($000s)	
	January 3, 1987	December 28, 1985
500 000 (1985 — 750 000) Cumulative Preference Shares at par value of $100 each	$50 000	$75 000
Nil (1985 — 20 334) Non-Voting, Redeemable, Non-Cumulative Preference Shares at par value of $1 000 each	—	20 334
	$50 000	$95 334

The 500 000 Cumulative Preference Shares bear a dividend entitlement of $\frac{1}{2}$ a chartered bank's prime lending rate plus $1\frac{1}{4}\%$. In the event of the default of the subsidiary on the dividend or redemption requirements of these shares, the parent's obligations relating thereto are secured by the collateral disclosed in note 4 in relation to bank indebtedness which ranks equally with bank indebtedness in all respects. Redemption is required in 1987 through 1989 at $25 000 000 annually. The first instalment of $25 000 000, due January 31, 1987, was paid prior to year end.

Effective December 29, 1985, the Non-Cumulative Preference Shares were redeemed and replaced by unsecured debt (see Note 4).

6. Share capital

The share capital of the Company at the end of the indicated fiscal periods is as follows:

Authorized	January 3, 1987	December 28, 1985
Cumulative Redeemable Convertible Preference Shares of the par value of $5 each redeemable at par		
5½% Class C	600 000	600 000
5½% Class D	400 000	400 000
Cumulative Redeemable Second Preference Shares of the par value of $100 each	200 000	200 000
Preference Shares of the par value of $25 each, issuable in series	10 000 000	10 000 000
Subordinated redeemable preference shares of the par value of $1 each, redeemable at par	1 025 542	1 025 542
Non-Voting Equity Shares without par value	25 000 000	25 000 000
Common shares without nominal or par value	25 000 000	25 000 000

		($000s)		
		January 3, 1987		December 28, 1985
Issued	Shares		Shares	
Class C and D				
Preference Shares	385 875	$ 1 929	385 875	$ 1 929
Second				
Preference Shares	200 000	20 000	200 000	20 000
Non-Voting				
Equity Shares	7 677 216	11 220	7 635 216	10 970
Common shares	7 677 216	11 220	7 635 216	10 970
		$44 369		$43 869

The Class C and Class D Convertible Preference Shares are inter-convertible at the option of the shareholder on a one-for-one basis and rank equally with respect to dividends and in all other respects.

On or before March 31, 1989, the Second Preference Shares are entitled to receive a stock dividend of two Common Shares and two Non-Voting Equity Shares for each Second Preference Share. Any redemptions prior to payment of the stock dividend require the Company to redeem these shares at their par value plus the issuance of the stock dividend.

After March 31, 1989, the Second Preference Shares are redeemable at their par value plus accrued and unpaid dividends. No cash dividends will accumulate on the

EXHIBIT 4 (continued)

Second Preference Shares until March 31, 1990, at which time dividends will commence, payable quarterly, at one-half the bank prime lending rate plus 3 percent. On March 31, 1990, the Company is required to redeem that portion of these shares having an aggregate par value plus accrued and unpaid dividends equal to the net proceeds received by the Company from the sale of certain assets as agreed upon by the Company and its bankers. The Class C and Class D Preference Shares and the Second Preference Shares will be redeemable in full in the event of any redemption, retraction or purchase for cancellation of any shares of the Company.

The Company has a common share option plan for designated directors, officers and certain managers of the Company and of subsidiary companies with a maximum of 10 percent of the issued Common Shares and Non-Voting Equity Shares reserved to meet potential rights under the plan. To date, options totalling 218 400 Common Shares and 221 400 Non-Voting Equity Shares have been granted, at various prices and times, to be exercised at any time during the three years after the option becomes exercisable. During the year, 42 000 Common Shares and 42 000 Non-Voting Equity Shares were issued under these options for proceeds of $500 790.

On July 14, 1986 the shareholders approved, and on July 30, 1986, confirmed a special resolution effecting the subdivision of the Common Shares of the Company into voting Common Shares and Non-Voting Equity Shares on the basis of one Common Share and one Non-Voting Equity Share for each Common Share outstanding. The Non-Voting Equity Shares are entitled to a preferential dividend of ten cents per annum and then share equally with the Common Shares in all further dividends. The Common Shares are convertible at any time to Non-Voting Equity Shares.

The Non-Voting Equity Shares contain provisions that if a non-exempt take over offer, as defined in the conditions, is made to buy Common Shares, then they are deemed to be converted to Common Shares for the purpose only of being tendered under the offer.

7. *Income taxes*

(a) Unrecorded investment tax credits of approximately $4 800 000 are available to offset future income tax liabilities and expire as follows:

1987	$2 200 000
1988	$ 500 000
1989 and later	$2 100 000

These credits, all arising prior to 1986, have not been reflected in these financial statements due to the uncertainty as to the amount that will finally be realized.

(b) The Company's provision for income taxes is different from the amount that would be obtained by using the customary corporate rate of 48%. This is due to the effect of amounts deductible for taxes that are not components of accounting income having a tax effect of approximately $1 000 000 (1985, $6 200 000), net of the tax effect of the non-deductibility of the dividends on the preference shares of subsidiary companies of approximately $2 500 000 (1985, $2 800 000).

8. Extraordinary items

	($000s)	
	Fiscal 1986	*Fiscal 1985*
Write-down of net book value on discontinued operations (less tax recovery of $510 000)	$ (594)	—
Gain on sale of assets	—	2 569
Write-down of investments	—	(962)
Recovery of income taxes on application of prior years' losses	$14 954	$1 276
	$14 360	$2 883

9. Earnings per share

	($000s)	
	Fiscal 1986	*Fiscal 1985*
Per Common Share		
Basic earnings		
Income before extraordinary items	$1.36	$0.42
Net income	2.30	0.61
Fully diluted		
Income before extraordinary items	1.27	0.40
Net income	2.14	0.57
Per Non-Voting Equity Share		
Basic earnings		
Income before extraordinary items	1.46	0.52
Net income	2.40	0.71
Fully diluted		
Income before extraordinary items	1.37	0.50
Net income	2.24	0.67

All calculations of earnings per share are after giving retroactive effect to the subdivision of one Common Share into one Common and one Non-Voting Equity Share effective August 15, 1986 (see note 6). Earnings per share on the Common Shares is calculated after taking into effect the preferential ten cent annual dividend on the Non-Voting Equity Shares. Fully diluted earnings per share is calculated after giving effect to the Common Shares and Non-Voting Equity Shares to be issued as stock dividends pursuant to the terms of the Second Preference Shares and under the Company's Stock Option Plan (note 6).

EXHIBIT 4 (continued)

10. *Cash from operations*

	($000s)	
	Fiscal 1986	*Fiscal 1985*
Income before extraordinary items	$21 764	$ 7 239
Charges (credits) to income not involving cash from operations		
Dividends on preference shares of subsidiary companies	4 977	5 932
Depreciation and amortization	13 098	14 731
Loss on sale of fixed assets	882	409
Non-cash income taxes	21 866	305
Share of affiliated companies' net earnings	(297)	(204)
	62 290	28 412
Interest on long-term debt	7 598	7 485
Net change in non-cash working capital balances related to operations		
Inventories	(11 602)	23 588
Accounts receivable, payable and other	8 980	4 310
	$67 266	$63 795

11. Segmented information

The Company is primarily engaged in the seafood industry which involves purchasing or harvesting, processing and marketing of seafood. Operations and identifiable assets by geographic region for the periods indicated are as follows:

	($000s)	
	Fiscal 1986	*Fiscal 1985*
Net sales		
Canadian operations		
To Canadian markets	$154 573	$139 353
To International markets	50 953	40 387
To United States markets	69 522	55 775
Inter-segment	111 421	95 853
United States operations		
To United States markets	241 367	219 193
Inter-segment	7 344	4 360
	635 180	554 921
Less inter-segment	118 765	100 213
Consolidated net sales	$516 415	$454 708
Segment contribution to income		
Canadian operations	$ 51 960	$ 11 537
United States operations	7 351	1 234
	59 311	12 771
Add (deduct) inter-segment	(5 261)	1 339
	54 050	14 110
Share of affiliated companies' net earnings	347	204
Dividends on preference shares of subsidiary companies	(4 977)	(5 932)
Profit sharing contribution	(4 942)	(838)
Income tax expense	(22 714)	(305)
Extraordinary items	14 360	2 883
Net income	$ 36 124	$ 10 122
Assets		
Canadian operations	$199 870	$181 702
United States operations	88 541	70 396
	$288 411	$252 098

Inter-segment sales are valued at market prices reduced by selling costs.

EXHIBIT 4 (continued)

12. *Commitments and contingent liabilities*

(a) Based on the most recent actuarial review an unfunded liability of $415 000 for an executive and management pension plan is being funded and amortized by the Company in equal amounts to 1990.

(b) Employees of the Company meeting specified eligibility requirements may partici-pate in an Employees' Savings and Profit Sharing Retirement Fund covering employ-ees of the Company and its subsidiaries. Participation in the Plan requires a contribution from the employee. The Company contributes an amount equal to 10% of its consolidated income from operations before income taxes but after inclusion of its share of affiliated companies' net earnings and deduction of dividends on preference shares of subsidiary companies.

(c) Operating lease commitments approximate $1 200 000 per year over each of the next five years and result principally from leases for office premises.

(d) The Company has been named as one of eleven defendants in an action by Cambridge Reinsurance Limited ("Cambridge"), through its liquidator. Cambridge is a former affiliate of the Company in Bermuda. The action alleges that the Com-pany was a party to certain actions that damaged Cambridge. Management believes the action is without merit and accordingly no provision has been made for any possible damages that may be awarded.

In addition, the Company is involved in litigation on various other matters, none of which is considered by management as likely to result in any significant losses to the Company.

EXHIBIT 4 (continued)

Report of Management Responsibilities
Auditors' Report

The management of National Sea Products Limited includes corporate executives, operating and financial managers and other personnel working full-time on Company business. The statements have been prepared in accordance with generally accepted accounting principles consistently applied, using management's best estimates and judgements, where appropriate. The financial information elsewhere in this report is consistent with the statements.

Management has established a system of internal control which it believes provides reasonable assurance that, in all material respects, assets are maintained and accounted for in accordance with management's authorizations, and transactions are recorded accurately on the Company's books and records. The Company's internal audit program is designed for constant evaluation of the adequacy and effectiveness of the internal controls. Audits measure adherence to established policies and procedures.

The Audit Committee of the Board of Directors is composed of five outside directors. The committee meets periodically with management, internal auditors and independent chartered accountants to review the work of each and to satisfy itself that the respective parties are properly discharging their responsibilities. The independent chartered accountants and the internal auditors have full and free access to the Audit Committee at any time. In addition, the Audit Committee reports its findings to the Board of Directors which reviews and approves the consolidated financial statements.

To the Shareholders of
National Sea Products Limited:

We have examined the consolidated balance sheet of National Sea Products Limited as at January 3, 1987 and the consolidated statements of income, retained earnings and changes in financial position for the fifty-three weeks then ended. Our examination was made in accordance with generally accepted auditing standards, and accordingly included such tests and other procedures as we considered necessary in the circumstances.

In our opinion, these consolidated financial statements present fairly the financial position of the company as at January 3, 1987 and the results of its operations and the changes in its financial position for the fifty-three weeks then ended in accordance with generally accepted accounting principles applied on a basis consistent with that of the preceding period.

EXHIBIT 5
NATIONAL SEA PRODUCTS LIMITED

Summary Financial Information
for the Years 1983–1987

	1986	1985	1984	1983	1982
Net sales	$516 415	454 708	404 964	452 158	386 231
Income (loss) before income taxes and extraordinary items	$ 44 478	7 544	(11 485)	(25 568)	1 020
Income (loss) before extraordinary items	$ 21 764	7 239	(9 529)	(20 278)	937
Net income (loss)	$ 36 124	10 122	(18 994)	(17 353)	1 030
Capital additions	$ 22 986	8 299	23 033	14 891	23 819
Basic earnings per common share:					
Before extraordinary items	+$ 1.36	0.42	(0.72)	(2.25)	0.04
After extraordinary items	+$ 2.30	0.61	(1.37)	(1.93)	0.05
Basic earnings per non-voting equity share:					
Before extraordinary items	+$ 1.46	0.52	(0.62)	(2.15)	0.14
After extraordinary items	+$ 2.40	0.71	(1.27)	(1.83)	0.15
Working capital	$ 96 792	91 638	76 788	13 285	22 321
Cash position	$ 9 035	7 670	(35 017)	(92 519)	(94 669)
Ratio of current assets to current liabilities	+$ 2.66	3.13	2.06	1.10	1.16
Fixed assets after depreciation	$117 403	109 505	118 568	112 556	111 174
Total assets	$288 411	252 098	276 450	270 857	291 250
Long-term debt	$ 87 637	65 261	67 767	112 174	100 805
Preference shares of subsidiary companies	$ 50 000	95 334	95 334	–	–
Common shareholders' equity	$ 60 716	26 590	17 644	22 114	39 573
Total shareholders' equity	$ 82 645	48 519	39 573	24 043	41 502
Dividends on C&D preference shares	$ 106	106	106	106	106
Dividends on common and non-voting equity shares	$ 2 302	764	–	–	–
Dividends paid per common share	+$ 0.10	0.10	–	–	–
Dividends paid per non-voting equity share	+$ 0.20	–	–	–	–
Number of common shares outstanding at period end	$ 7 677	7 635	7 635	4 635	4 635
Number of non-voting equity shares outstanding at period end	$ 7 677	–	–	–	–
Fish landings (000 kilos)	$159 000	169 000	158 000	143 000	161 000

(All amounts in thousands except as indicated +)
All per share amounts are after giving retroactive effect to the subdivision of one Common Share into one Common and one Non-Voting Equity Share
Effective August 15, 1986.

EXHIBIT 6
NATIONAL SEA PRODUCTS LIMITED

Forecasted Income Statement and Balance Sheet
Year Ended December 31, 1987
($000)

Forecasted Income Statement

Net sales		$ 550 000
Cost of sales		410 000
		140 000
Operating expenses	$ 59 600	
Depreciation & amortization	14 000	
Interest expenses	10 400	84 000
		56 000
Profit sharing		5 600
		50 400
Taxes (12 000 current, 11 000 deferred)		23 000
Net income		27 000
Less		
Preferred dividends		(106)
Common dividends		(2 350)
Increase in retained earnings		24 554

Forecasted Balance Sheet
as of December 31, 1987
($000)

Current assets		Current liabilities	
Cash	$ 2 000	Bank loan	$ 14 000
Accounts receivable	48 000	Accounts payable	47 000
Inventory	104 000	Current installment	
Other current	10 000	Long term debt	7 000
Fixed assets	122 000	Long term debt	103 000
Other assets	15 000	Deferred tax	17 000
		Share capital	49 000
		Retained earnings	64 000
	$301 000		$301 000

EXHIBIT 7
NATIONAL SEA PRODUCTS LIMITED

Selected Exchange Rates
for 1985 to October 1987

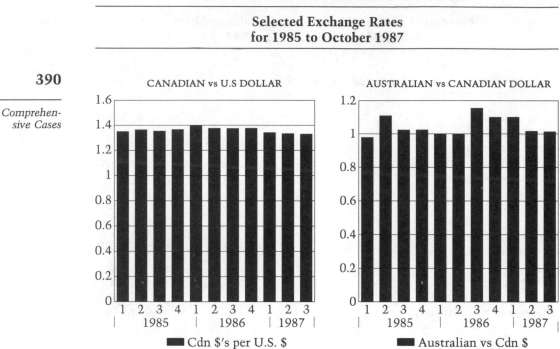

Source: Inter'l Financial Statistics

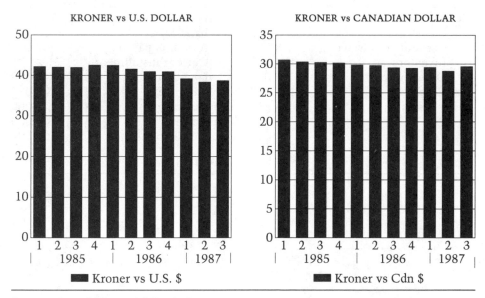

Source: Inter'l Financial Statistics

EXHIBIT 7 (Continued)

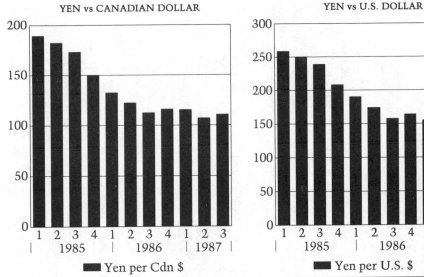

YEN vs CANADIAN DOLLAR

YEN vs U.S. DOLLAR

Yen per Cdn $ Yen per U.S. $

Source: Inter'l Financial Statistics

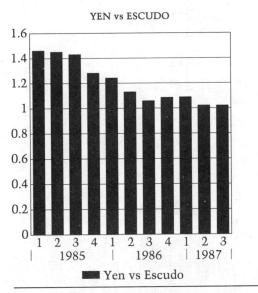

YEN vs ESCUDO

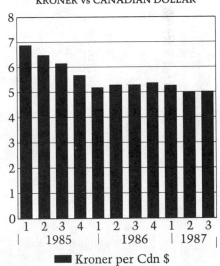

KRONER vs CANADIAN DOLLAR

Yen vs Escudo   Kroner per Cdn $

Source: Inter'l Financial Statistics

EXHIBIT 8
NATIONAL SEA PRODUCTS LIMITED

**Selected Exchange Rate and Interest Rate Information
as of November 4, 1987**

		Forecasts								
		1988				1989				Source of
	Current	Q_1	Q_2	Q_3	Q_4	Q_1	Q_2	Q_3	Q_4	Forecast
Canadian $	1.3275	1.32	1.32	1.317	1.312	1.310	1.310	1.307	1.307	E[1]
		1.318	1.319	1.319	1.321	1.322	1.322	1.320	1.319	C[2]
Bank rate	8.09	9.99	10.23	10.25	10.21	9.99	9.78	9.75	9.67	E
		9.82	9.83	9.77	9.97	10.47	10.68	10.87	10.96	C
Prime rate	9.75	10.41	10.44	10.41	10.61	11.09	11.30	11.49	11.59	E
90 day corporate paper	8.75	9.68	9.92	9.93	9.89	9.68	9.46	9.43	9.35	E
		9.69	9.70	9.64	9.84	10.35	10.56	10.75	10.84	C
Long term (20 yr) industrial bonds	11.23	12.29	12.32	12.34	12.26	11.57	11.11	11.00	11.00	E
		11.53	11.62	11.63	11.65	11.71	11.76	11.86	11.95	C
Bankers' (90 day) Acceptances	8.50									
LIBOR (3 mo)	7.56									

Sources:

[1] The Royal Bank of Canada, *Econoscope*, Forecast as at October 1987, p. 14, 17.
[2] The Conference Board of Canada, "Canadian Outlook", Forecast as at October 2, 1987, p.16, 35.
[3] Rate on high quality 5 year industrial bonds was 10.6%.

EXHIBIT 9

NATIONAL SEA PRODUCTS LIMITED

Selected Financial Information Relating
to Firms Which are Roughly Comparable to National Sea

	National Sea	Fisheries Products	Quaker Oats	Campbell Soup
Return on total assets[1]	.075	.111	.100	.114
Return on equity[2]	.263	.146	.166	.176
Dividends per common share[3]	$0.10	$0.26[4]	$110.00	$0.39[5]
Earnings per common share[3]	$1.27	$1.94	$130.17	$1.20
Payout ratio[6]	.08	.13	.85	.33
Capital structure (%)				
Long term debt	38.1	7.6	—	15.4
Preferred shares	31.2	—	—	—
Deferred tax	4.3	—	9.2	5.8
Non voting common	4.9	—	—	—
Common	4.9	69.0	3.9	1.9
Retained earnings	16.9	23.4	85.6	76.9
Other	−0.3	—	1.3	—

[1] Earnings after tax and before extraordinary items/total assets
[2] Earnings after tax and before extraordinary items/total equity
[3] Fully diluted after tax and before extraordinary items
[4] Indicated annual dividend $0.56
[5] Indicated annual dividend $0.42
[6] Dividends per common share/fully diluted EPS after tax and before extraordinary items

EXHIBIT 10
NATIONAL SEA PRODUCTS LIMITED

Stock Price Behavior of National Sea Products and the TSE 300 Index January 1986–October 1987

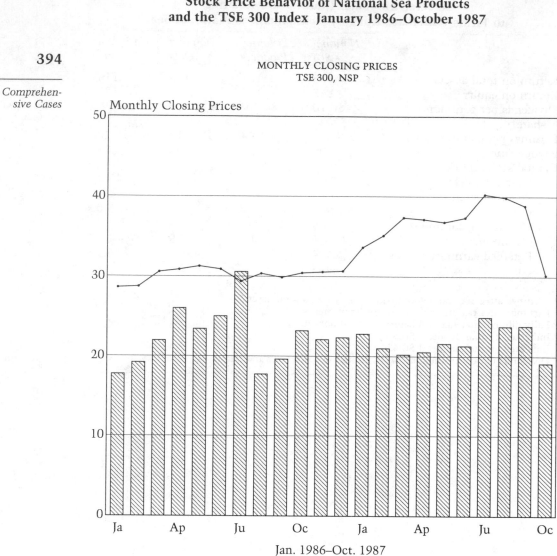

MONTHLY CLOSING PRICES
TSE 300, NSP

Jan. 1986–Oct. 1987

TSE 300 * 0.01   NSP

Data Source: TSE/Western Database

Note: The TSE 300 Index was divided by 100 for ease of comparison.

EXHIBIT 11
NATIONAL SEA PRODUCTS LIMITED

1987 Stock Price Behavior of National Sea Products, Fishery Products International Limited and the TSE 300 Index

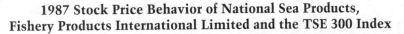

MONTHLY CLOSING PRICES
TSE 300, NSP, NSP.A, FPL

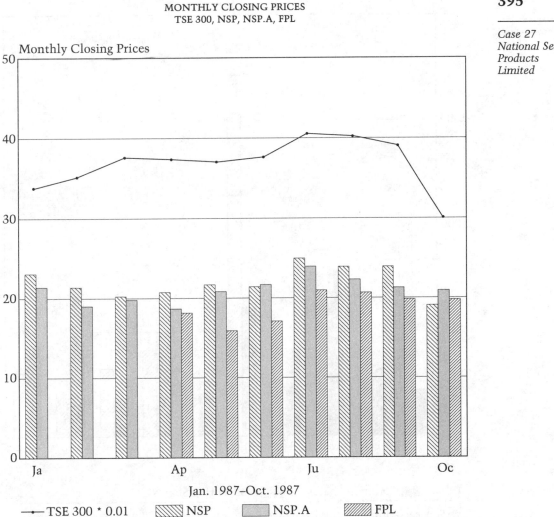

Monthly Closing Prices

Jan. 1987–Oct. 1987

— TSE 300 * 0.01   NSP   NSP.A   FPL

Data Source: TSE/Western Database

Note: The TSE 300 Index was divided by 100 for ease of comparison.

EXHIBIT 12
NATIONAL SEA PRODUCTS LIMITED

**Monthly Volume of National Sea Products'
Shares Traded on the TSE During 1987**

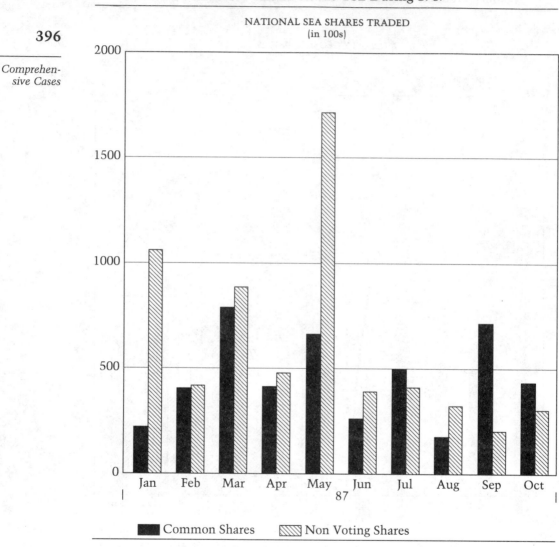

NATIONAL SEA SHARES TRADED
(in 100s)

Common Shares  Non Voting Shares

Source: Toronto Stock Exchange Review

EXHIBIT 13

NATIONAL SEA PRODUCTS LIMITED

Index of the Relative Prices of Poultry and Fresh Fish
January 1985—October 1987

QUARTERLY FISH AND POULTRY PRICES

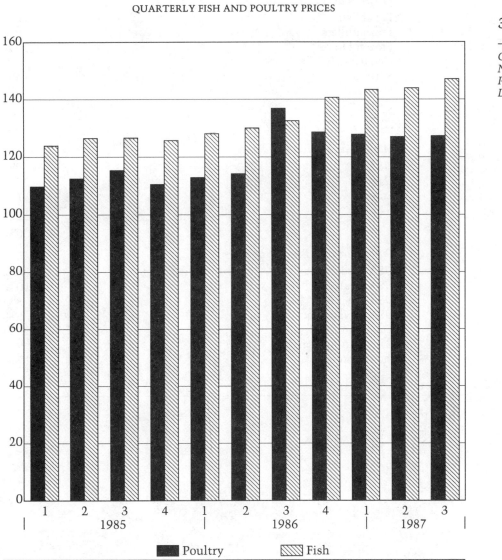

Source: Statistics Canada CPI

EXHIBIT 14
NATIONAL SEA PRODUCTS LIMITED

Major Products Produced and Markets Served by National Sea Products

Products as a Percent of Sales

Fresh fish	10%
Frozen fillets	30%
Frozen blocks	22%
Cooked fish	23%
Shrimp	4%
Lobster	5%
Other	6%
	100%

Markets as a Percent of Sales

USA	59%
Canada	24%
Europe	7%
Asia	10%
	100%

Customers as a Percent of Sales

USA foodservice	36%
USA retail	10%
USA fresh fish	8%
USA private label	5%
Canadian retail	15%
Canadian foodservice	9%
International	17%
	100%

EXHIBIT 15
NATIONAL SEA PRODUCTS LIMITED

Selected Capital Expenditure Projects
for the Coming Year
($millions)

Carried forward		4.0
Profit maintenance		17.0
Non profit		4.0
Profit improvement		
Factory trawler	30.0	
Louisburg plant remodel	15.0	
Boxing program	4.5	
Meal plant improvements	2.5	
Auto packaging equipment	1.0	
Freezer equipment	1.0	54.0
Possible acquisitions		
Brittaine Export (France)	7.0	
Treasure Isle Shrimp (Florida)	12.0	
Argentine Acquisition	12.0	31.0
		110.0

PART ELEVEN

Foreign Exchange Management

WRIGHT-ANDERSON MACHINES

Paul Fitzpatrick, vice-president of finance for Wright-Anderson Machines, was working late one evening in March 1987. Wright-Anderson Machines was a Canadian manufacturer of heavy industrial equipment with revenues in Canadian dollars. In early April 1981, the company had borrowed SF 60 million at six percent fixed with a six-year maturity. At that time the Canadian dollar equivalent of the loan was about $37 million. Now the loan was approaching maturity, and as there were no resources available to retire it, it would have to be rolled over. It was Paul's responsibility to decide on the best way to refinance the loan.

Paul was considering a variety of currencies and maturities for the purpose of refinancing. Specifically he was considering using SF, DM, $US, or $CAN, and in maturities of six months, or one, three, or five years. He also thought about dividing the SF 60 million loan among currencies and maturities in minimum packages of SF five million. The plethora of options was confounding.

Earlier that day Paul had contacted his banker and received the following information on current fixed rate borrowing costs.

	6 Mos.	1 Yr.	3 Yr.	5 Yr.
SF	5.25	5.25	5.50	5.75
DM	5.80	6.00	6.00	6.20
US	8.60	8.66	8.70	8.75
CDN	9.20	9.37	9.75	10.00

Paul also inquired about current spot and forward exchange rates and found they were as follows:

Term	$US/SF	$US/DM	$CDN/$US
Spot	.6644	.5511	1.3051
3 Mos.	.6731	.5588	1.3067
6 Mos.	.6735	.5584	1.3079
12 Mos.	.6855	.5650	1.3115

Forward rates beyond twelve months were usually available, but the market was less liquid.

To provide a bit of historical perspective, the bank gave Paul the following spot exchange rates in effect at the dates indicated:

		$CDN/SF
April	1981	.6198
	1982	.6361
	1983	.5927
	1984	.5928
	1985	.5223
	1986	.7204
March	1987	.8666

After sharpening his pencil, Paul got to work. A decision had to be made soon and Paul wanted to make sure his decision was a good one.

WATERSIDE FURNITURE COMPANY

Amy Hurst, President and principal share holder of Waterside Furniture Company Limited, allowed herself a congratulatory smile as she replaced the receiver on the phone. Hurst had just confirmed an order dated July 3, 1989 with Staub Rummel of West Germany for the purchase of a state of the art thermal plastic coating application system. Although the negotiations had been difficult at times, Hurst was satisfied that she had succeeded in acquiring the machine at the best possible price.

In 1977 Waterside Furniture of Barrie, Ontario, had expanded its operations to include the production of high quality, moulded plastic leisure furniture for pool and patio use. Ten years later company sales were about equally divided between the new line and the traditional wood dining room and bedroom furniture.

The purchase of the new equipment would increase Waterside's capacity to produce the outdoor line by about 50 percent. For the past two seasons, sales had been constrained by lack of production facilities, and Hurst was eager to expand. Due to recent high rates of growth the firm was very short of working capital and was using a 20 percent hurdle rate for new capital investments. Waterside's tax rate was 40 percent. Income statements and balance sheets for Waterside are found in Exhibits 1 and 2.

The terms of the machinery deal were as follows:

Price	DM	2 000 000
Terms		
Deposit with order	DM	200 000
On Shipment	DM	400 000
90 days after shipment date	DM	600 000
270 days after shipment date	DM	800 000

Staub Rummel estimated a 90 day period from receipt of the order deposit to shipment date, and offered a 3 percent discount on the full price for a cash settlement on shipment date. Hurst was anxious to ensure that the final all in cost of the equipment was as low as possible. Tight working capital conditions meant that if the cash discount were to be taken, the money would have to be borrowed. Interest payments only on any loan taken could be paid out of the company's small cash balances. The approximately $1,500,000 for the machinery would eventually be available from settlement of a successful lawsuit against a competitor launched two years previously for patent infringement. The date for settlement had been set for July 9, 1990.

Hurst had been in discussion with a chartered bank lending officer to determine the best way to finance the purchase of the machinery prior to the lawsuit settlement. The bank representative had provided her with the information on exchange rates and interest rates shown in Exhibit 3. For computational convenience, Hurst decided for a first cut to ignore bid/offer spreads and to use mid-market foreign exchange rates for calculating the differences between order financing alternatives. These rates, as developed by Hurst, are shown in Exhibit 4. Eurocurrency loans denominated in pounds Sterling, Swiss francs or Deutschemarks were available at fixed LIBOR. The rate quoted is an annual rate. Interest would be payable quarterly in arrears. The Eurocurrency borrowing rate for Waterside would be the LIBOR shown plus 75 basis points. The Canadian dollar deposit rate is a Banker's Acceptance rate, which would be available to Waterside on surplus funds. The bank representative indicated that Waterside could borrow Canadian dollars at prime plus 50 basis points, on a discount basis for up to one year. That is, the interest would be deducted from loan proceeds at the beginning of the loan period. From their discussions the following alternatives emerged.

Option 1

Skip the discount. When the DM payments became due, Hurst could buy DM as required at spot prices and fund with Canadian dollar loans arranged at that time. Loans would be discounted and repaid from the lawsuit settlement in July, 1990.

Option 2

Take advantage of the 3 percent cash discount and avoid both foreign exchange and interest rate exposure by arranging a single one year loan denominated in Canadian dollars. The proceeds of the loan would be converted to DM at the spot rate. After making the initial downpayment the remaining DM would be invested for three months at the DM deposit rate shown in Exhibit 3 to yield the required DM on day 90.

Option 3

Use option 2 except borrow one year Swiss francs or Sterling rather than Canadian dollars. Fully cover foreign exchange exposure by buying the francs or Sterling forward as required to meet the interest (quarterly) and principal (end of period) payments. Assume the Canadian dollar cost of the quarterly interest payments can be taken out of working capital when required at no explicit borrowing cost.

Option 4

Skip the discount. Borrow a single Canadian dollar loan now, convert to DM at the current spot rate, pay the deposit and invest the balance of the DM proceeds in Germany to come due at 90 days, 180 days, and 360 days as required.

Option 5

Skip the discount. Buy DM now on the forward market for delivery when needed for DM payments. Borrow a single one year Canadian funds loan now and invest the unused balances until needed to meet forward contracts. This "overborrowing" avoids interest rate exposure at the cost of the borrowing-deposit spread on the unused balances.

Before making any decision, Ms. Hurst decided to calculate the all in cost and assess the risk of each alternative. As a base from which to compare the alternatives, she decided to use the 2,000,000 DM price expressed in Canadian dollars at spot as the "cost" of the order, or the value to be financed. The "cost" of each alternative would then be the discount rate which made the present value of all its future dollar cash flows equal to the order value.

EXHIBIT 1

WATERSIDE FURNITURE COMPANY

Income Statements
(C$000)

	1988	1987
Sales	$67 172	$57 825
Cost of goods sold	51 358	44 658
Marketing, general & admin.	10 694	8 373
Depreciation	597	399
Interest	866	248
	63 515	53 678
Earnings before income taxes and extraordinary	3 657	4 147
Income taxes		
Current	879	1 297
Deferred	732	687
	1 611	1 984
Earnings before extraordinary	2 046	2 163
Reduction in income tax as a result of loss carry forward	552	427
Net income	$ 2 598	$ 2 590
Statement of retained earnings		
Retained earnings, beginning of year	$ 1 423	$- 867
Add net earnings	2 598	2 590
	4 021	1 723
Deduct dividends	425	300
Retained earnings, end of year	$ 3 596	$ 1 423

EXHIBIT 2

WATERSIDE FURNITURE COMPANY

Balance Sheets
(C$000)

	December 31	
	1988	*1987*
Assets		
Current		
Cash	$ –	$ 2 853
Accounts receivable	5 687	5 473
Inventory	8 490	7 006
Prepaid expenses	175	158
	14 352	15 490
Long term receivables	1 500	600
Fixed		
Land	514	75
Buildings	3 933	2 997
Machinery & equipment	4 940	4 196
	9 387	7 268
Less: accumulated depreciation	4 927	4 340
	4 460	2 928
TOTAL ASSETS	$20 312	$19 018
Liabilities		
Current		
Bank indebtedness	690	–
Accounts payable & accrued	3 412	3 992
Sales & other taxes payable	851	1 525
LT debt due within 1 year	1 290	–
Dividends payable	91	89
Deferred income tax (current)	73	199
	6 407	5 805
Long term debt	4 038	5 800
Deferred income taxes	670	418
	11 115	12 023
Shareholders Equity		
Capital	5 601	5 572
Retained earnings	3 596	1 423
	9 197	6 995
TOTAL LIABILITIES & EQUITY	$20 312	$19 018

EXHIBIT 3
WATERSIDE FURNITURE COMPANY

Selected Foreign Exchange and Interest Rates, July 3, 1989

Exchange Rates	Spot	3 Mo	6 Mo	9 Mo	12 Mo
Sterling	1.6233/43	−195/−192	−249/−243	−311/−307	−379/−372
Swiss Franc	1.6170/80	−79/−76	−150/−144	−219/−211	−285/−275
DM	1.8780/87	−95/−92	−164/−158	−230/−222	−295/−285
$ Canadian	1.1886/91	95/98	159/163	222/220	287/297

All rates quoted are currency units/US$, except for Sterling which is quoted US$/Pound Sterling

Borrowing Rates (Libor Offer)	3 Mo	6 Mo	9 Mo	12 Mo
Sterling	13.68	12.02	11.43	11.15
Swiss Franc	6.84	6.81	6.73	6.70
DM	6.87	6.87	6.87	6.87
US Dollar	8.81	8.71	8.61	8.50
Cdn Dollar Bank Prime	12.04	11.72	11.38	11.07

Deposit Rates (Libor Bid)	3 Mo	6 Mo	9 Mo	12 Mo
Sterling	13.56	11.92	11.33	11.05
Swiss Franc	6.72	6.68	6.61	6.58
DM	6.75	6.75	6.75	6.75
US Dollar	8.68	8.56	8.47	8.37
Cdn Dollar B/A's	12.01	11.67	11.34	11.02

EXHIBIT 4
WATERSIDE FURNITURE COMPANY

Amy Hurst's Table of Mid-Market Rates

	Spot	3 Mo	6 Mo	9 Mo	12 Mo
Sterling	1.6238	−193	−246	−309	−377
Swiss Franc	1.6175	−77	−147	−215	−280
DM	1.8784	−93	−161	−226	−290
$ Canadian	1.1888	96	161	221	292

GRAPPLEGROMMET CORPORATION

In early January 1988, Jordan Mills, the president of GrappleGrommet Corporation (GGC) was considering establishing a manufacturing facility and subsidiary in the Republic of Torsa. This facility would allow GGC to supply the growing markets for grapple grommets in Torsa and in nearby Batavia. Engineering estimated that the facility could be in production by January 1989 if a decision to go ahead was made before February.

Project Overview

The plant would cost and have depreciable-assets of $800,000 (LC[1] 4,000,000) and be incorporated as a wholly owned subsidiary of GGC. The facility would not require any capital additions for at least 7 years. All working capital requirements would be met by borrowing at the local level. Land and site improvements would be provided by ANWEP, the industrial development arm of the Torsa government, and be leased for 5 years at nominal cost.

Although GGC anticipated a project life in excess of 10 years, the Torsa Government insisted that the subsidiary be sold to ANWEP after 5 years for LC 4,000,000.

The government would guarantee the remittance in dollars to the parent company of 100% of the subsidiary accounting profits together with an annual management fee, all subject to a 15.0% withholding tax. Depreciation was not permitted to be repatriated as an operating cash flow although the accumulated depreciation would be recovered in the final sale to ANWEP.

GGC's after tax hurdle rate for these types of projects was 25.0%, assuming no project specific (i.e. not guaranteed by GGC) financing.

---

[1] LC = Local Currency; the currency in use in Torsa.

Variable Costs

Some raw materials were available locally in Torsa but a few raw materials had to be sourced from Canada. Engineering estimated that unit variable costs would be as follows:

From Torsa
- Raw Materials   87.00   LC/Unit
- Labour   34.00   LC/Unit

From Canada
- Raw Materials   23.00 $/Unit

Note: All above costs at 1989 price levels.

Fixed Costs

Fixed costs were forecast as follows in 1989 LC units:

Management Fees:	LC 500 000
Selling and General Administration:	LC 200 000
Depreciation:	LC 400 000

Management Fees were negotiated between GGC and the ANWEP and are in lieu of any royalties. These fees would be fixed for five years.

Selling and General Administration costs are expected to rise with local inflation. Land and site improvement lease payments are included in these costs.

Depreciation, based on historic cost would be on a straight-line basis for 10 years.

Sales Volumes and Prices

Marketing estimates that base unit sales volumes would be as follows for the Torsa and Batavia markets.

	1989	1990	1991	1992	1993
Torsa	2 000	2 500	3 000	4 000	5 000
Batavia	1 000	1 250	1 500	1 800	2 200

These volumes were based upon 1989 prices of:

Torsa	LC	870.00 per unit
Batavia	EC[2]	290.00 per unit

with the assumption that prices for 1990 through 1993 will be simply adjusted for inflation in each of the local markets.

---

[2] EC = Export Currency; the currency in use in Batavia

In the Batavia market, Economics anticipated that a real price increase (i.e. above the local inflation rate) of 1.00% would cause a unit volume decrease of 2.50%. The Torsa pricing structure (i.e. no change in price except for inflation) was part of the agreement with ANWEP, and not subject to direct control by GGC.

Due to the possibility of dumping charges being laid against GGC, prices for the Batavia market were to be Torsa prices converted to the Batavia currency (EC) at current spot prices.

The addition of the Torsa facility would not affect GGC's sales from existing production facilities.

Inflation and Exchange Rates

GGC's Economic Planning group had forecast inflation rates and exchange rates for Canada, Torsa and Batavia. Given the difficulty of forecasting in the volatile Torsa market, three scenarios were presented with associated probabilities.

Economics forecasted future exchange rates based on differential inflation rates with a correction to reflect anticipated imperfections in the adjustment process. The correction factors used were 1.10 for LC/$ and 0.95 for LC/EC. The forecasts of inflation, exchange rates, and unit export sales volumes (to Batavia) are all shown in Appendix I. The Batavia unit sales are the base sales forecast modified to reflect:

(1) Real price change over time in the Batavia market. The price in Torsa is assumed to adjust exactly for inflation but the Batavian price is the Torsa price at current exchange rates, and this exchange rate is not forecast to track differential inflation exactly (see paragraph above).

(2) The elasticity of demand in Batavia as described above based on the forecast real price changes.

Taxation

GGC had negotiated the following tax rates in Torsa.

Income Tax:	25.0%	of accounting profit after allowance for 10 year straight line depreciation.
Withholding Tax:	15.0%	of dividends and fees.

In Canada, GGC was subject to corporate income tax at a 45% rate[3].

---

[3] For purposes of this exercise, assume that Canadian tax is based on *all* earnings (before any tax) regardless of where the income was earned. A credit up to the applicable Canadian taxes payable is given for any foreign taxes (both income and withholding) paid. See example presented in appendix II.

LC Financing Option

ANWEP has offered to provide five year fixed rate local currency financing of LC 2,000,000 at 20%, with repayment of the principal on sale of the business to ANWEP. Interest would be paid annually in arrears, and would be deductible from local income for tax purposes. Ms. Mills considered this rate to be quite high, relative to current Canadian dollar borrowing costs in the 11–13% range.

APPENDIX 1
Economic Planning Forecasts of Inflation and Exchange Rates for the period 1988 – 1993

Most Likely Scenario

Probability: 60%

Exchange Rates (Average exchange rate throughout the year)

	1988	1989	1990	1991	1992	1993
LC/$	5.00	6.25	7.81	9.76	12.19	15.23
LC/EC		3.00	3.75	4.68	5.85	7.31
Exports (Units)		1 000	1 220	1 421	1 660	1 972

Inflation Rate — Torsa 30.0% (per year)

High Local Inflation

Probability: 30%

Exchange Rates (Average exchange rate throughout the year)

	1988	1989	1990	1991	1992	1993
LC/$	5.00	7.80	12.17	18.99	29.63	46.23
LC/EC		3.00	4.58	6.99	10.66	16.26
Exports (Units)		1 000	1 195	1 366	1 553	1 791

Inflation Rate — Torsa 60.0% (per year)

Low Local Inflation

Probability: 10%

Exchange Rates (Average exchange rate throughout the year)

	1988	1989	1990	1991	1992	1993
LC/$	5.00	5.47	5.98	6.54	7.15	7.82
LC/EC		3.00	3.33	3.70	4.11	4.56
Exports (Units)		1 000	1 232	1 460	1 728	2 077

Inflation Rate — Torsa 15.0% (per year)
Inflation Rate — Canada and Batavia
Inflation in Canada and Batavia is expected to remain constant regardless of the scenario projected for Torsa.

Canada   — 6% (per year)
Batavia   — 3% (per year)

APPENDIX II
Example Calculation of Taxes on Cash Flow to Parent

Assumptions: Before tax income (in Torsa) of 1000 LCs.
Torsa income tax rate is 25 percent.
Withholding tax of 15 percent.
Canadian tax rate is 45 percent.
Exchange rate of LC/CDN$ = 5.00

E.B.T.	1 000	LC	
Income Tax	250	LC	.25 × 1 000
	750	LC	
Withholding Tax	112.5	LC	.15 × 750
Net Cash Flow to Parent Country	637.5	LC	750 − 112.5
	127.5	CDN$	637.5/5.00
E.B.T.	200	CDN$	1 000/5.00
CDN Tax Payable	90	CDN$	.45 × 200
Less Credits:			
Torsa Income Tax	50	CDN$	250/5.00
Withholding Tax	22.5	CDN$	112.5/5.00
Net CDN Tax Payable	17.5	CDN$	90 − 50 − 22.5
Net After Tax Cash Flow to Parent	110	CDN$	127.5 − 17.5